Shojo Beat

Stepping on Roses

Vol. 2

Story & Art by
Rinko Ueda

Stepping on Roses

Volume 2
CONTENTS

Story Thus Far

Sumi Kitamura lives a life of poverty, but she loves and cares for the young orphans that her elder brother Eisuke brings home. One day when one of the children gets sick, Sumi receives help from Nozomu Ijuin, a young man whom she becomes attracted to. Still, she is forced to sell herself in order to protect the children and repay Eisuke's debts. Soichiro Ashida, the heir to a wealthy conglomerate, agrees to her price and asks her to marry him so that he can secure his inheritance. But at their housewarming party, Sumi is reunited with Nozomu! Moreover, Nozomu invites Sumi to a party at his house, so she must present herself as a refined lady.
Now the day for Sumi to go to Nozomu's house has arrived at last...

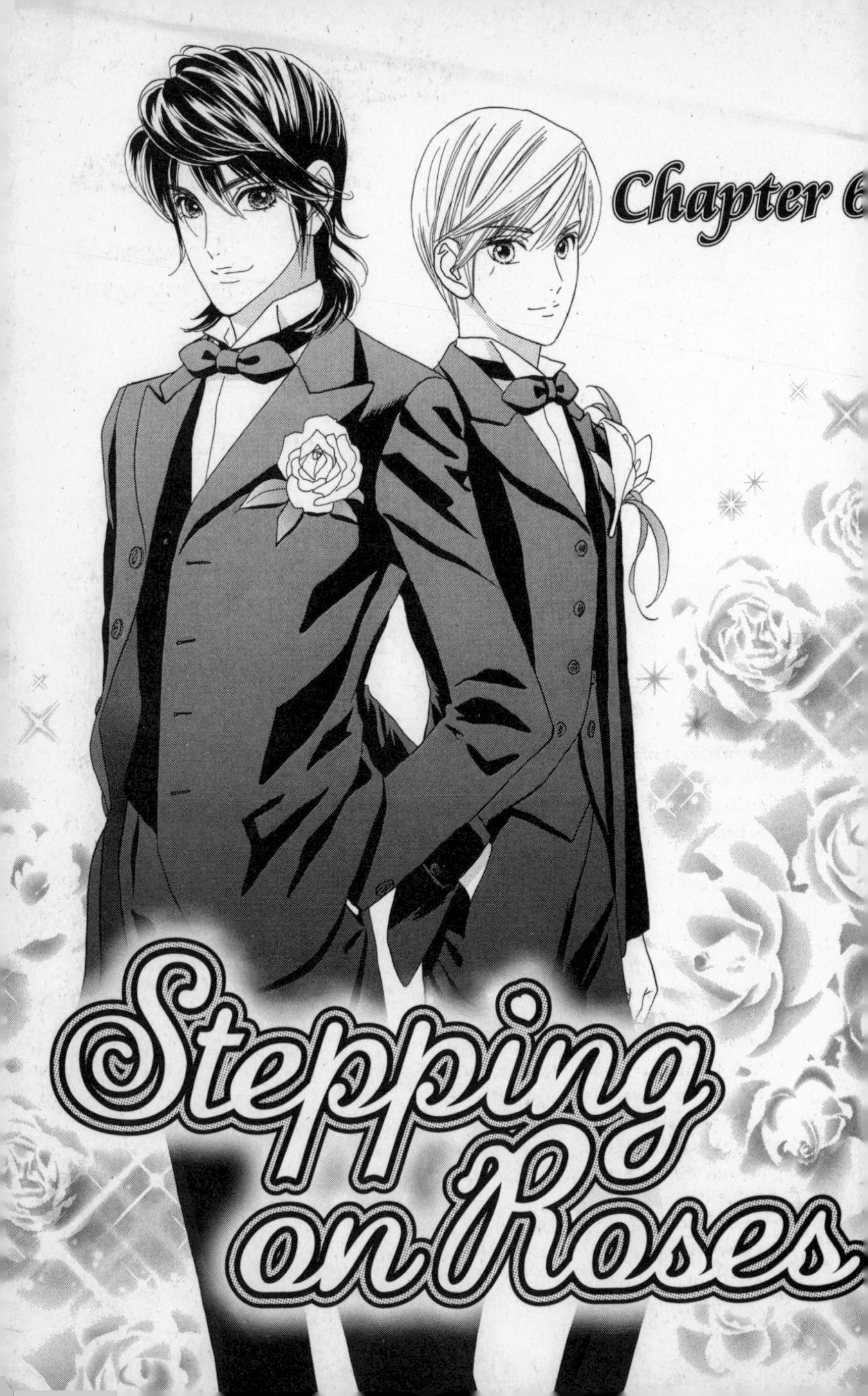
Chapter 6
Stepping on Roses

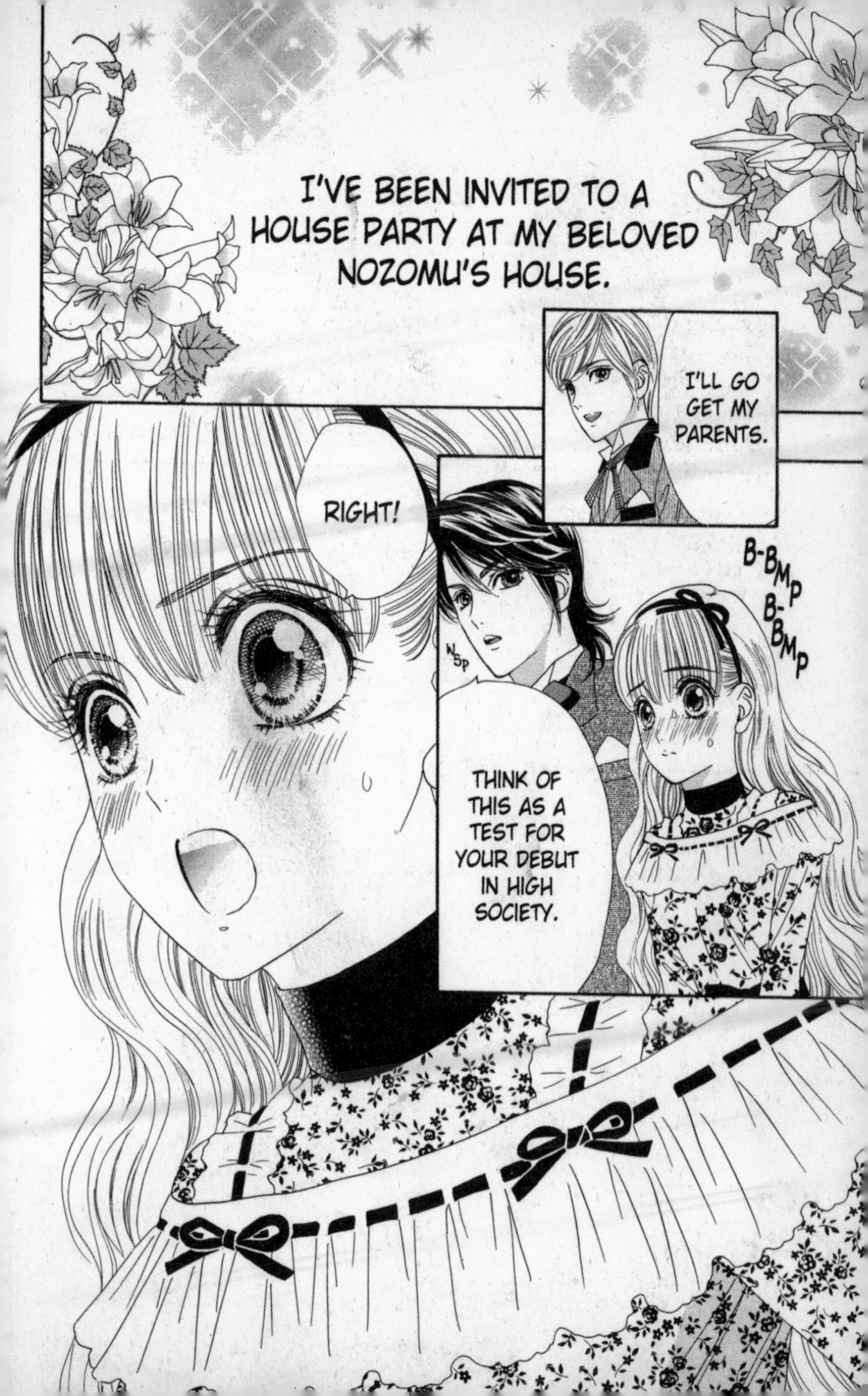
I'VE BEEN INVITED TO A HOUSE PARTY AT MY BELOVED NOZOMU'S HOUSE.
I'LL GO GET MY PARENTS.
B-BMP B-BMP
NSP
THINK OF THIS AS A TEST FOR YOUR DEBUT IN HIGH SOCIETY.
RIGHT!

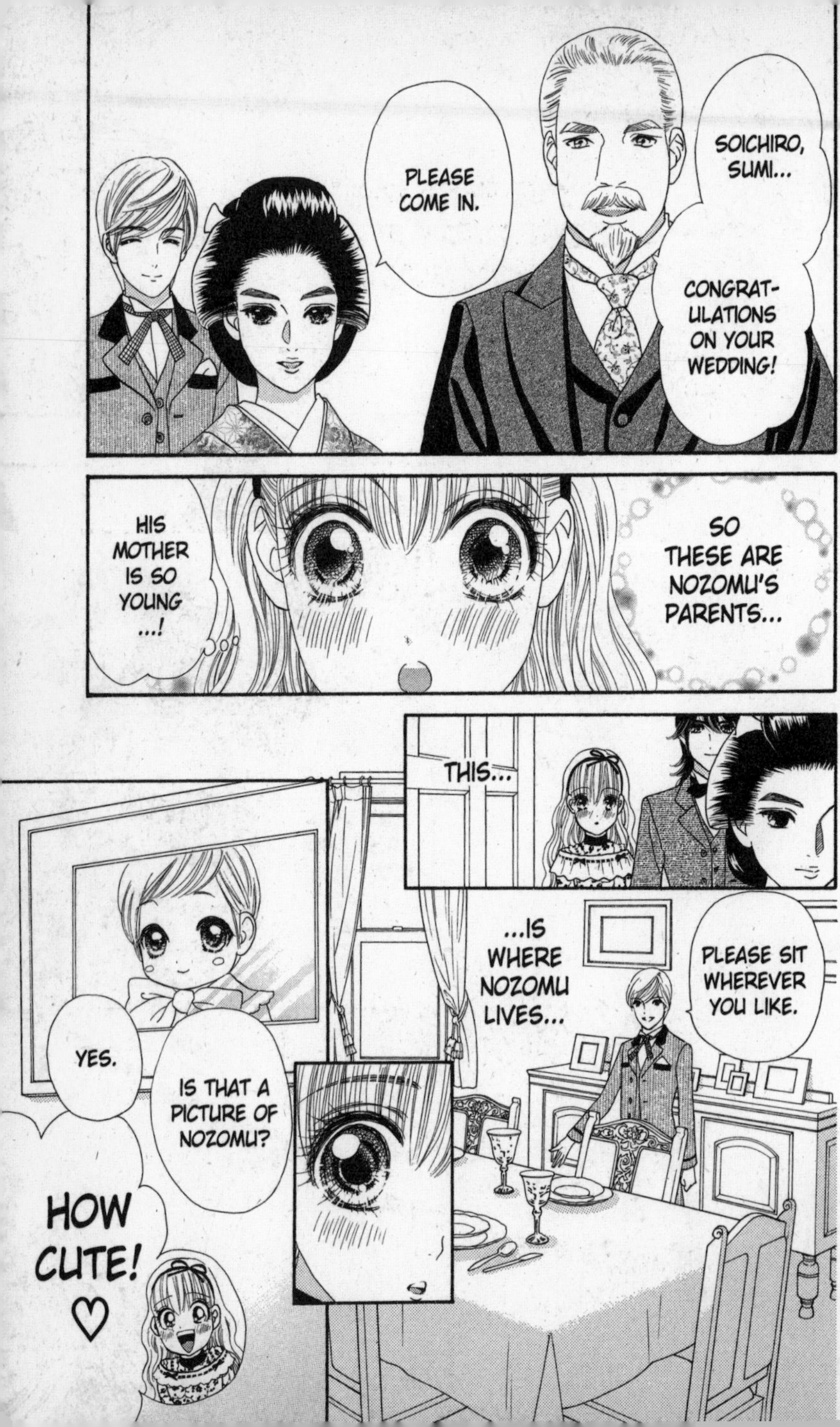
SOICHIRO, SUMI...
CONGRAT-ULATIONS ON YOUR WEDDING!
PLEASE COME IN.
SO THESE ARE NOZOMU'S PARENTS...
HIS MOTHER IS SO YOUNG ...!
THIS...
...IS WHERE NOZOMU LIVES...
PLEASE SIT WHEREVER YOU LIKE.
IS THAT A PICTURE OF NOZOMU?
YES.
HOW CUTE! ♡

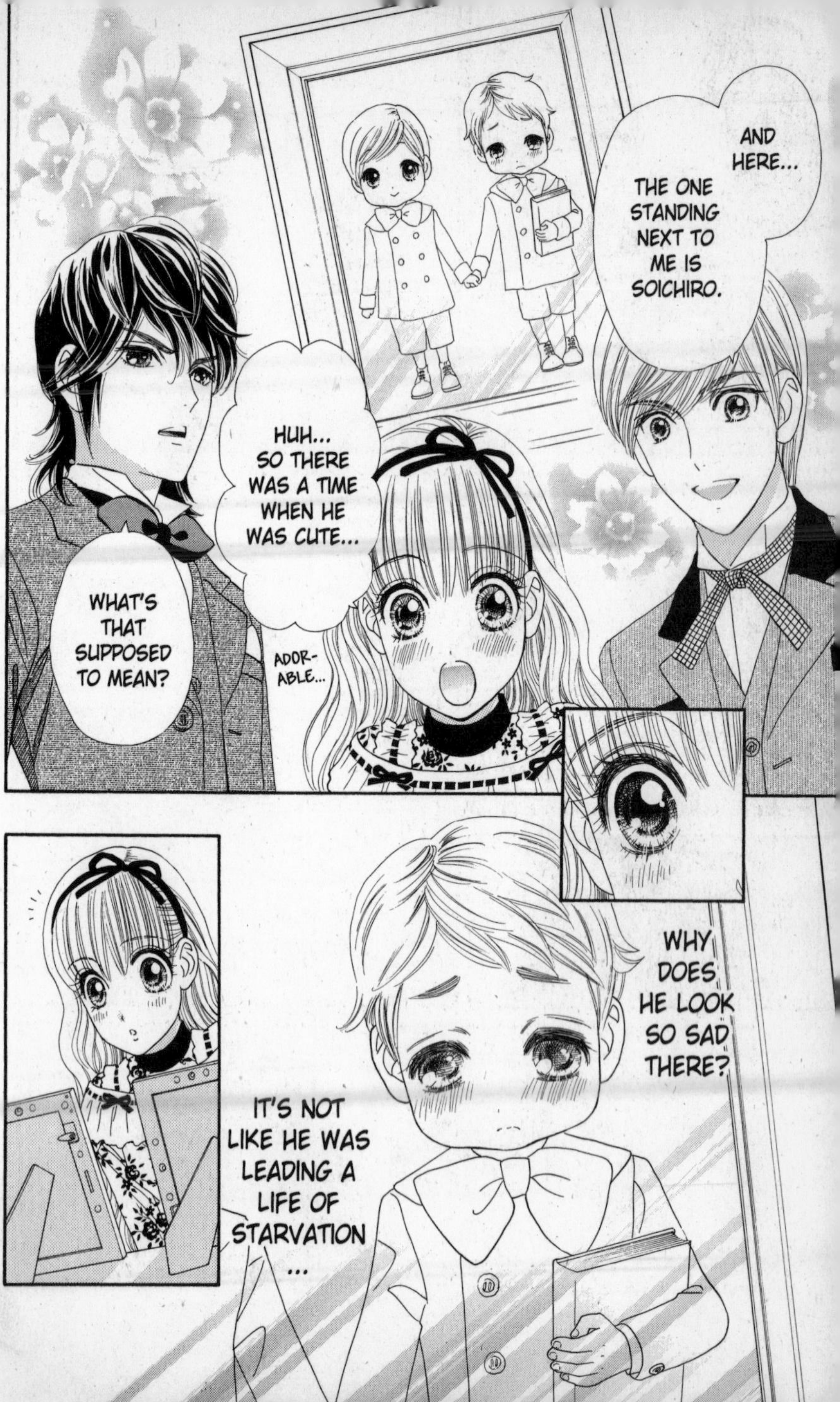
AND HERE...
THE ONE STANDING NEXT TO ME IS SOICHIRO.
HUH... SO THERE WAS A TIME WHEN HE WAS CUTE...
ADOR-ABLE...
WHAT'S THAT SUPPOSED TO MEAN?
WHY DOES HE LOOK SO SAD THERE?
IT'S NOT LIKE HE WAS LEADING A LIFE OF STARVATION...

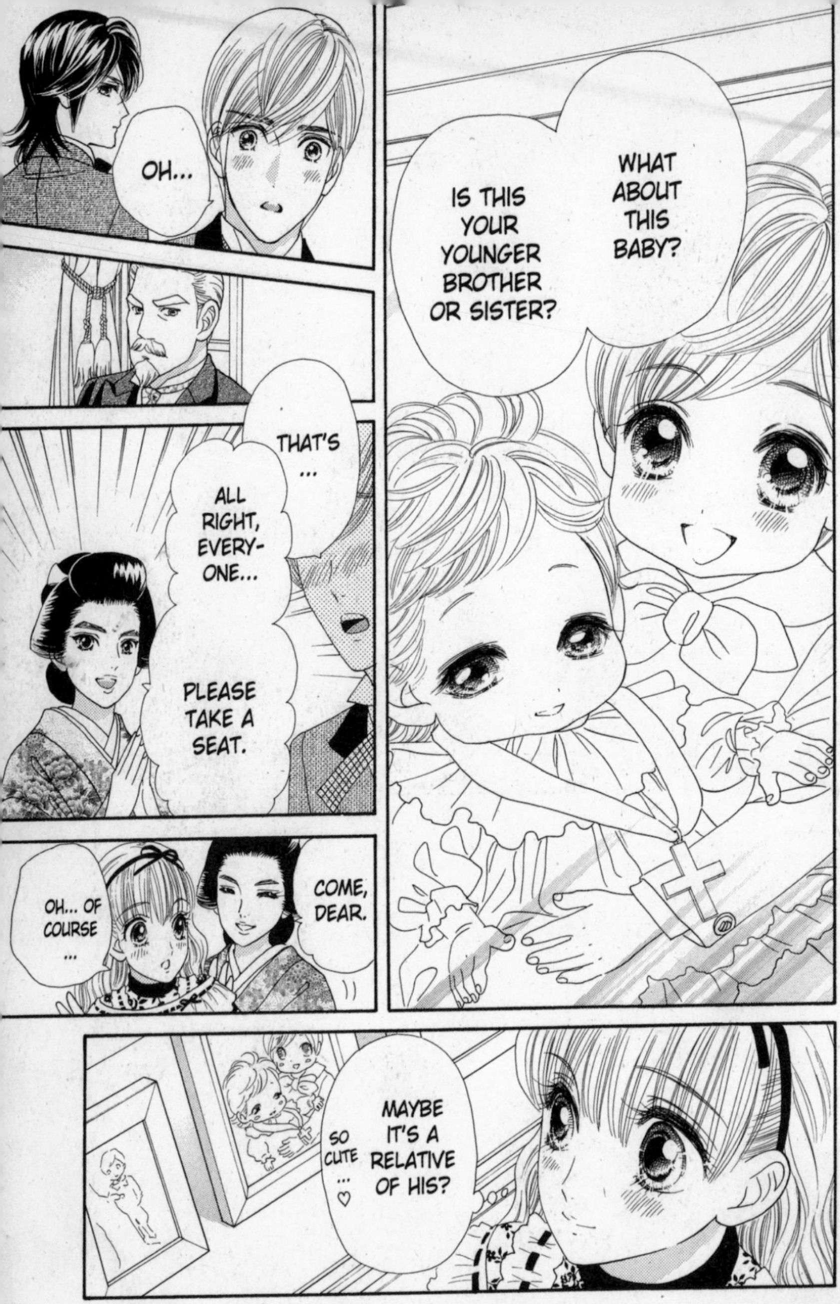
WHAT ABOUT THIS BABY?
IS THIS YOUR YOUNGER BROTHER OR SISTER?
OH...
THAT'S ...
ALL RIGHT, EVERY-ONE...
PLEASE TAKE A SEAT.
COME, DEAR.
OH... OF COURSE ...
MAYBE IT'S A RELATIVE OF HIS?
SO CUTE ... ♡

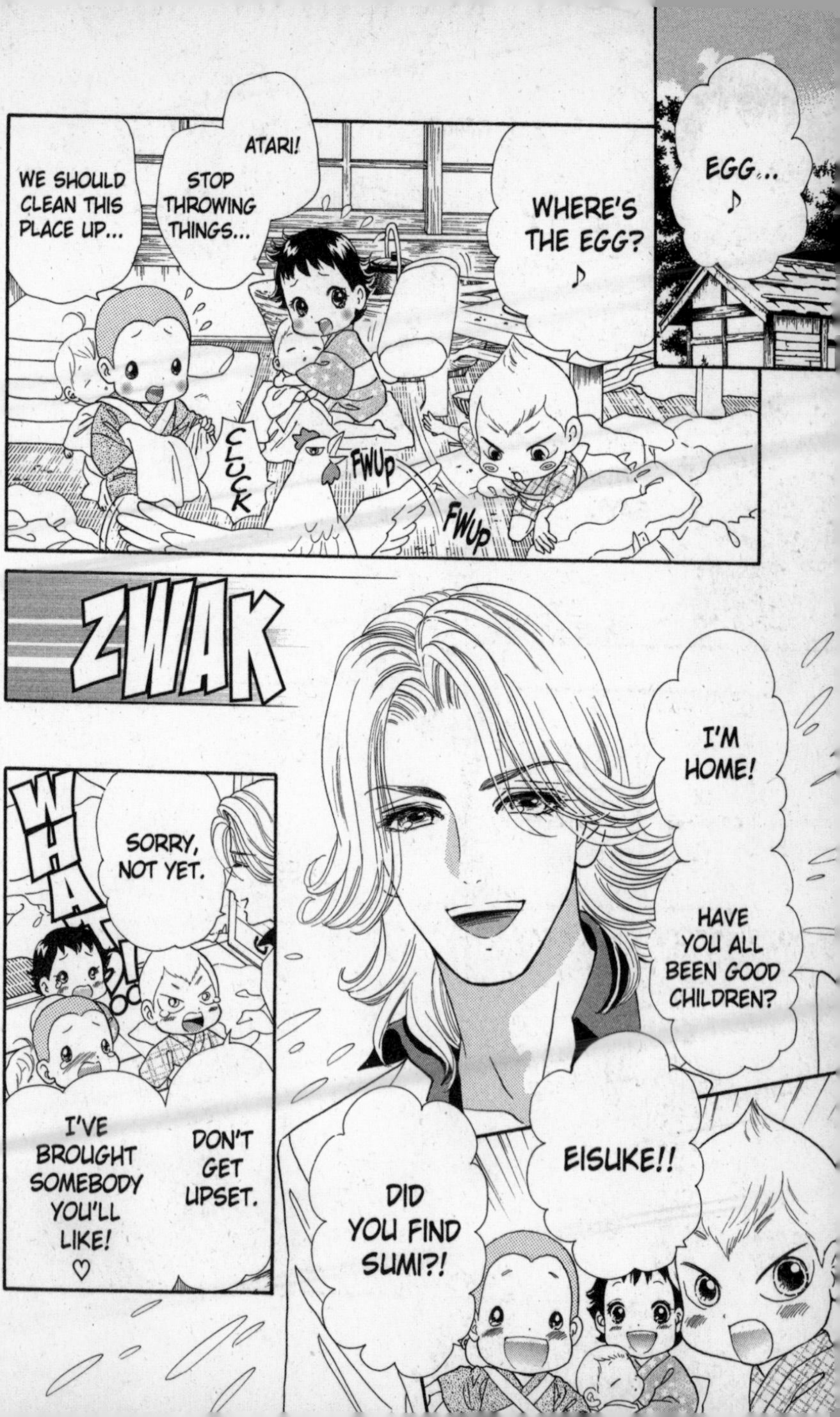
EGG... ♪
WHERE'S THE EGG? ♪
ATARI! STOP THROWING THINGS...
WE SHOULD CLEAN THIS PLACE UP...
CLUCK
FWUP
FWUP
ZWAK
I'M HOME!
HAVE YOU ALL BEEN GOOD CHILDREN?
EISUKE!!
DID YOU FIND SUMI?!
WHAT?!
SORRY, NOT YET.
DON'T GET UPSET.
I'VE BROUGHT SOMEBODY YOU'LL LIKE! ♡

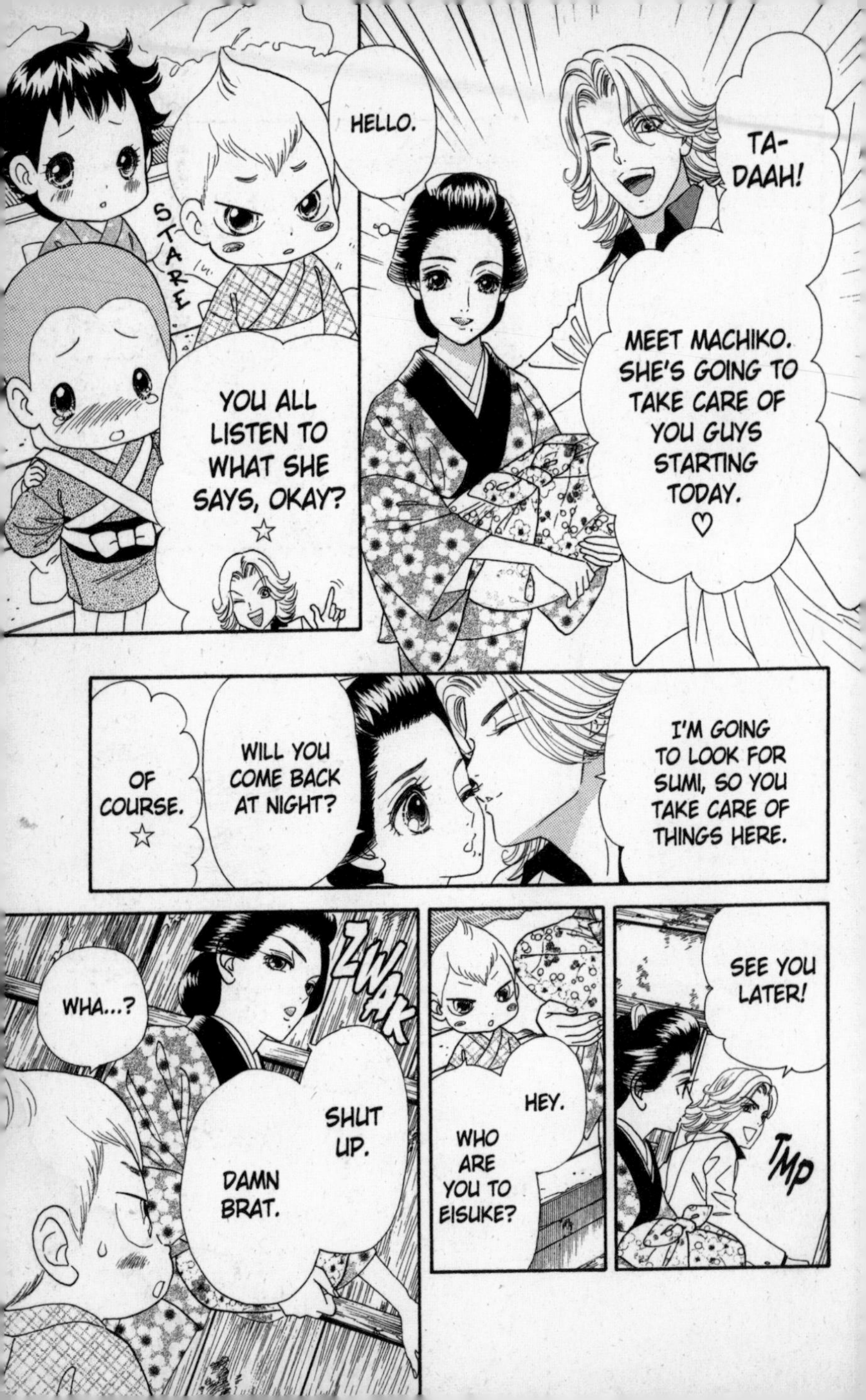
TA-DAAH!
MEET MACHIKO. SHE'S GOING TO TAKE CARE OF YOU GUYS STARTING TODAY. ♡
HELLO.
STARE
YOU ALL LISTEN TO WHAT SHE SAYS, OKAY? ☆
I'M GOING TO LOOK FOR SUMI, SO YOU TAKE CARE OF THINGS HERE.
WILL YOU COME BACK AT NIGHT?
OF COURSE. ☆
SEE YOU LATER!
TMP
HEY.
WHO ARE YOU TO EISUKE?
ZWAK
WHA...?
SHUT UP.
DAMN BRAT.

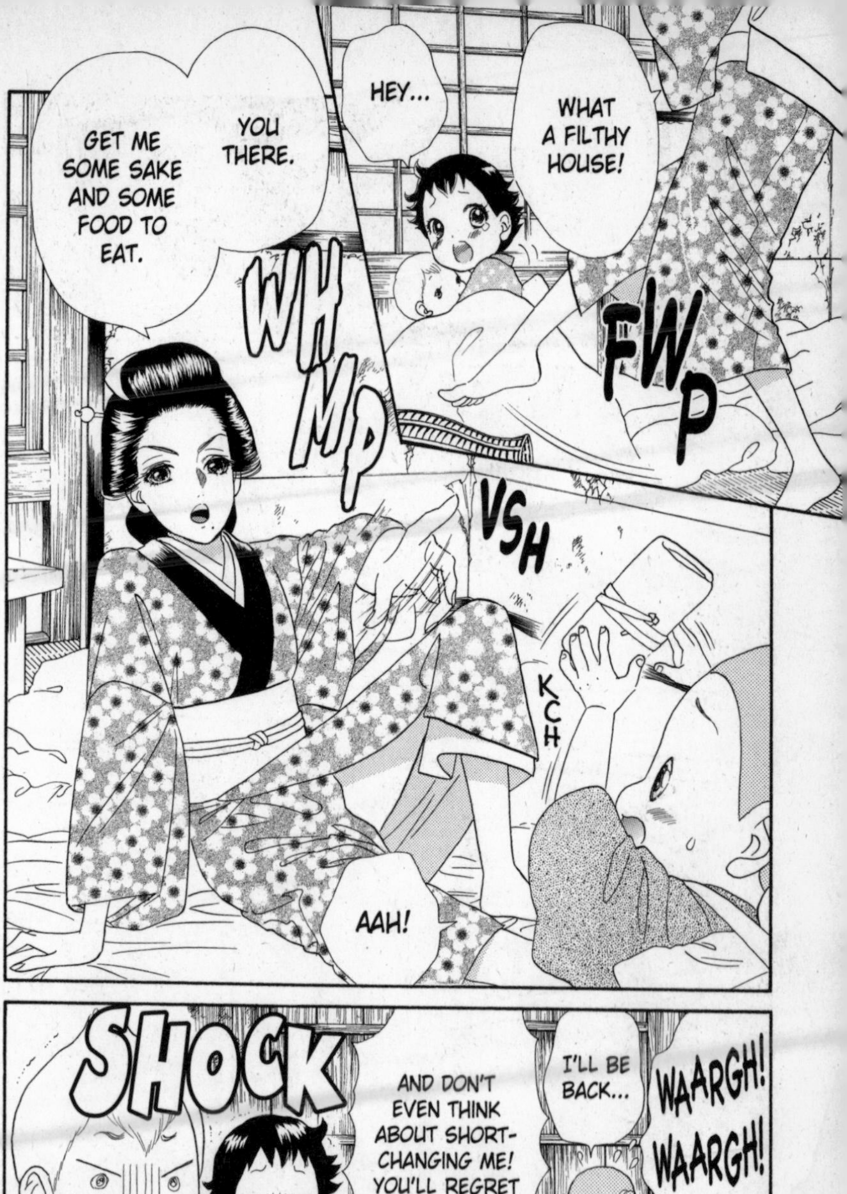
WHAT A FILTHY HOUSE!
HEY...
FWP
YOU THERE.
GET ME SOME SAKE AND SOME FOOD TO EAT.
WHMP
VSH
KCH
AAH!
WAARGH! WAARGH!
I'LL BE BACK...
AND DON'T EVEN THINK ABOUT SHORT-CHANGING ME! YOU'LL REGRET IT, I PROMISE!!
SHOCK

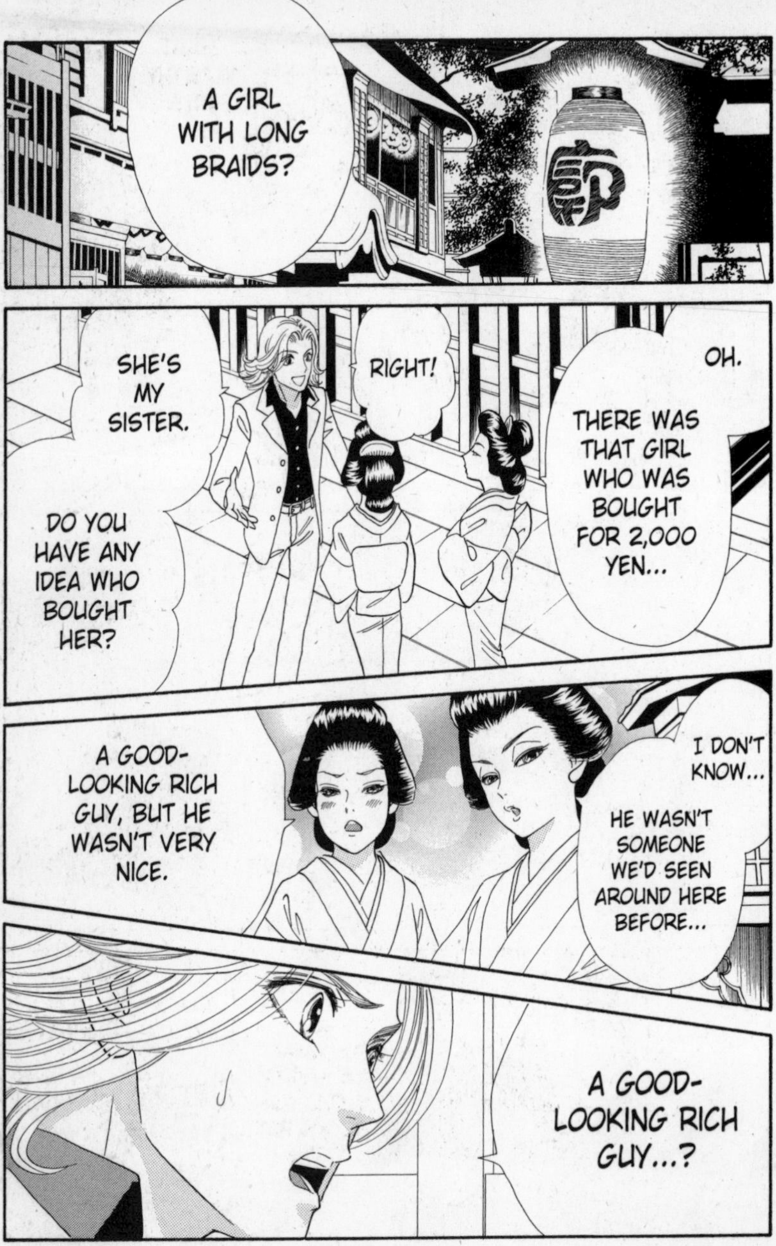
A GIRL WITH LONG BRAIDS?
OH.
THERE WAS THAT GIRL WHO WAS BOUGHT FOR 2,000 YEN...
RIGHT!
SHE'S MY SISTER.
DO YOU HAVE ANY IDEA WHO BOUGHT HER?
I DON'T KNOW...
HE WASN'T SOMEONE WE'D SEEN AROUND HERE BEFORE...
A GOOD-LOOKING RICH GUY, BUT HE WASN'T VERY NICE.
A GOOD-LOOKING RICH GUY...?

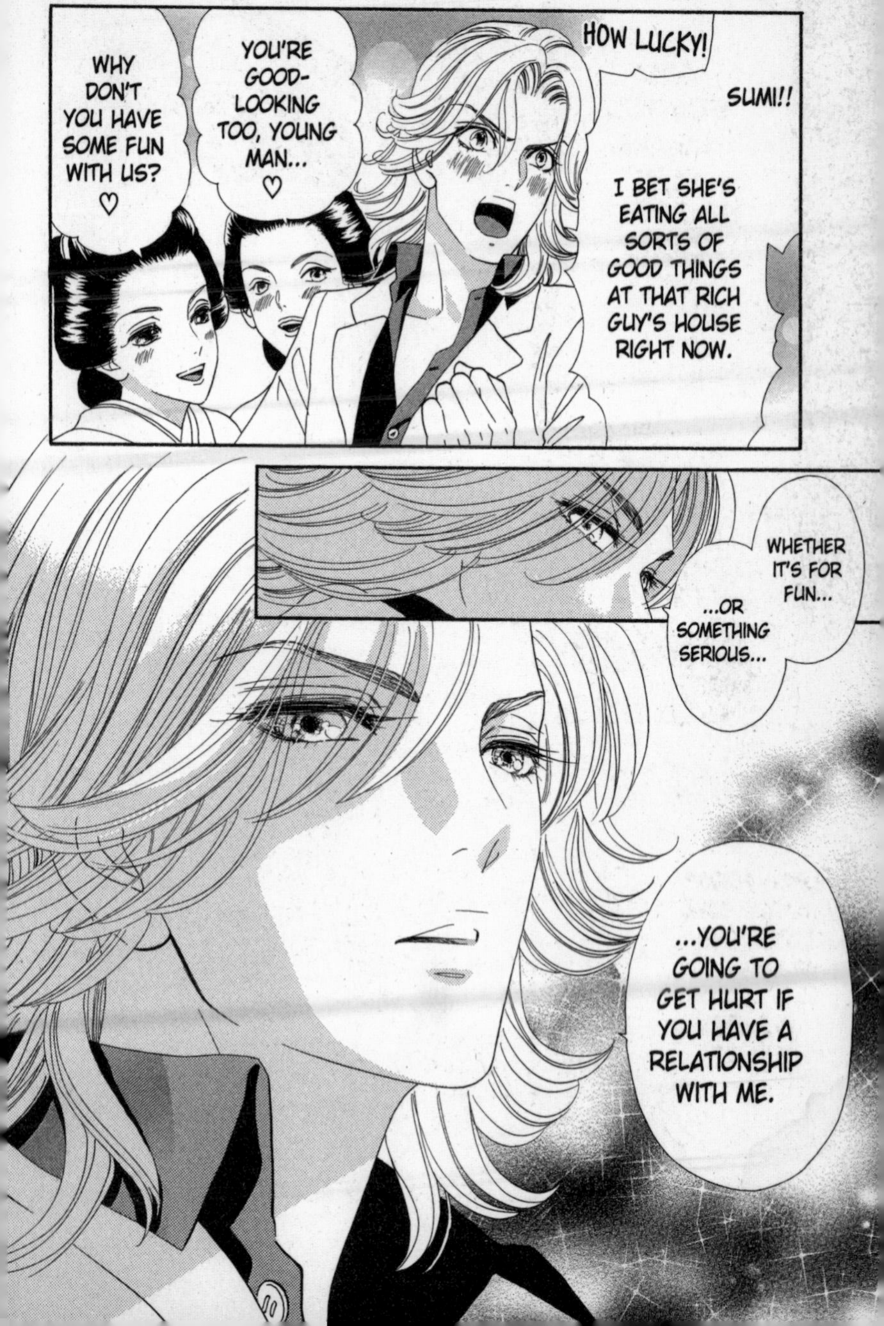
SUMI!!
I BET SHE'S EATING ALL SORTS OF GOOD THINGS AT THAT RICH GUY'S HOUSE RIGHT NOW.
HOW LUCKY!
YOU'RE GOOD-LOOKING TOO, YOUNG MAN... ♡
WHY DON'T YOU HAVE SOME FUN WITH US? ♡
WHETHER IT'S FOR FUN...
...OR SOMETHING SERIOUS...
...YOU'RE GOING TO GET HURT IF YOU HAVE A RELATIONSHIP WITH ME.

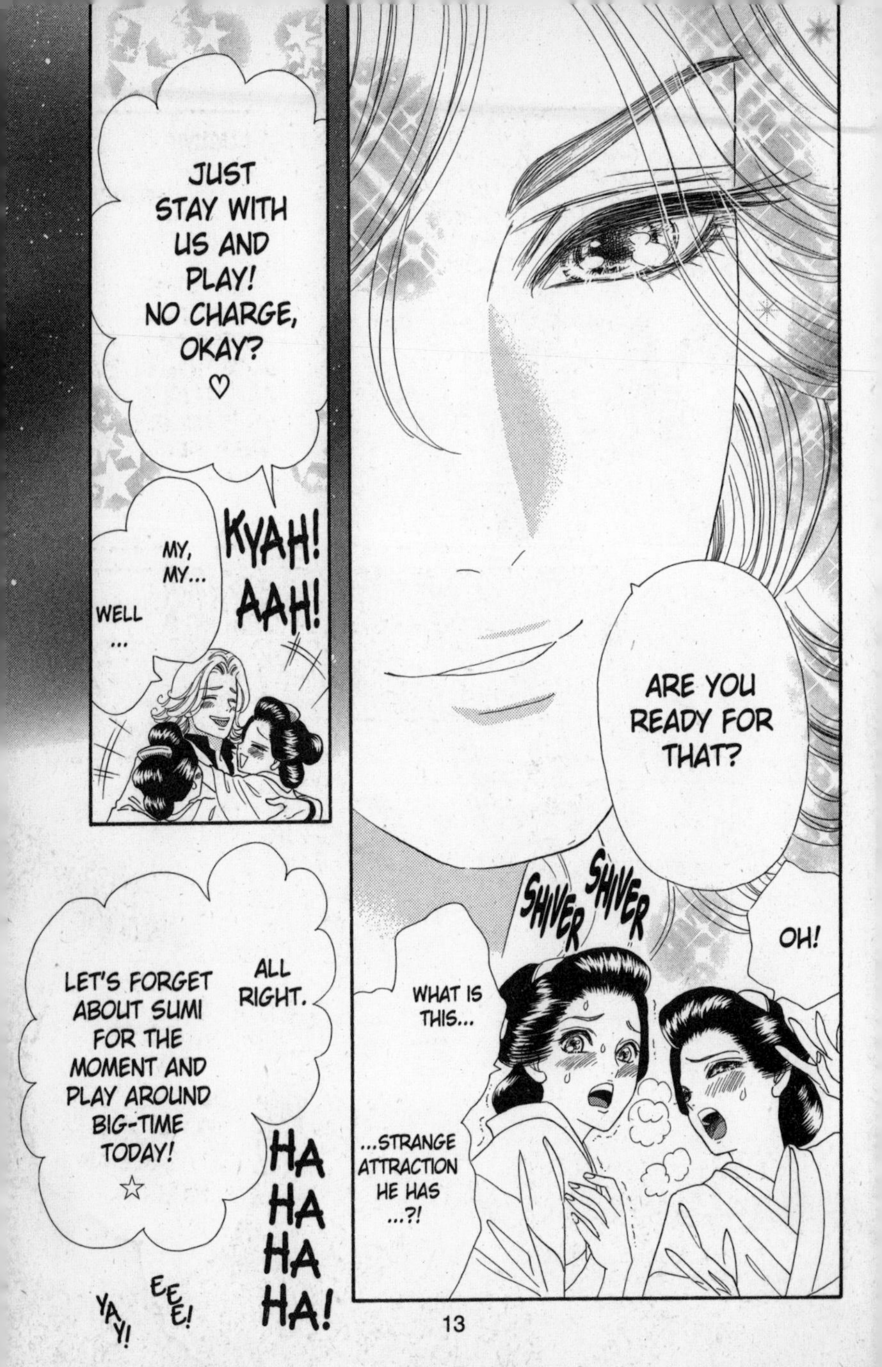
ARE YOU READY FOR THAT?
SHIVER SHIVER
OH!
WHAT IS THIS...
...STRANGE ATTRACTION HE HAS ...?!
JUST STAY WITH US AND PLAY! NO CHARGE, OKAY? ♡
KYAH! AAH!
MY, MY...
WELL ...
ALL RIGHT.
LET'S FORGET ABOUT SUMI FOR THE MOMENT AND PLAY AROUND BIG-TIME TODAY! ☆
HA HA HA HA!
EEE!
YAY!

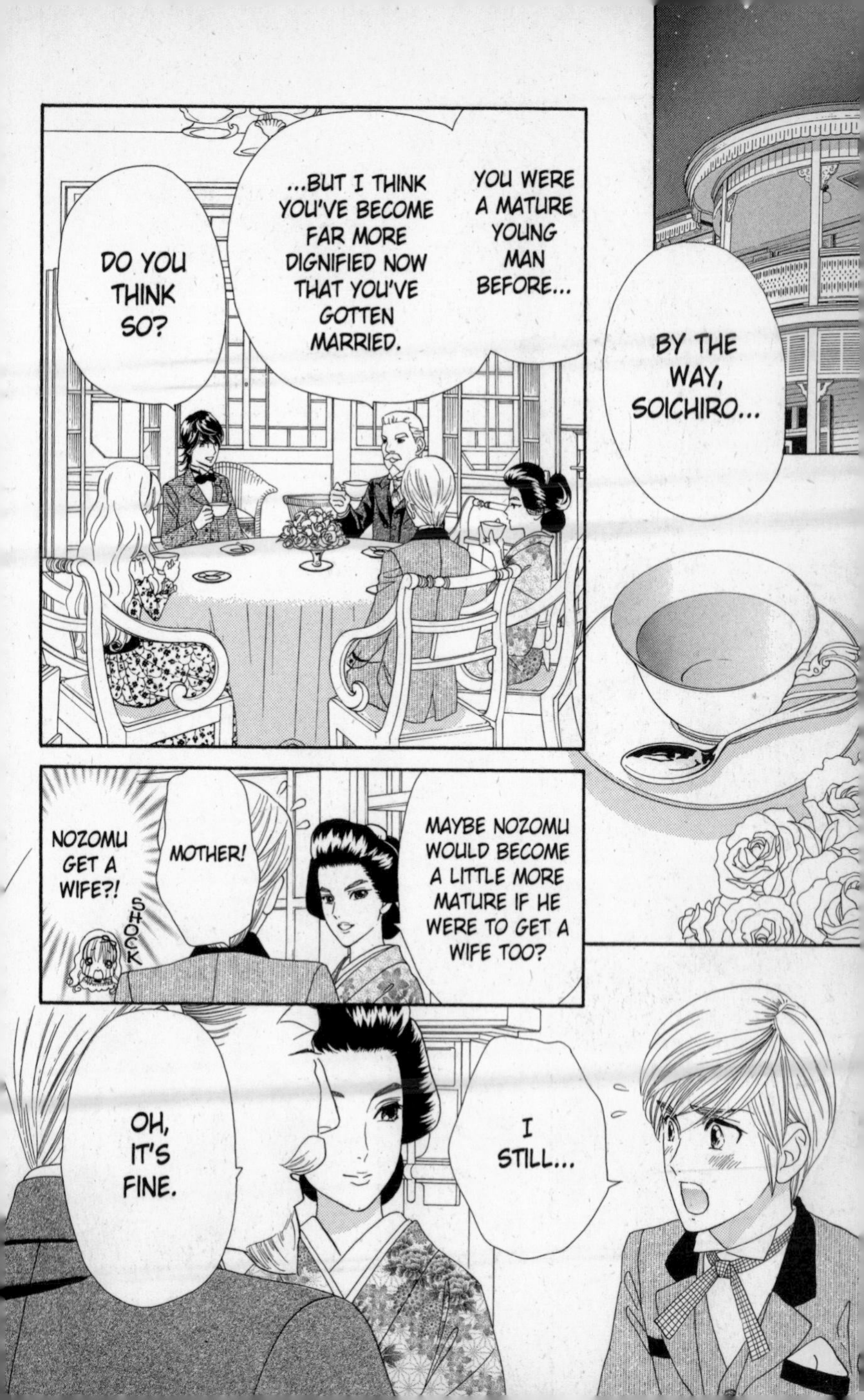
BY THE WAY, SOICHIRO...
YOU WERE A MATURE YOUNG MAN BEFORE...
...BUT I THINK YOU'VE BECOME FAR MORE DIGNIFIED NOW THAT YOU'VE GOTTEN MARRIED.
DO YOU THINK SO?
MAYBE NOZOMU WOULD BECOME A LITTLE MORE MATURE IF HE WERE TO GET A WIFE TOO?
MOTHER!
NOZOMU GET A WIFE?!
SHOCK
I STILL...
OH, IT'S FINE.

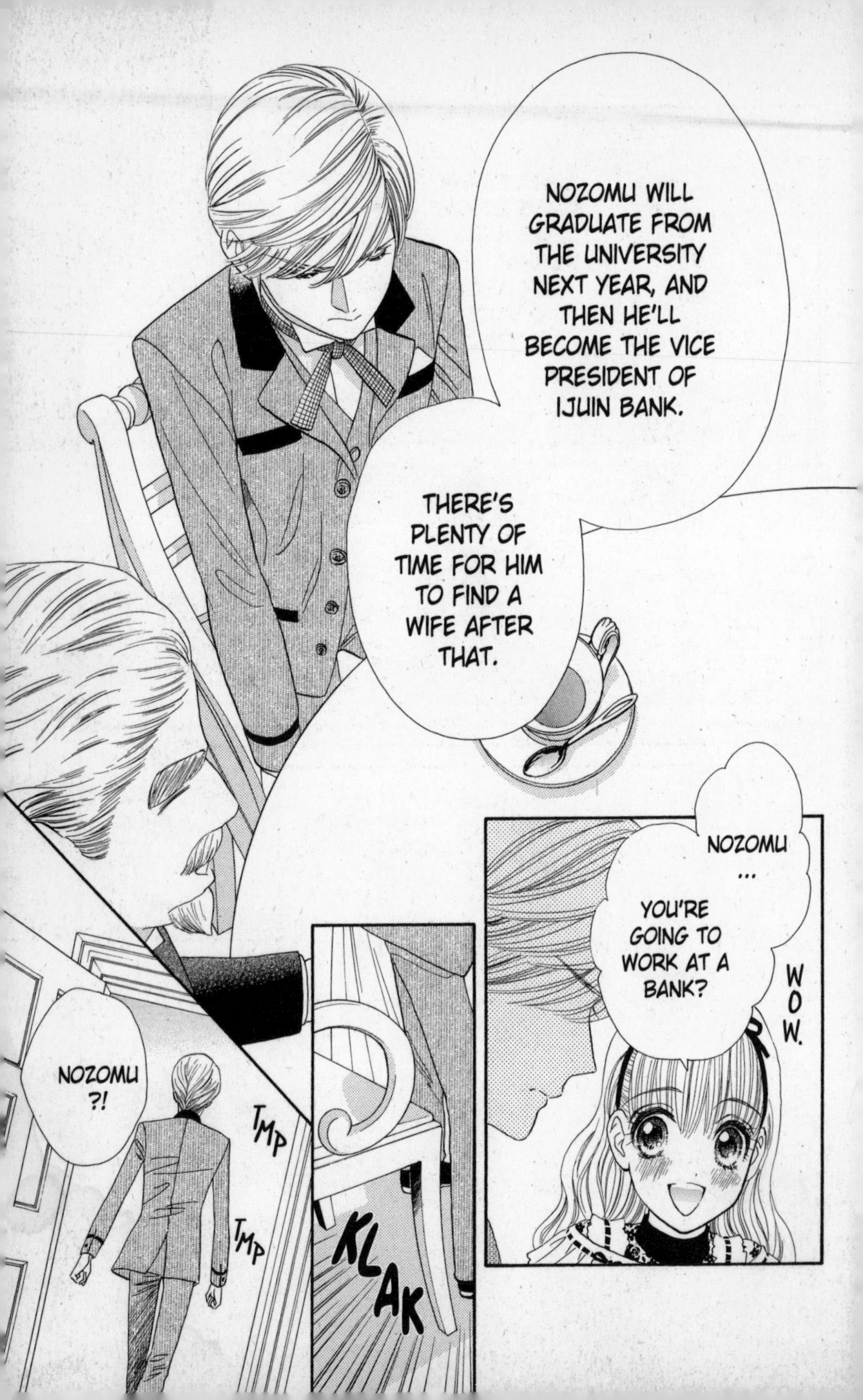
NOZOMU WILL GRADUATE FROM THE UNIVERSITY NEXT YEAR, AND THEN HE'LL BECOME THE VICE PRESIDENT OF IJUIN BANK.
THERE'S PLENTY OF TIME FOR HIM TO FIND A WIFE AFTER THAT.
NOZOMU ...
YOU'RE GOING TO WORK AT A BANK?
WOW.
KLAK
TMP
TMP
NOZOMU ?!

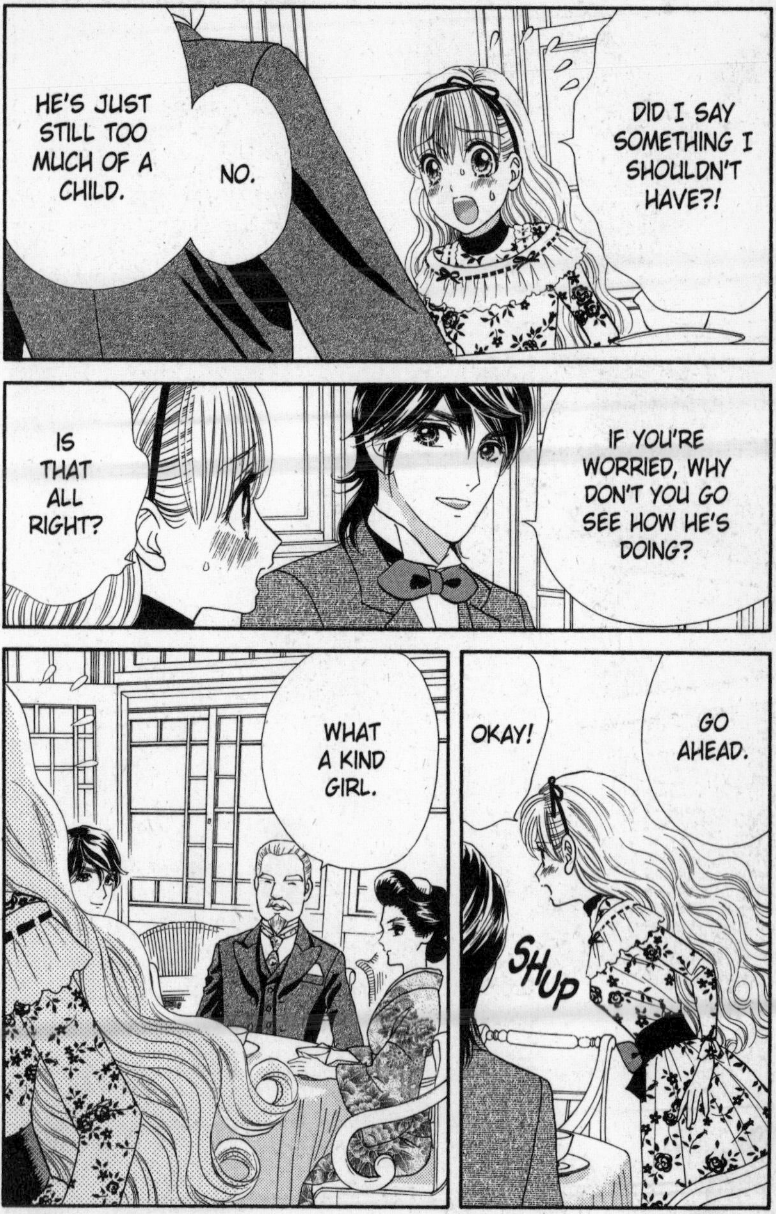
DID I SAY SOMETHING I SHOULDN'T HAVE?!
NO.
HE'S JUST STILL TOO MUCH OF A CHILD.
IF YOU'RE WORRIED, WHY DON'T YOU GO SEE HOW HE'S DOING?
IS THAT ALL RIGHT?
GO AHEAD.
OKAY!
SHUP
WHAT A KIND GIRL.

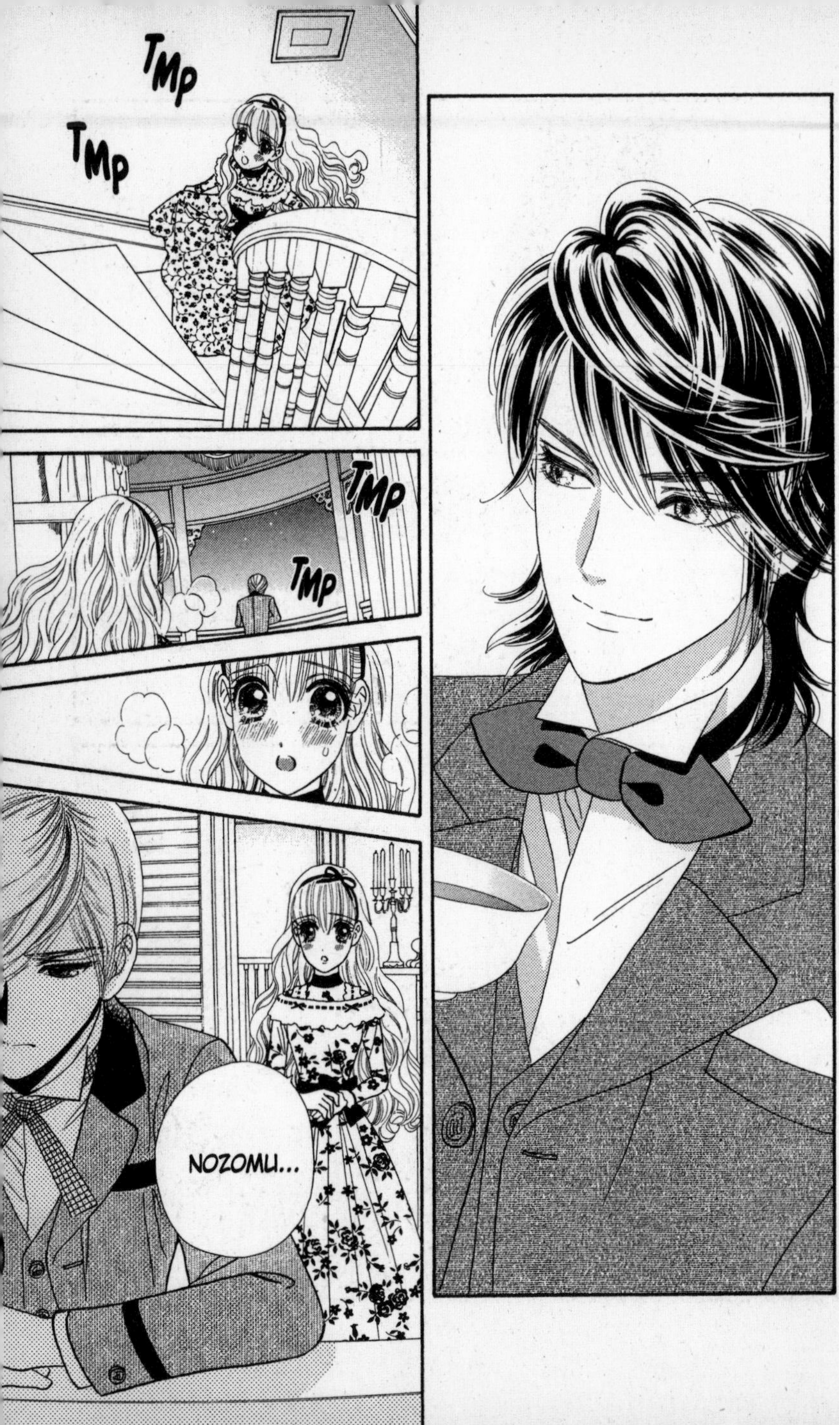
TMP
TMP
TMP
TMP
NOZOMU...

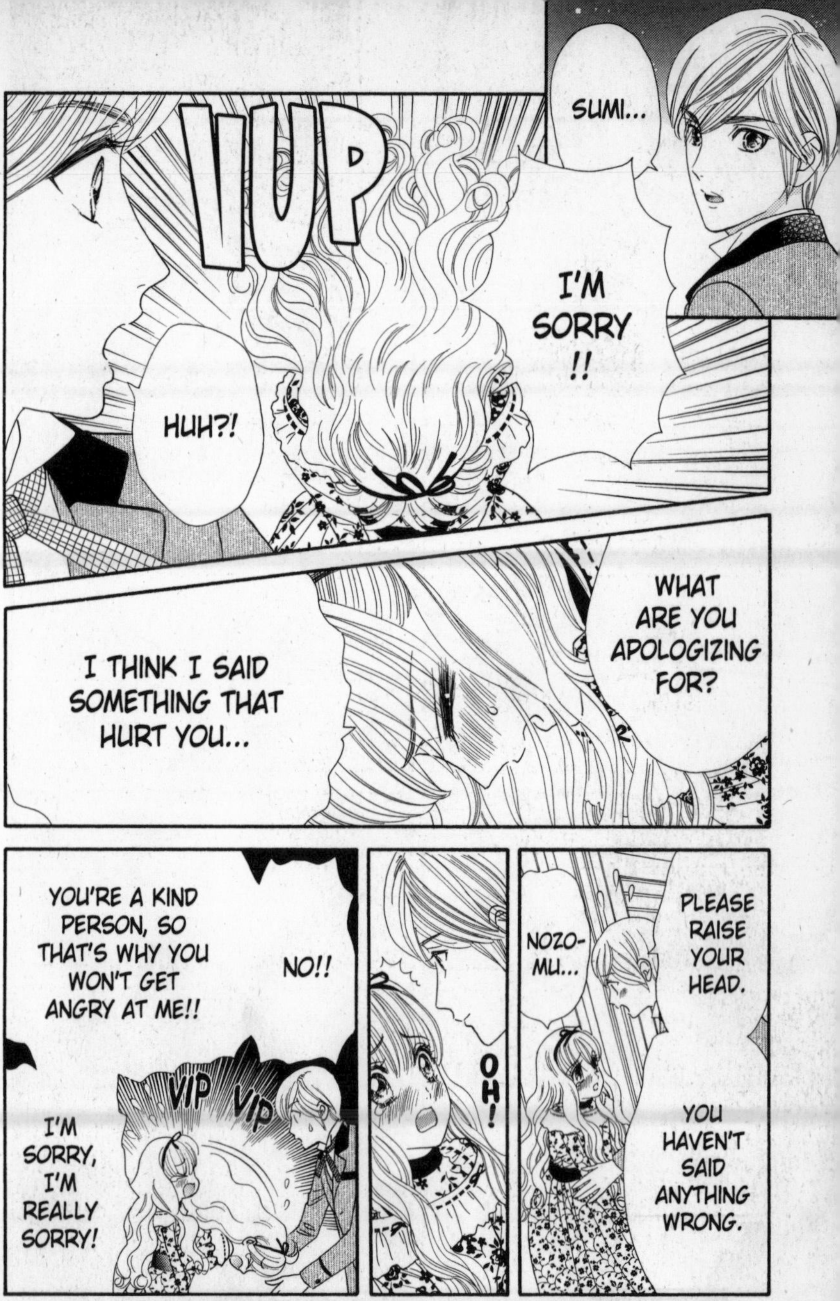
SUMI...
I'M SORRY !!
VUP
HUH?!
WHAT ARE YOU APOLOGIZING FOR?
I THINK I SAID SOMETHING THAT HURT YOU...
PLEASE RAISE YOUR HEAD.
NOZO-MU...
YOU HAVEN'T SAID ANYTHING WRONG.
OH!
NO!!
YOU'RE A KIND PERSON, SO THAT'S WHY YOU WON'T GET ANGRY AT ME!!
VIP VIP
I'M SORRY, I'M REALLY SORRY!

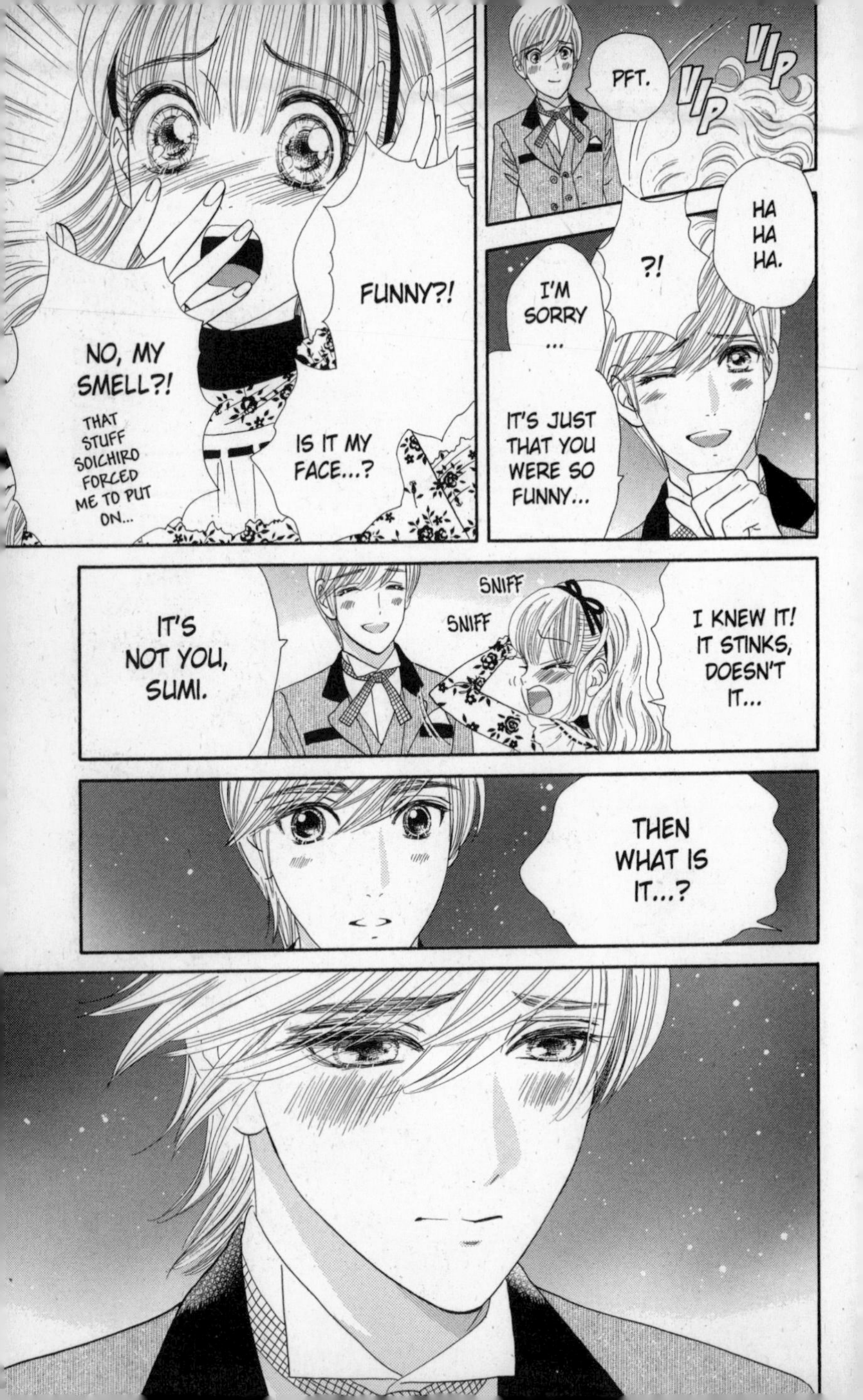
PFT.
VIP VIP
HA HA HA.
?!
I'M SORRY...
IT'S JUST THAT YOU WERE SO FUNNY...
FUNNY?!
IS IT MY FACE...?
NO, MY SMELL?!
THAT STUFF SOICHIRO FORCED ME TO PUT ON...
I KNEW IT! IT STINKS, DOESN'T IT...
SNIFF
SNIFF
IT'S NOT YOU, SUMI.
THEN WHAT IS IT...?

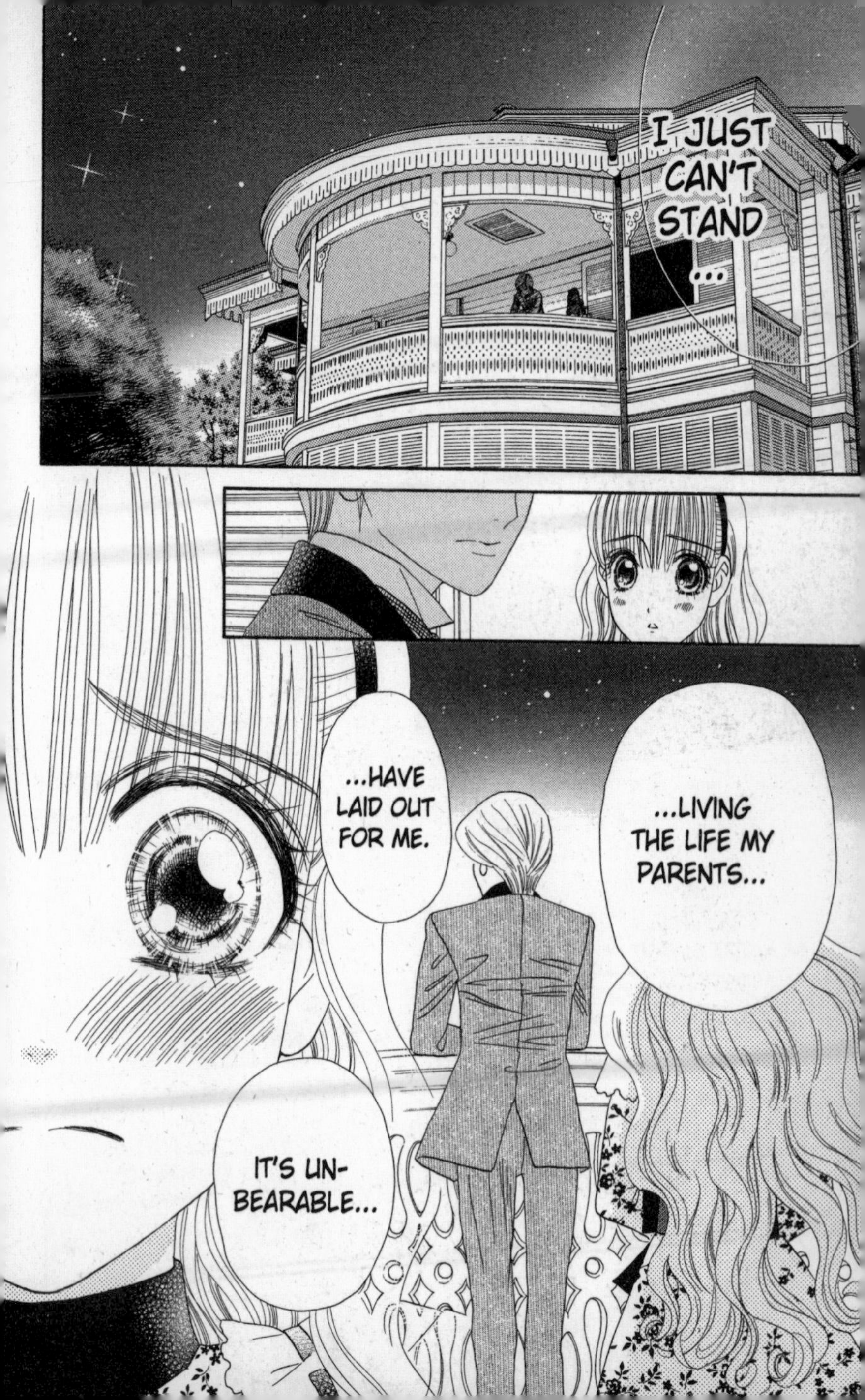
I JUST CAN'T STAND ...
...LIVING THE LIFE MY PARENTS...
...HAVE LAID OUT FOR ME.
IT'S UN-BEARABLE...

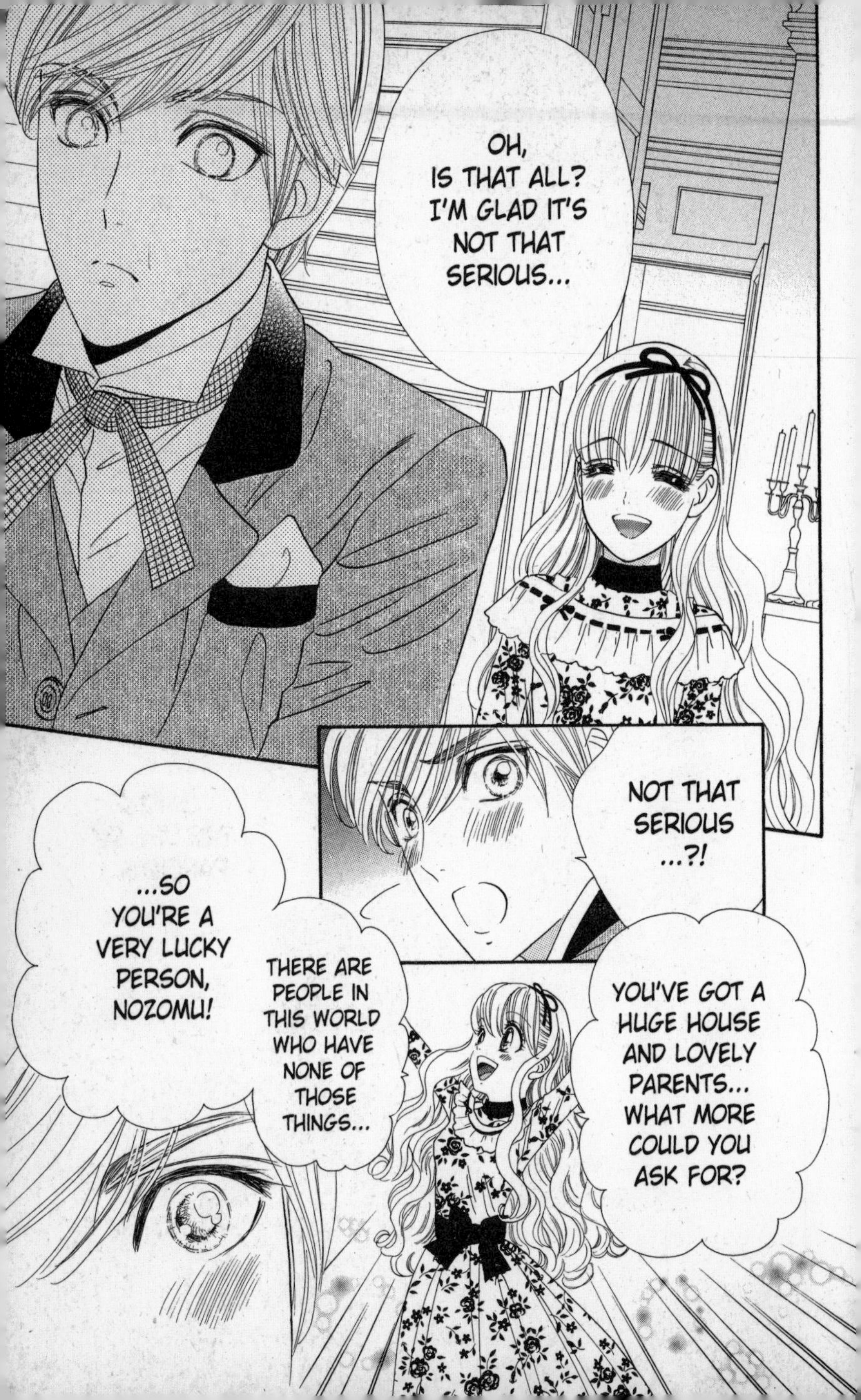
OH, IS THAT ALL? I'M GLAD IT'S NOT THAT SERIOUS...
NOT THAT SERIOUS ...?!
YOU'VE GOT A HUGE HOUSE AND LOVELY PARENTS... WHAT MORE COULD YOU ASK FOR?
THERE ARE PEOPLE IN THIS WORLD WHO HAVE NONE OF THOSE THINGS...
...SO YOU'RE A VERY LUCKY PERSON, NOZOMU!

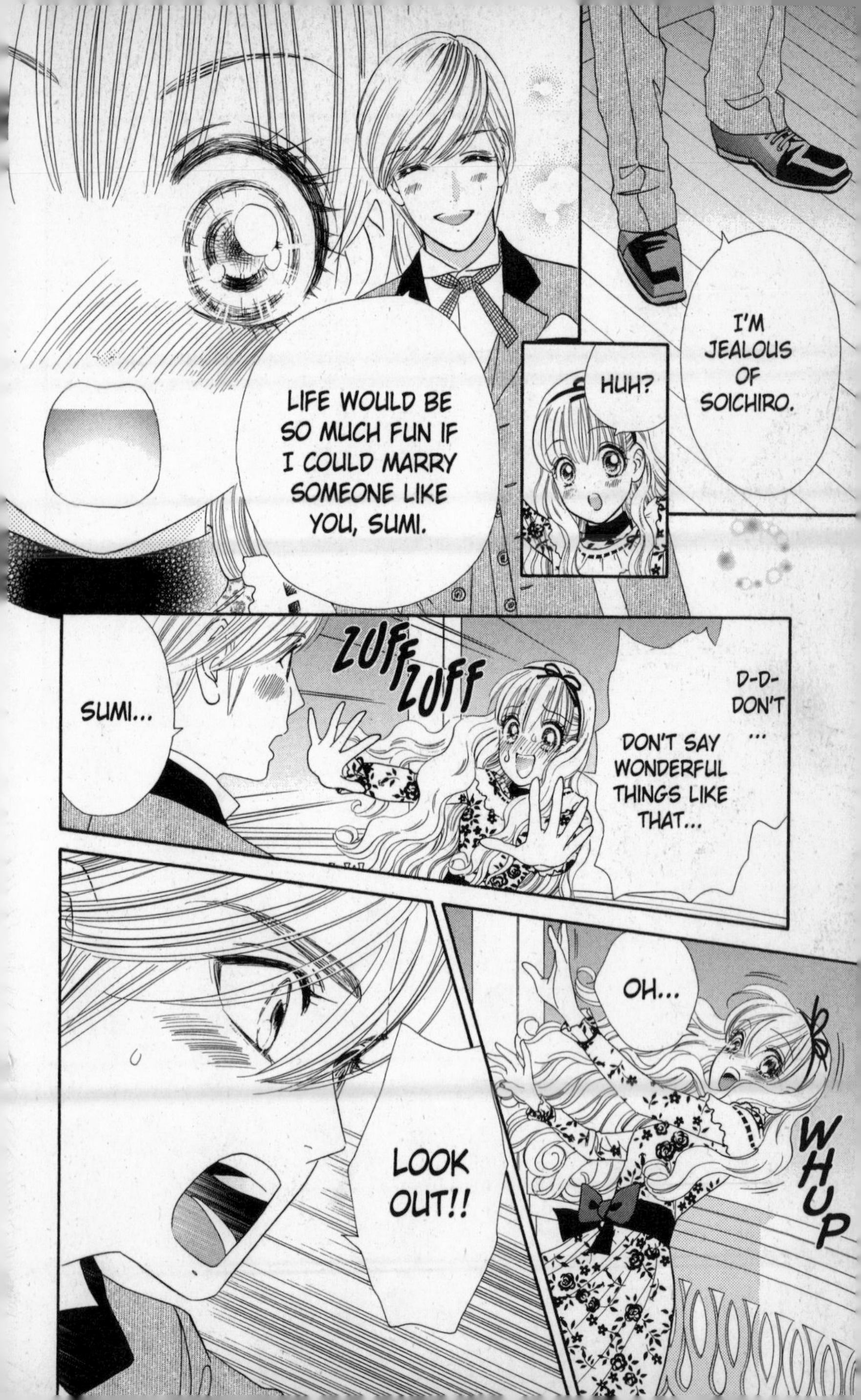
I'M JEALOUS OF SOICHIRO.
HUH?
LIFE WOULD BE SO MUCH FUN IF I COULD MARRY SOMEONE LIKE YOU, SUMI.
D-D-DON'T...
DON'T SAY WONDERFUL THINGS LIKE THAT...
ZUFF ZUFF
SUMI...
OH...
WHUP
LOOK OUT!!

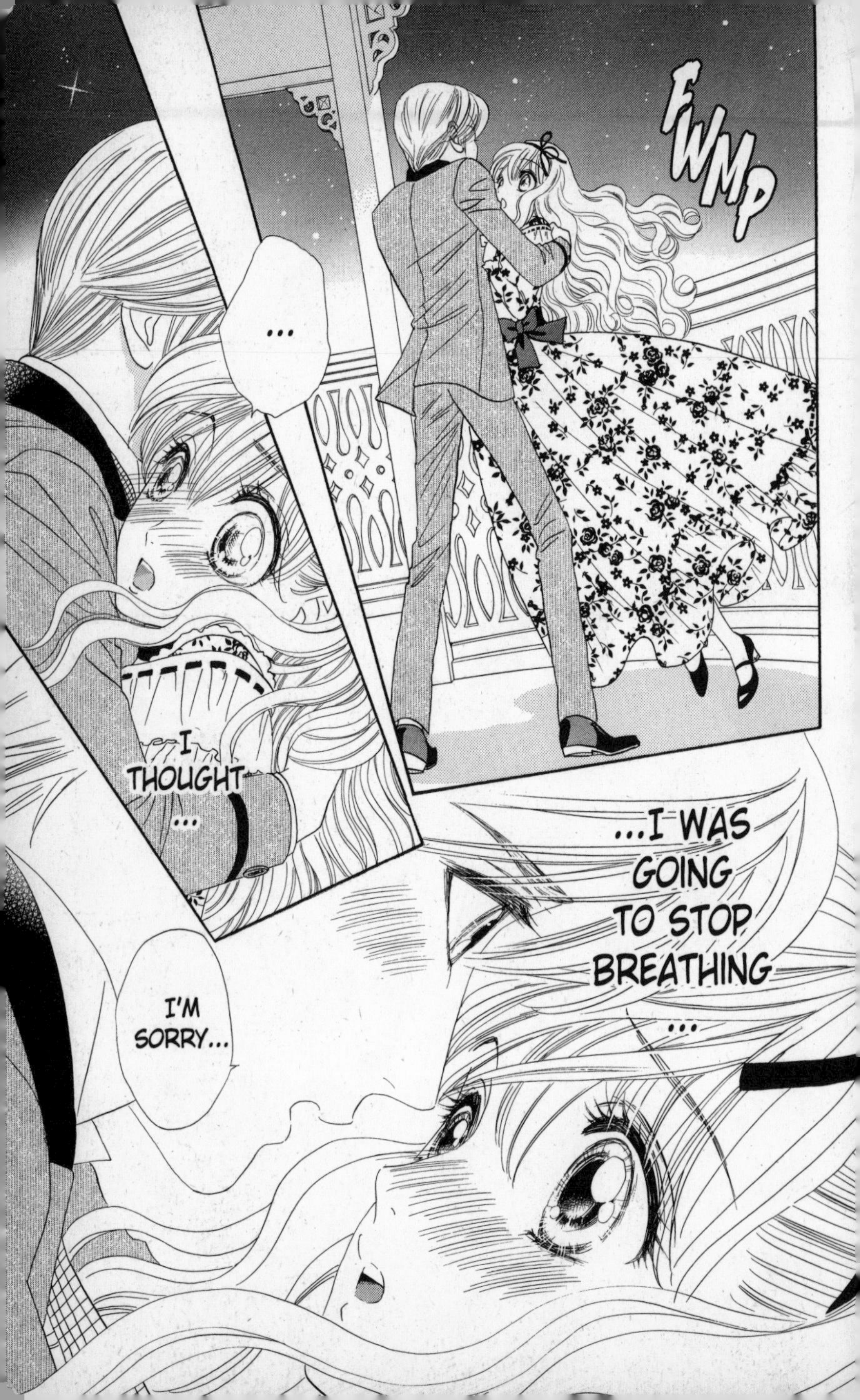
FWMP
...
I THOUGHT ...
...I WAS GOING TO STOP BREATHING ...
I'M SORRY...

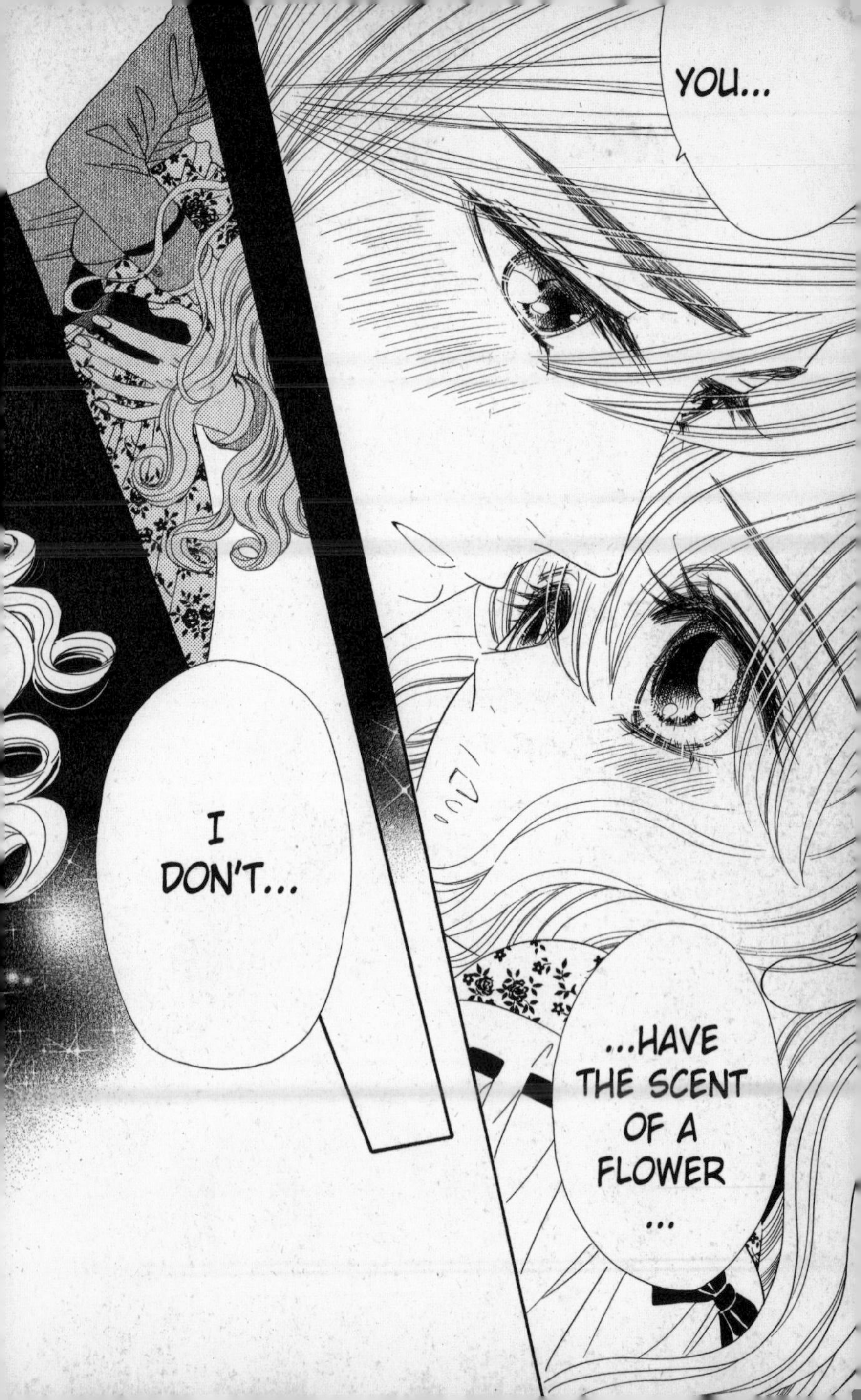
YOU...
...HAVE THE SCENT OF A FLOWER ...
I DON'T...

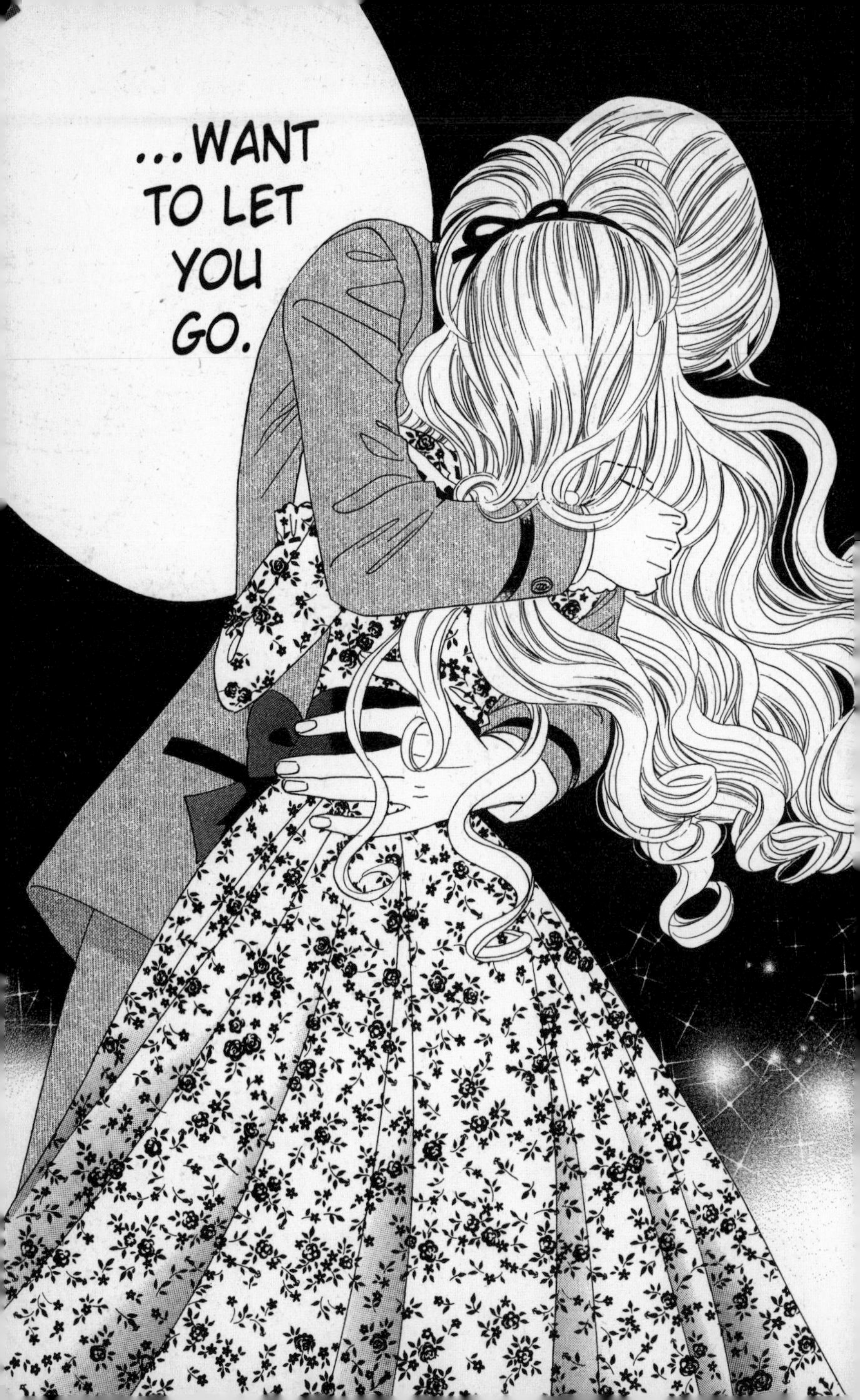
...WANT TO LET YOU GO.

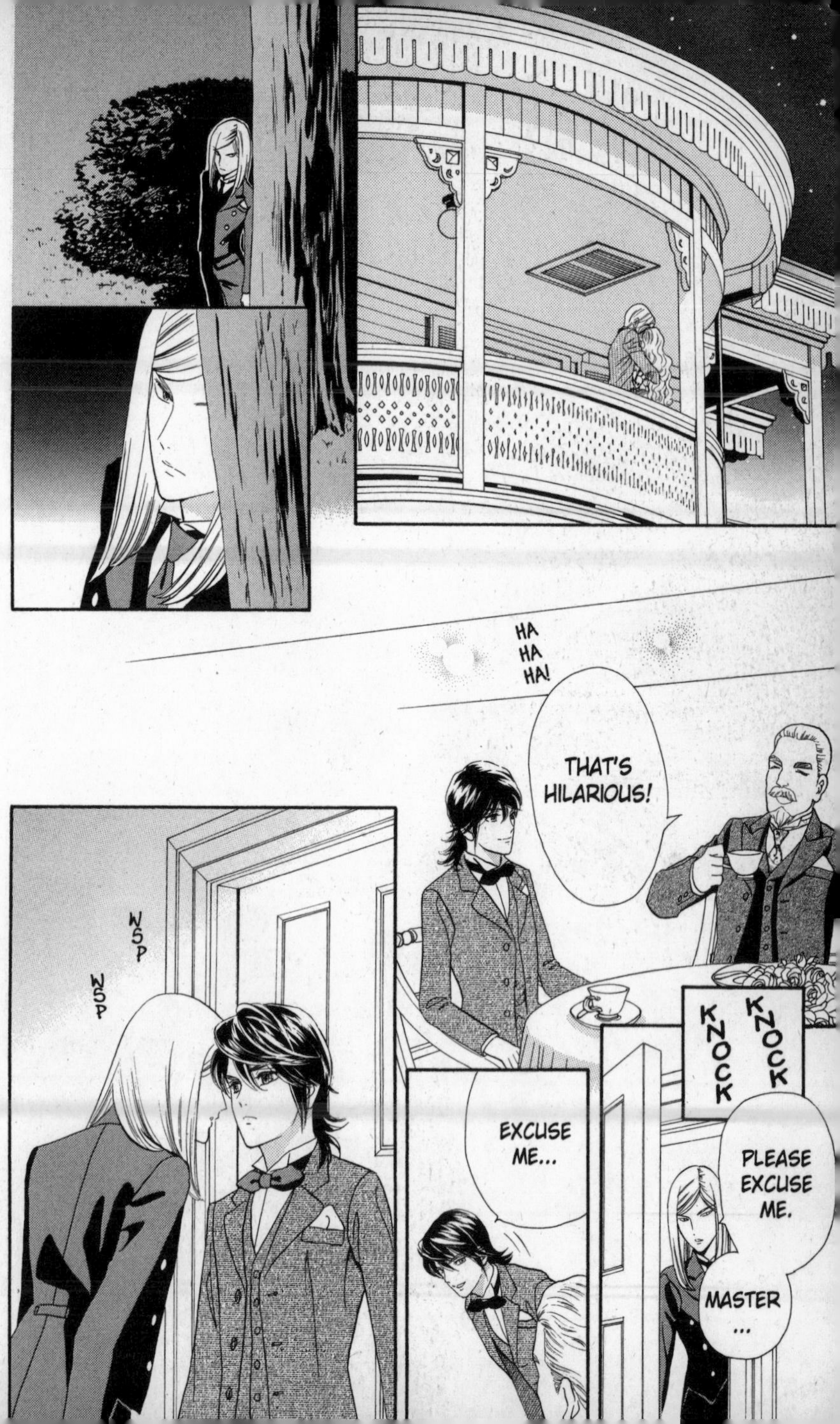
HA HA HA!
THAT'S HILARIOUS!
KNOCK KNOCK
PLEASE EXCUSE ME.
MASTER...
EXCUSE ME...
WSP WSP

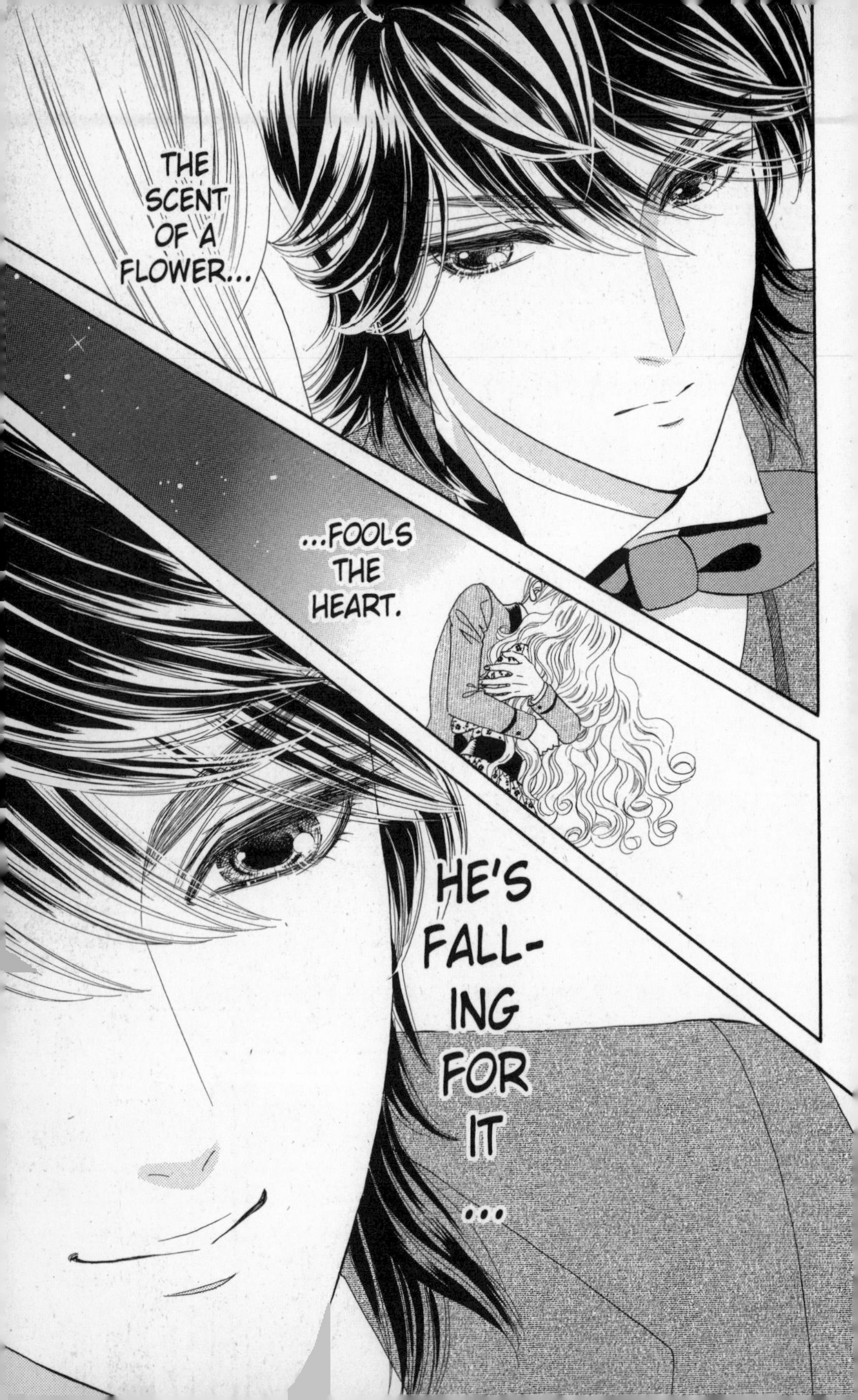
THE SCENT OF A FLOWER...
...FOOLS THE HEART.
HE'S FALL-ING FOR IT ...

No.

STEPPING ON ROSES BACKSTAGE SECTION!!

Date

HELLO, IT'S UE-RIN!!

THANK YOU VERY MUCH FOR PICKING UP VOLUME 2.
EVEN I WAS SURPRISED AT HOW THE STORY IN THIS VOLUME TURNED OUT.

I WAS IN MUCH AGONY DURING THE PREPARATION PERIOD FOR *STEPPING ON ROSES* BECAUSE I WASN'T ABLE TO DECIDE ON THE TITLE OF THIS SERIES AS WELL AS THE NAMES OF THE MAIN CHARACTERS.

UP UNTIL NOW, MOST OF THE CHARACTERS IN *RYO* AND *TAIL OF THE MOON* WERE PEOPLE WHO REALLY EXISTED, LIKE YOSHITSUNE, BENKEI AND HATTORI HANZO, SO I DIDN'T REALLY HAVE TO WORK THAT HARD ON NAMING THE CHARACTERS.

BUT IN THIS SERIES, EVERYONE IS A FICTIONAL CHARACTER, AND I HAD TO COME UP WITH NAMES FOR ALL OF THEM.
I COULDN'T GIVE THEM POPULAR MODERN NAMES OR SIMPLY NAME THEM ON A WHIM SINCE I OBVIOUSLY COULDN'T RENAME THEM ONCE THEIR NAMES WERE SET. I WAS AT A COMPLETE LOSS FROM THE PRESSURE OF NOT HAVING CHOSEN THEIR NAMES EVEN AT THE LAST MINUTE.

BUT JUST THEN, A SAVIOR APPEARED BEFORE POOR DISTRESSED UE-RIN!!

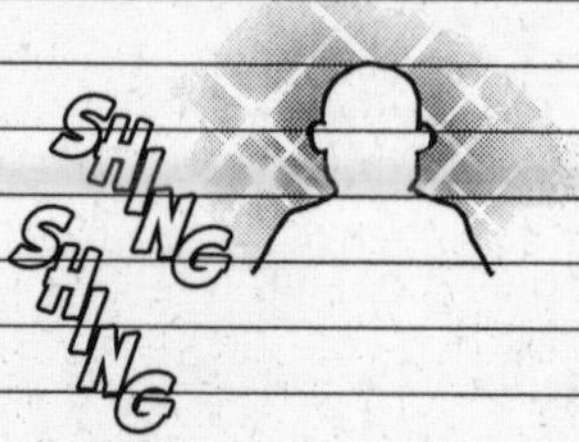
SHING
SHING

TO BE CONTINUED!!

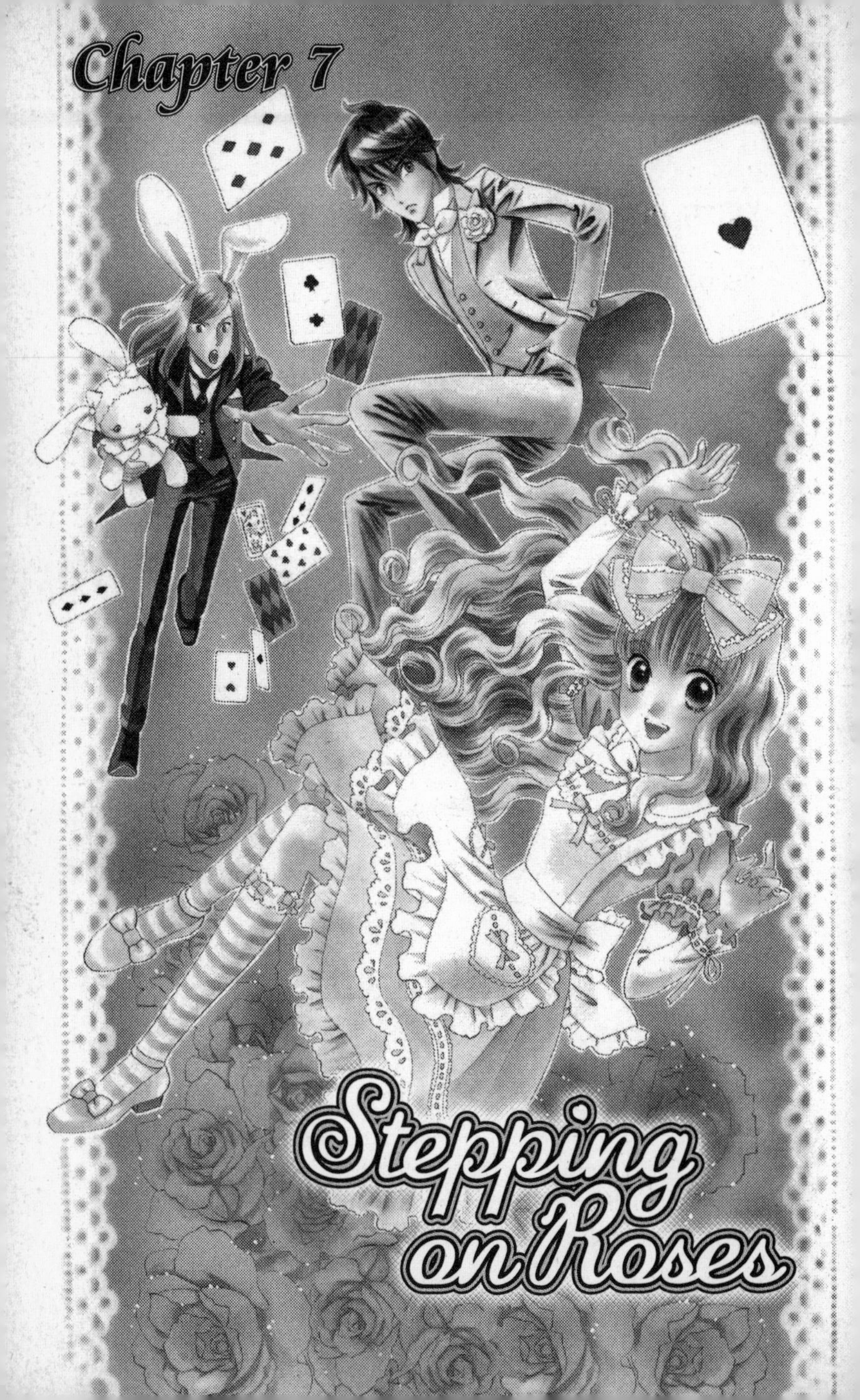
Chapter 7
Stepping on Roses

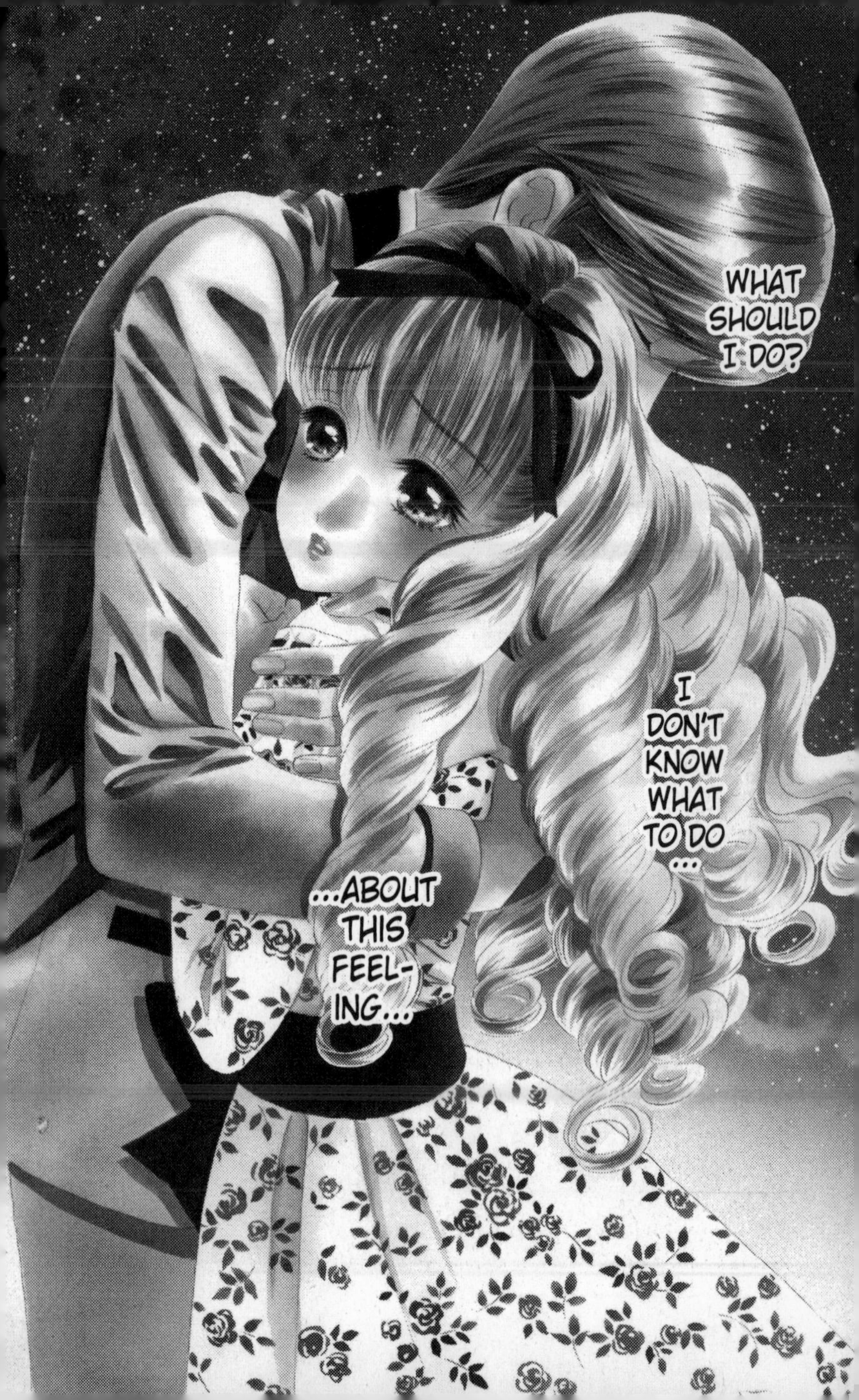
WHAT SHOULD I DO?
I DON'T KNOW WHAT TO DO...
...ABOUT THIS FEEL-ING...

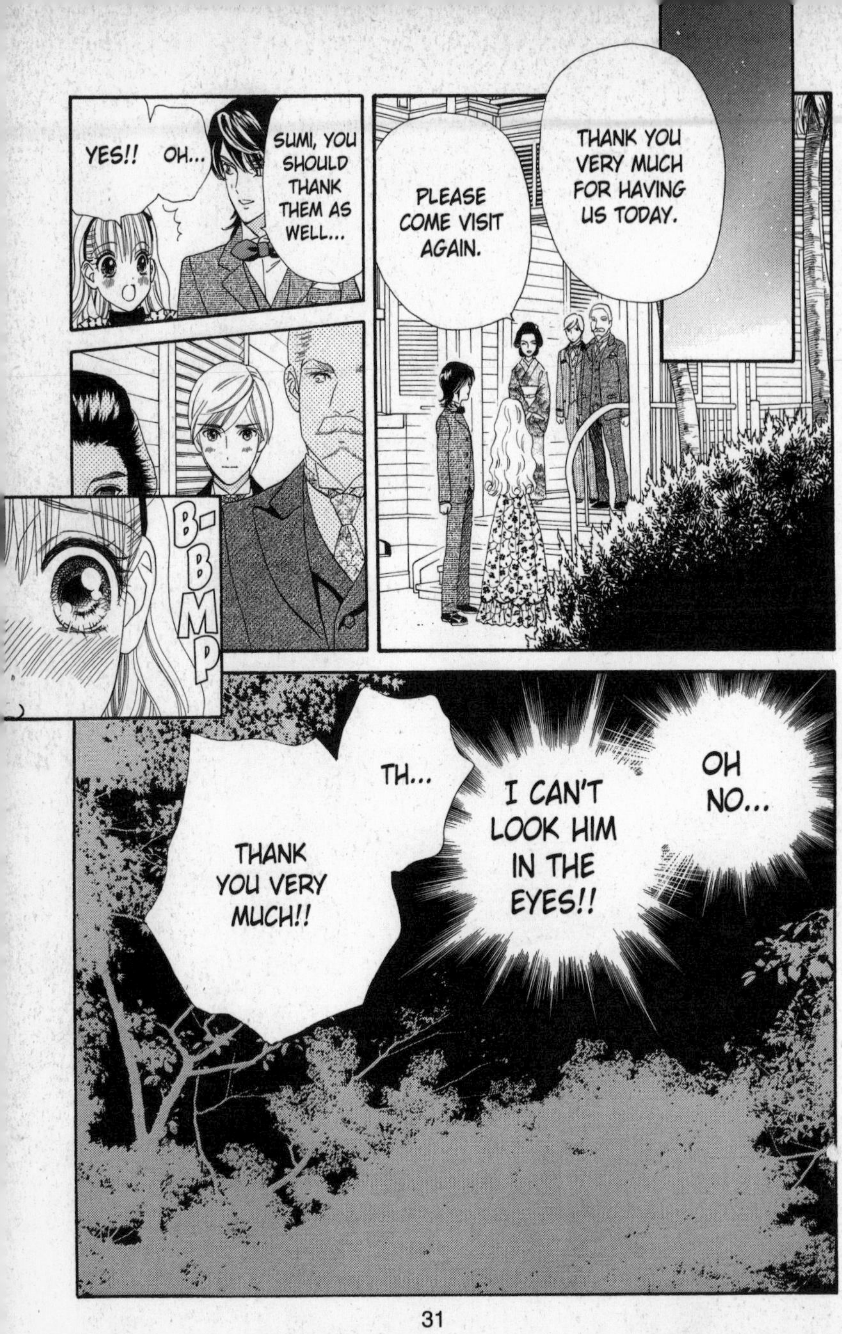
THANK YOU VERY MUCH FOR HAVING US TODAY.
PLEASE COME VISIT AGAIN.
SUMI, YOU SHOULD THANK THEM AS WELL...
YES!! OH...
B-BMP
OH NO...
I CAN'T LOOK HIM IN THE EYES!!
TH...
THANK YOU VERY MUCH!!

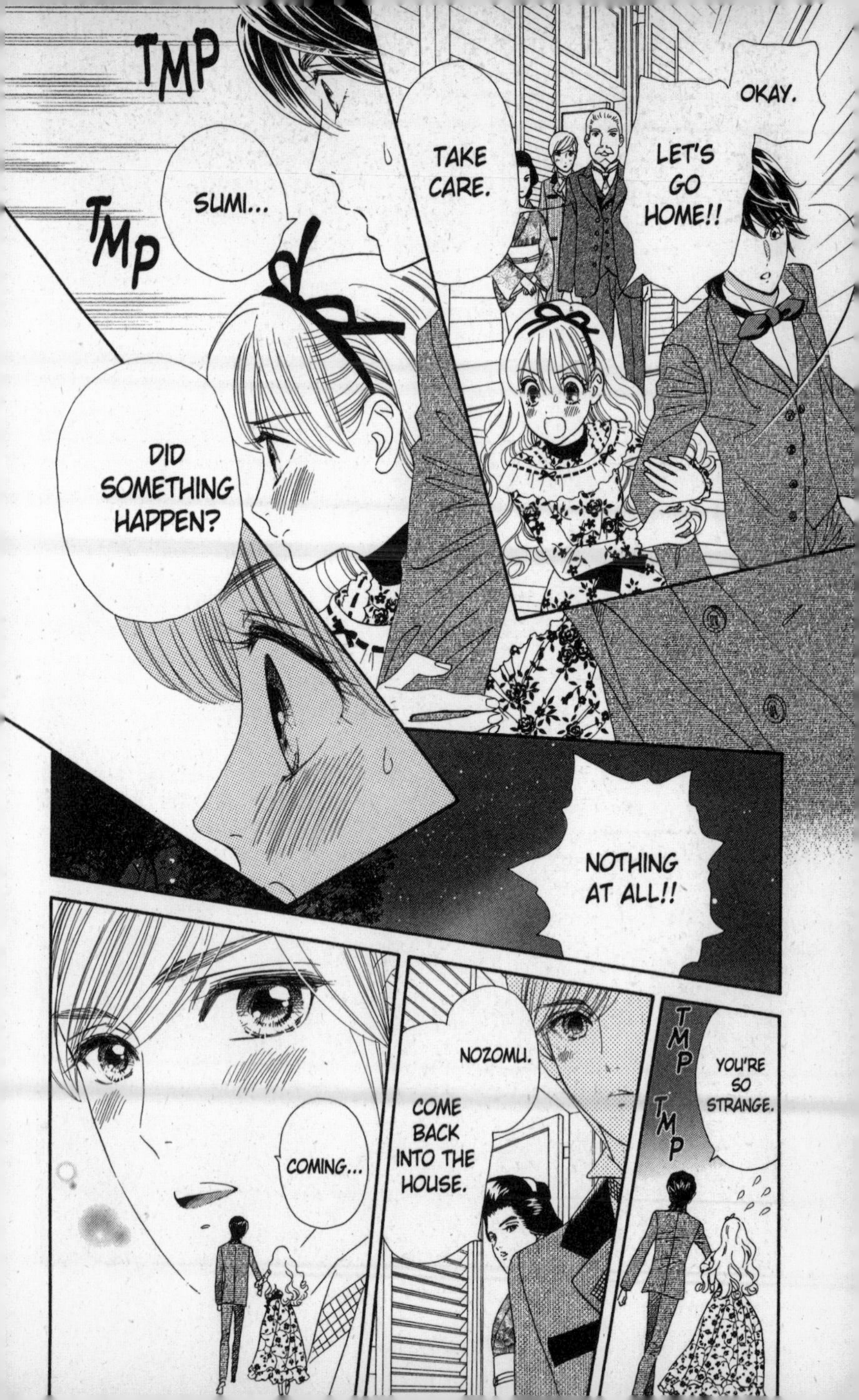
OKAY.
LET'S GO HOME!!
TAKE CARE.
TMP
SUMI...
TMP
DID SOMETHING HAPPEN?
NOTHING AT ALL!!
TMP TMP
YOU'RE SO STRANGE.
NOZOMU.
COME BACK INTO THE HOUSE.
COMING...

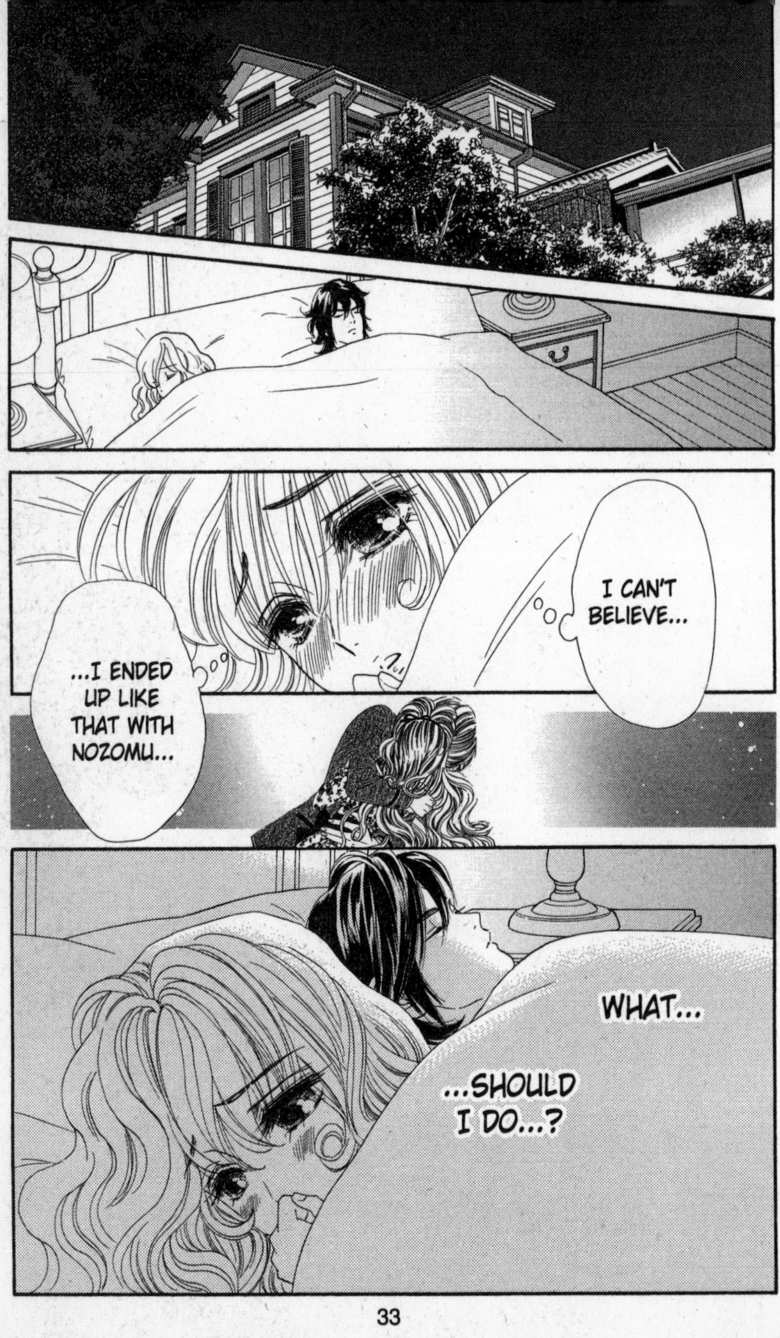
I CAN'T BELIEVE...
...I ENDED UP LIKE THAT WITH NOZOMU...
WHAT...
...SHOULD I DO...?

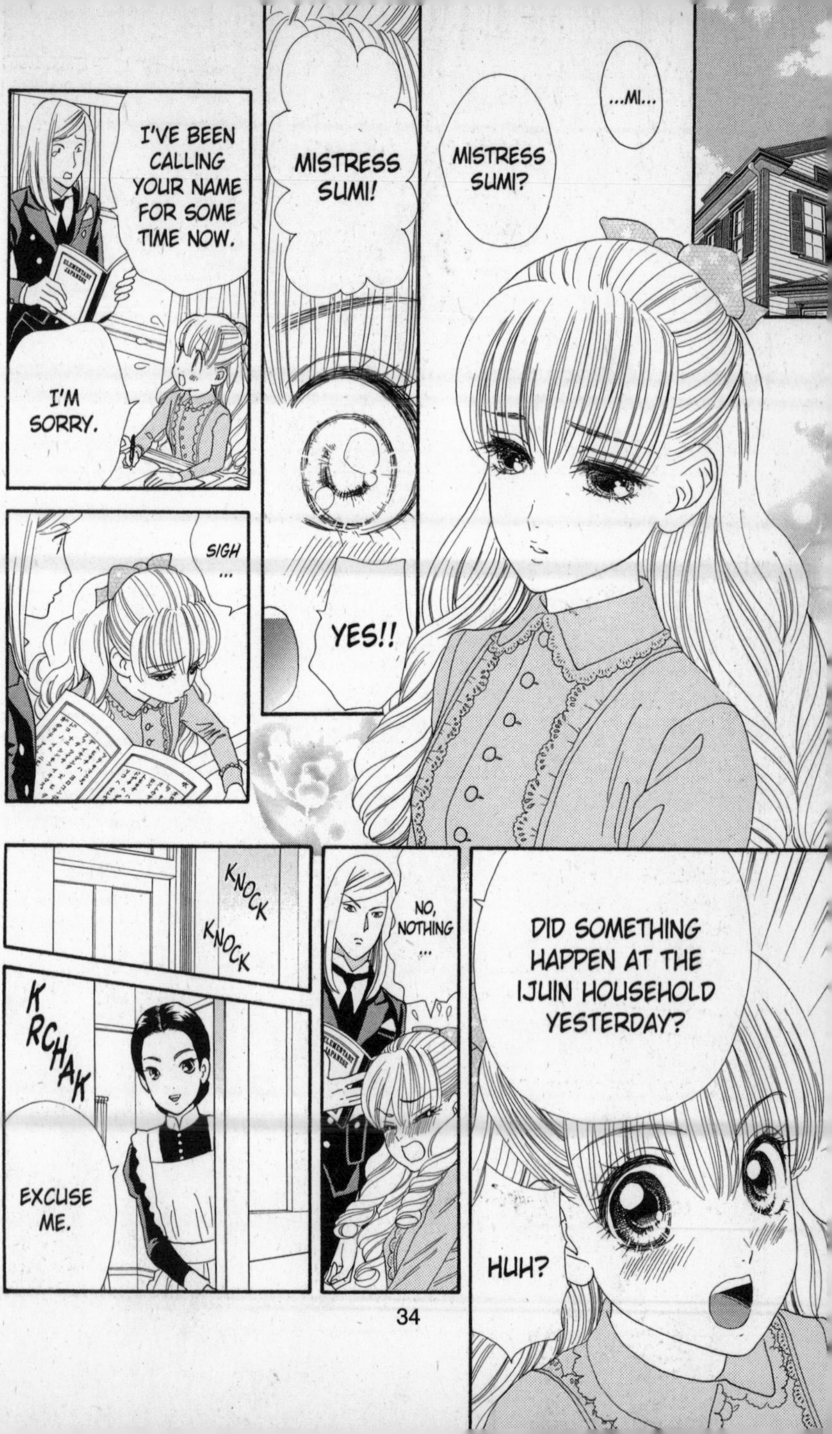
...MI...
MISTRESS SUMI?
MISTRESS SUMI!
YES!!
I'VE BEEN CALLING YOUR NAME FOR SOME TIME NOW.
ELEMENTARY JAPANESE
I'M SORRY.
SIGH...
DID SOMETHING HAPPEN AT THE IJUIN HOUSEHOLD YESTERDAY?
HUH?
NO, NOTHING...
ELEMENTARY JAPANESE
KNOCK
KNOCK
KRCHAK
EXCUSE ME.

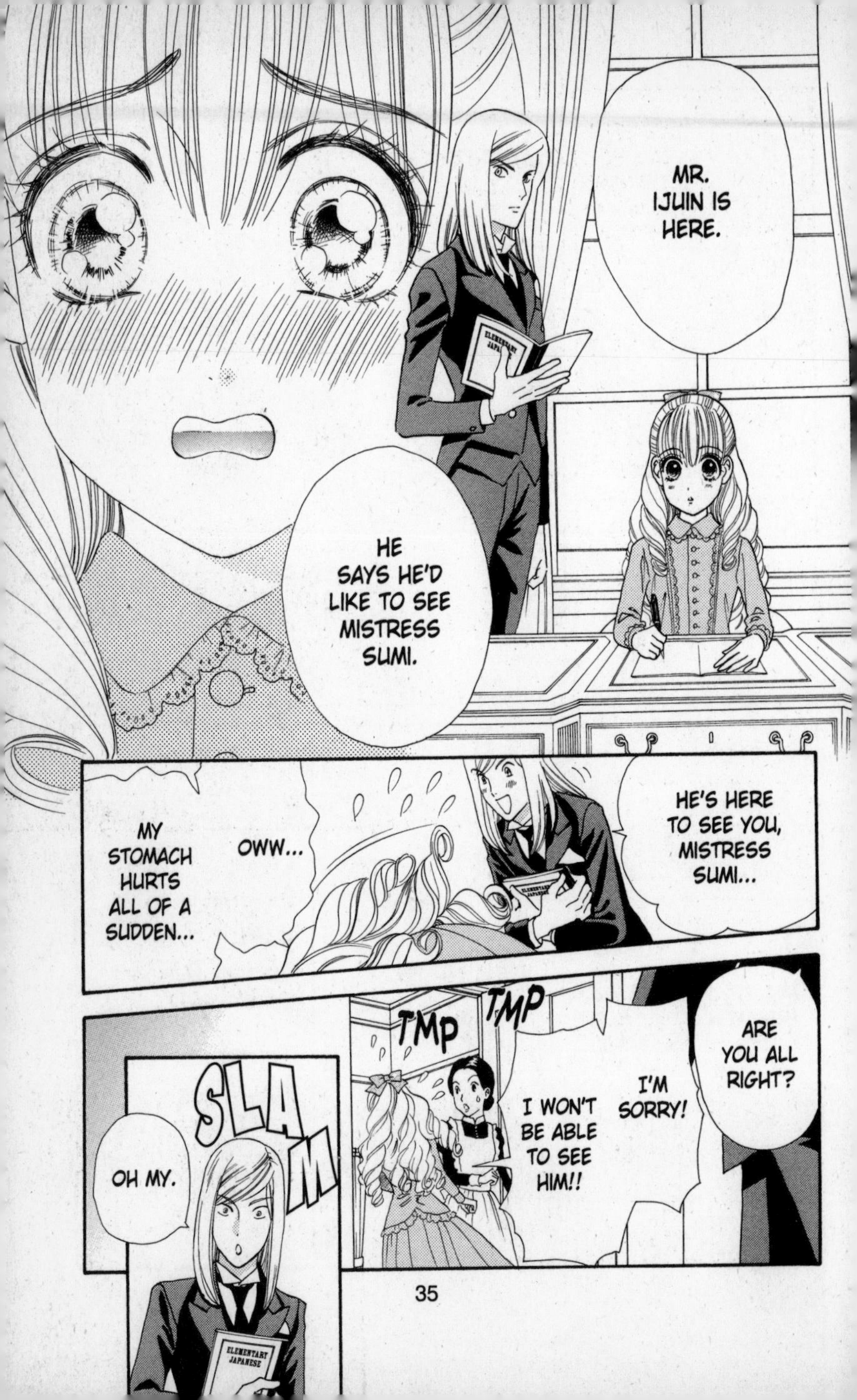
MR. IJUIN IS HERE.
HE SAYS HE'D LIKE TO SEE MISTRESS SUMI.
HE'S HERE TO SEE YOU, MISTRESS SUMI...
OWW...
MY STOMACH HURTS ALL OF A SUDDEN...
TMP
TMP
ARE YOU ALL RIGHT?
I'M SORRY!
I WON'T BE ABLE TO SEE HIM!!
SLAM
OH MY.
ELEMENTARY JAPANESE

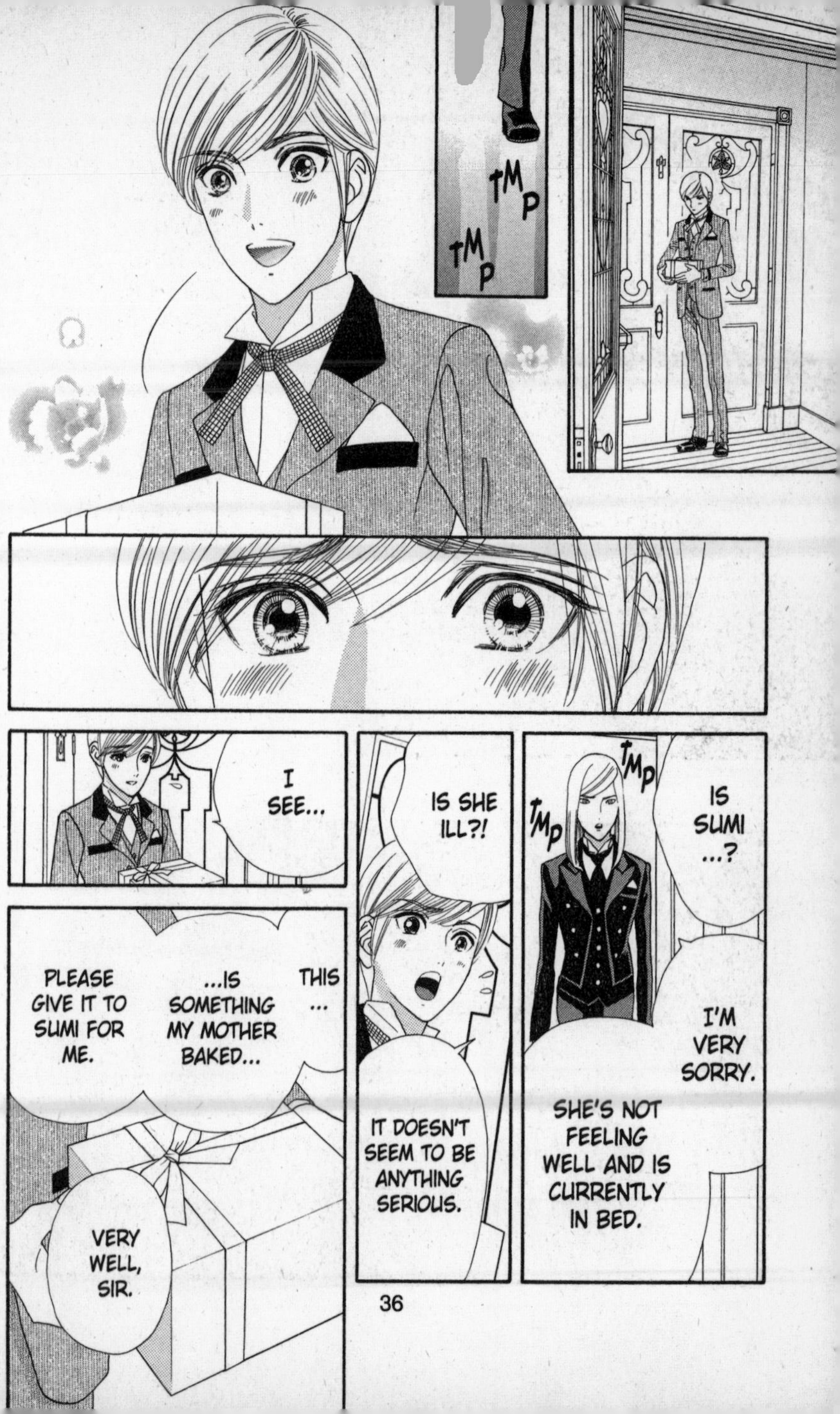

TMP
TMP
TMP
TMP
IS SUMI ...?
I'M VERY SORRY.
SHE'S NOT FEELING WELL AND IS CURRENTLY IN BED.
IS SHE ILL?!
IT DOESN'T SEEM TO BE ANYTHING SERIOUS.
I SEE...
THIS ...
...IS SOMETHING MY MOTHER BAKED...
PLEASE GIVE IT TO SUMI FOR ME.
VERY WELL, SIR.

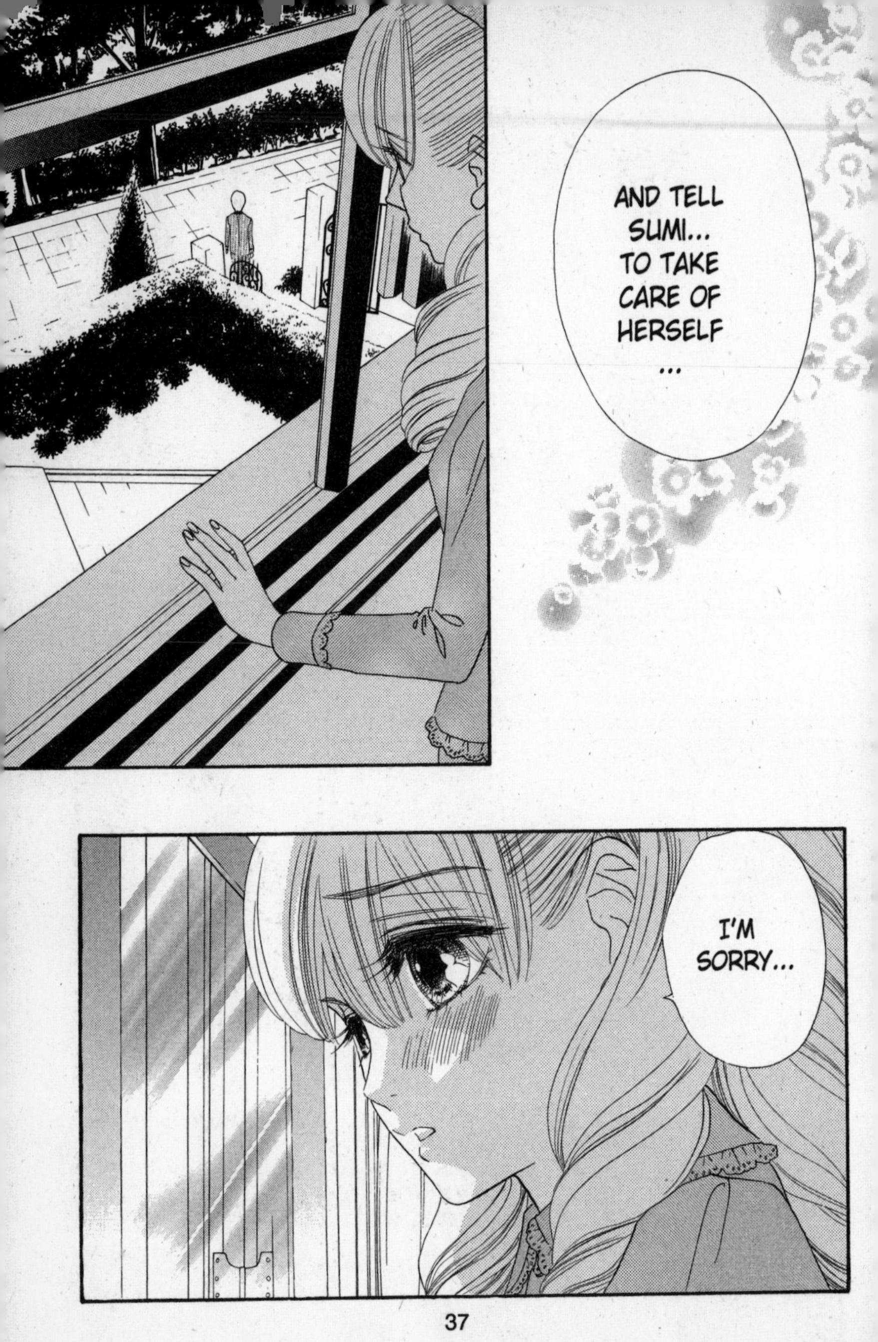
AND TELL SUMI... TO TAKE CARE OF HERSELF ...
I'M SORRY...

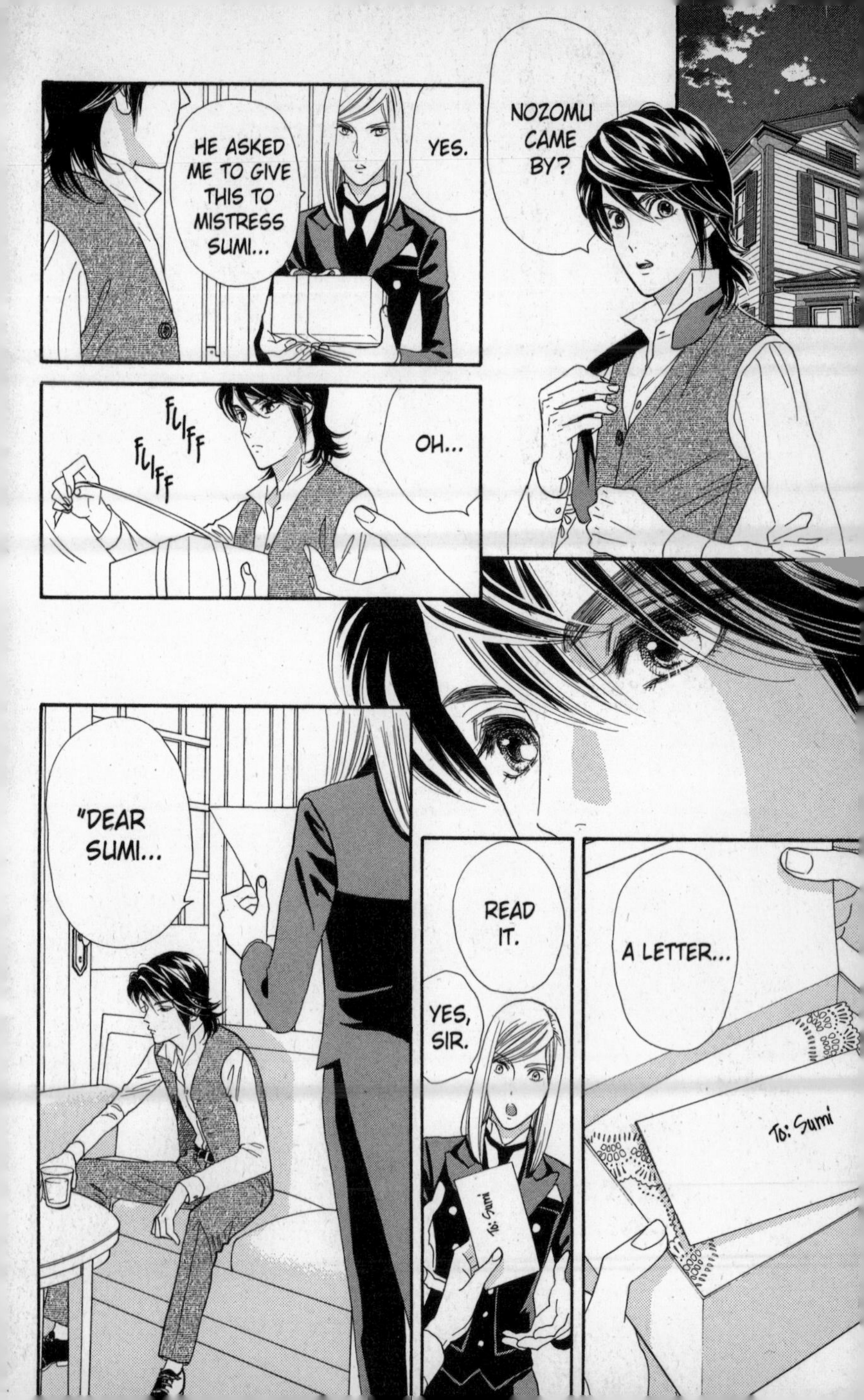
NOZOMU CAME BY?
YES.
HE ASKED ME TO GIVE THIS TO MISTRESS SUMI...
OH...
FLIFF
FLIFF
A LETTER...
To: Sumi
READ IT.
YES, SIR.
To: Sumi
"DEAR SUMI...

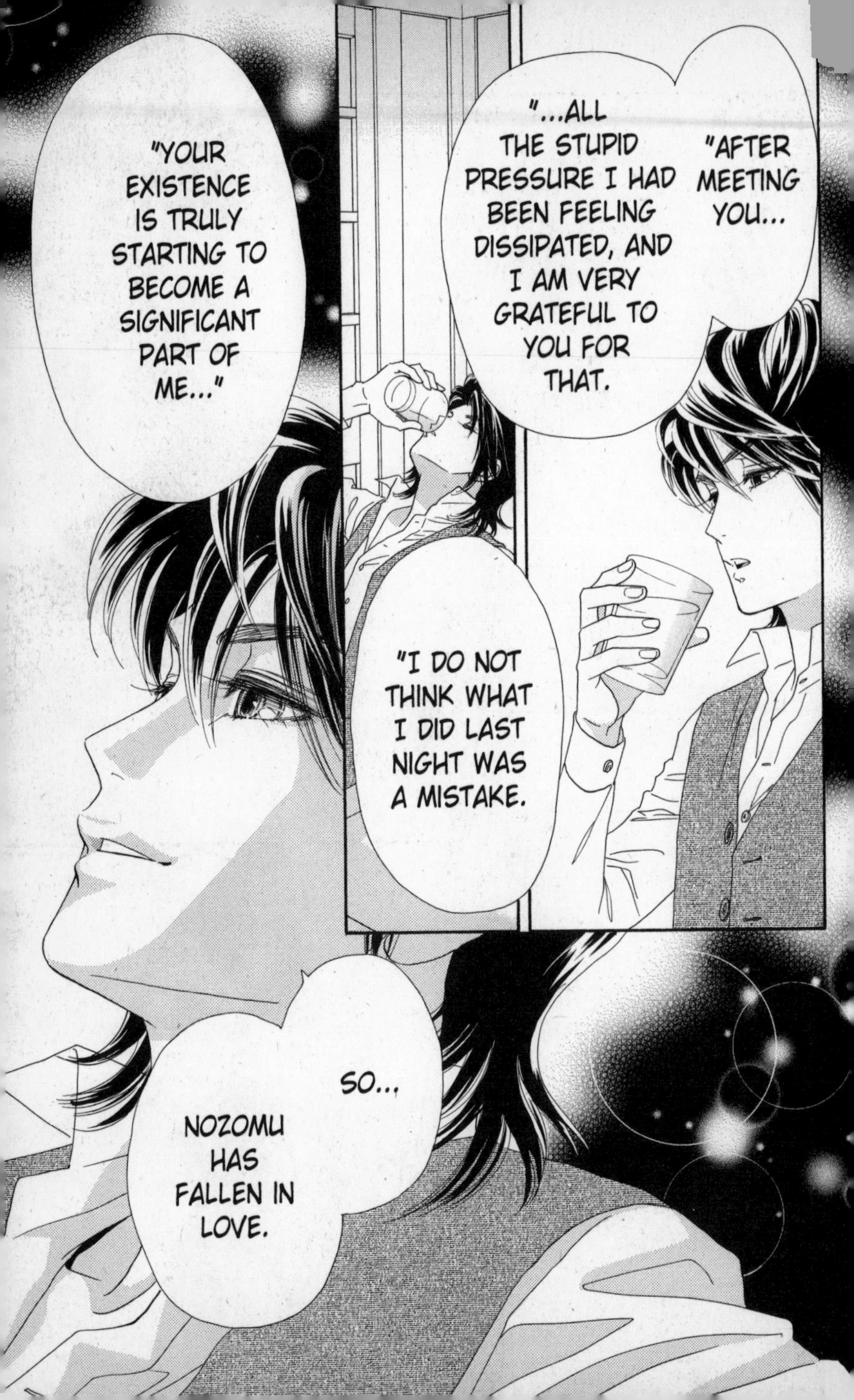
"AFTER MEETING YOU...
"...ALL THE STUPID PRESSURE I HAD BEEN FEELING DISSIPATED, AND I AM VERY GRATEFUL TO YOU FOR THAT.
"I DO NOT THINK WHAT I DID LAST NIGHT WAS A MISTAKE.
"YOUR EXISTENCE IS TRULY STARTING TO BECOME A SIGNIFICANT PART OF ME..."
SO...,
NOZOMU HAS FALLEN IN LOVE.

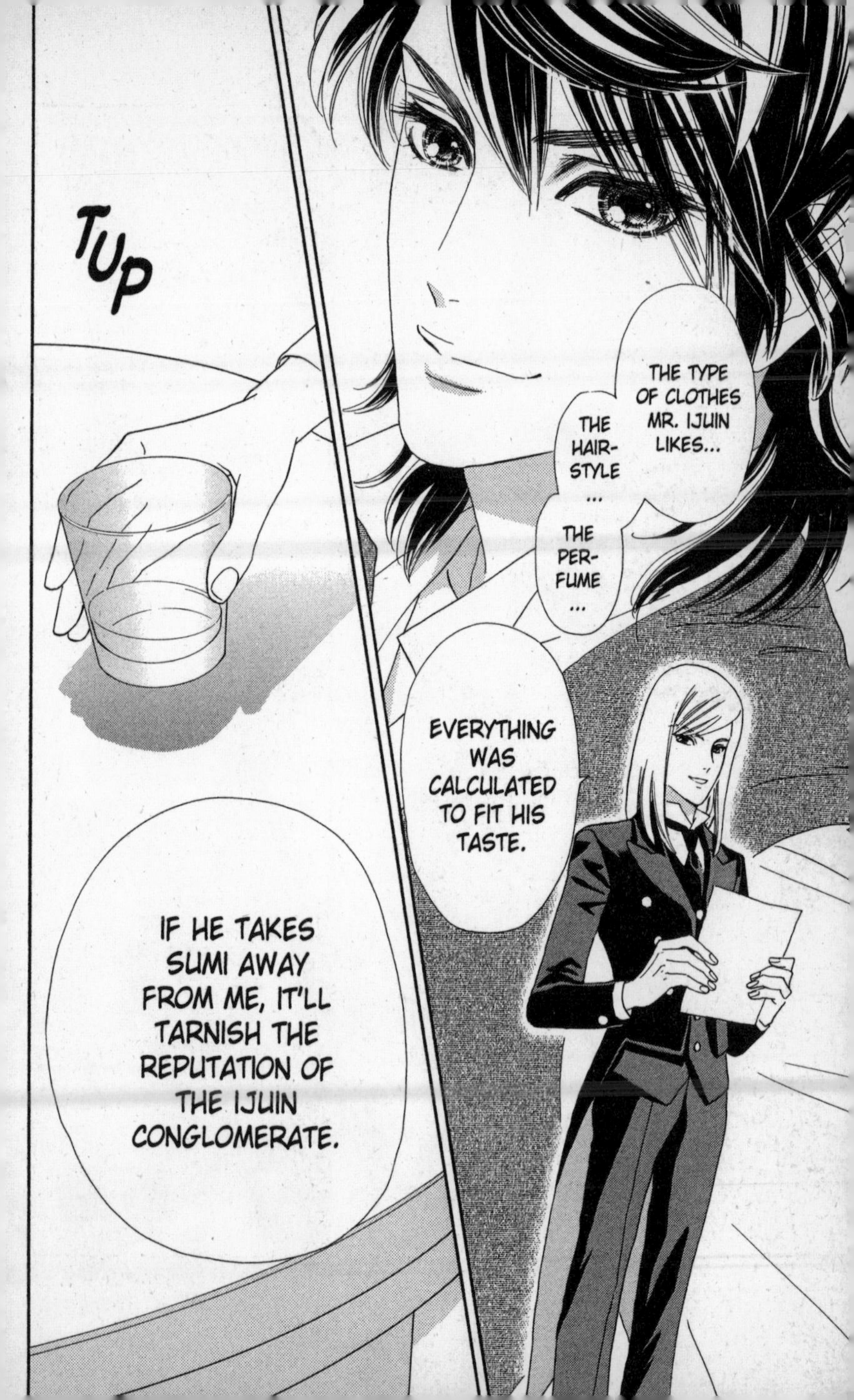
THE TYPE OF CLOTHES MR. IJUIN LIKES...
THE HAIR-STYLE...
THE PER-FUME...
EVERYTHING WAS CALCULATED TO FIT HIS TASTE.
TUP
IF HE TAKES SUMI AWAY FROM ME, IT'LL TARNISH THE REPUTATION OF THE IJUIN CONGLOMERATE.

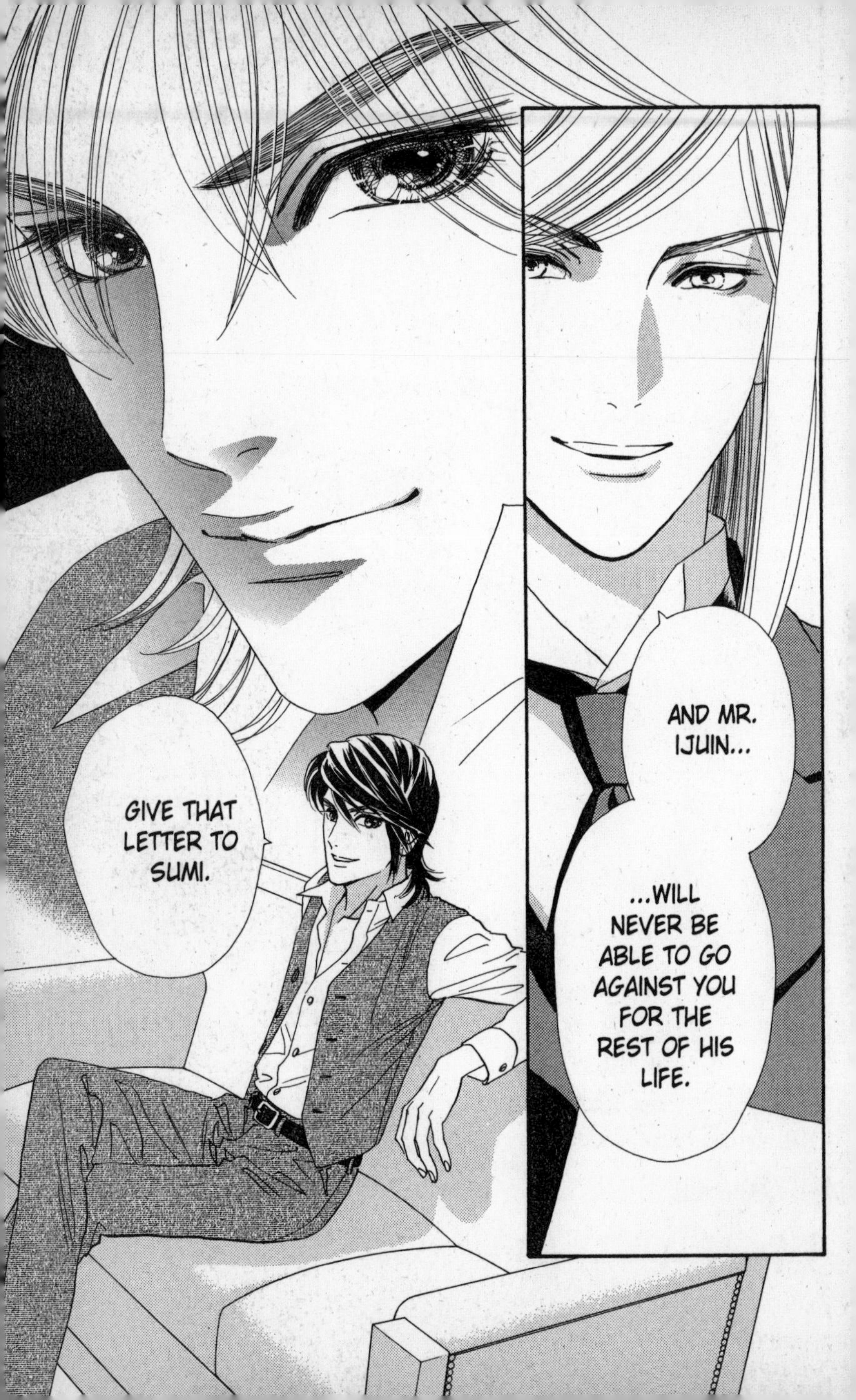
AND MR. IJUIN...
...WILL NEVER BE ABLE TO GO AGAINST YOU FOR THE REST OF HIS LIFE.
GIVE THAT LETTER TO SUMI.

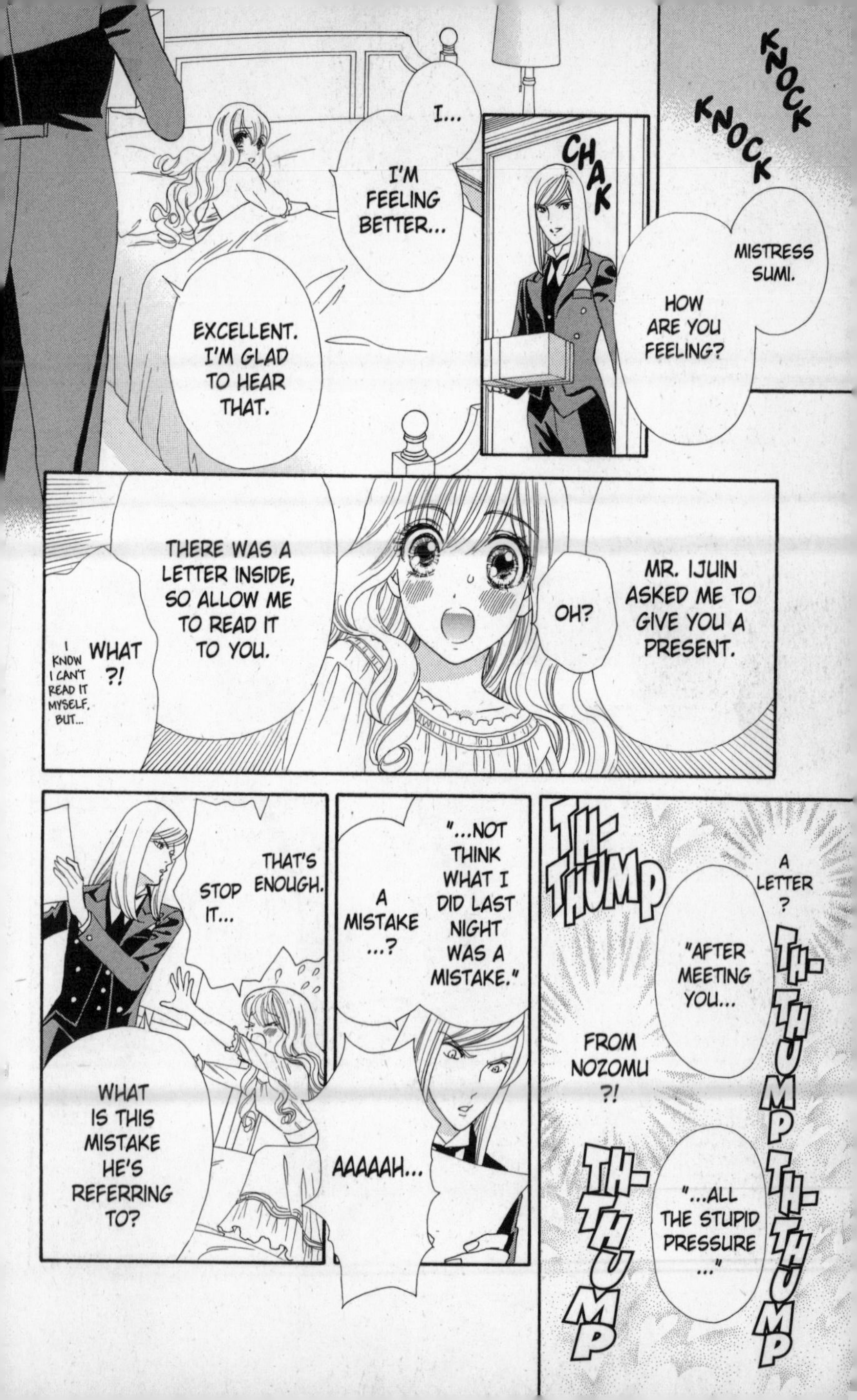
KNOCK
KNOCK
CHAK
MISTRESS SUMI.
HOW ARE YOU FEELING?
I...
I'M FEELING BETTER...
EXCELLENT. I'M GLAD TO HEAR THAT.
MR. IJUIN ASKED ME TO GIVE YOU A PRESENT.
OH?
THERE WAS A LETTER INSIDE, SO ALLOW ME TO READ IT TO YOU.
WHAT ?!
I KNOW I CAN'T READ IT MYSELF, BUT...
TH-THUMP
A LETTER ?
"AFTER MEETING YOU...
FROM NOZOMU ?!
TH-THUMP
TH-THUMP
"...ALL THE STUPID PRESSURE ..."
TH-THUMP
"...NOT THINK WHAT I DID LAST NIGHT WAS A MISTAKE."
A MISTAKE ...?
AAAAAH...
THAT'S ENOUGH.
STOP IT...
WHAT IS THIS MISTAKE HE'S REFERRING TO?

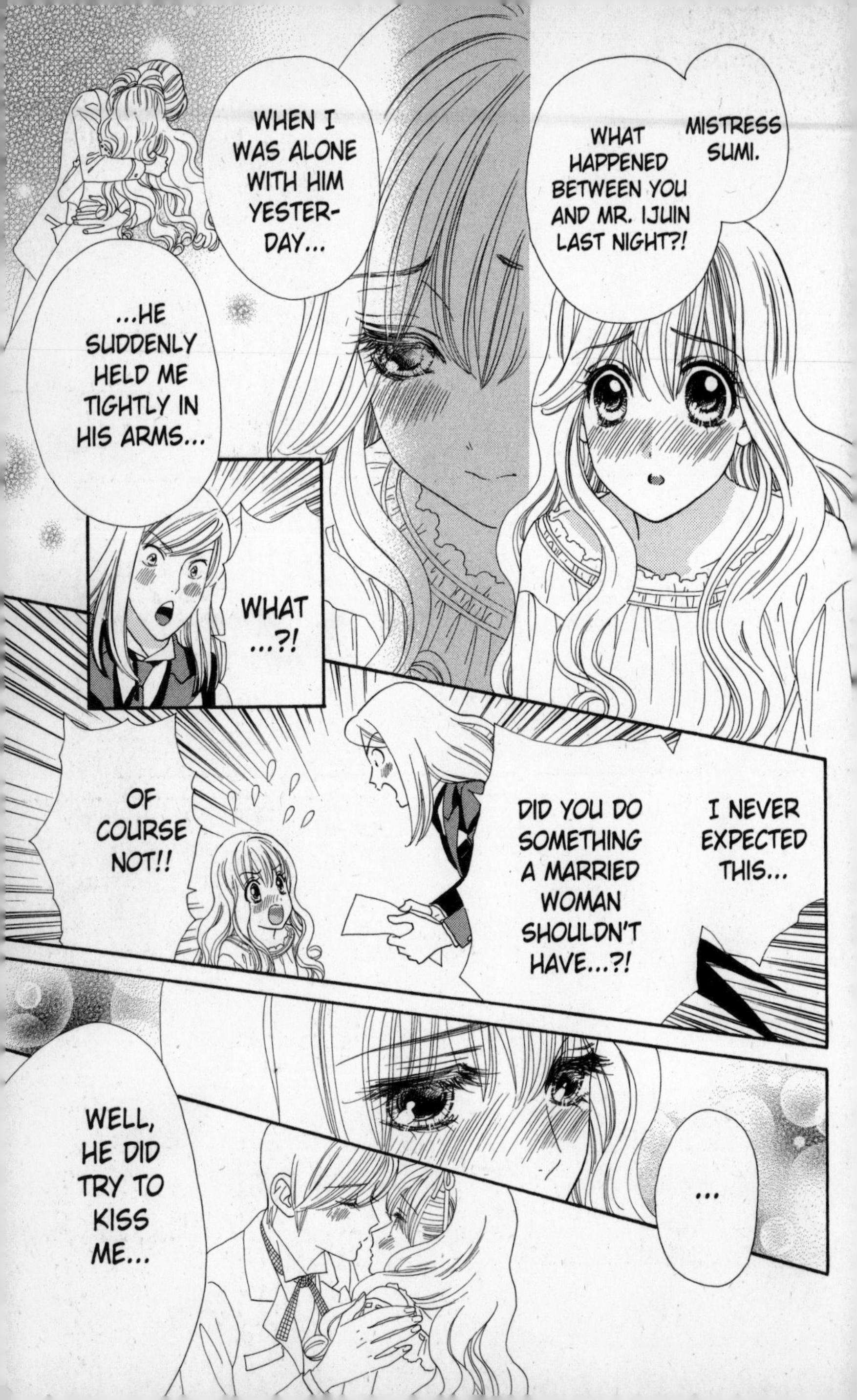
MISTRESS SUMI.
WHAT HAPPENED BETWEEN YOU AND MR. IJUIN LAST NIGHT?!
WHEN I WAS ALONE WITH HIM YESTER-DAY...
...HE SUDDENLY HELD ME TIGHTLY IN HIS ARMS...
WHAT ...?!
I NEVER EXPECTED THIS...
DID YOU DO SOMETHING A MARRIED WOMAN SHOULDN'T HAVE...?!
OF COURSE NOT!!
...
WELL, HE DID TRY TO KISS ME...

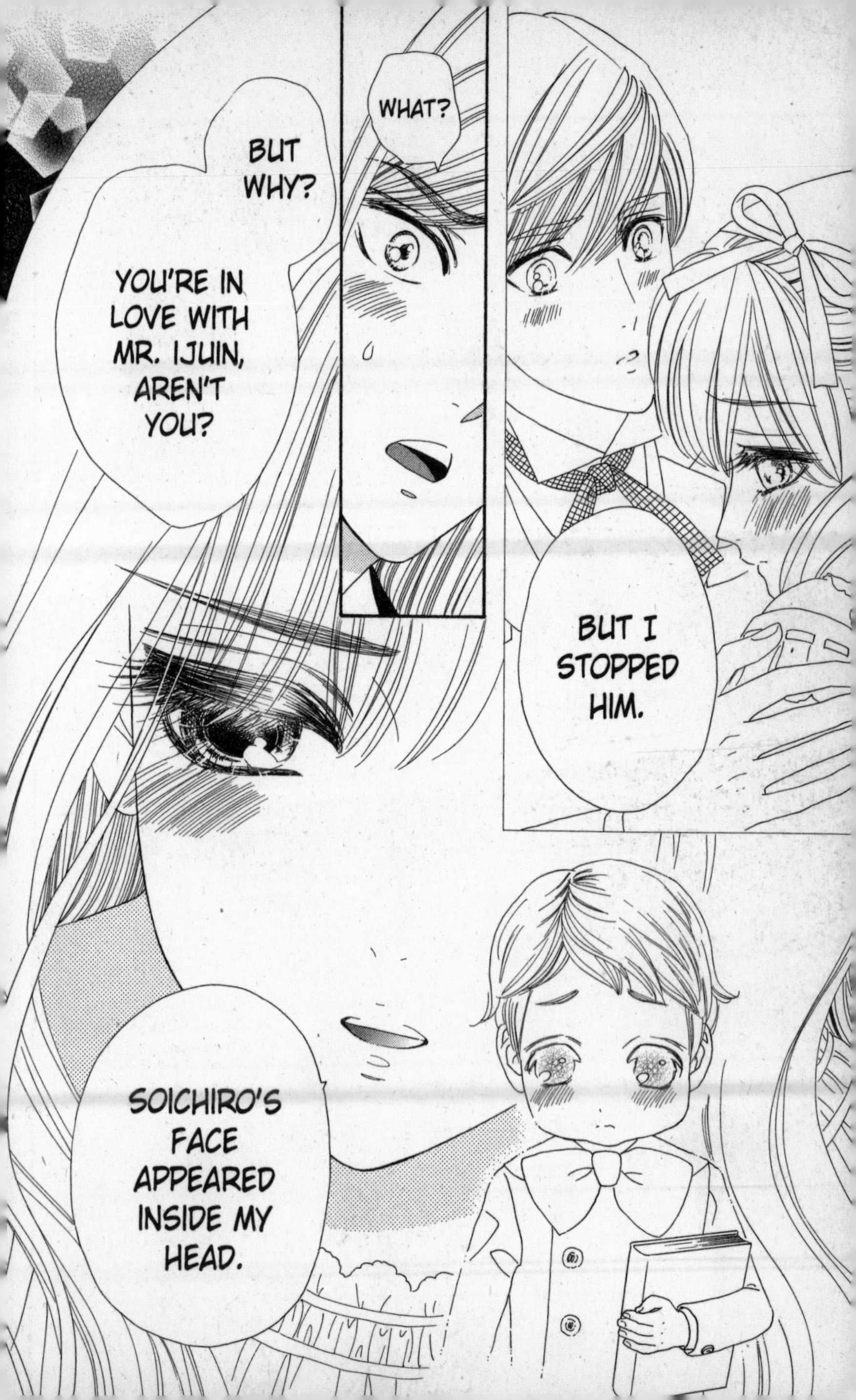
BUT WHY?
YOU'RE IN LOVE WITH MR. IJUIN, AREN'T YOU?
WHAT?
BUT I STOPPED HIM.
SOICHIRO'S FACE APPEARED INSIDE MY HEAD.

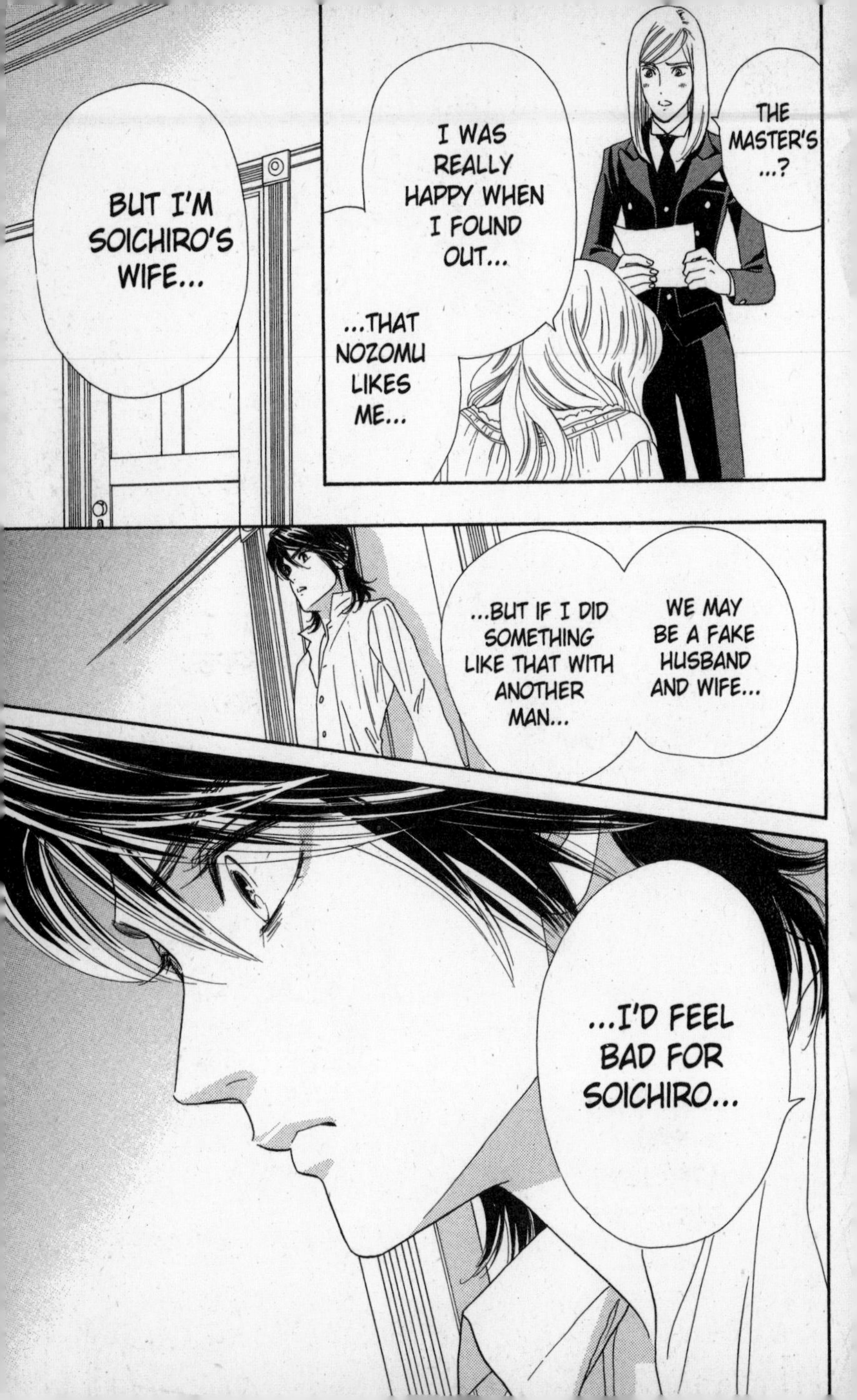
THE MASTER'S ...?
I WAS REALLY HAPPY WHEN I FOUND OUT...
...THAT NOZOMU LIKES ME...
BUT I'M SOICHIRO'S WIFE...
WE MAY BE A FAKE HUSBAND AND WIFE...
...BUT IF I DID SOMETHING LIKE THAT WITH ANOTHER MAN...
...I'D FEEL BAD FOR SOICHIRO...

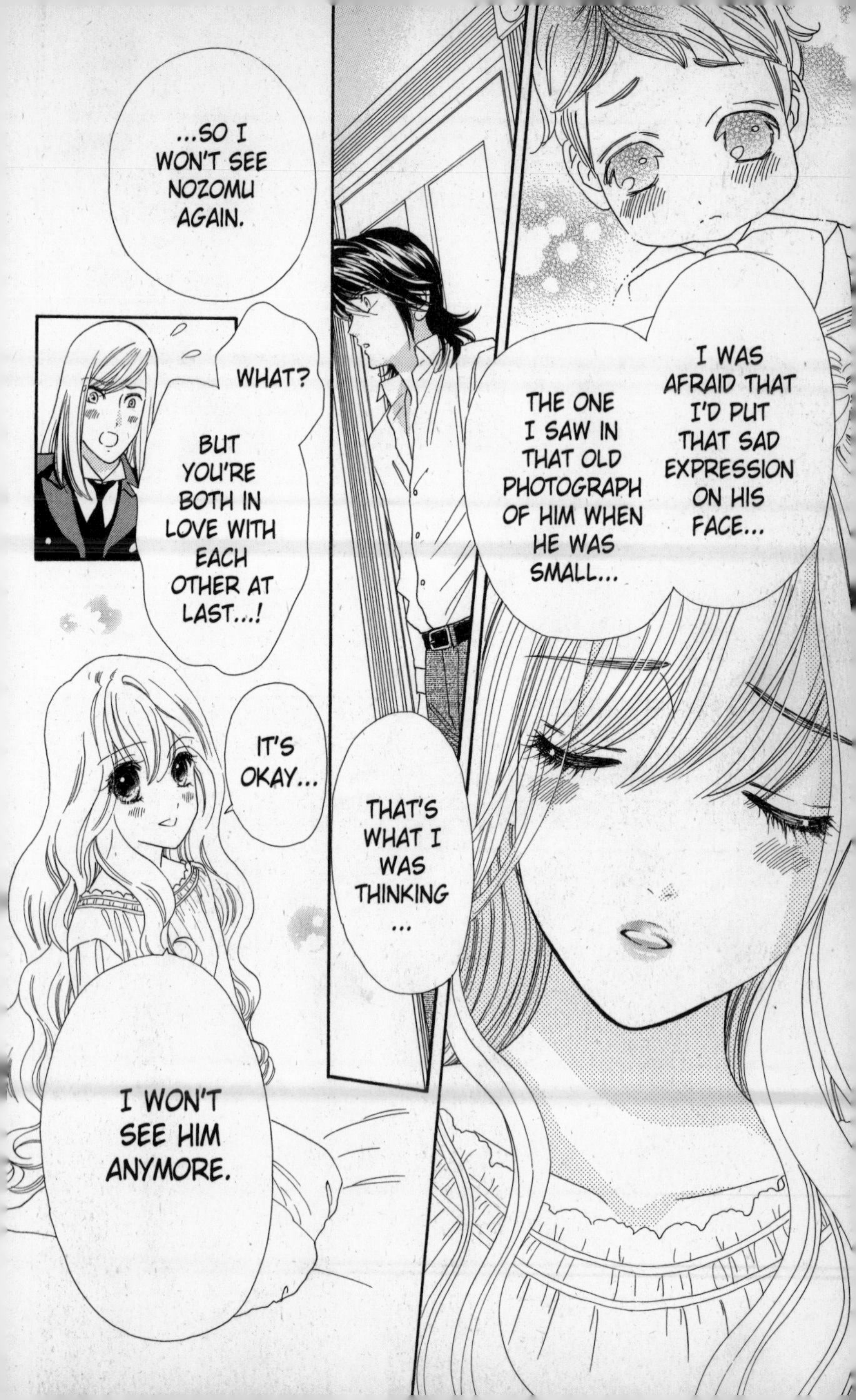
I WAS AFRAID THAT I'D PUT THAT SAD EXPRESSION ON HIS FACE...
THE ONE I SAW IN THAT OLD PHOTOGRAPH OF HIM WHEN HE WAS SMALL...
THAT'S WHAT I WAS THINKING...
...SO I WON'T SEE NOZOMU AGAIN.
WHAT?
BUT YOU'RE BOTH IN LOVE WITH EACH OTHER AT LAST...!
IT'S OKAY...
I WON'T SEE HIM ANYMORE.

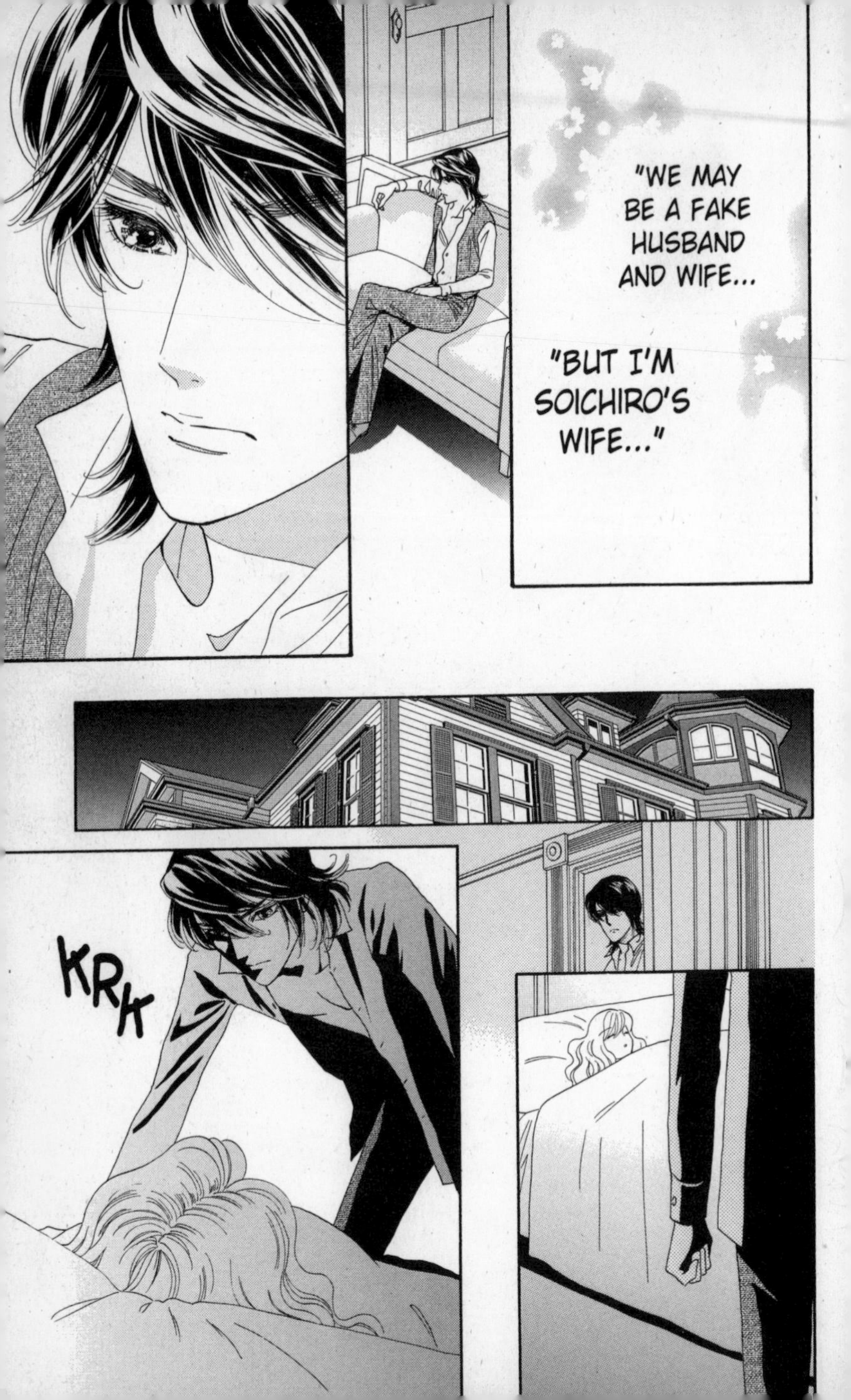
"WE MAY BE A FAKE HUSBAND AND WIFE...
"BUT I'M SOICHIRO'S WIFE..."
KRK

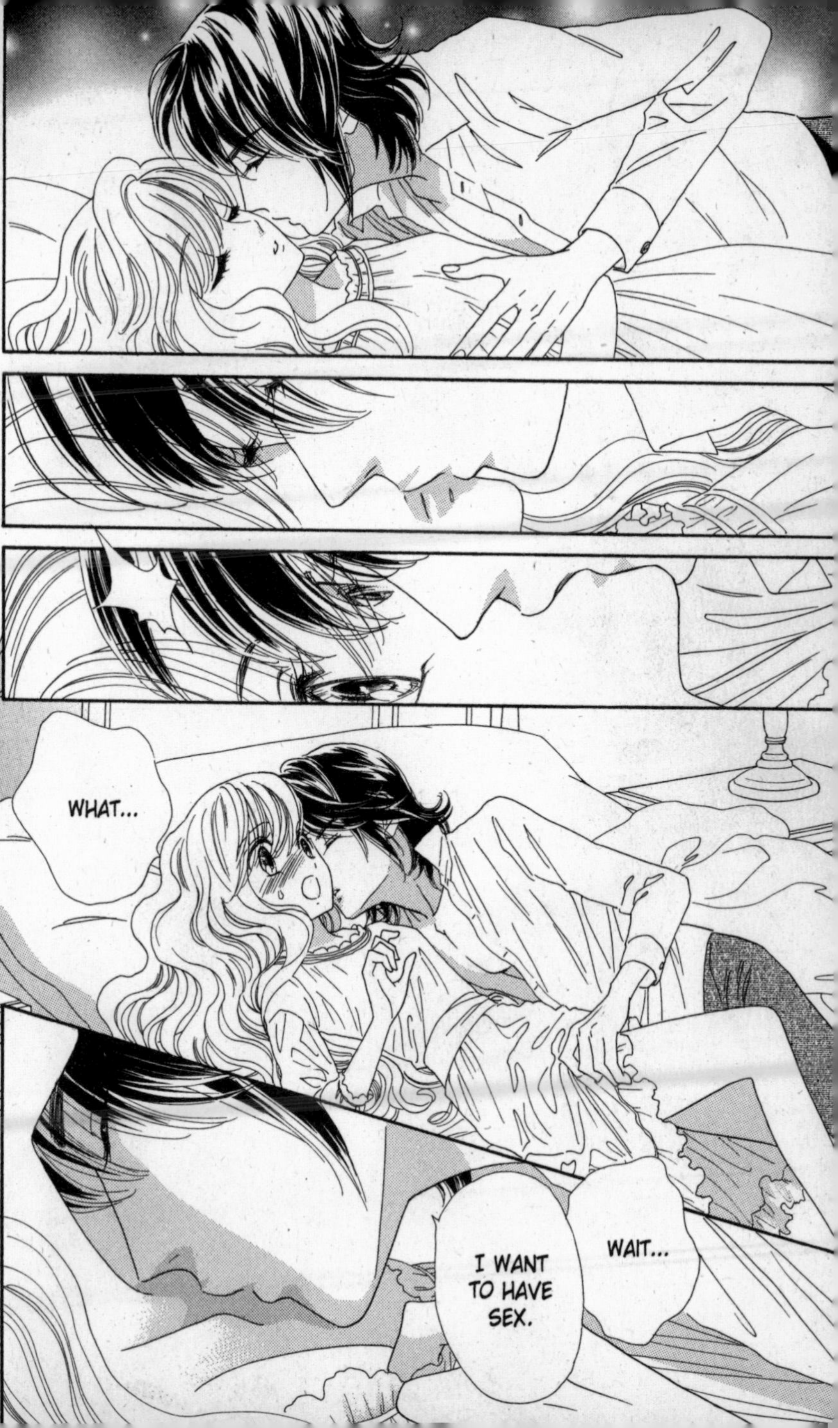
WHAT...
WAIT...
I WANT TO HAVE SEX.

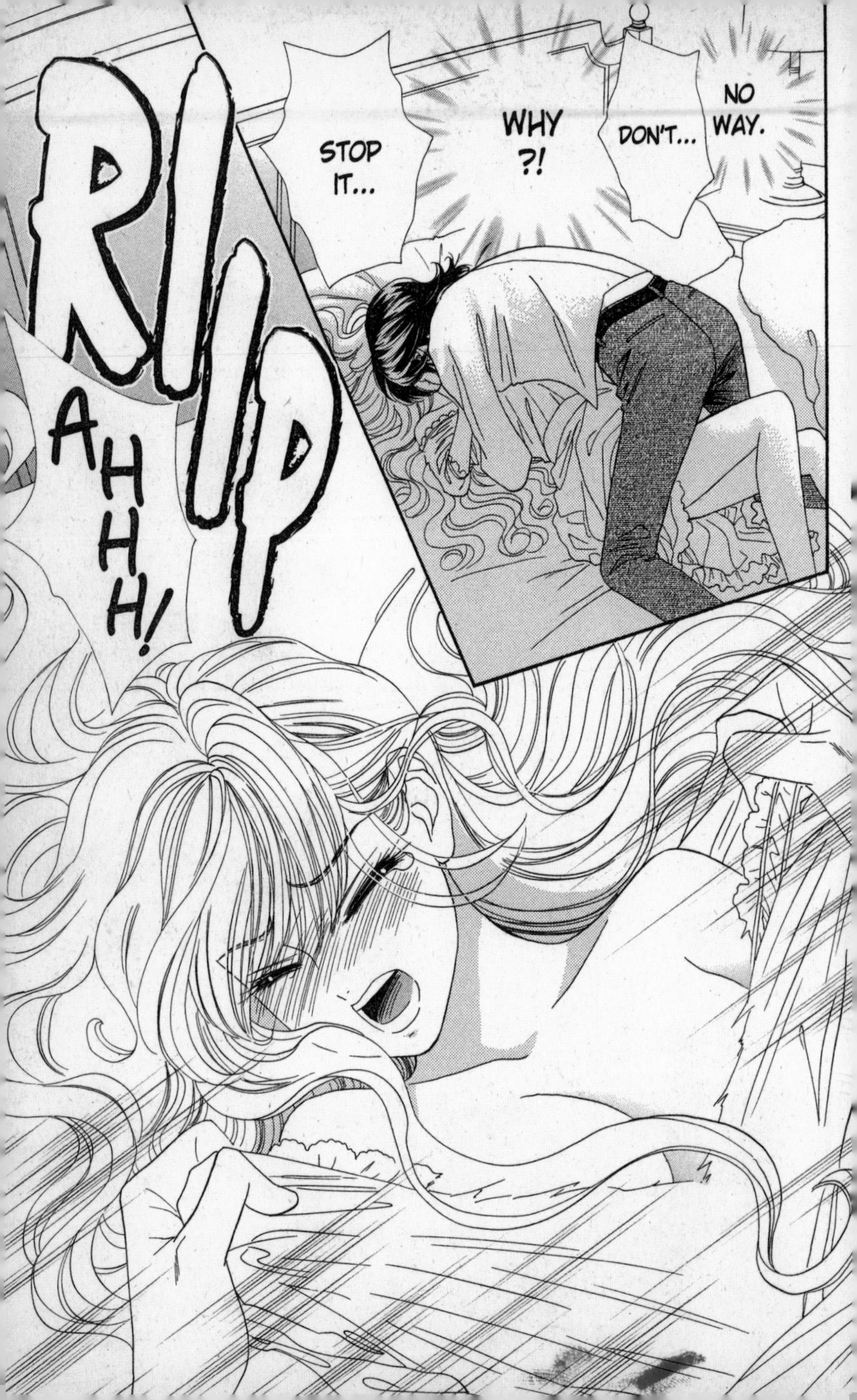
NO WAY.
DON'T...
WHY?!
STOP IT...
RIIP
AHHH!

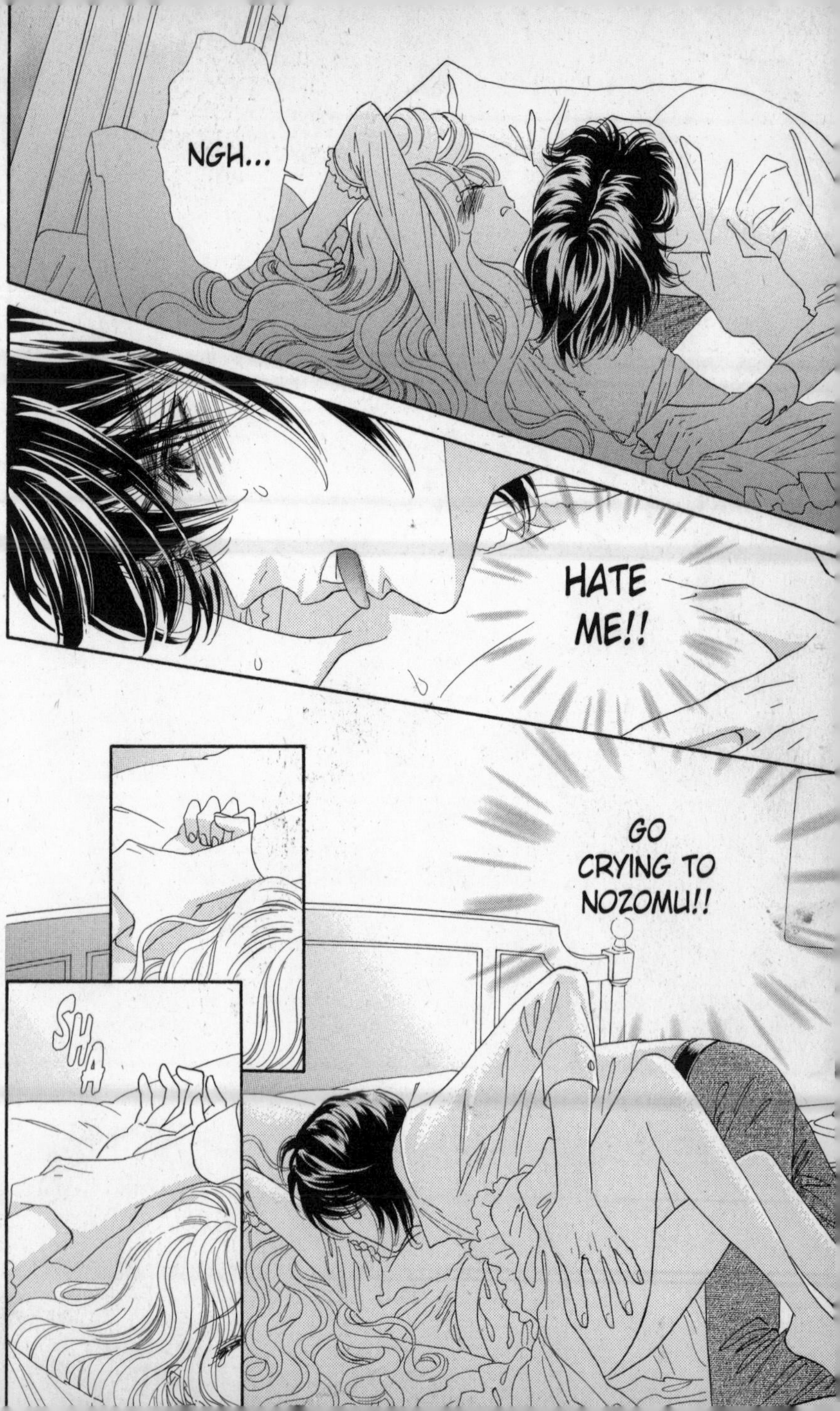
NGH...
HATE ME!!
GO CRYING TO NOZOMU!!
SHA

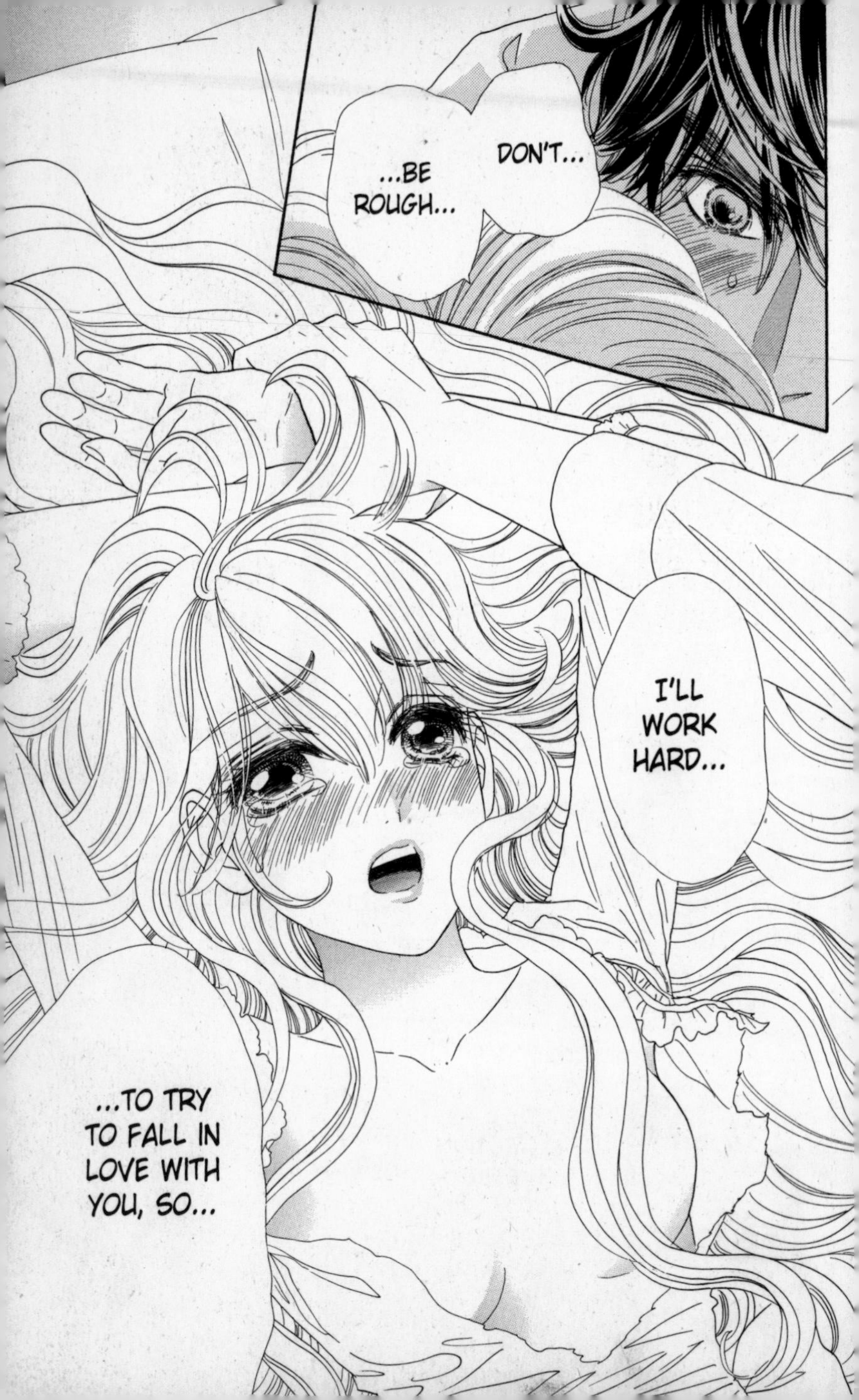
DON'T...
...BE ROUGH...
I'LL WORK HARD...
...TO TRY TO FALL IN LOVE WITH YOU, SO...

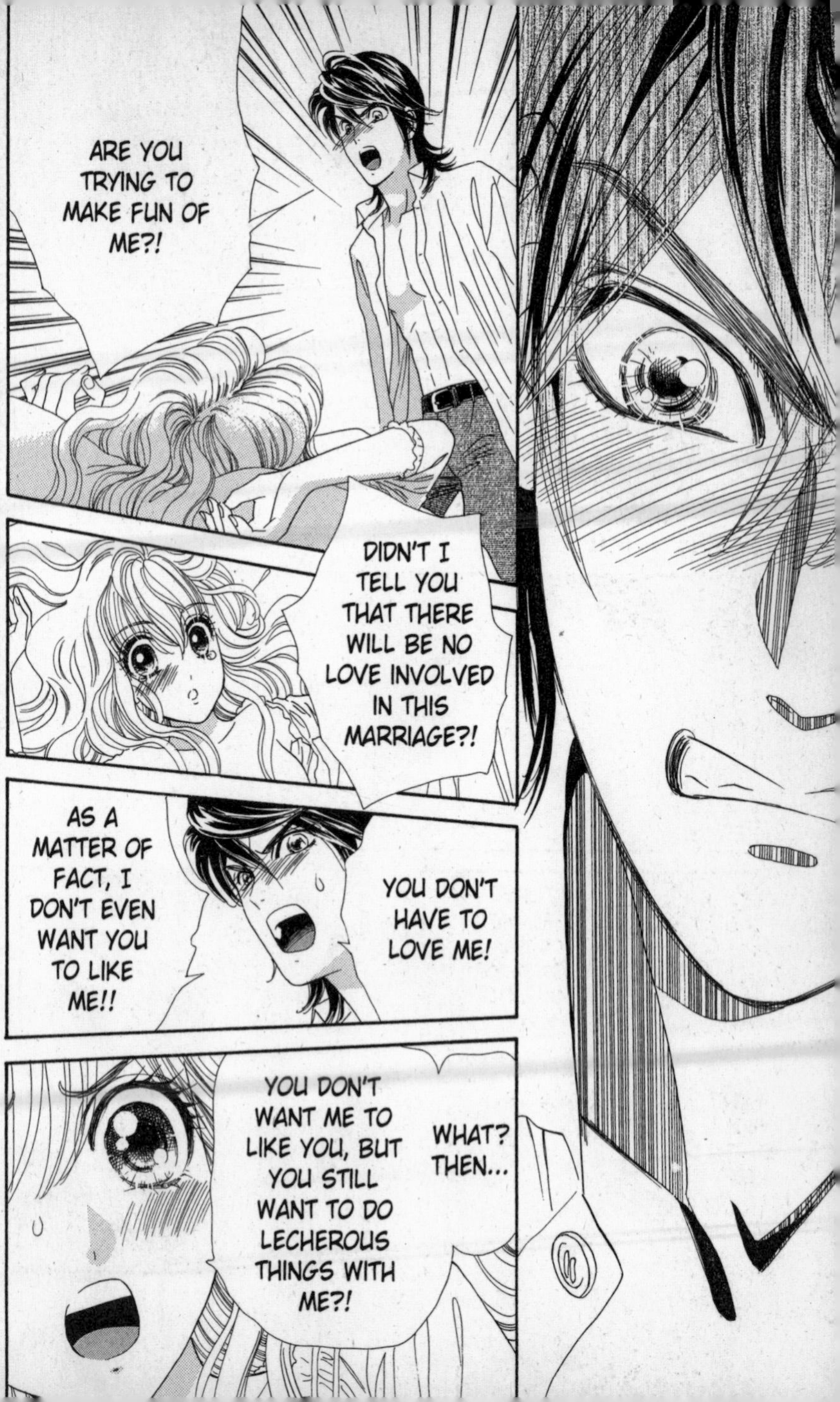
ARE YOU TRYING TO MAKE FUN OF ME?!
DIDN'T I TELL YOU THAT THERE WILL BE NO LOVE INVOLVED IN THIS MARRIAGE?!
YOU DON'T HAVE TO LOVE ME!
AS A MATTER OF FACT, I DON'T EVEN WANT YOU TO LIKE ME!!
WHAT? THEN...
YOU DON'T WANT ME TO LIKE YOU, BUT YOU STILL WANT TO DO LECHEROUS THINGS WITH ME?!

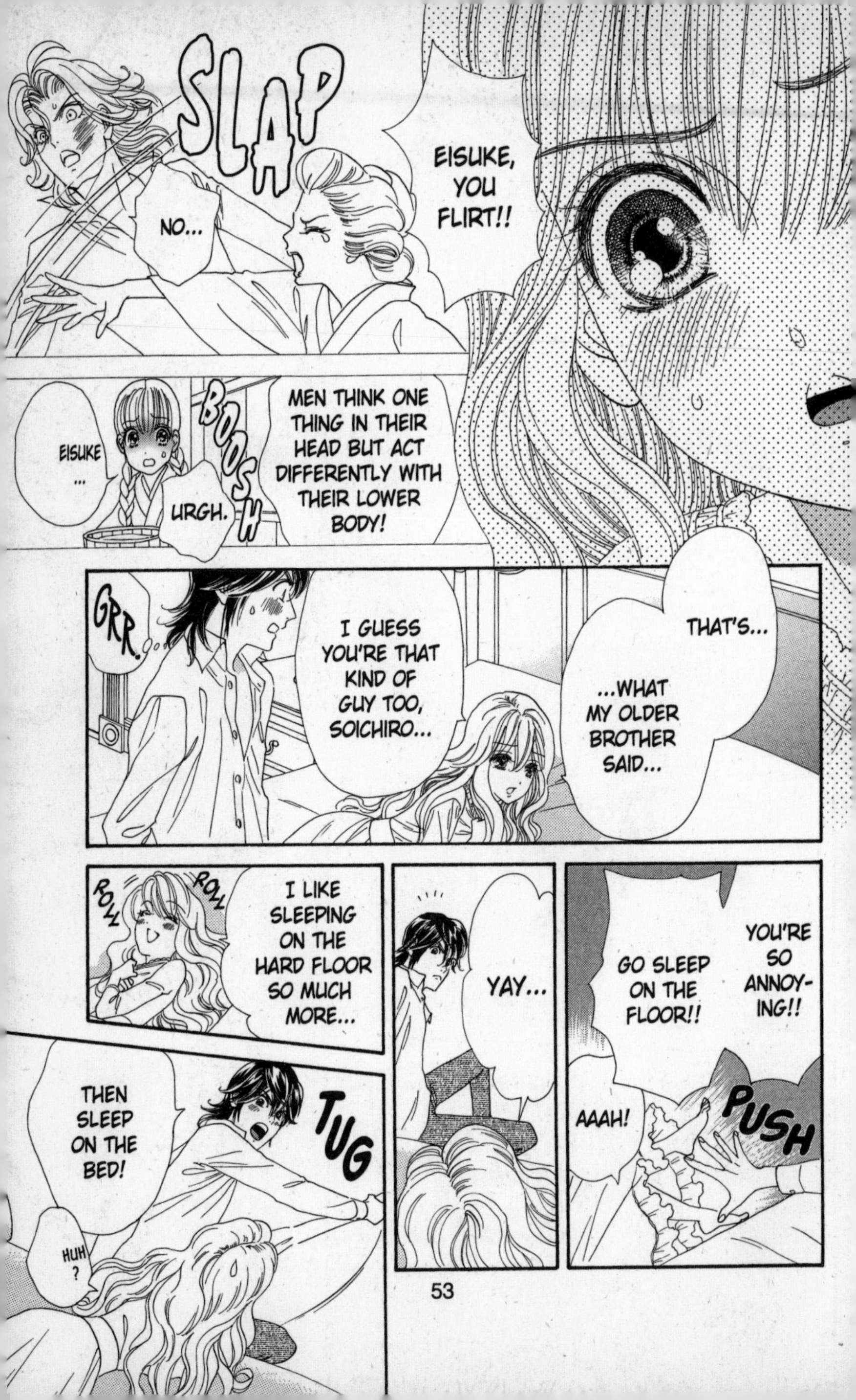
EISUKE, YOU FLIRT!!
SLAP
NO...
MEN THINK ONE THING IN THEIR HEAD BUT ACT DIFFERENTLY WITH THEIR LOWER BODY!
BOOSH
URGH.
EISUKE ...
THAT'S...
...WHAT MY OLDER BROTHER SAID...
I GUESS YOU'RE THAT KIND OF GUY TOO, SOICHIRO...
GRR.
YOU'RE SO ANNOY-ING!!
GO SLEEP ON THE FLOOR!!
PUSH
AAAH!
YAY...
I LIKE SLEEPING ON THE HARD FLOOR SO MUCH MORE...
ROLL
ROLL
THEN SLEEP ON THE BED!
TUG
HUH ?

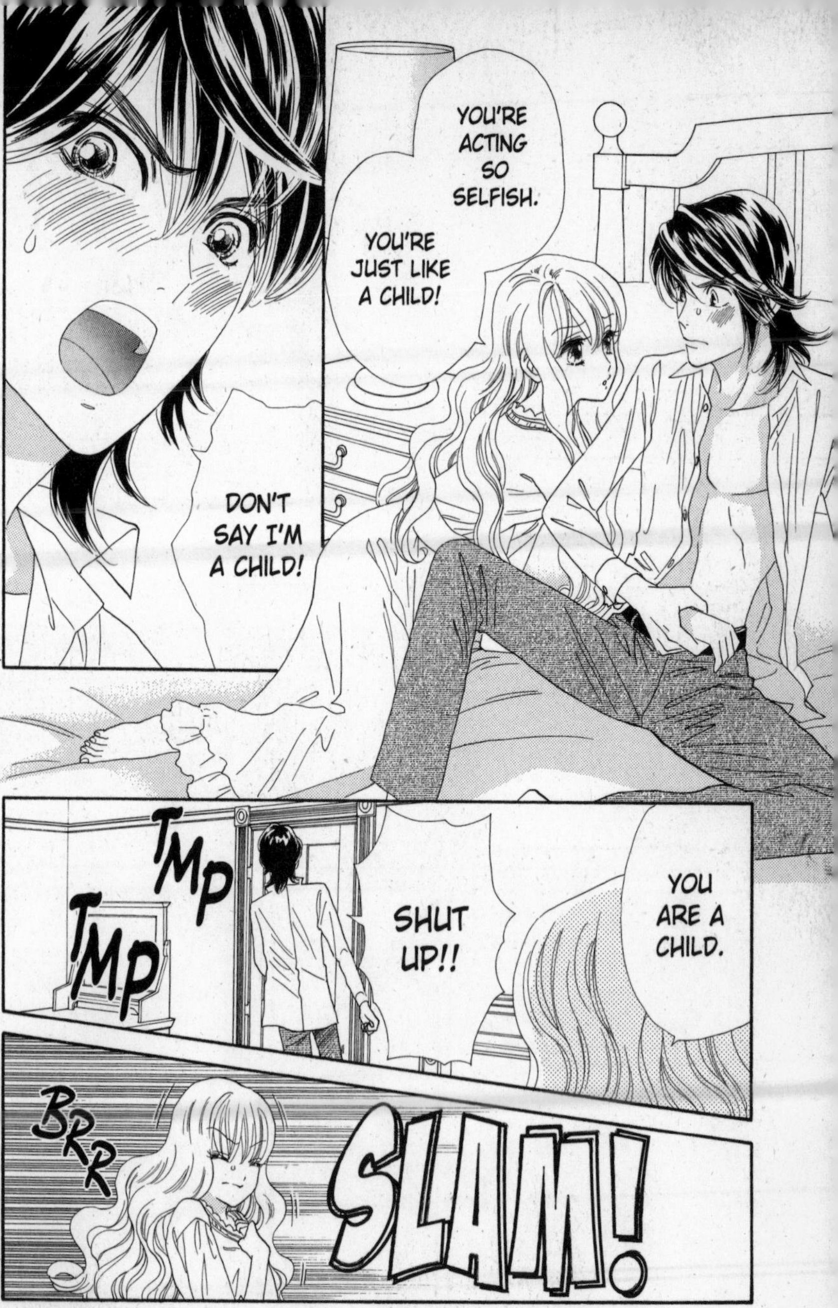
YOU'RE ACTING SO SELFISH.
YOU'RE JUST LIKE A CHILD!
DON'T SAY I'M A CHILD!
YOU ARE A CHILD.
SHUT UP!!
TMP
TMP
SLAM!
BRR

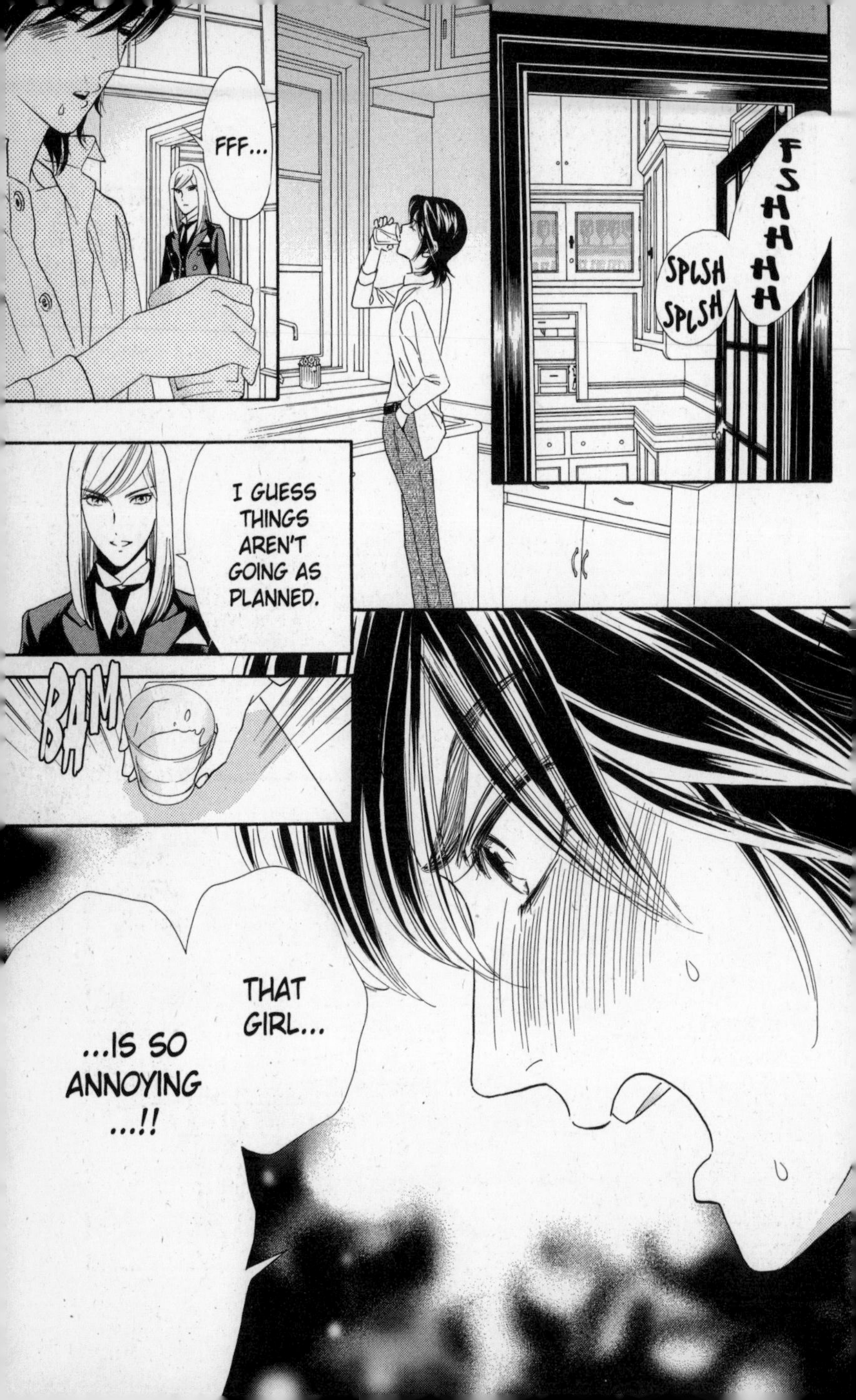
FSHHHH
SPLSH SPLSH
FFF...
I GUESS THINGS AREN'T GOING AS PLANNED.
BAM
THAT GIRL...
...IS SO ANNOYING ...!!

STEPPING ON ROSES BACKSTAGE SECTION!!

WHICH ABBREVIATES TO STEP STAGE☆②

No.

Date

DURING SPRING 2007, A THANK-YOU PARTY WAS HELD BY SHUEISHA FOR ALL THE SHOJO MANGA ARTISTS. AT THE AFTER-PARTY, MR. T, WHO WAS THE CHIEF EDITOR OF *RIBON* THEN, WAS SITTING ACROSS FROM ME. HE USED TO BE AN EDITOR FOR *MARGARET*, BUT IT HAD BEEN SOME TIME SINCE I HAD LAST TALKED TO HIM. DURING OUR CONVERSATION, I TOLD HIM, "I'M HAVING TROUBLE COMING UP WITH THE NAMES OF THE CHARACTERS FOR MY NEW SERIES THAT'S SET IN THE MEIJI ERA." MR. T SUDDENLY SAID, "THEN THE GIRL'S NAME SHOULD BE SUMI. WRITTEN AS '純'."

HE CONTINUED WITH, "THE ELDER BROTHER WILL BE CALLED EISUKE. SOUNDS POSH, DON'T YOU THINK?" IT REALLY DOES SOUND POSH!! SO I IMMEDIATELY PULLED OUT MY NOTEBOOK AND STARTED WRITING ON IT.

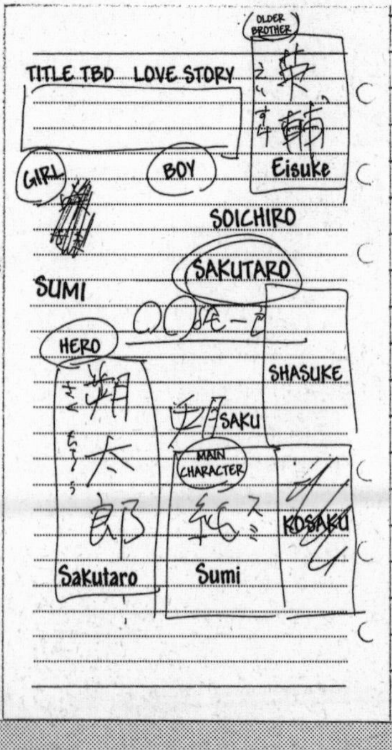
OLDER BROTHER
TITLE TBD LOVE STORY
Eisuke
GIRL
BOY
SOICHIRO
SAKUTARO
SUMI
HERO
SHASUKE
SAKU
MAIN CHARACTER
KOSAKU
Sakutaro
Sumi

← THIS IS THE ACTUAL NOTE I WROTE.

CHECK OUT THE NAME "SAKUTARO" AT THE BOTTOM. SOICHIRO WAS ACTUALLY NAMED SAKUTARO BACK THEN.

BECAUSE HE IS THE ELDEST SON, I WANTED TO INCLUDE "TARO" OR "ICHIRO" IN HIS NAME. I DECIDED TO CHANGE HIS NAME TO SOICHIRO RIGHT BEFORE THE DEADLINE.

WHEN I MET MR. T AGAIN AT THE THANK-YOU PARTY IN 2008, I SAID, "THANK YOU VERY MUCH FOR NAMING MY CHARACTERS." BUT HE REPLIED, "HUH? I DON'T REMEMBER DOING THAT AT ALL."

NEVERTHELESS, IT WAS STILL A LIFESAVER FOR ME. THANK YOU VERY MUCH!

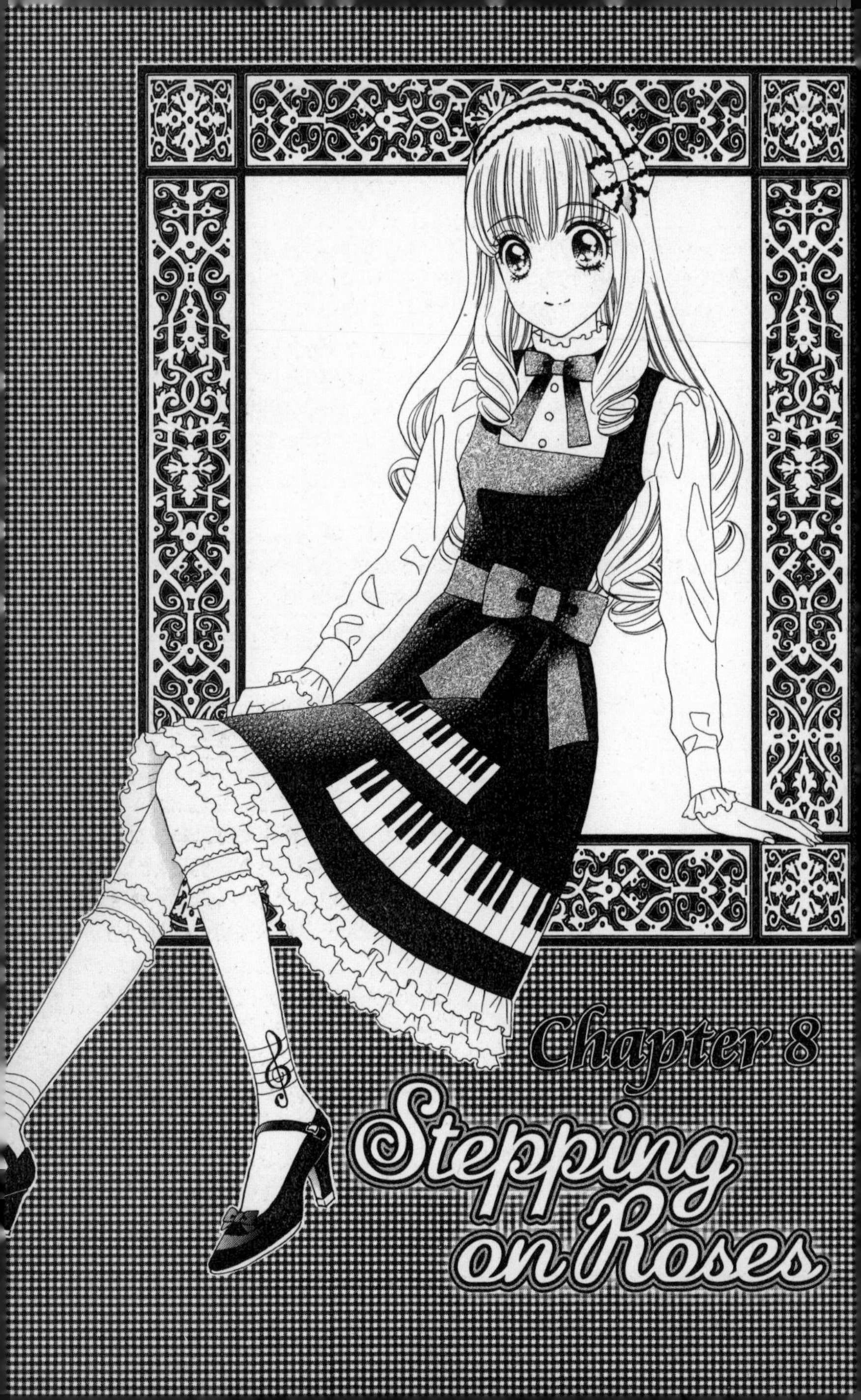
Chapter 8
Stepping on Roses

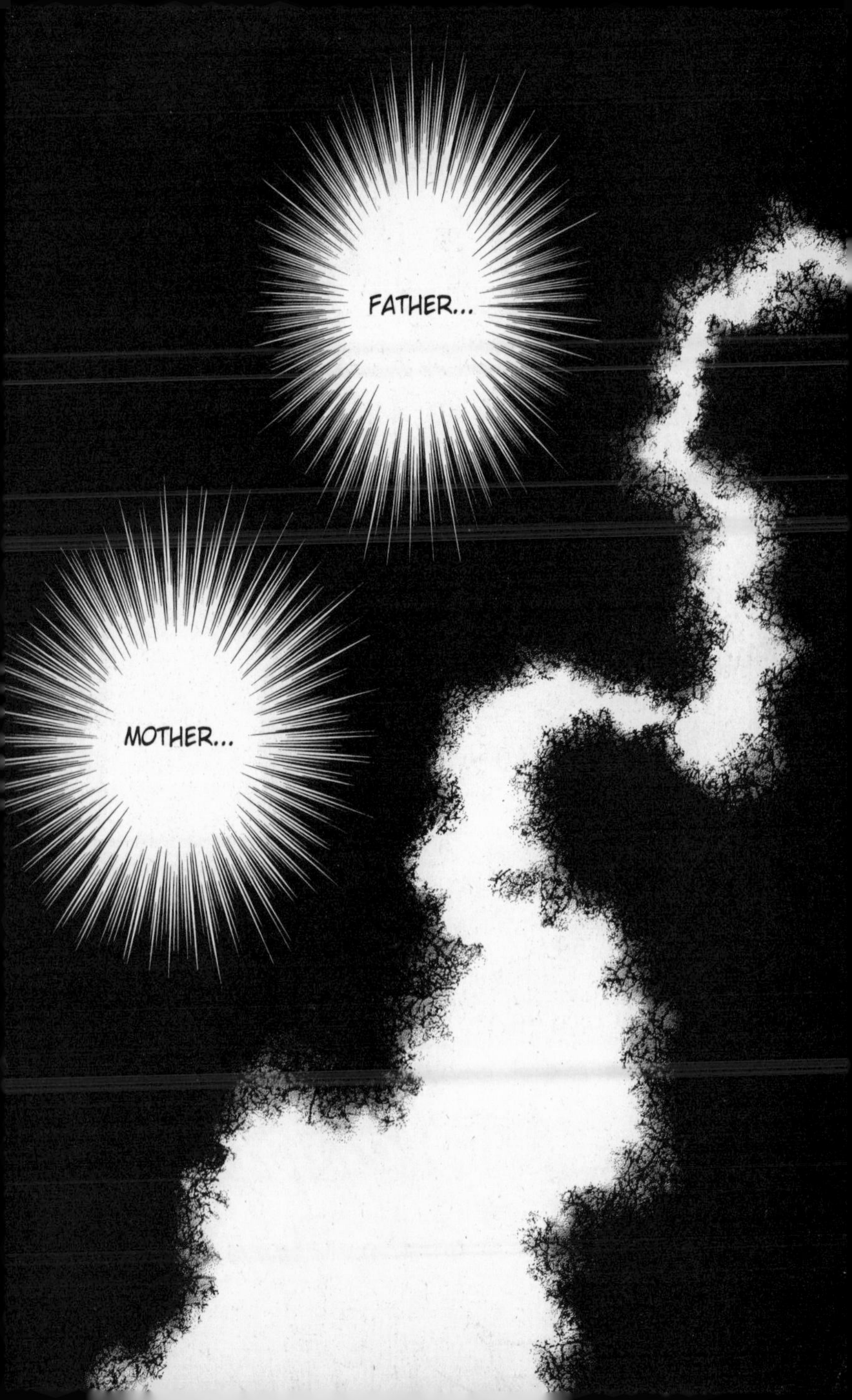
FATHER...
MOTHER...

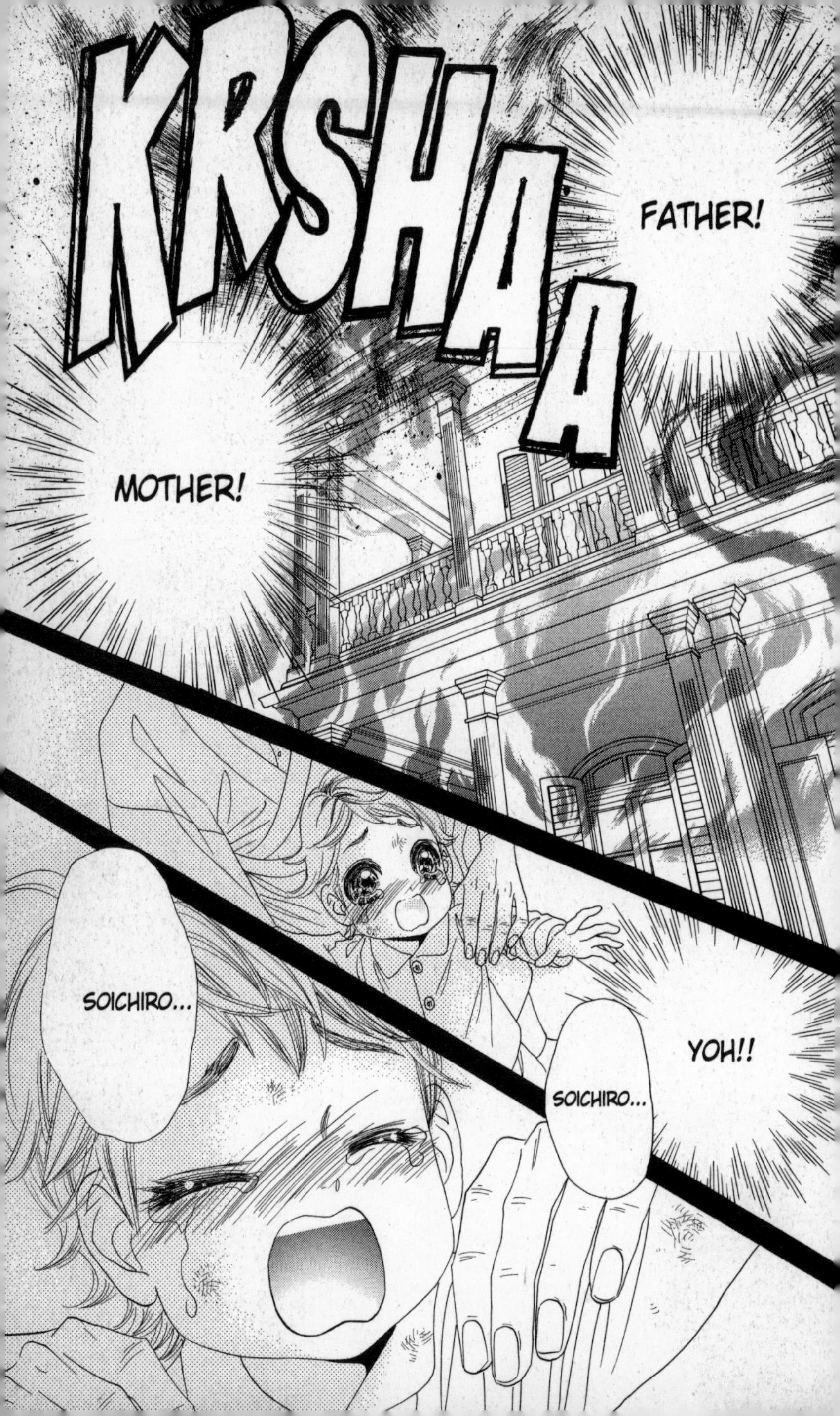
KRSHAA
FATHER!
MOTHER!
YOH!!
SOICHIRO...
SOICHIRO...

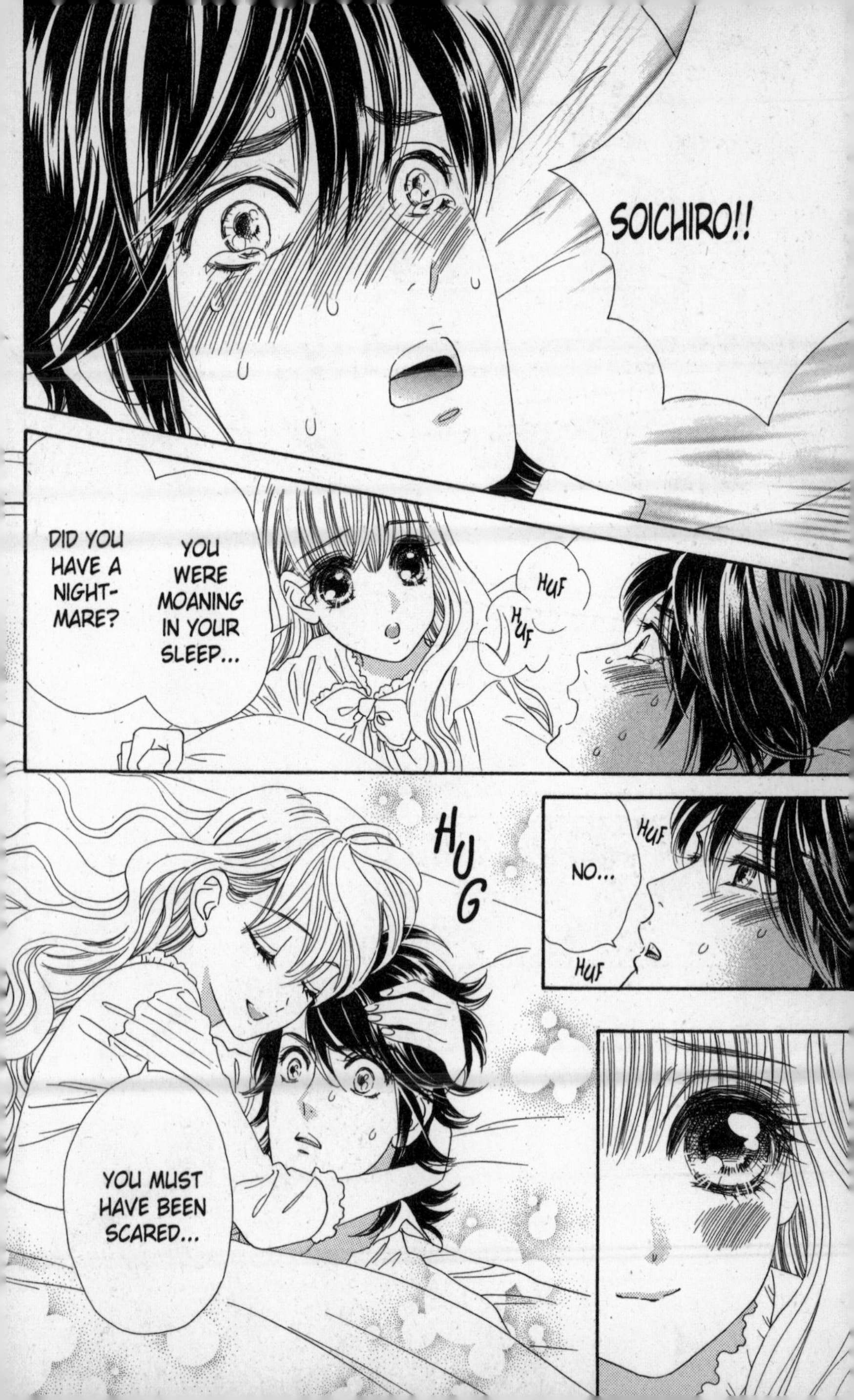
SOICHIRO!!
HUF
HUF
YOU WERE MOANING IN YOUR SLEEP...
DID YOU HAVE A NIGHTMARE?
HUF
NO...
HUF
HUG
YOU MUST HAVE BEEN SCARED...

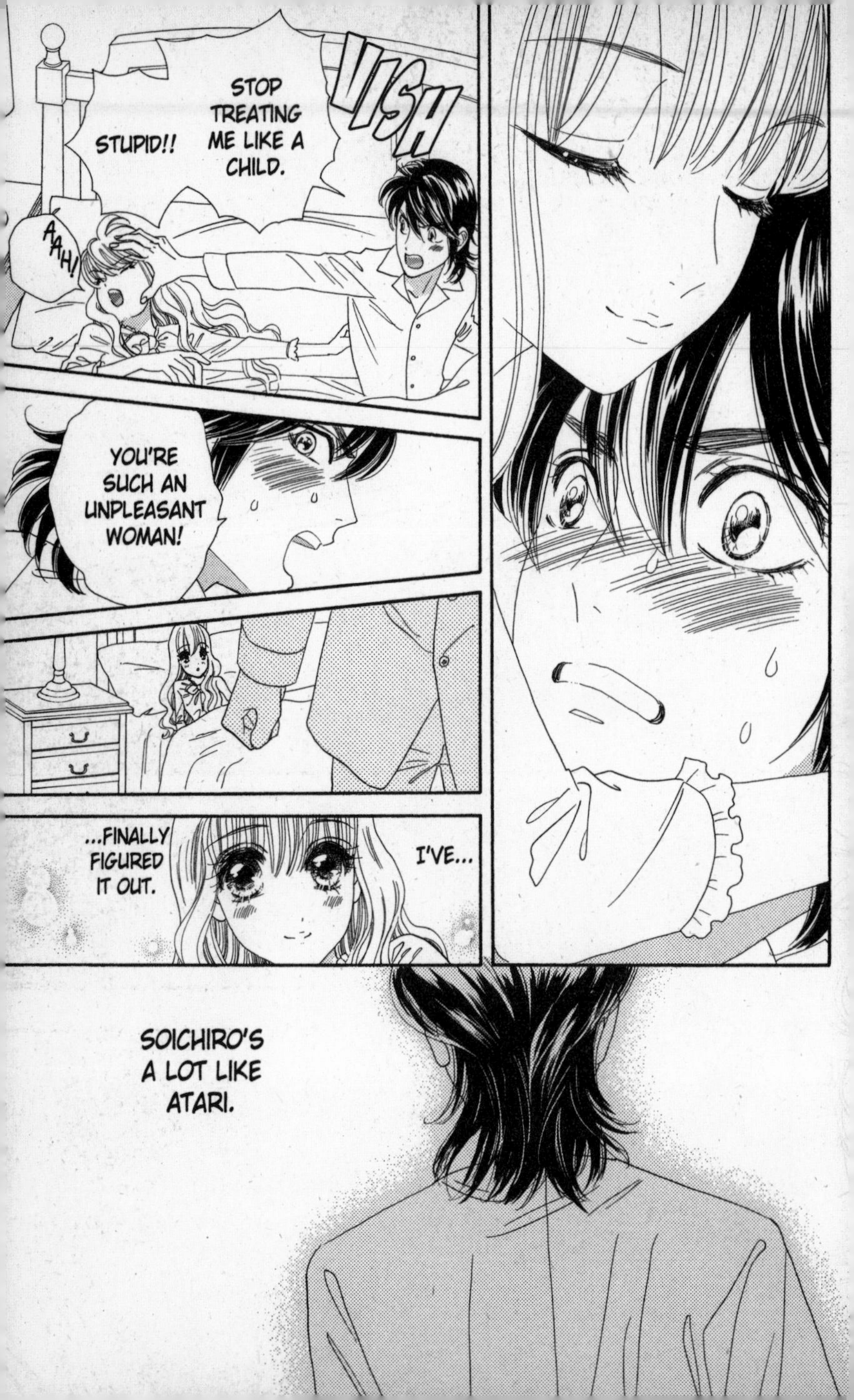
VISH
STOP TREATING ME LIKE A CHILD.
STUPID!!
AAH!
YOU'RE SUCH AN UNPLEASANT WOMAN!
I'VE...
...FINALLY FIGURED IT OUT.
SOICHIRO'S A LOT LIKE ATARI.

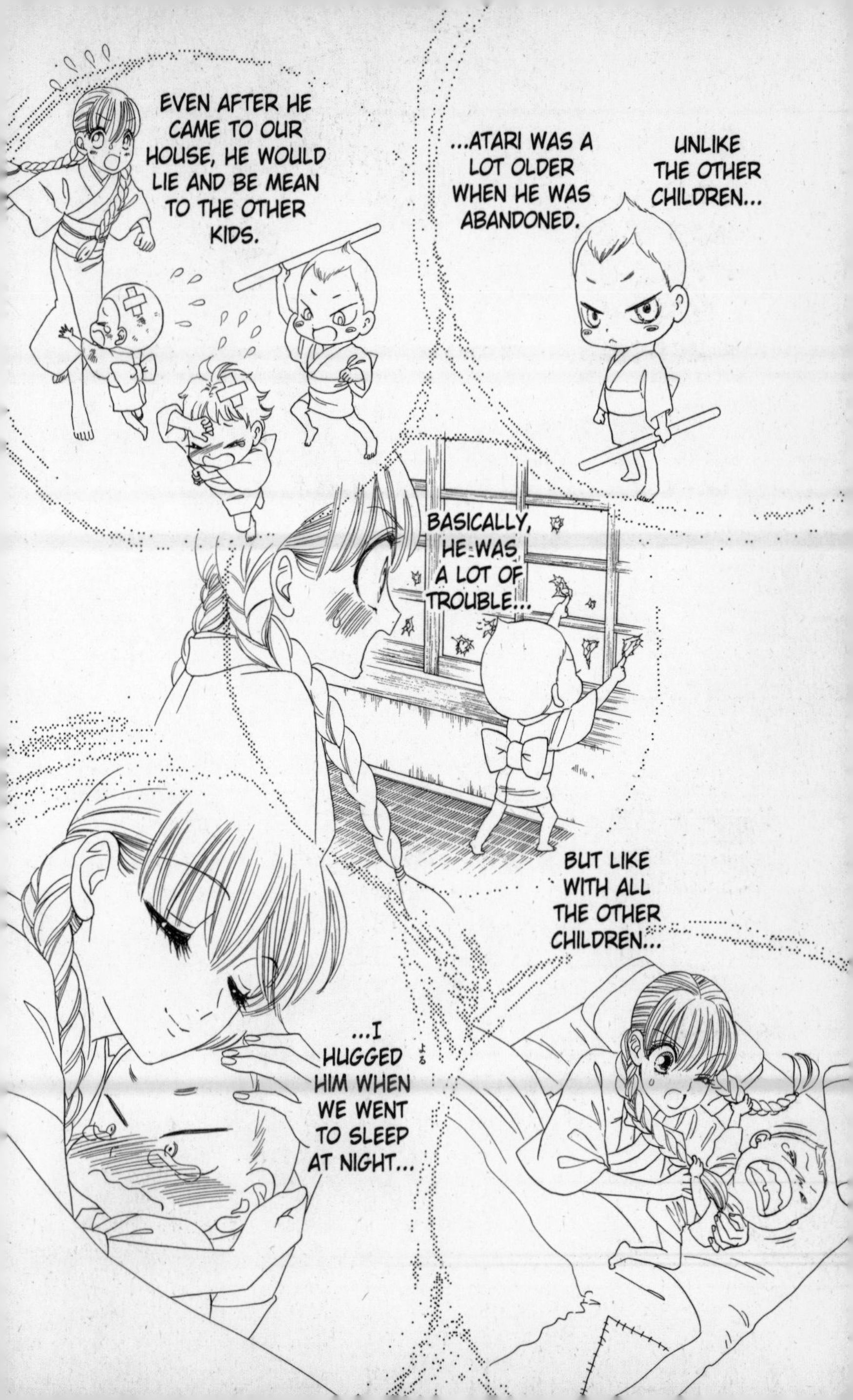
UNLIKE THE OTHER CHILDREN...
...ATARI WAS A LOT OLDER WHEN HE WAS ABANDONED.
EVEN AFTER HE CAME TO OUR HOUSE, HE WOULD LIE AND BE MEAN TO THE OTHER KIDS.
BASICALLY, HE WAS A LOT OF TROUBLE...
BUT LIKE WITH ALL THE OTHER CHILDREN...
...I HUGGED HIM WHEN WE WENT TO SLEEP AT NIGHT...

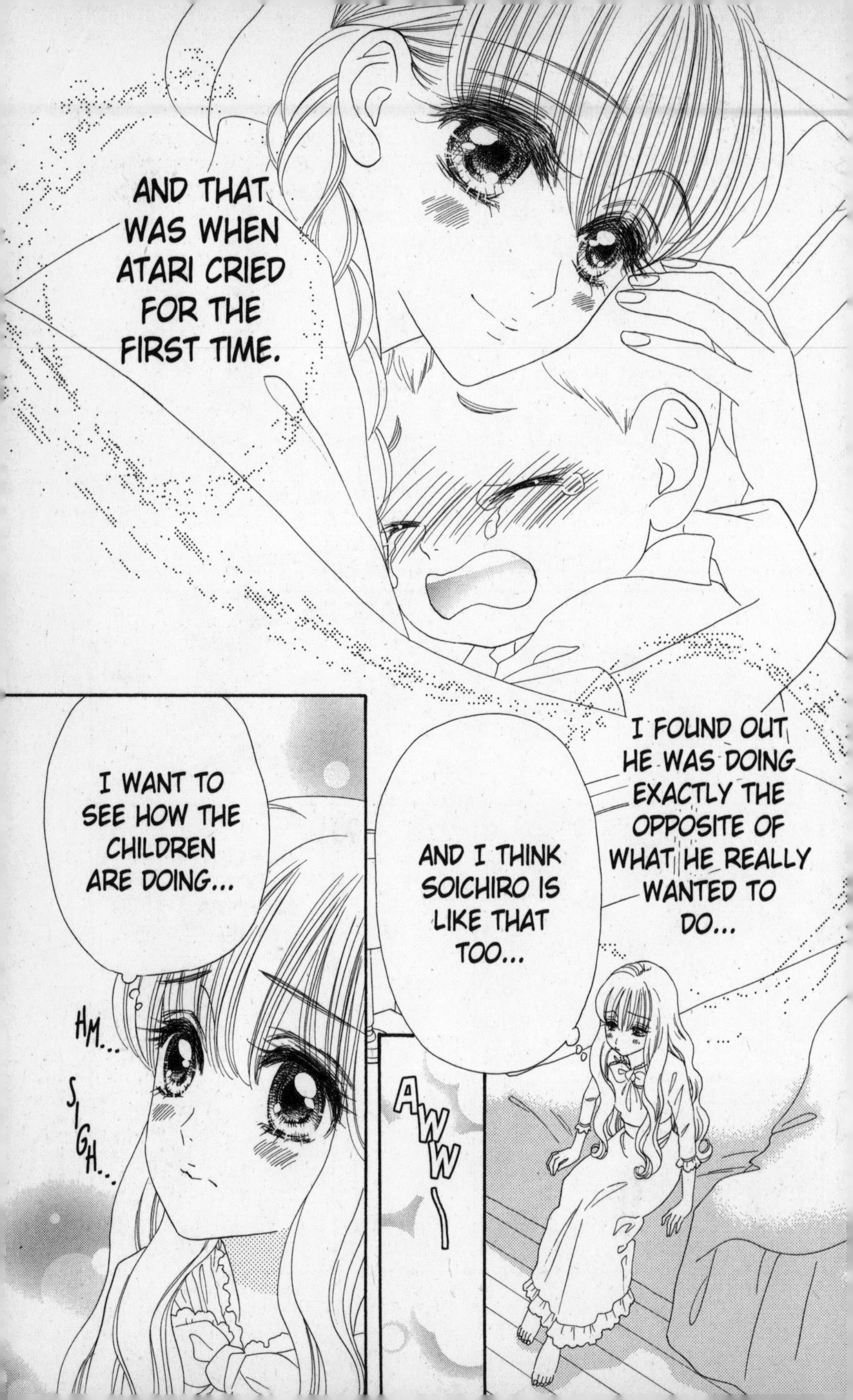
AND THAT WAS WHEN ATARI CRIED FOR THE FIRST TIME.
I FOUND OUT HE WAS DOING EXACTLY THE OPPOSITE OF WHAT HE REALLY WANTED TO DO...
AND I THINK SOICHIRO IS LIKE THAT TOO...
AWW
I WANT TO SEE HOW THE CHILDREN ARE DOING...
HM...
SIGH...

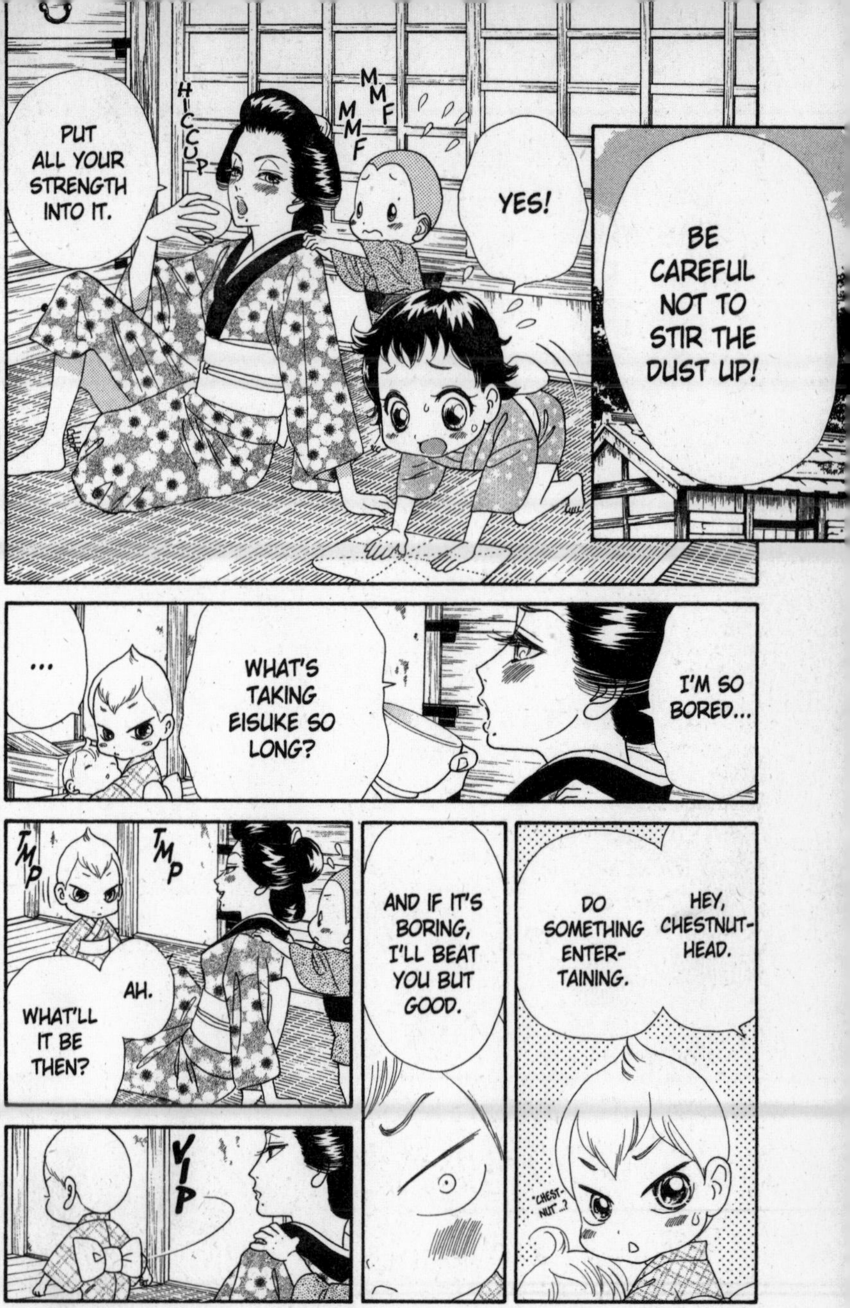
BE CAREFUL NOT TO STIR THE DUST UP!
YES!
MMF MMF
HICCUP
PUT ALL YOUR STRENGTH INTO IT.
I'M SO BORED...
WHAT'S TAKING EISUKE SO LONG?
...
HEY, CHESTNUT-HEAD.
DO SOMETHING ENTERTAINING.
"CHEST-NUT"...?
AND IF IT'S BORING, I'LL BEAT YOU BUT GOOD.
TMP
TMP
AH.
WHAT'LL IT BE THEN?
VIP

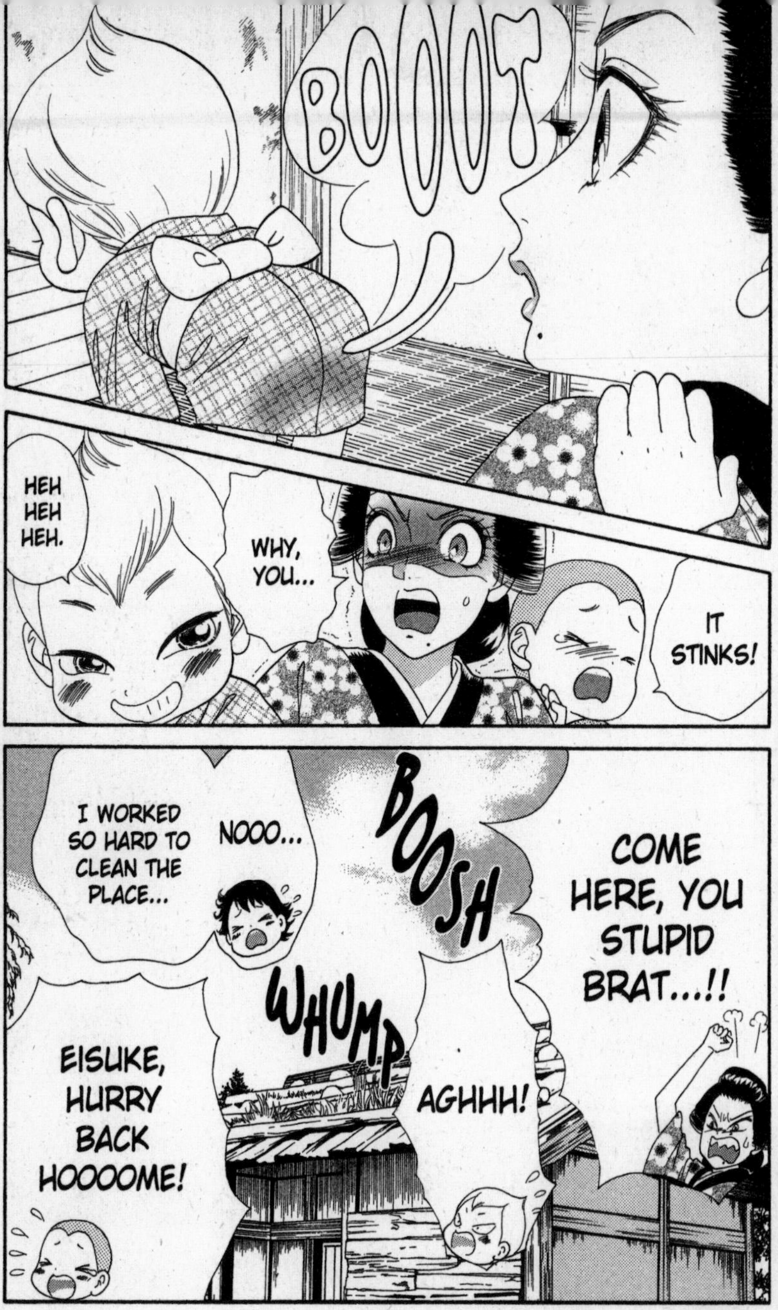
BOOOT
IT STINKS!
WHY, YOU...
HEH HEH HEH.
COME HERE, YOU STUPID BRAT...!!
BOOSH
AGHHH!
WHUMP
NOOO...
I WORKED SO HARD TO CLEAN THE PLACE...
EISUKE, HURRY BACK HOOOOME!

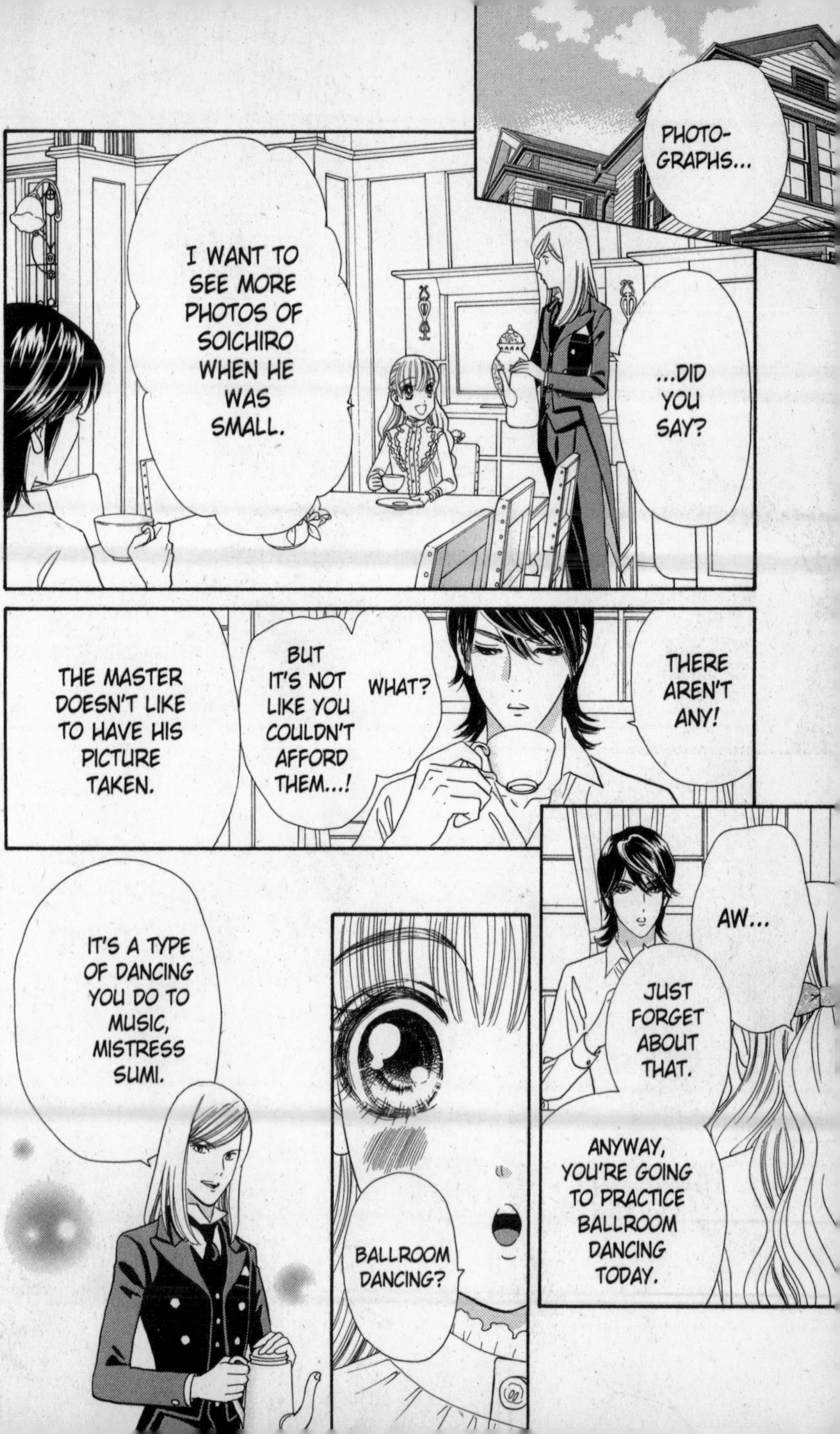
PHOTO-GRAPHS...
I WANT TO SEE MORE PHOTOS OF SOICHIRO WHEN HE WAS SMALL.
...DID YOU SAY?
THERE AREN'T ANY!
WHAT?
BUT IT'S NOT LIKE YOU COULDN'T AFFORD THEM...!
THE MASTER DOESN'T LIKE TO HAVE HIS PICTURE TAKEN.
AW...
JUST FORGET ABOUT THAT.
ANYWAY, YOU'RE GOING TO PRACTICE BALLROOM DANCING TODAY.
BALLROOM DANCING?
IT'S A TYPE OF DANCING YOU DO TO MUSIC, MISTRESS SUMI.

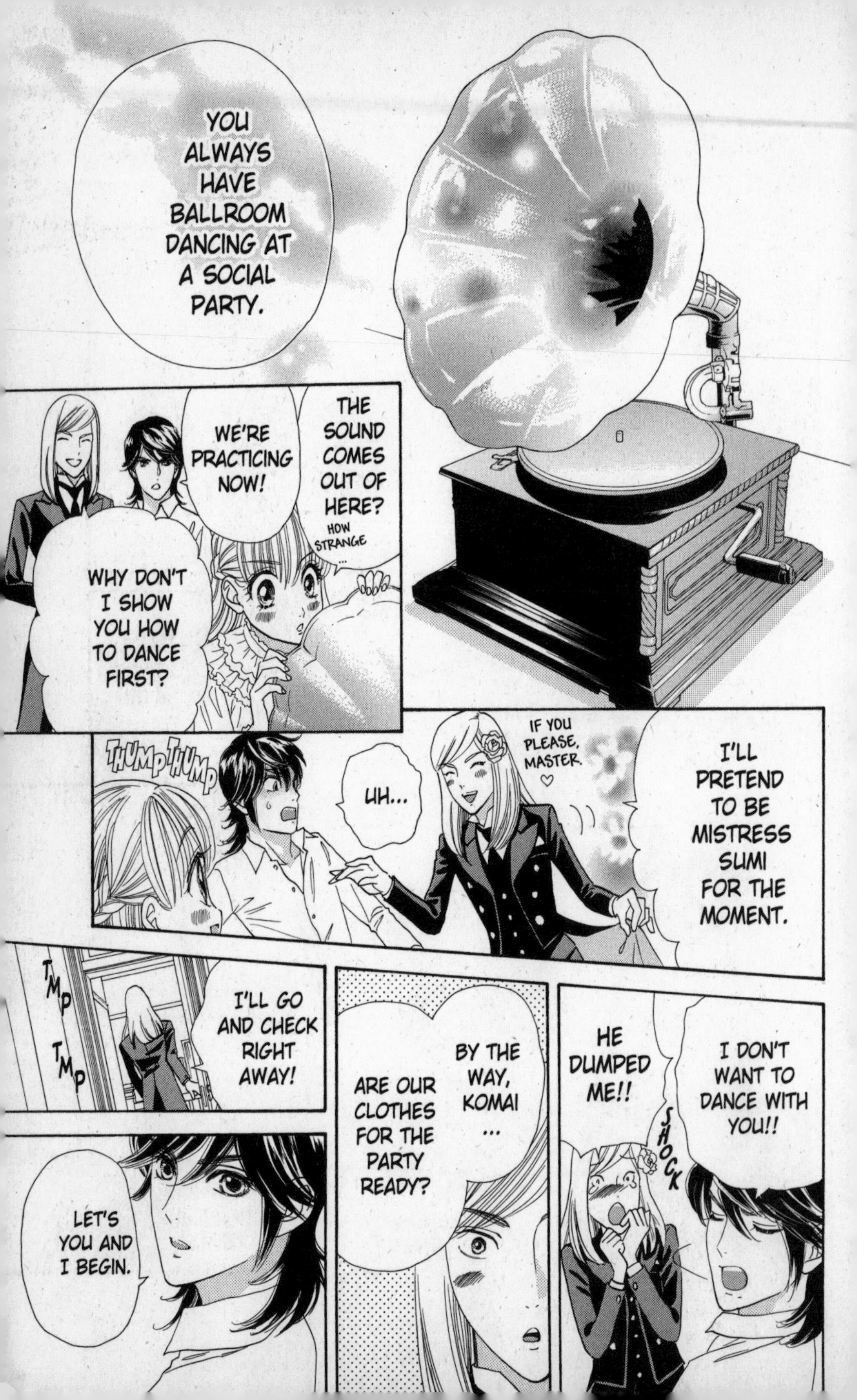
YOU ALWAYS HAVE BALLROOM DANCING AT A SOCIAL PARTY.
THE SOUND COMES OUT OF HERE?
HOW STRANGE ...
WE'RE PRACTICING NOW!
WHY DON'T I SHOW YOU HOW TO DANCE FIRST?
I'LL PRETEND TO BE MISTRESS SUMI FOR THE MOMENT.
IF YOU PLEASE, MASTER. ♡
UH...
THUMP THUMP
I DON'T WANT TO DANCE WITH YOU!!
SHOCK
HE DUMPED ME!!
BY THE WAY, KOMAI ...
ARE OUR CLOTHES FOR THE PARTY READY?
I'LL GO AND CHECK RIGHT AWAY!
TMP TMP
LET'S YOU AND I BEGIN.

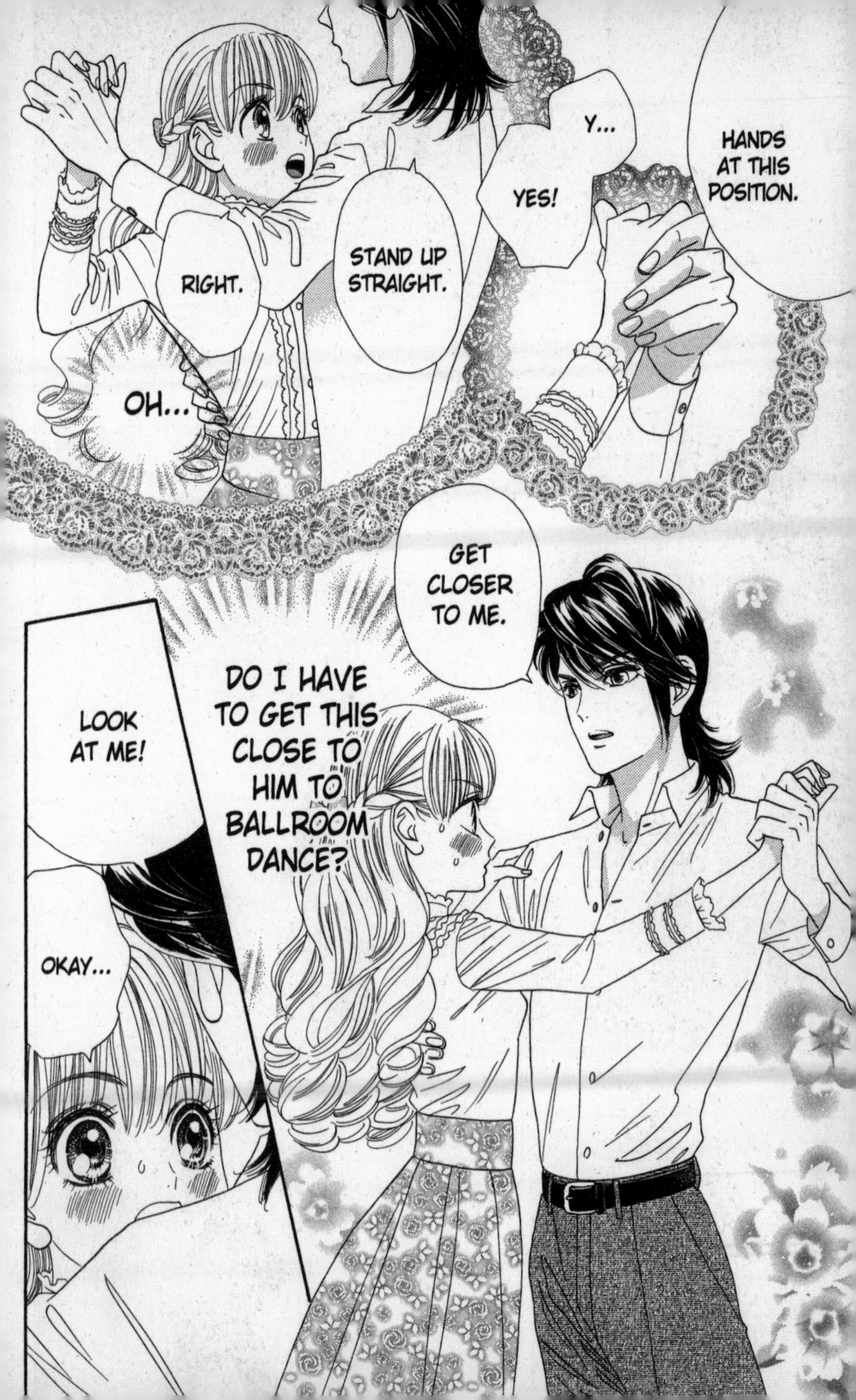
HANDS AT THIS POSITION.
Y...
YES!
STAND UP STRAIGHT.
RIGHT.
OH...
GET CLOSER TO ME.
DO I HAVE TO GET THIS CLOSE TO HIM TO BALLROOM DANCE?
LOOK AT ME!
OKAY...

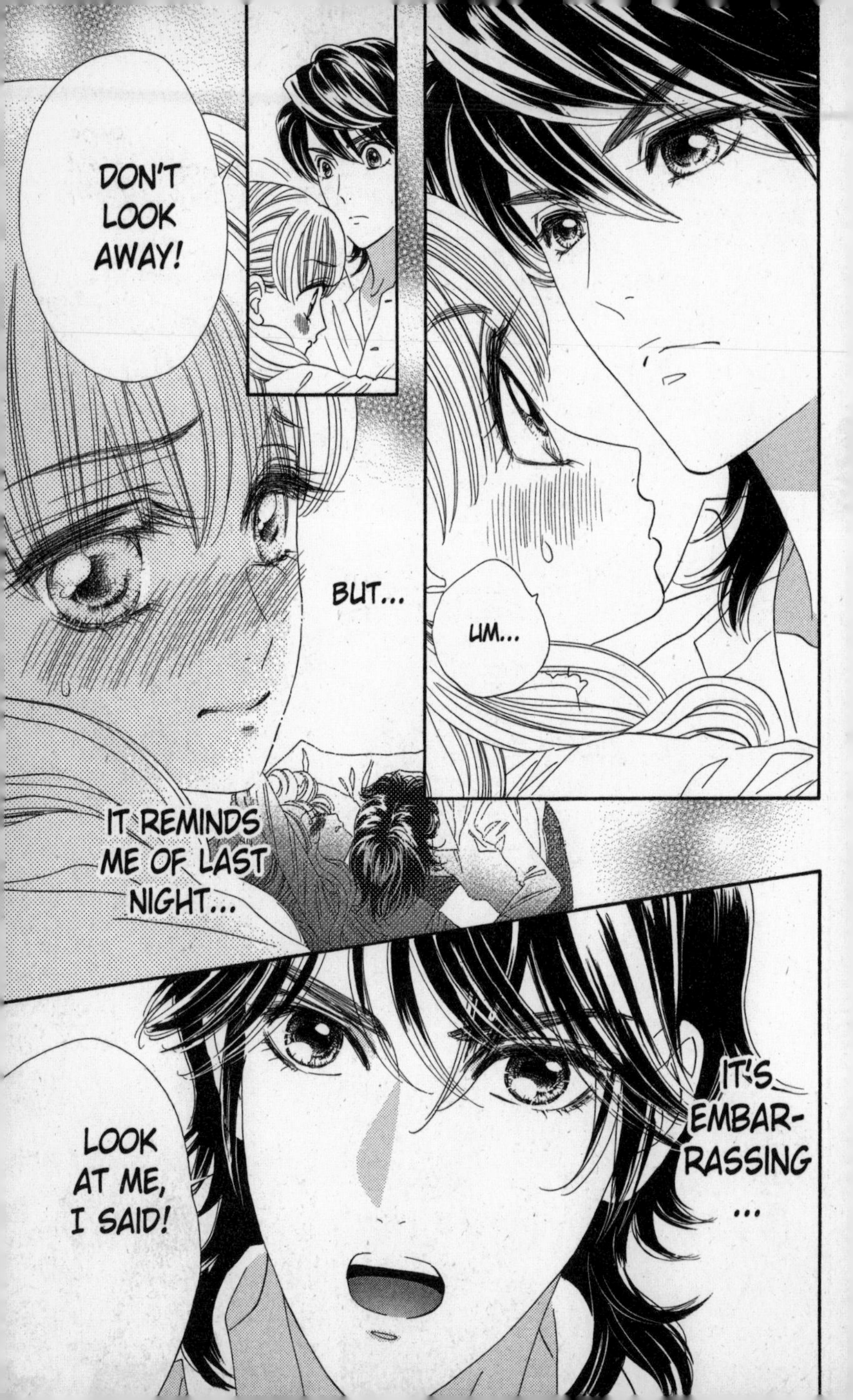
UM...
DON'T LOOK AWAY!
BUT...
IT REMINDS ME OF LAST NIGHT...
IT'S EMBARRASSING...
LOOK AT ME, I SAID!

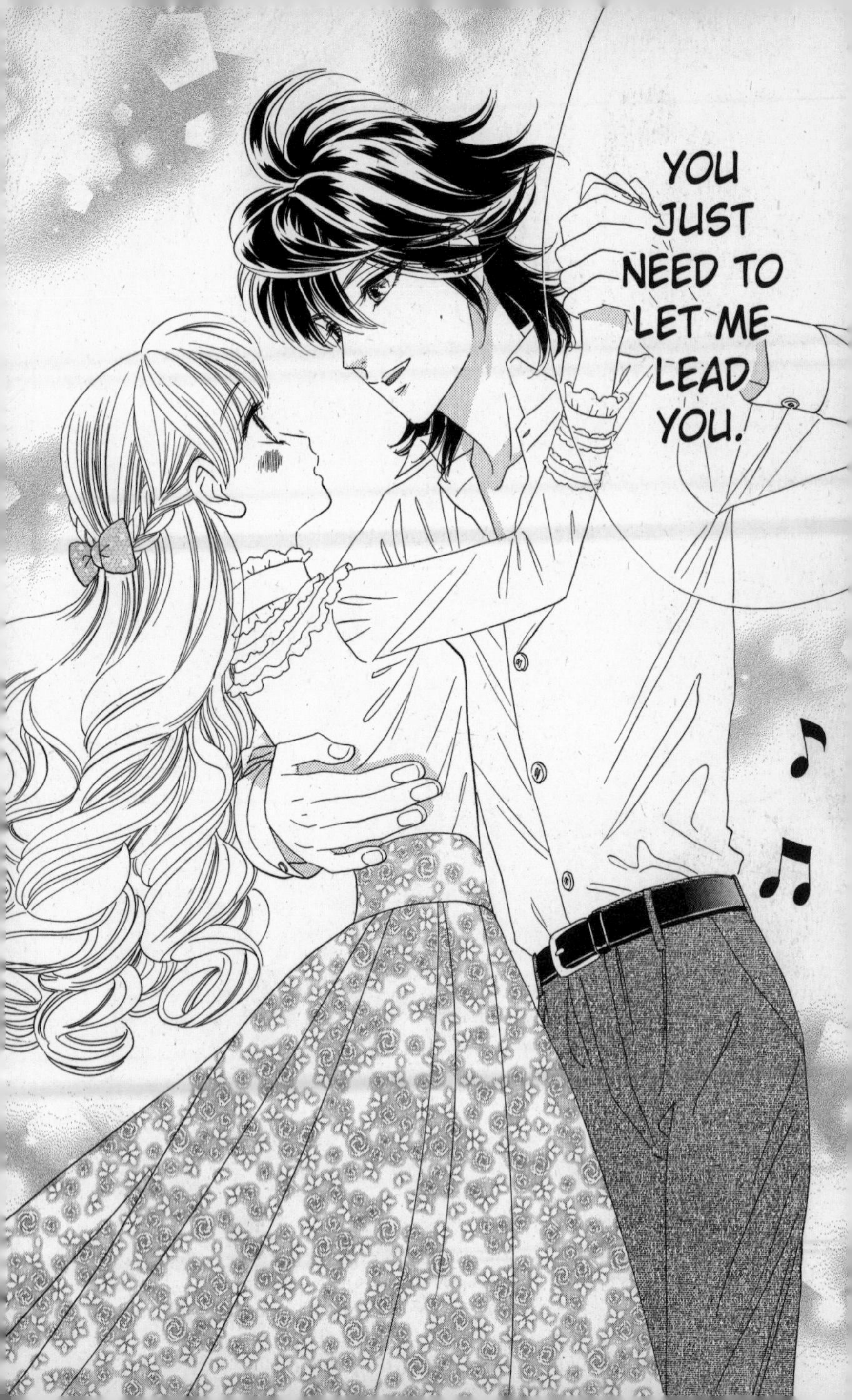
YOU JUST NEED TO LET ME LEAD YOU.

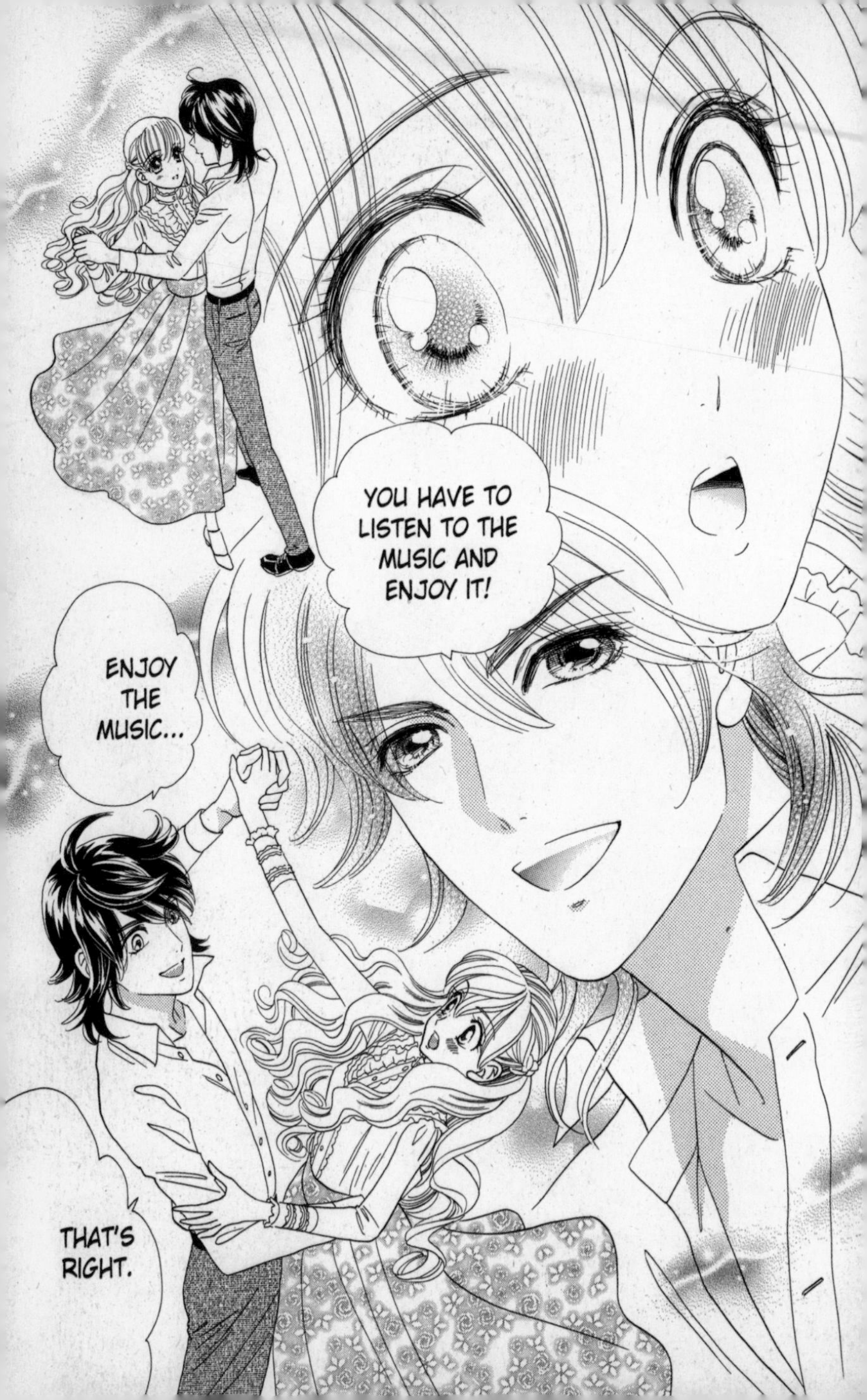
YOU HAVE TO LISTEN TO THE MUSIC AND ENJOY IT!
ENJOY THE MUSIC...
THAT'S RIGHT.

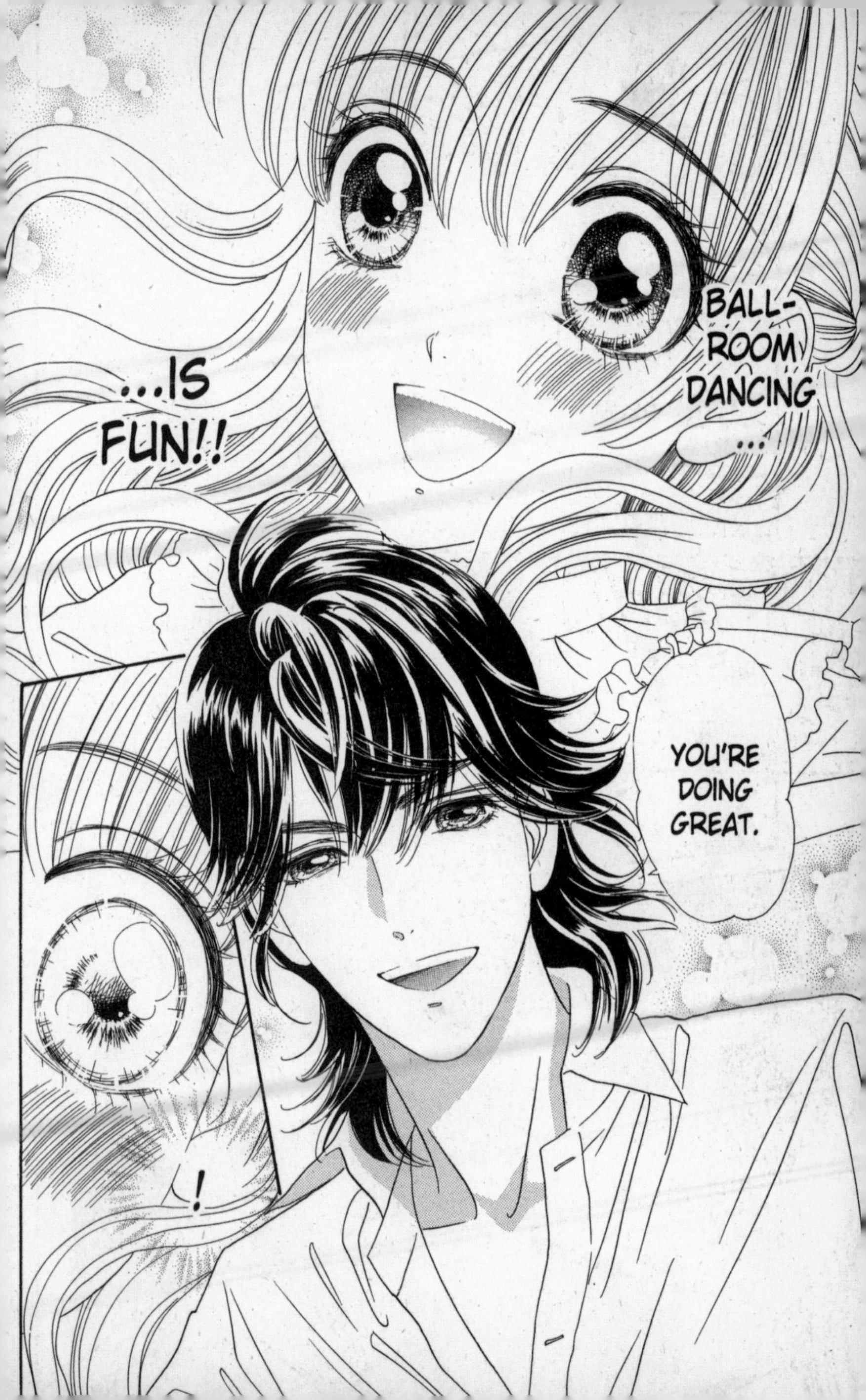
BALL-ROOM DANCING ...
...IS FUN!!
YOU'RE DOING GREAT.
!

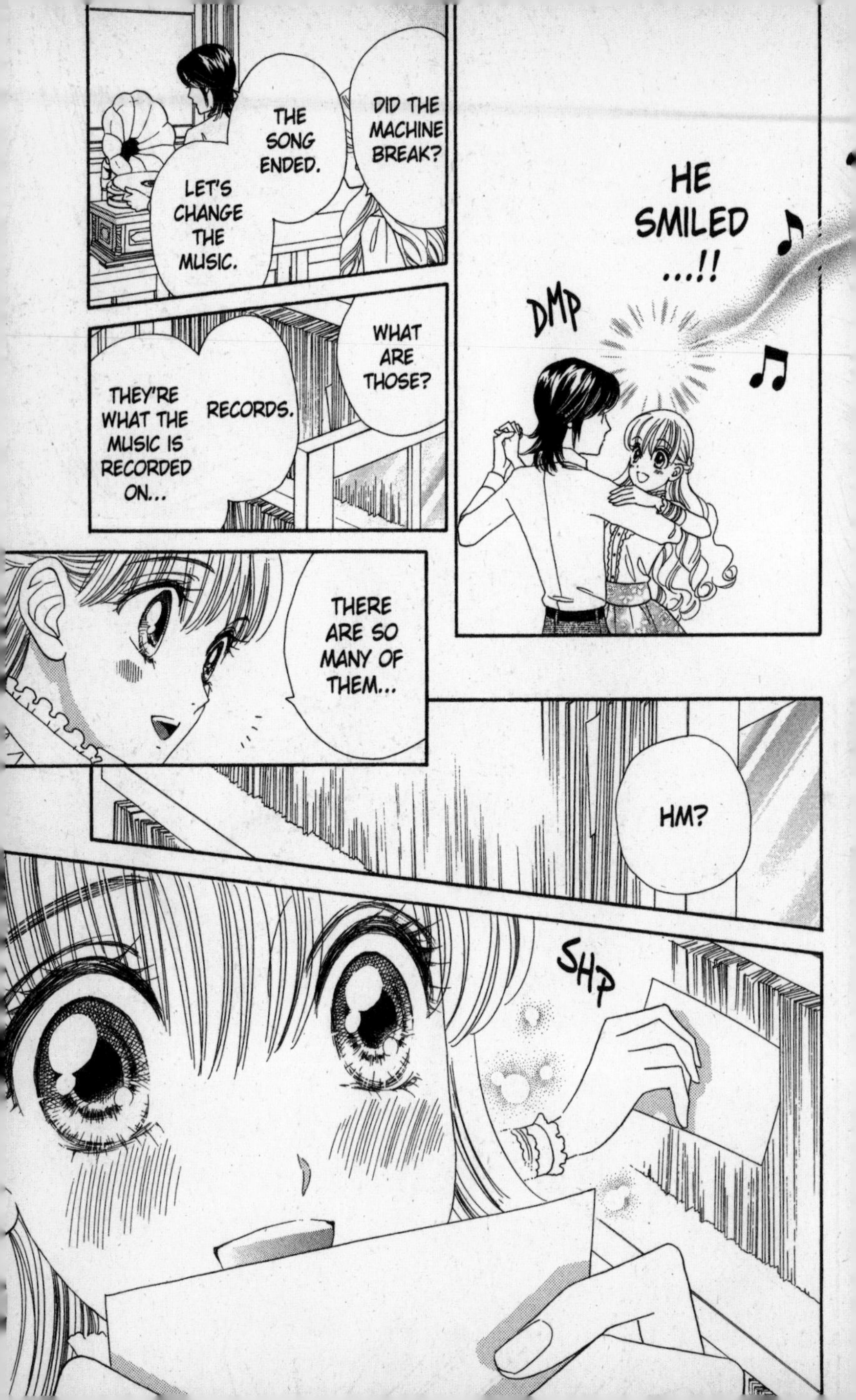

HE SMILED ...!!
DMP
DID THE MACHINE BREAK?
THE SONG ENDED.
LET'S CHANGE THE MUSIC.
WHAT ARE THOSE?
RECORDS.
THEY'RE WHAT THE MUSIC IS RECORDED ON...
THERE ARE SO MANY OF THEM...
HM?
SHP

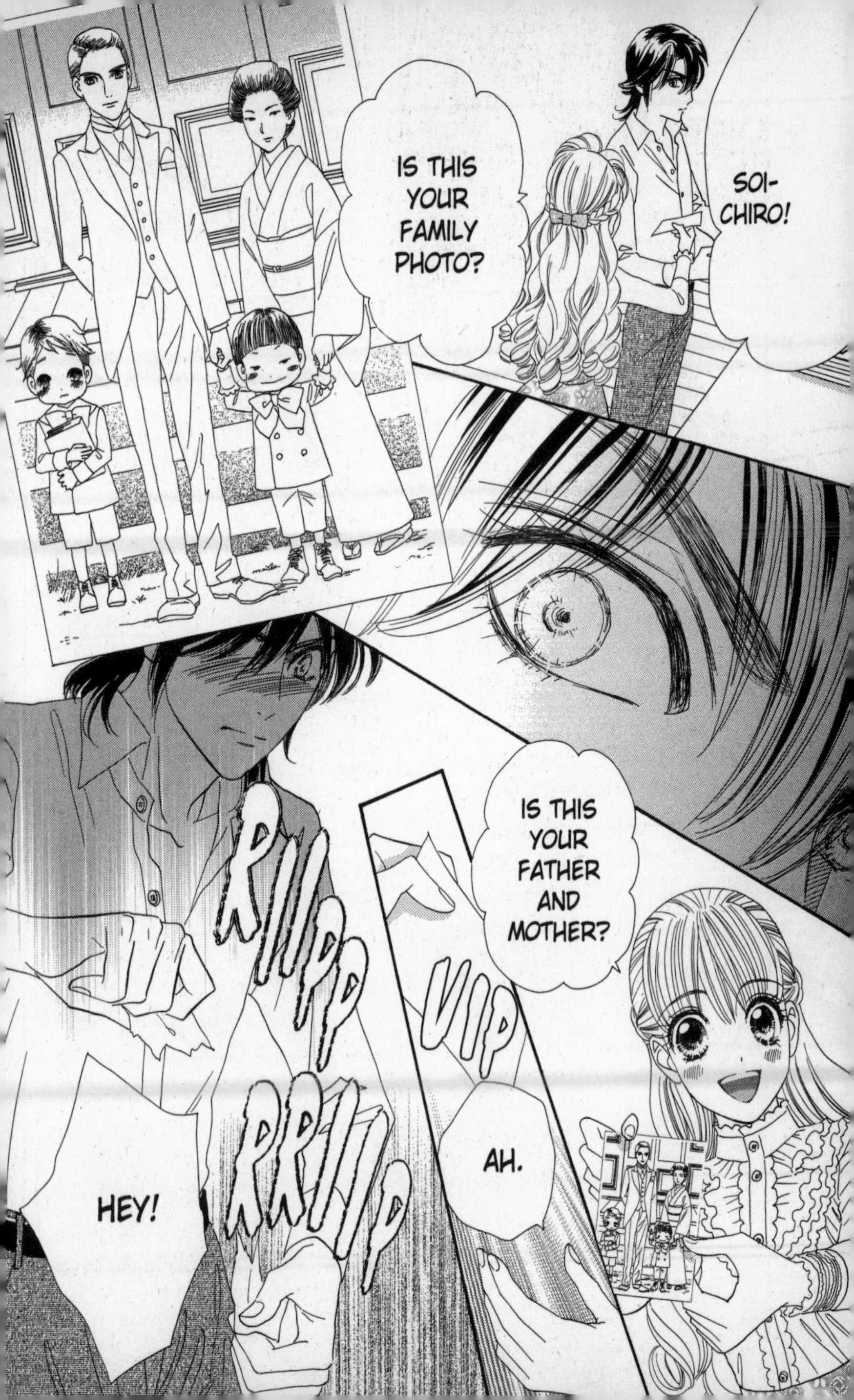
SOI-CHIRO!
IS THIS YOUR FAMILY PHOTO?
IS THIS YOUR FATHER AND MOTHER?
AH.
VIP
HEY!

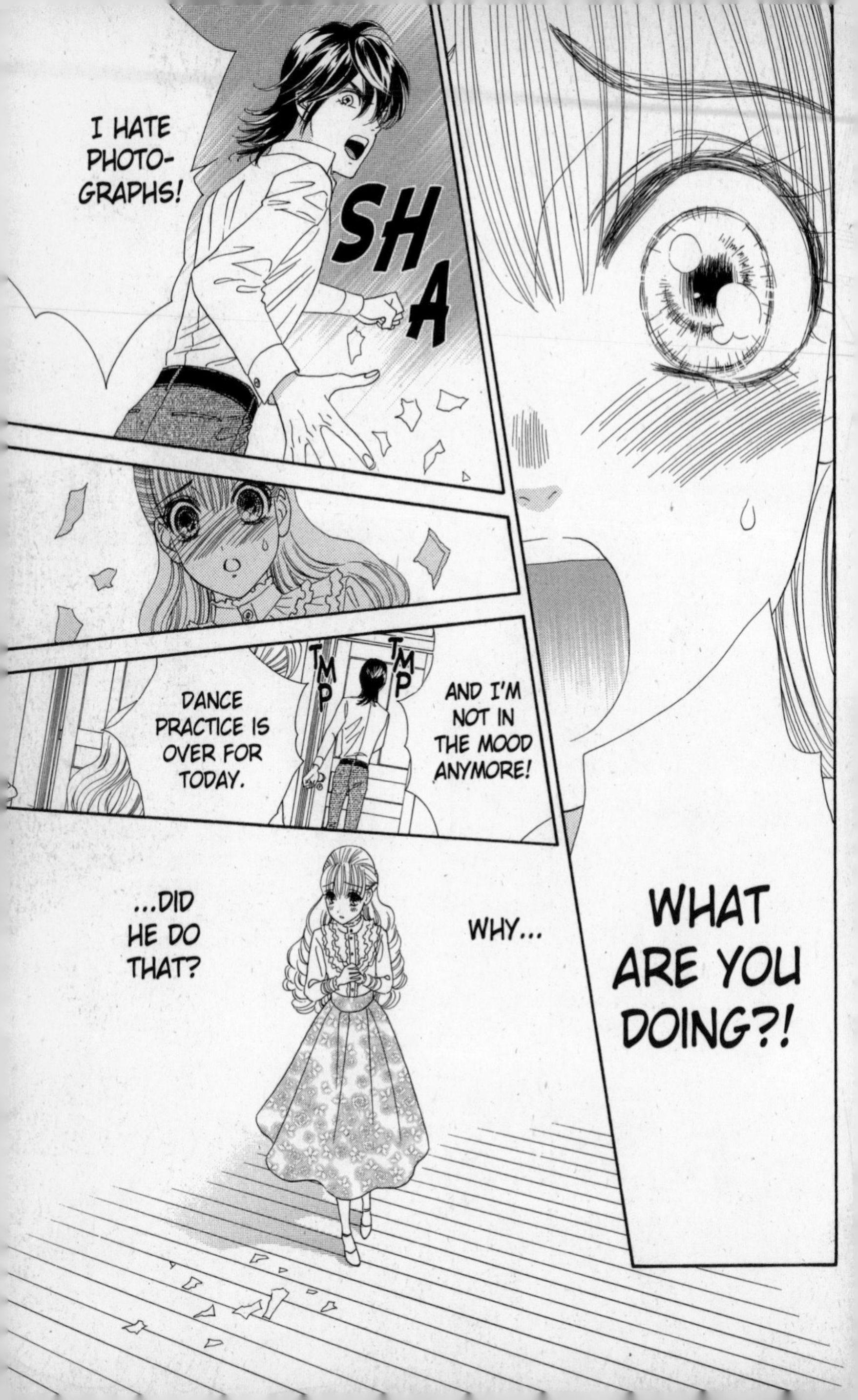
WHAT ARE YOU DOING?!
I HATE PHOTOGRAPHS!
SHA
TMP
AND I'M NOT IN THE MOOD ANYMORE!
TMP
DANCE PRACTICE IS OVER FOR TODAY.
WHY...
...DID HE DO THAT?

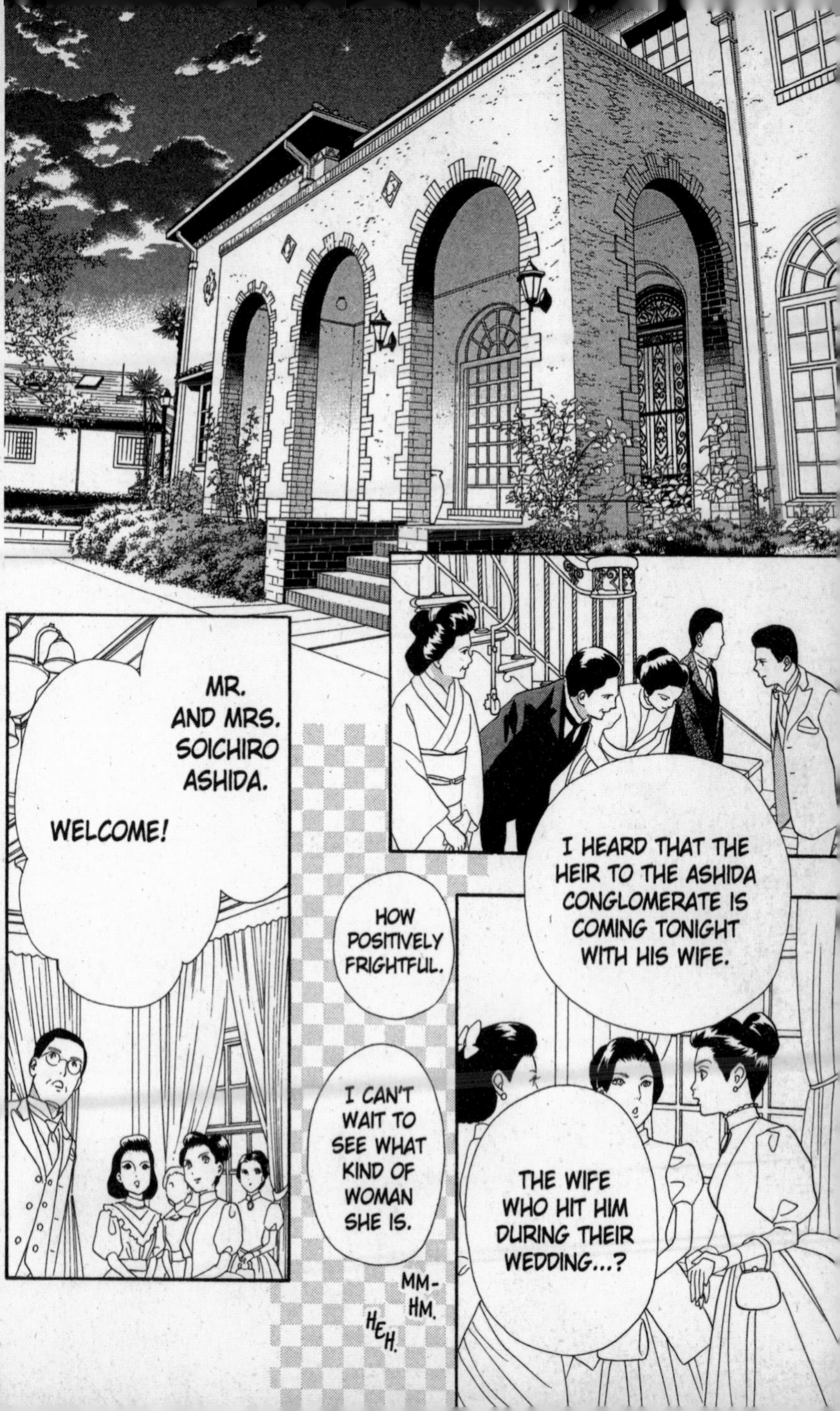
I HEARD THAT THE HEIR TO THE ASHIDA CONGLOMERATE IS COMING TONIGHT WITH HIS WIFE.
HOW POSITIVELY FRIGHTFUL.
THE WIFE WHO HIT HIM DURING THEIR WEDDING...?
I CAN'T WAIT TO SEE WHAT KIND OF WOMAN SHE IS.
MM-HM.
HEH.
MR. AND MRS. SOICHIRO ASHIDA.
WELCOME!

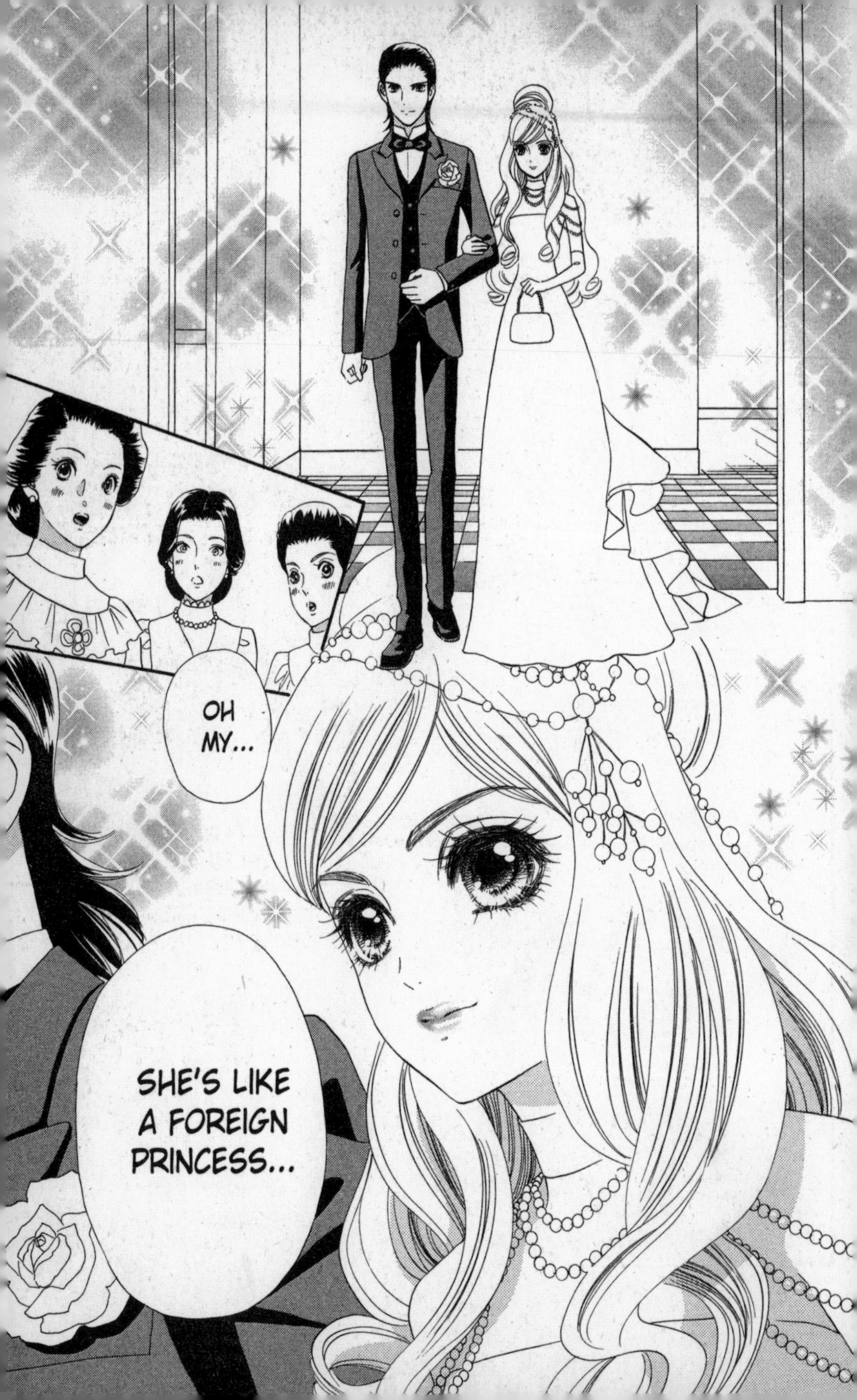
OH MY...
SHE'S LIKE A FOREIGN PRINCESS...

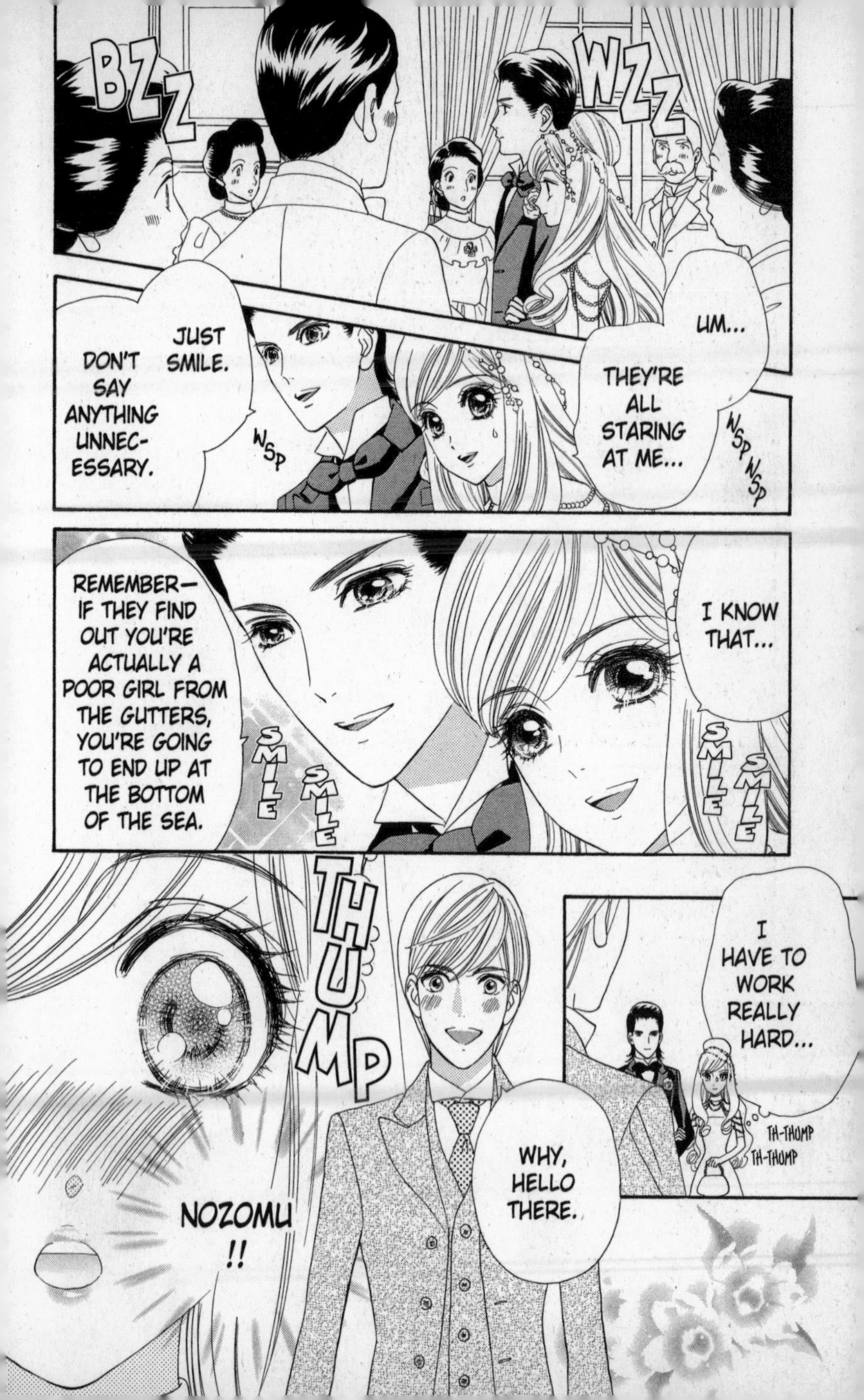
WZZ
BZZ
UM...
THEY'RE ALL STARING AT ME...
WSP WSP
WSP
JUST SMILE.
DON'T SAY ANYTHING UNNEC-ESSARY.
I KNOW THAT...
SMILE SMILE
REMEMBER—IF THEY FIND OUT YOU'RE ACTUALLY A POOR GIRL FROM THE GUTTERS, YOU'RE GOING TO END UP AT THE BOTTOM OF THE SEA.
SMILE SMILE
I HAVE TO WORK REALLY HARD...
TH-THOMP TH-THOMP
THUMP
WHY, HELLO THERE.
NOZOMU!!

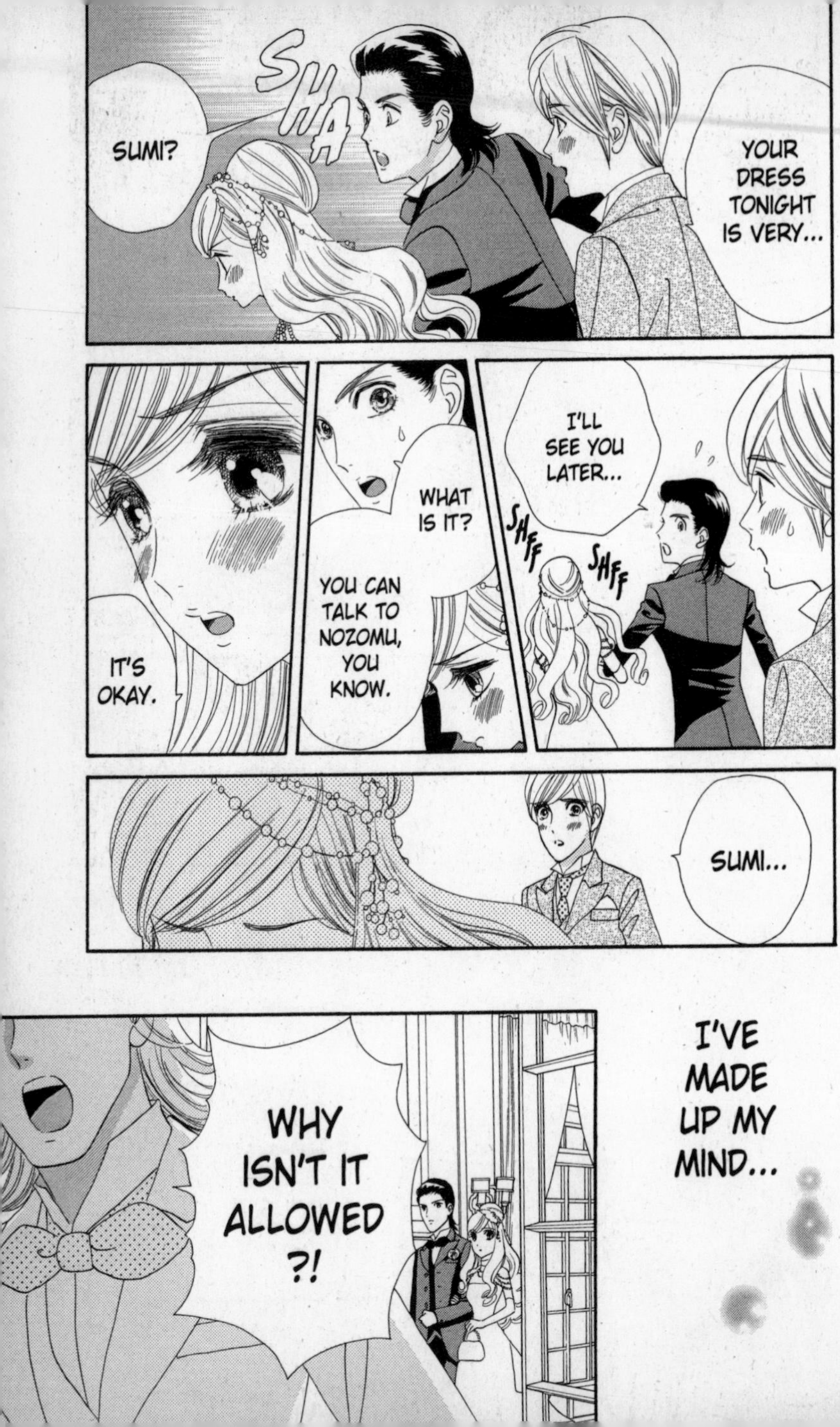
YOUR DRESS TONIGHT IS VERY...
SHA
SUMI?
I'LL SEE YOU LATER...
SHFF
SHFF
WHAT IS IT?
YOU CAN TALK TO NOZOMU, YOU KNOW.
IT'S OKAY.
SUMI...
I'VE MADE UP MY MIND...
WHY ISN'T IT ALLOWED?!

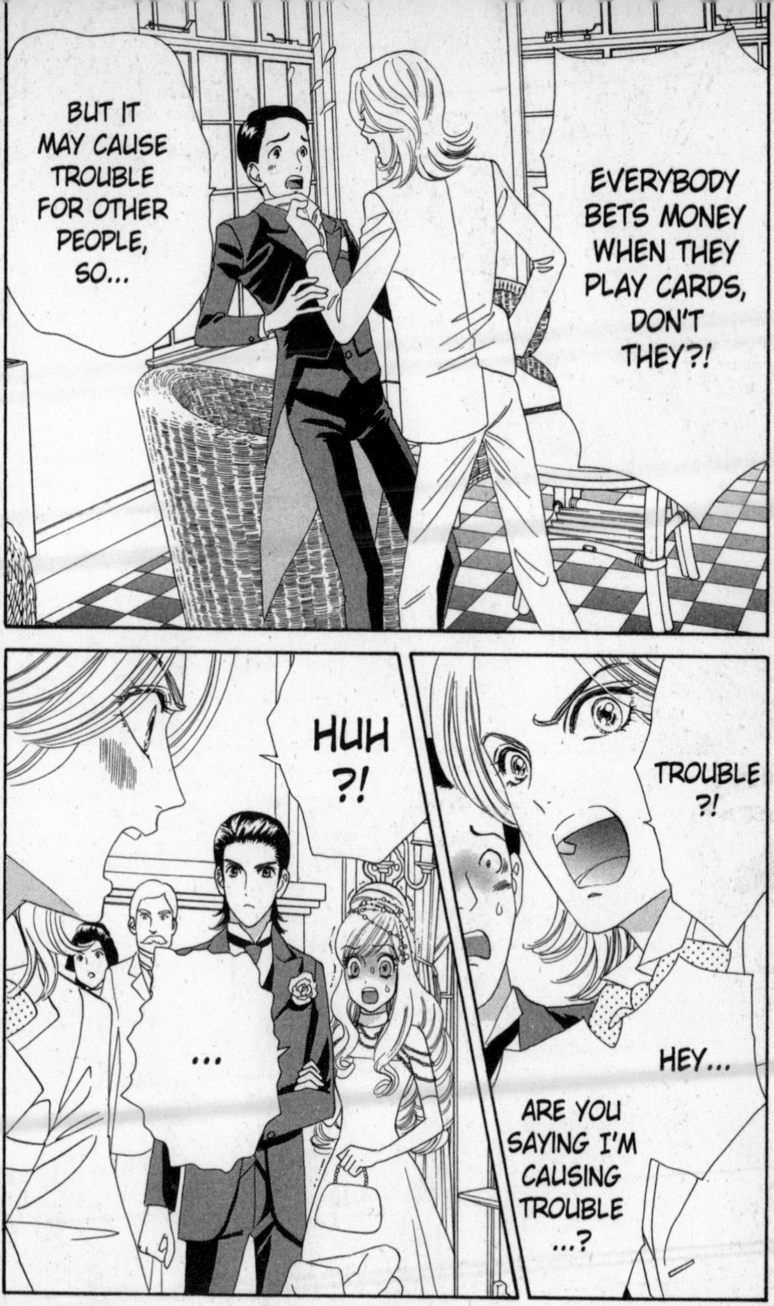
EVERYBODY BETS MONEY WHEN THEY PLAY CARDS, DON'T THEY?!
BUT IT MAY CAUSE TROUBLE FOR OTHER PEOPLE, SO...
TROUBLE ?!
HEY...
ARE YOU SAYING I'M CAUSING TROUBLE ...?
HUH ?!
...

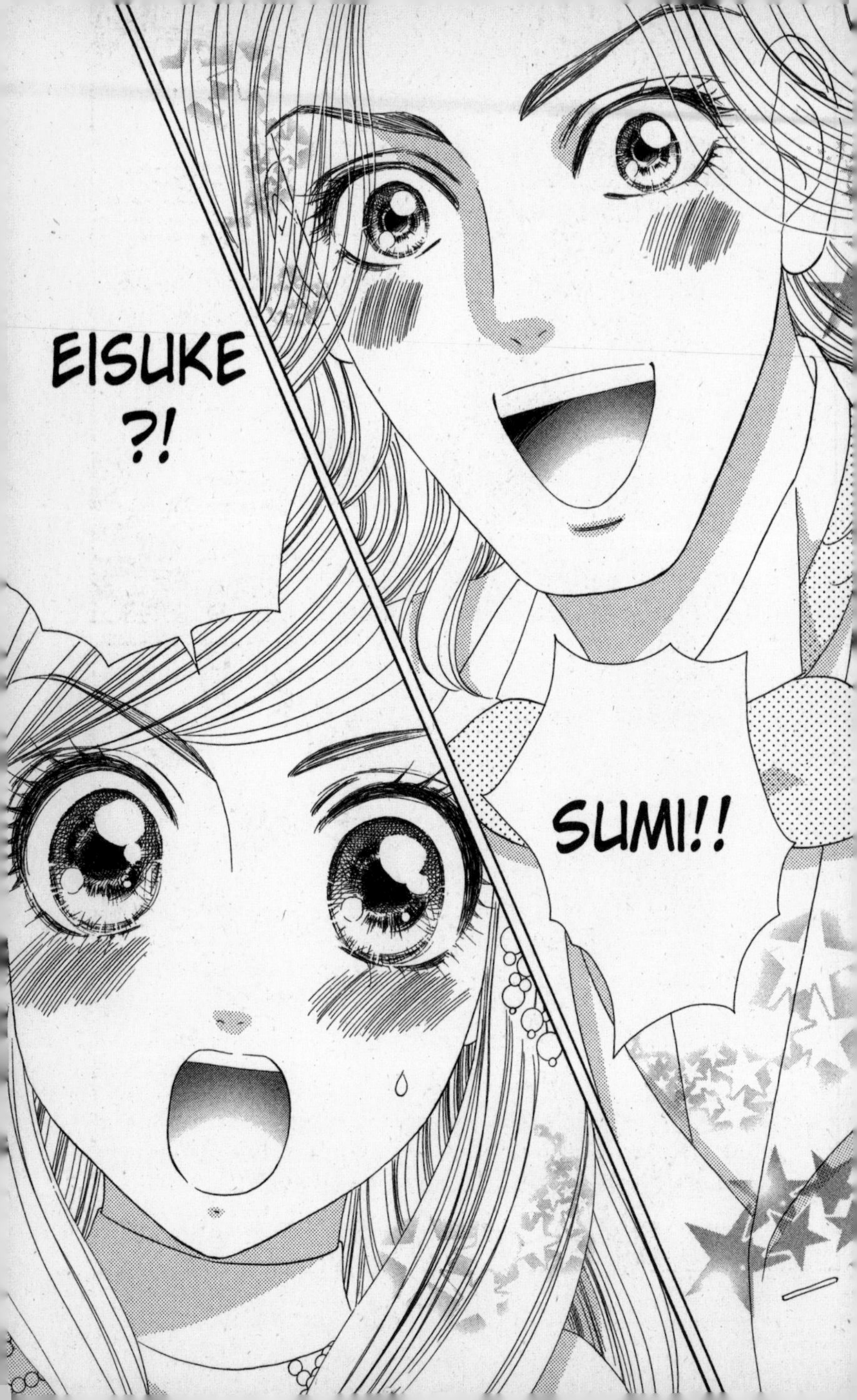
SUMI!!
EISUKE ?!

STEP STAGE★3

No.

THIS IS A ROUGH SKETCH I DREW WHILE PREPARING THE SERIES. Date

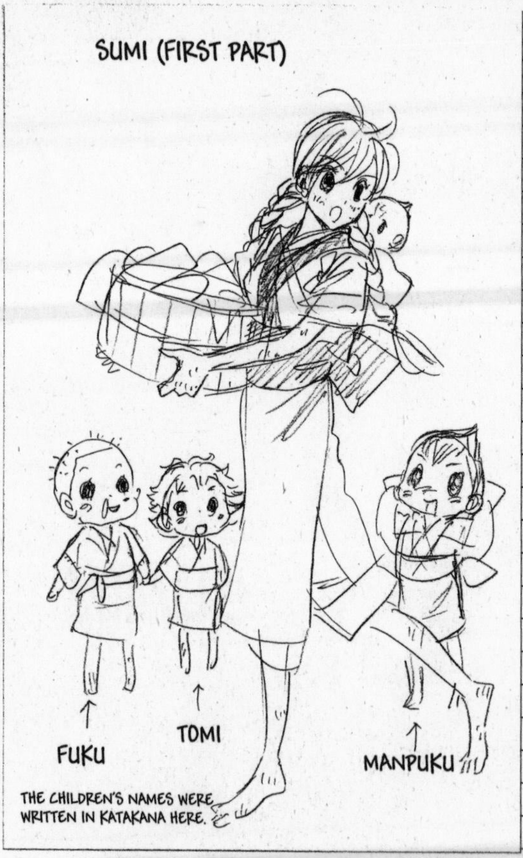
SUMI (FIRST PART)
FUKU
TOMI
MANPUKU
THE CHILDREN'S NAMES WERE WRITTEN IN KATAKANA HERE.

THE CHILD ON THE RIGHT IS THE ONE WHO BECOMES ATARI, BUT HIS NAME WAS "MANPUKU" BACK THEN.

THEIR NAMES ARE LIKE THIS BECAUSE EISUKE NAMED THEM WITH THE HOPE OF GETTING GOOD LUCK WITH HIS GAMBLING.

AFTER SEEING THIS ILLUSTRATION, MY EDITOR SAID, "I KNOW THEY'RE SUPPOSED TO BE POOR, BUT AREN'T THEY A LITTLE TOO GRUNGY? ESPECIALLY FUKU..." SO FOR THE ACTUAL SERIES, I DREW THEM A LITTLE CLEANER.

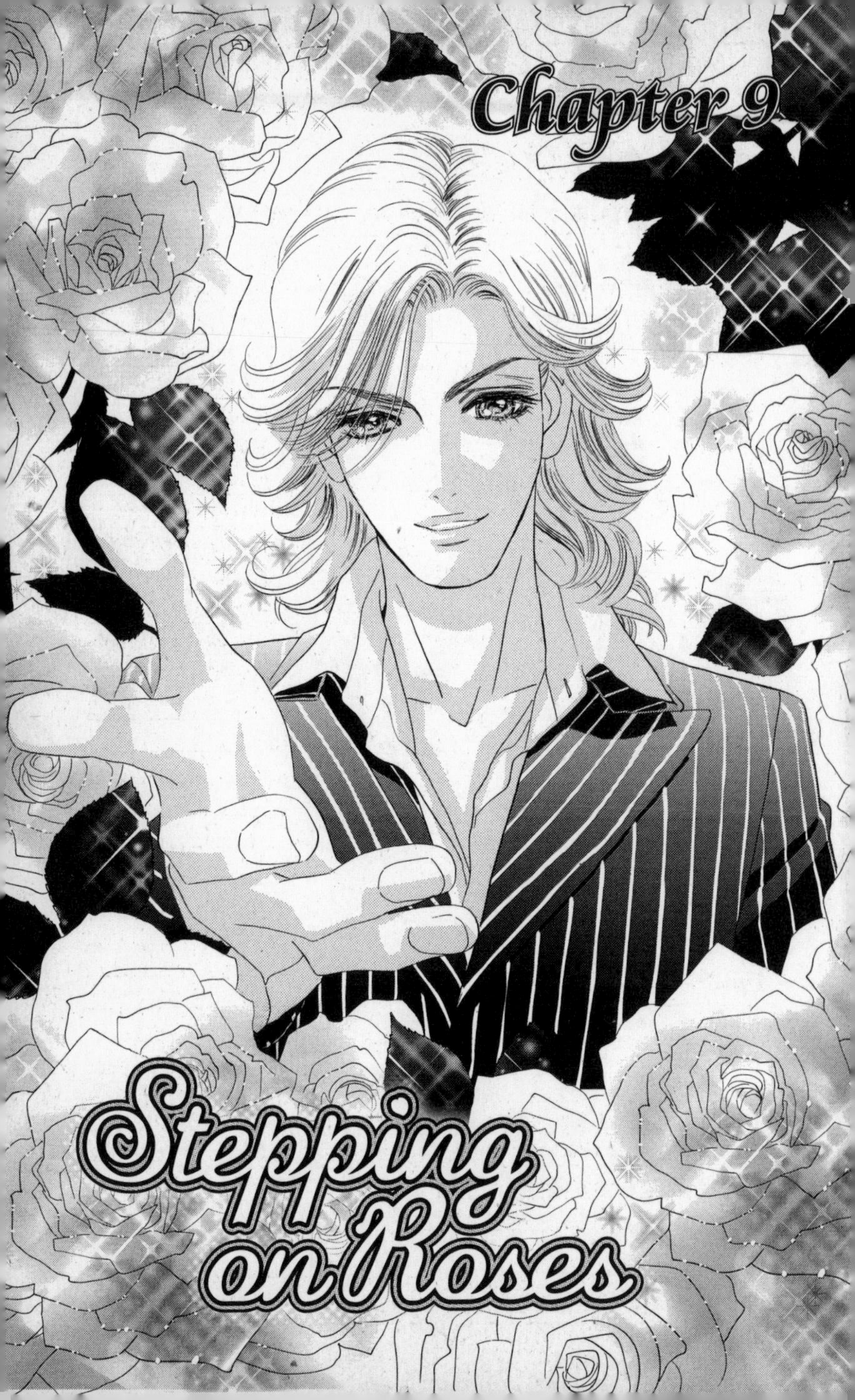
Chapter 9
Stepping on Roses

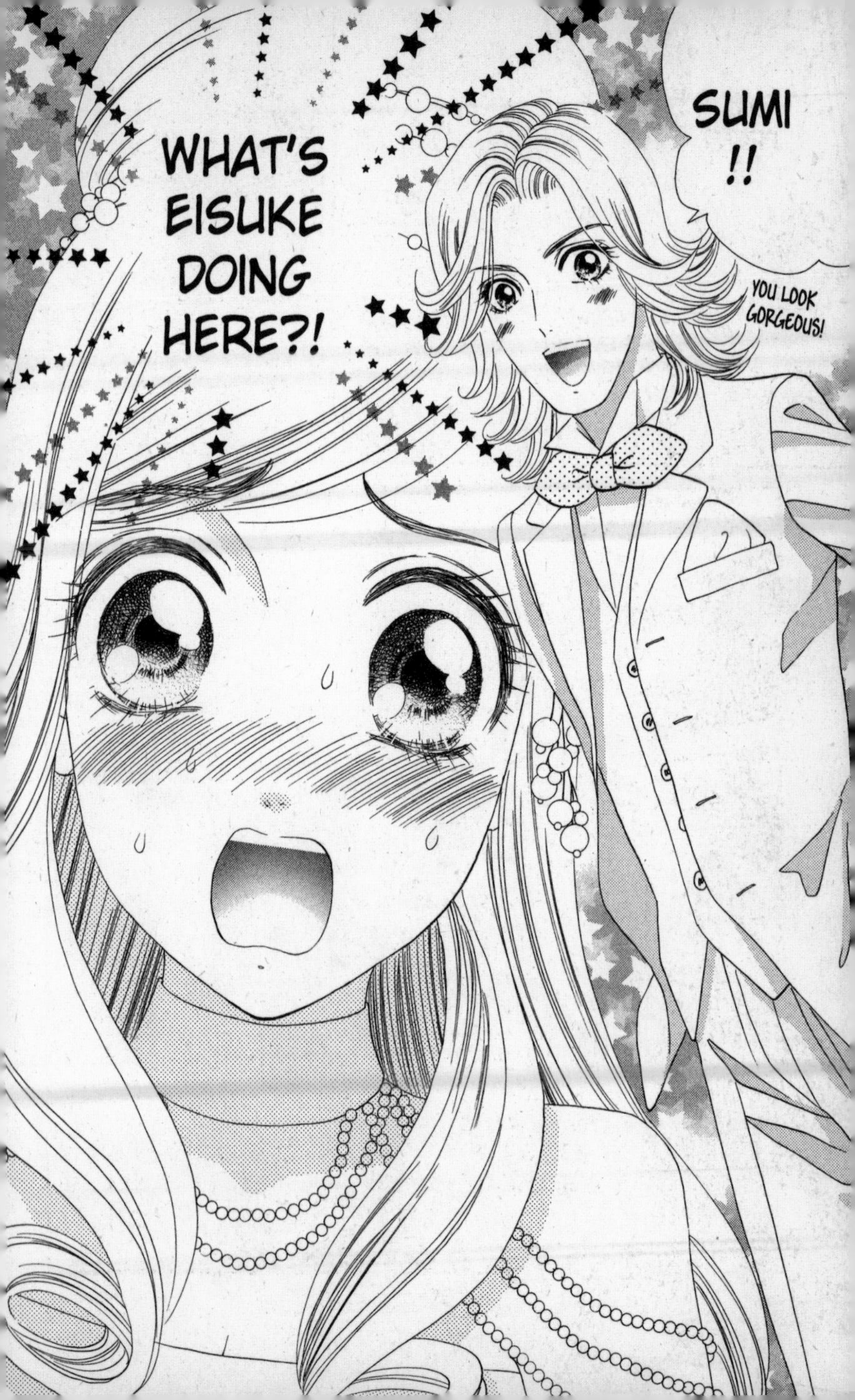
SUMI !!
YOU LOOK GORGEOUS!
WHAT'S EISUKE DOING HERE?!

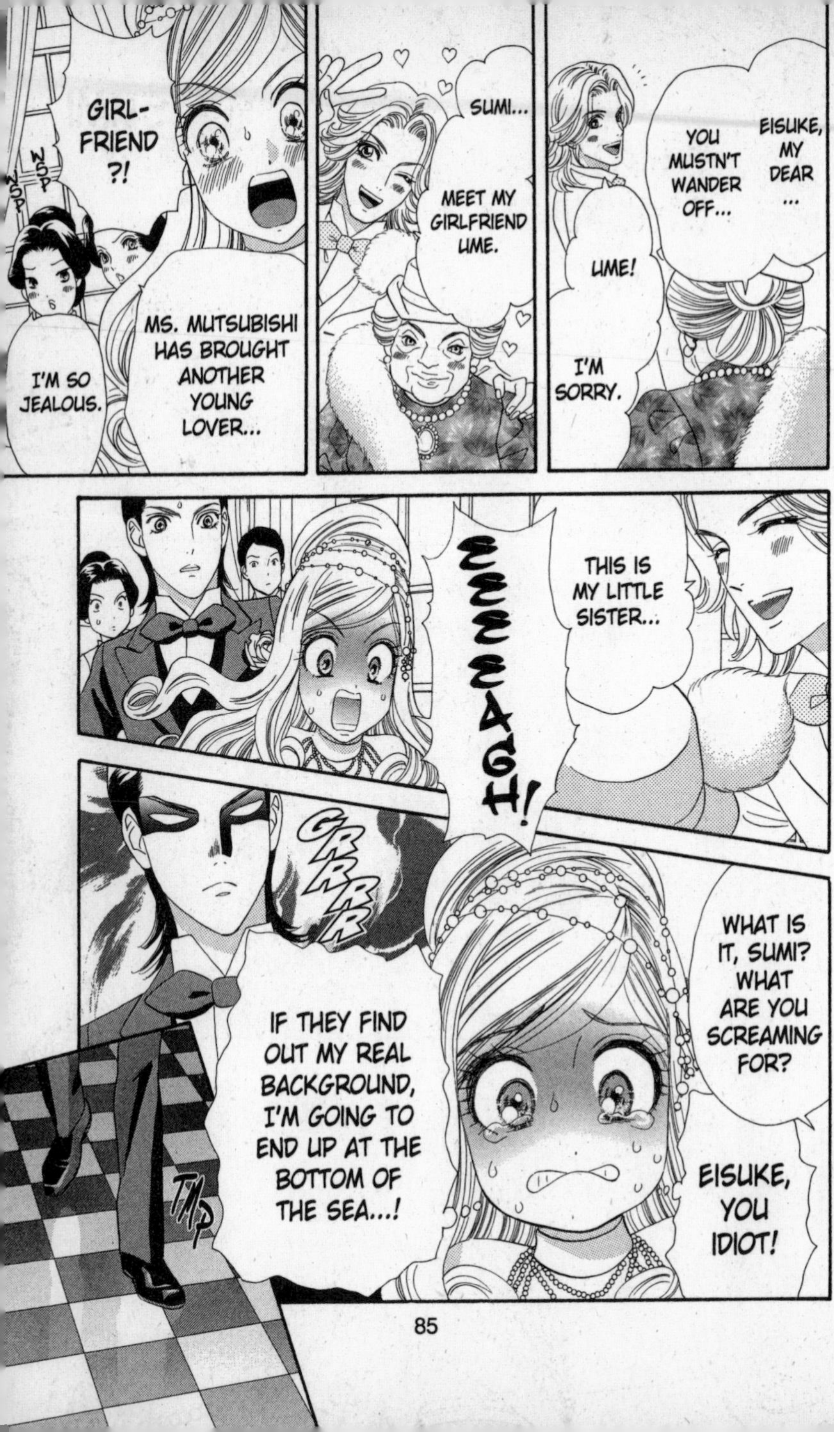
EISUKE, MY DEAR ...
YOU MUSTN'T WANDER OFF...
UME!
I'M SORRY.
SUMI...
MEET MY GIRLFRIEND UME.
GIRL-FRIEND ?!
WSP WSP
MS. MUTSUBISHI HAS BROUGHT ANOTHER YOUNG LOVER...
I'M SO JEALOUS.
THIS IS MY LITTLE SISTER...
EEEEAGH!
WHAT IS IT, SUMI? WHAT ARE YOU SCREAMING FOR?
EISUKE, YOU IDIOT!
GRRRR
IF THEY FIND OUT MY REAL BACKGROUND, I'M GOING TO END UP AT THE BOTTOM OF THE SEA...!
TMP

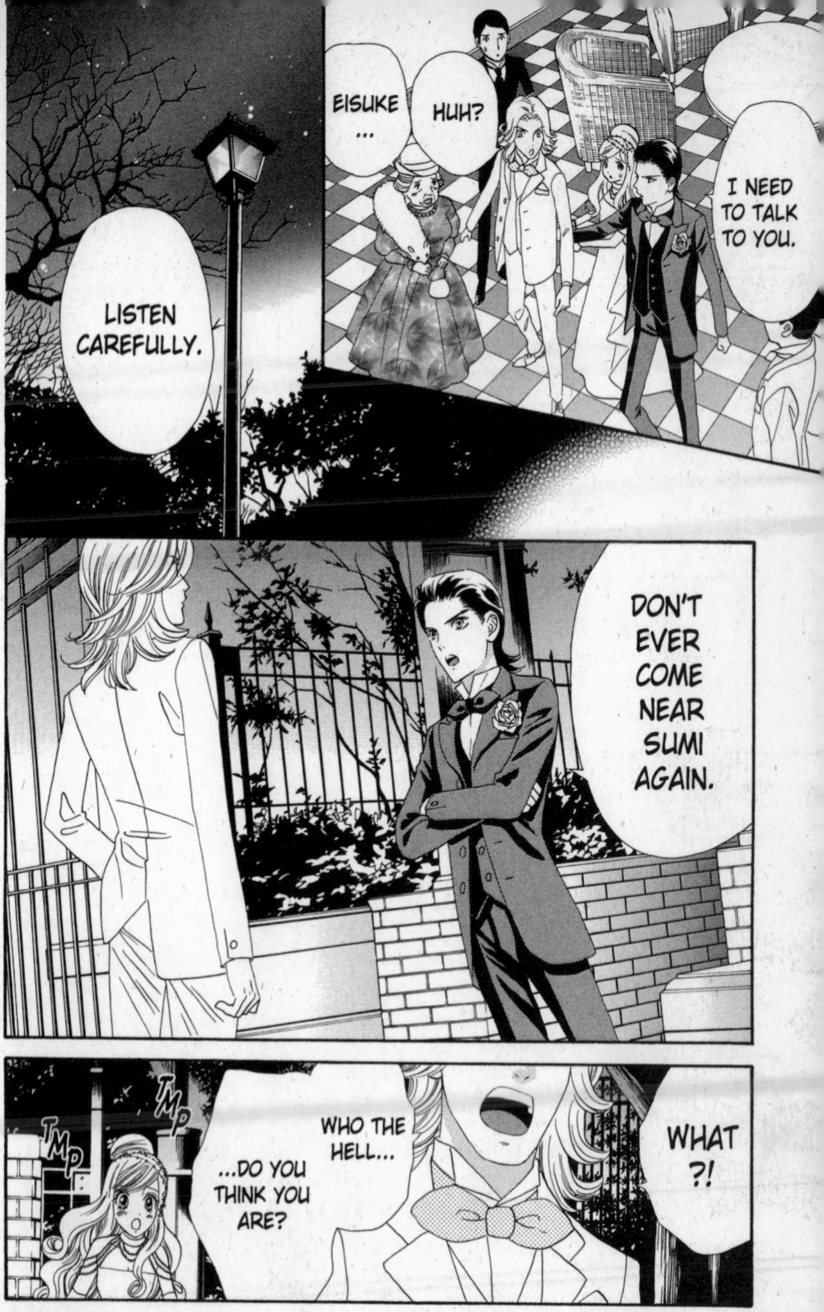
I NEED TO TALK TO YOU.
HUH?
EISUKE ...
LISTEN CAREFULLY.
DON'T EVER COME NEAR SUMI AGAIN.
WHAT?!
WHO THE HELL...
...DO YOU THINK YOU ARE?
TMP
TMP

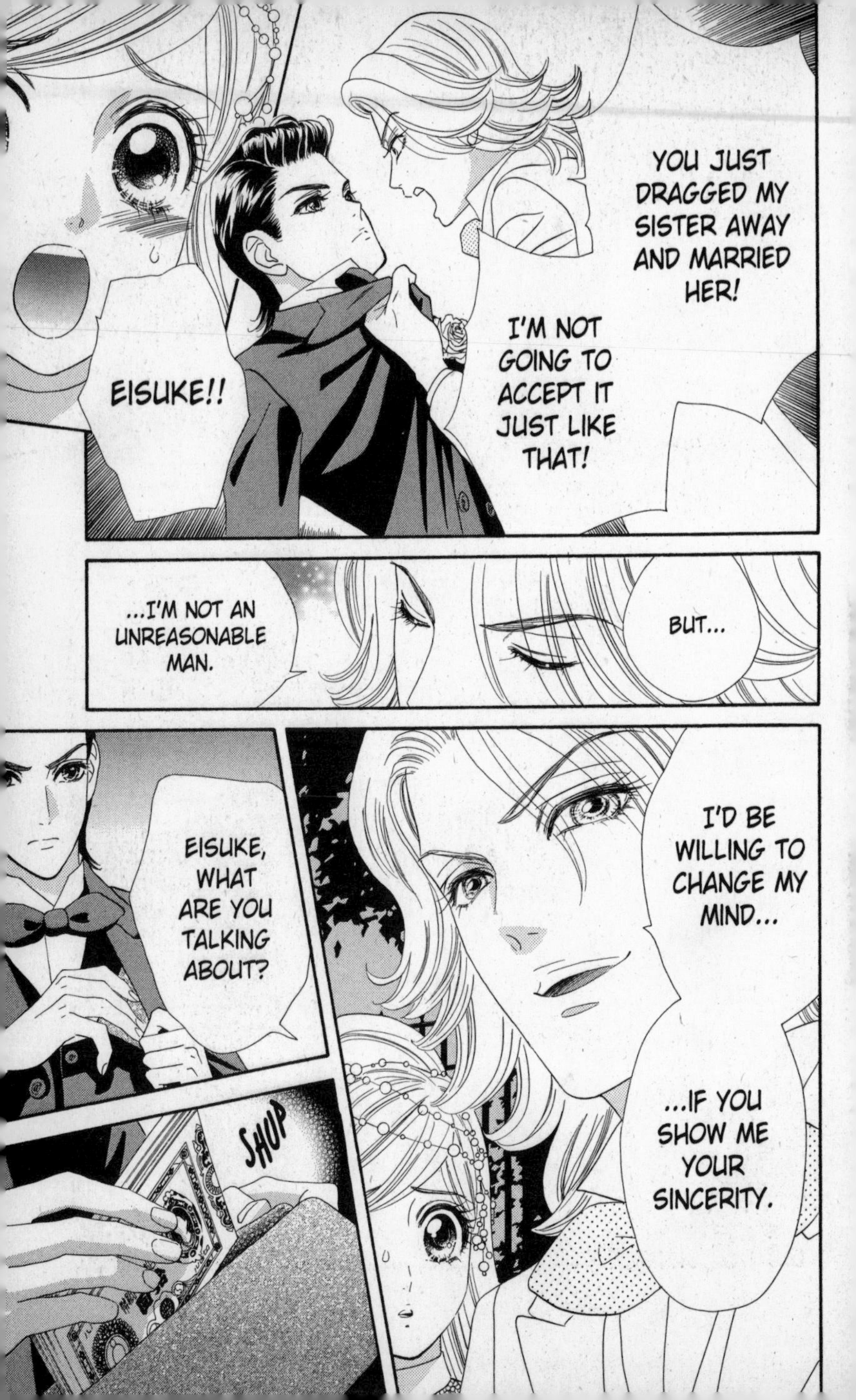
YOU JUST DRAGGED MY SISTER AWAY AND MARRIED HER!
I'M NOT GOING TO ACCEPT IT JUST LIKE THAT!
EISUKE!!
BUT...
...I'M NOT AN UNREASONABLE MAN.
I'D BE WILLING TO CHANGE MY MIND...
...IF YOU SHOW ME YOUR SINCERITY.
EISUKE, WHAT ARE YOU TALKING ABOUT?
SHUP

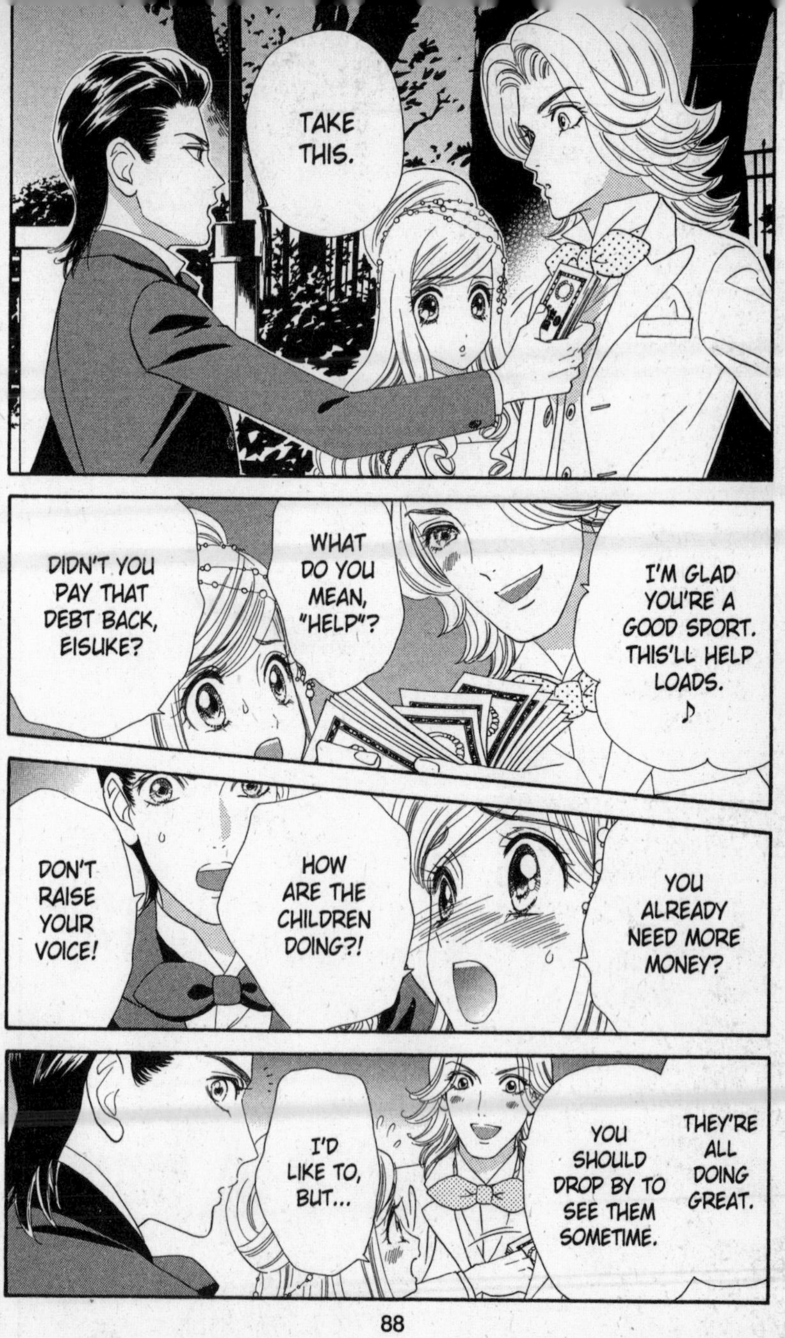
TAKE THIS.
I'M GLAD YOU'RE A GOOD SPORT. THIS'LL HELP LOADS. ♪
WHAT DO YOU MEAN, "HELP"?
DIDN'T YOU PAY THAT DEBT BACK, EISUKE?
YOU ALREADY NEED MORE MONEY?
HOW ARE THE CHILDREN DOING?!
DON'T RAISE YOUR VOICE!
THEY'RE ALL DOING GREAT.
YOU SHOULD DROP BY TO SEE THEM SOMETIME.
I'D LIKE TO, BUT...

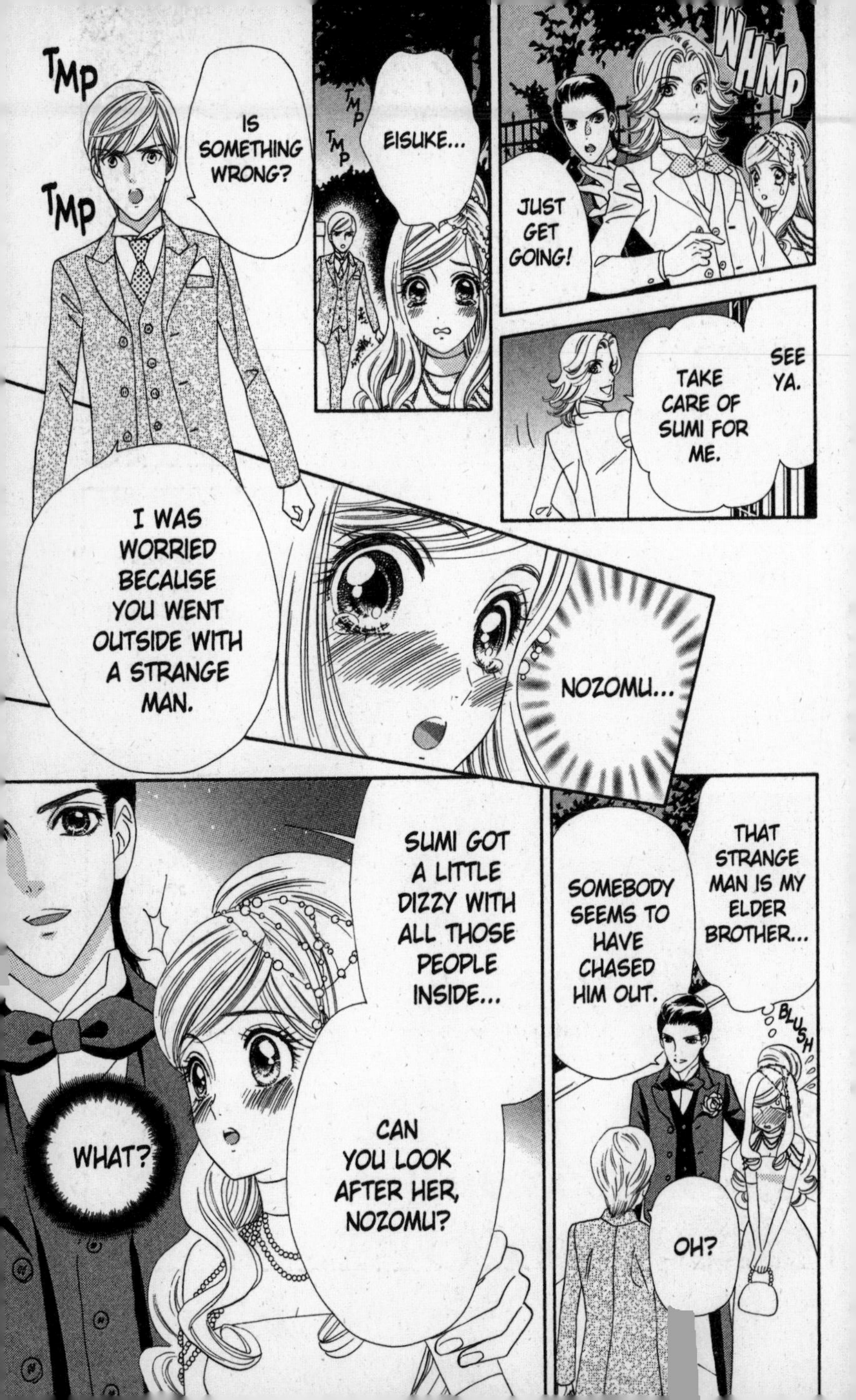
WHMP
JUST GET GOING!
SEE YA.
TAKE CARE OF SUMI FOR ME.
TMP TMP
EISUKE...
TMP
TMP
IS SOMETHING WRONG?
I WAS WORRIED BECAUSE YOU WENT OUTSIDE WITH A STRANGE MAN.
NOZOMU...
THAT STRANGE MAN IS MY ELDER BROTHER...
SOMEBODY SEEMS TO HAVE CHASED HIM OUT.
BLUSH
OH?
SUMI GOT A LITTLE DIZZY WITH ALL THOSE PEOPLE INSIDE...
CAN YOU LOOK AFTER HER, NOZOMU?
WHAT?

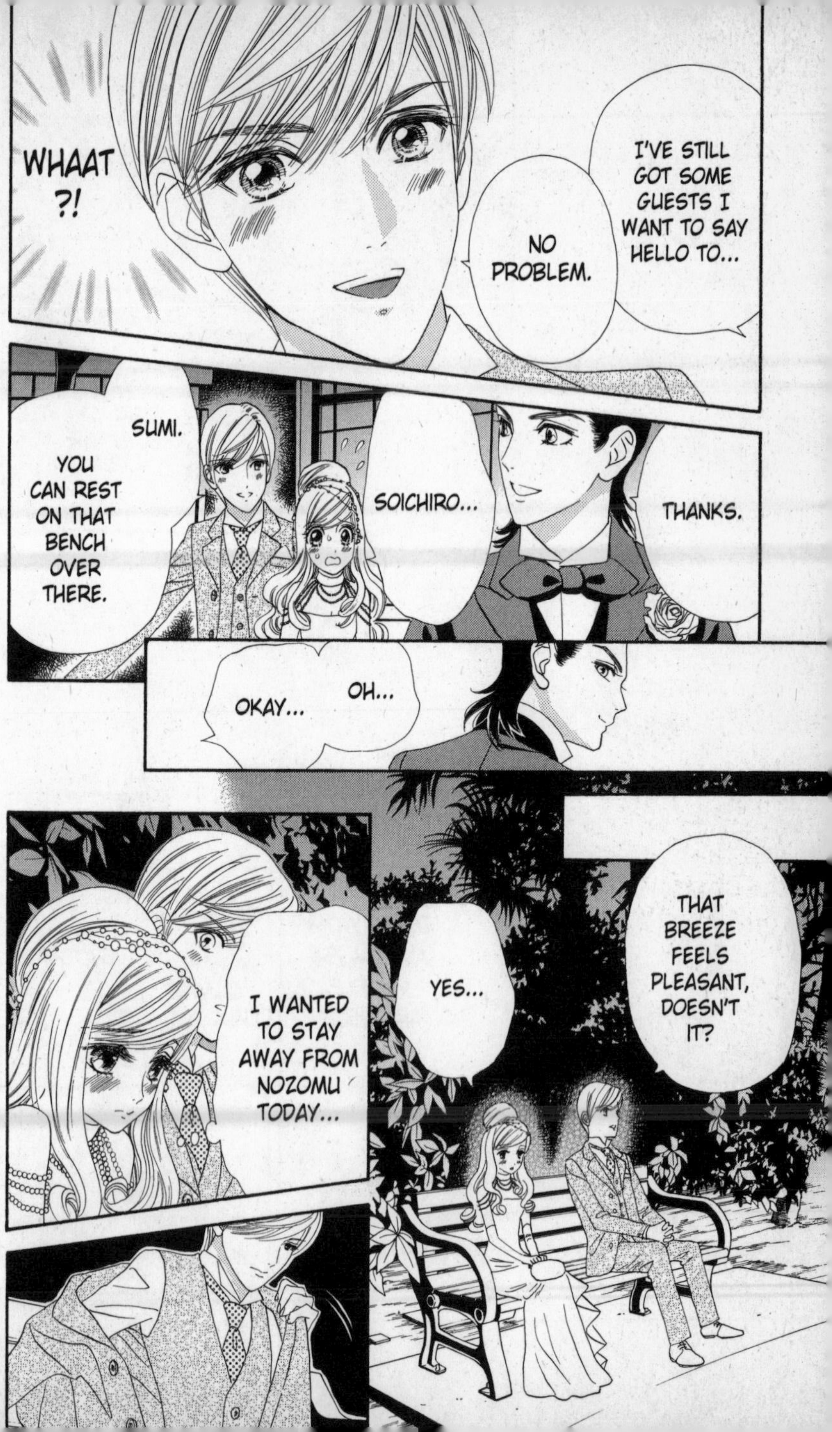
I'VE STILL GOT SOME GUESTS I WANT TO SAY HELLO TO...
NO PROBLEM.
WHAAT ?!
THANKS.
SOICHIRO...
SUMI.
YOU CAN REST ON THAT BENCH OVER THERE.
OH...
OKAY...
THAT BREEZE FEELS PLEASANT, DOESN'T IT?
YES...
I WANTED TO STAY AWAY FROM NOZOMU TODAY...

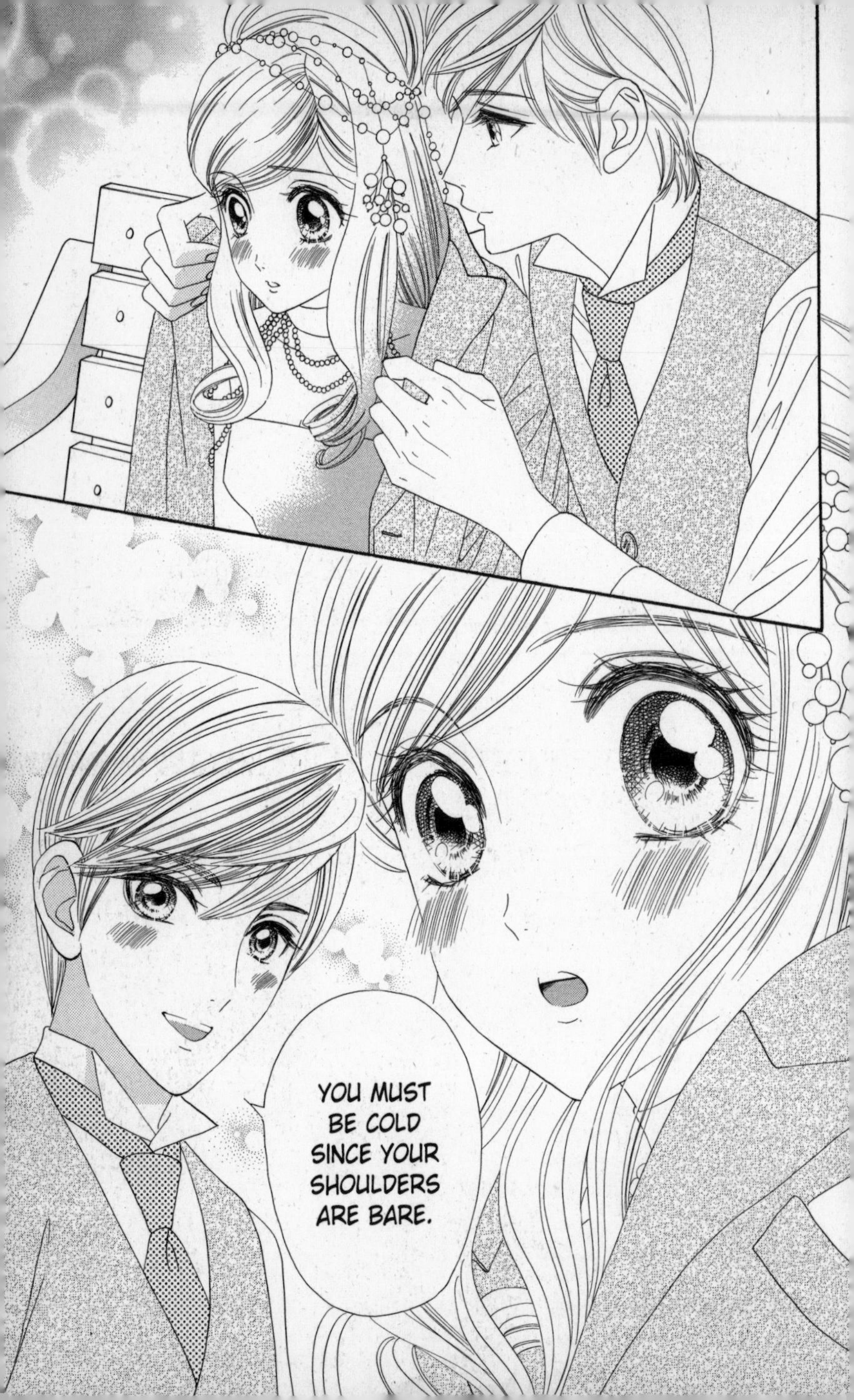
YOU MUST BE COLD SINCE YOUR SHOULDERS ARE BARE.

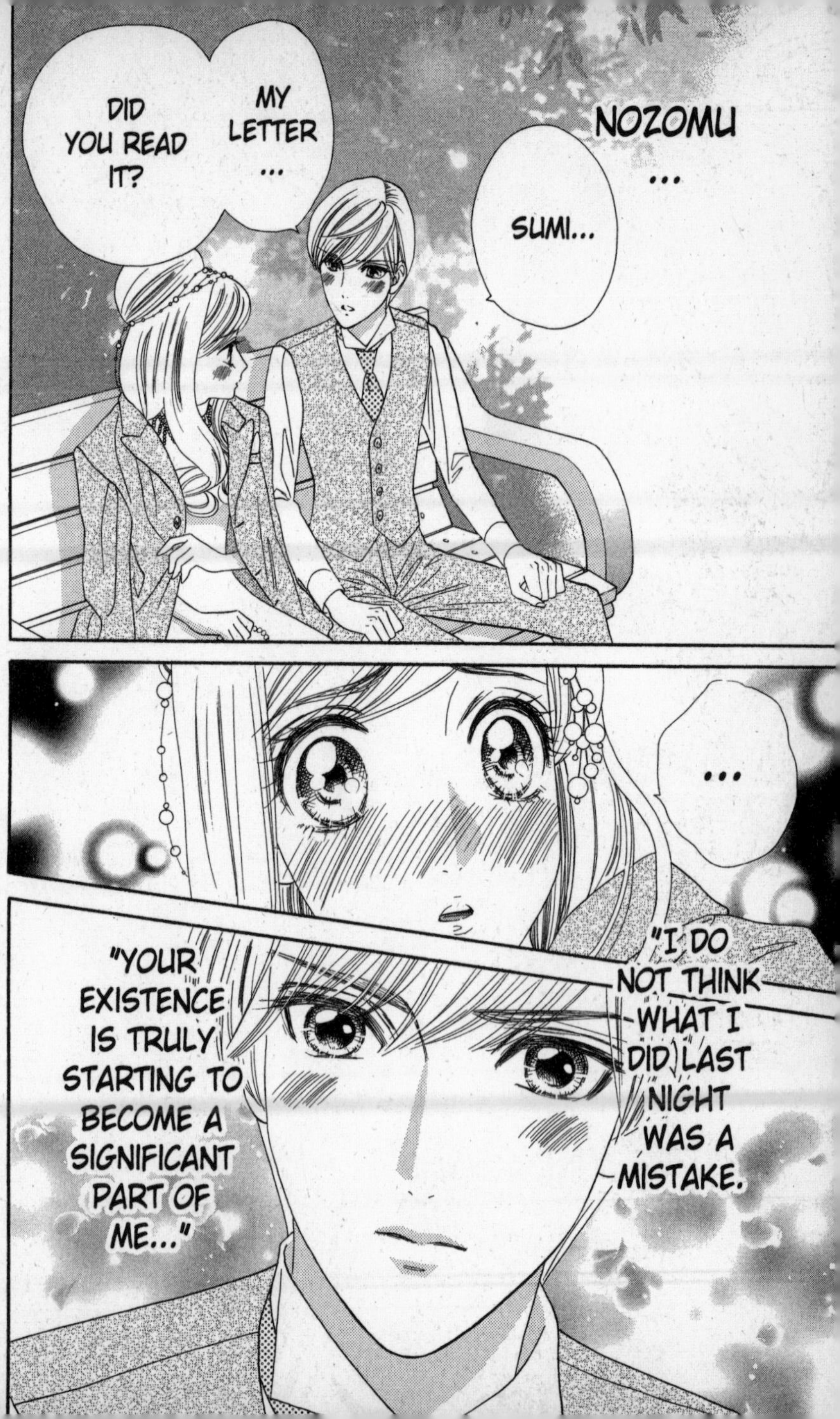

NOZOMU ...
SUMI...
MY LETTER ...
DID YOU READ IT?
...
"I DO NOT THINK WHAT I DID LAST NIGHT WAS A MISTAKE.
"YOUR EXISTENCE IS TRULY STARTING TO BECOME A SIGNIFICANT PART OF ME..."

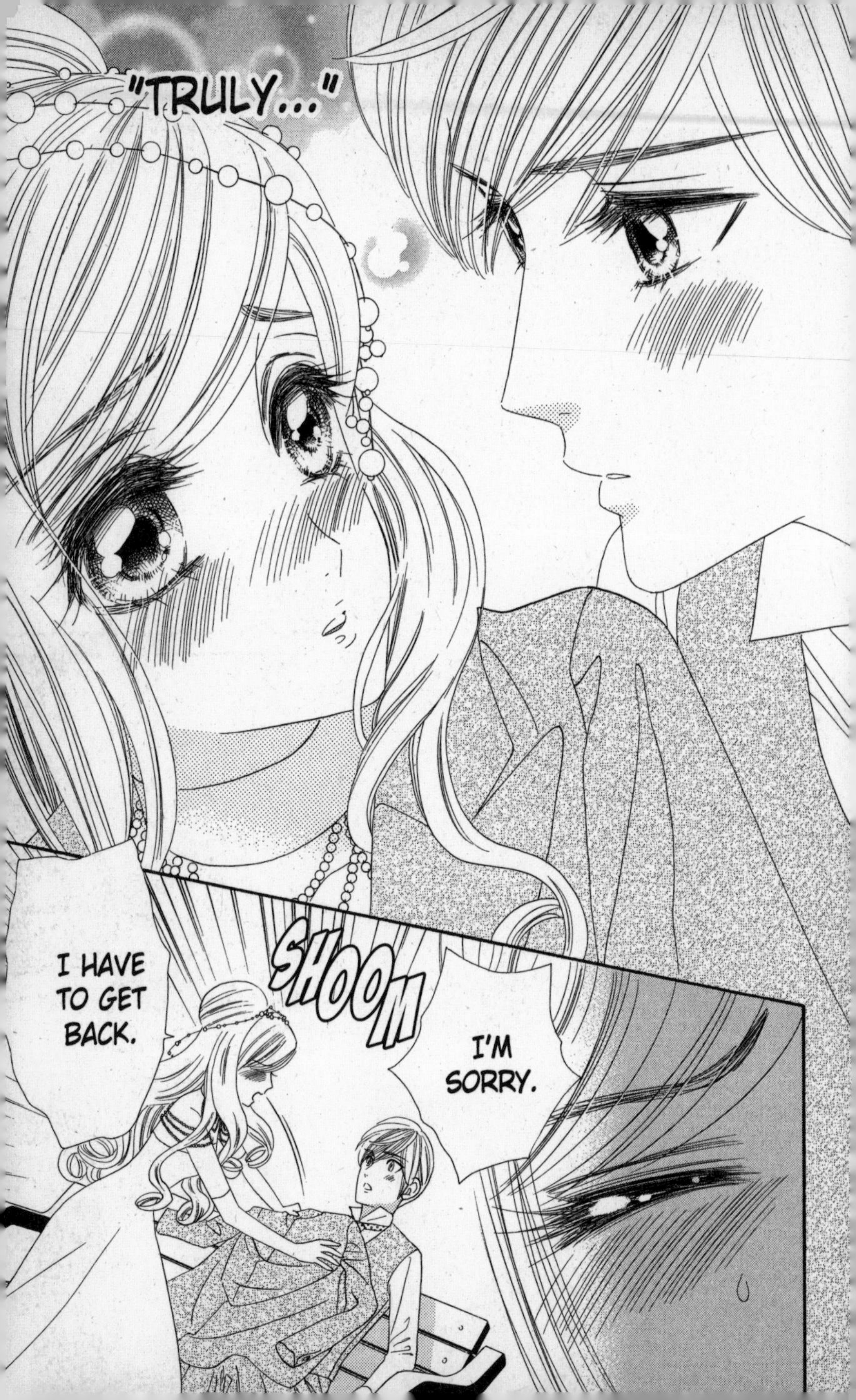
"TRULY..."
I'M SORRY.
SHOOM
I HAVE TO GET BACK.

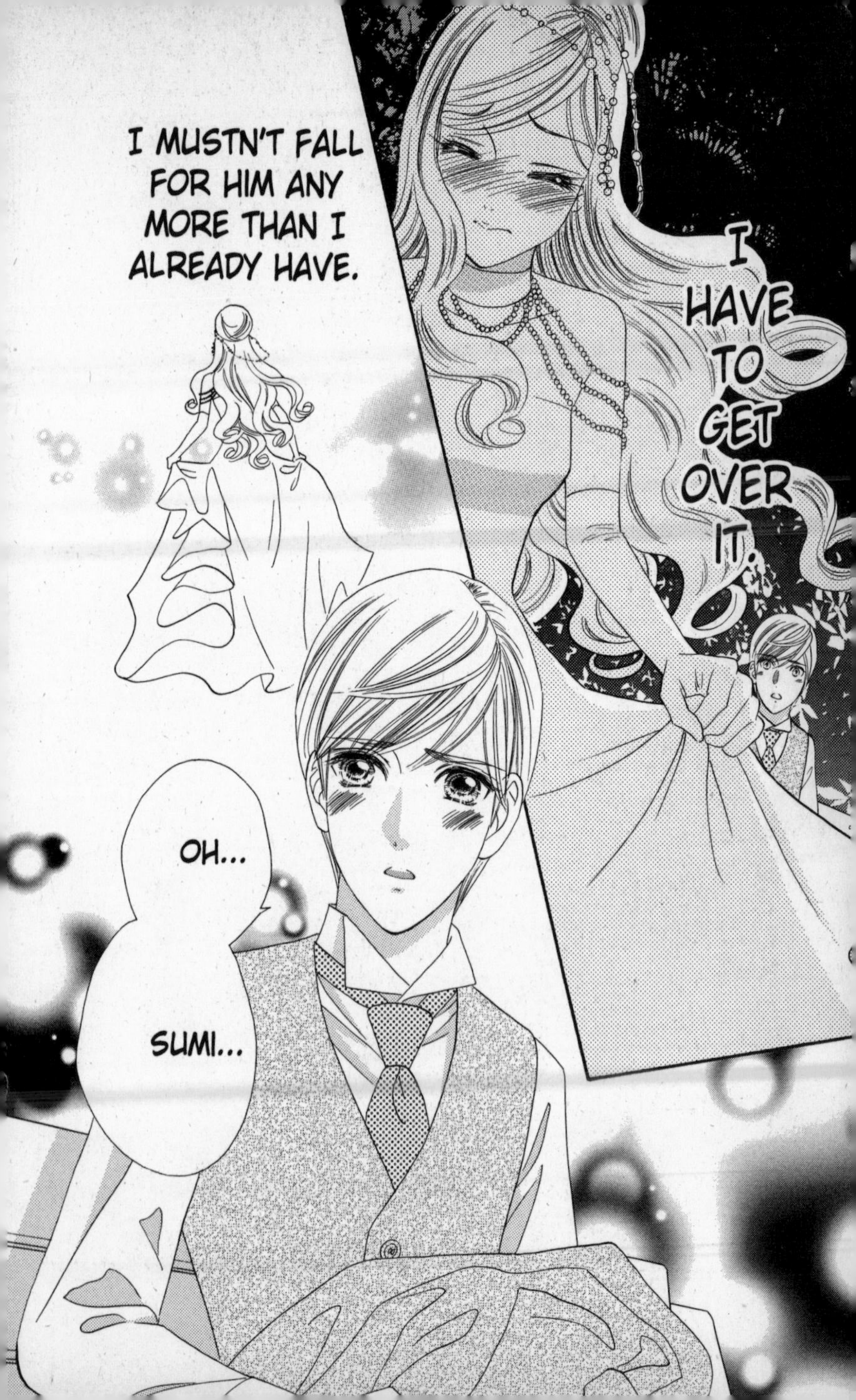
I HAVE TO GET OVER IT.
I MUSTN'T FALL FOR HIM ANY MORE THAN I ALREADY HAVE.
OH...
SUMI...

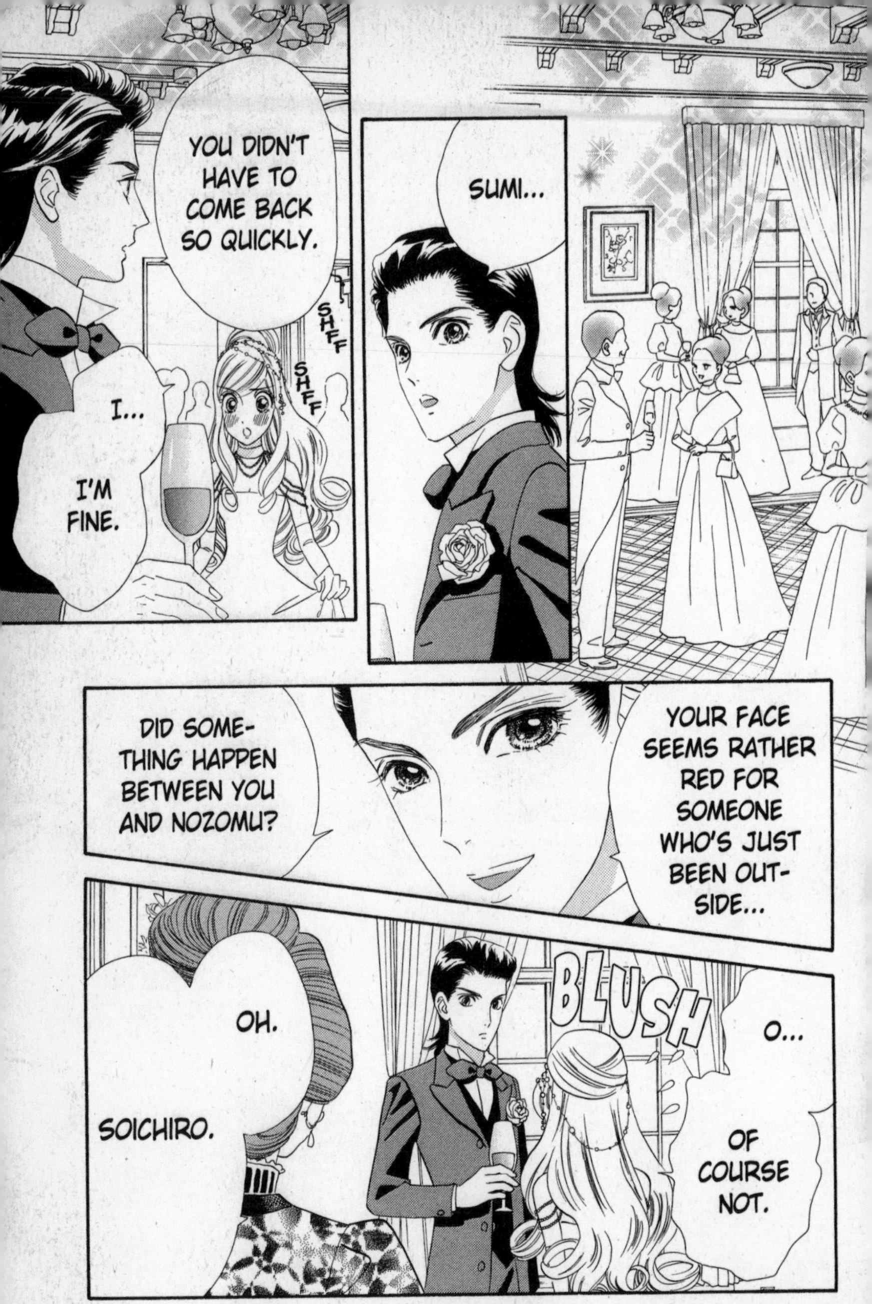
SUMI...
YOU DIDN'T HAVE TO COME BACK SO QUICKLY.
SHFF
SHFF
I...
I'M FINE.
YOUR FACE SEEMS RATHER RED FOR SOMEONE WHO'S JUST BEEN OUT-SIDE...
DID SOME-THING HAPPEN BETWEEN YOU AND NOZOMU?
BLUSH
O...
OF COURSE NOT.
OH.
SOICHIRO.

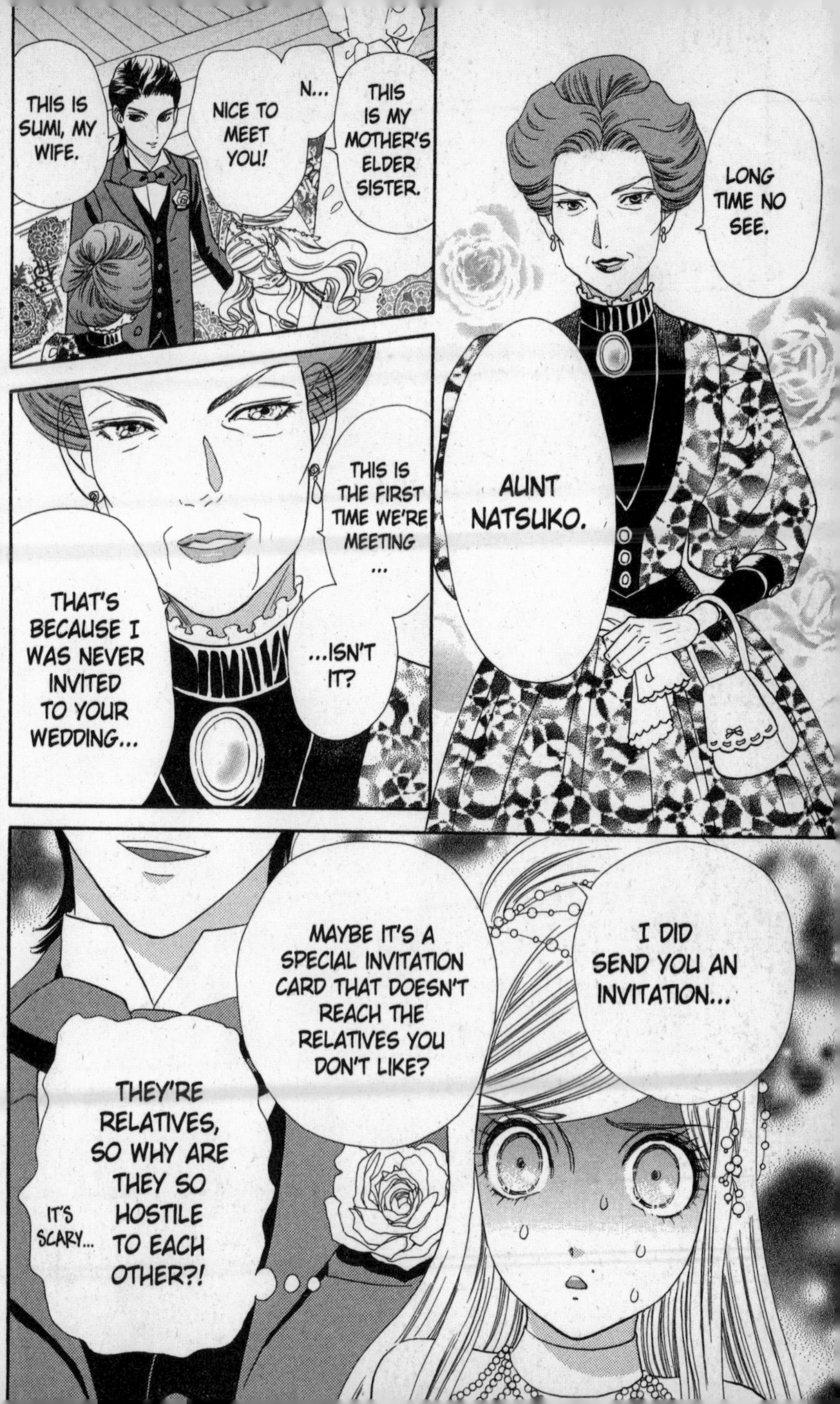
LONG TIME NO SEE.
AUNT NATSUKO.
THIS IS MY MOTHER'S ELDER SISTER.
N...
NICE TO MEET YOU!
THIS IS SUMI, MY WIFE.
THIS IS THE FIRST TIME WE'RE MEETING ...
...ISN'T IT?
THAT'S BECAUSE I WAS NEVER INVITED TO YOUR WEDDING...
I DID SEND YOU AN INVITATION...
MAYBE IT'S A SPECIAL INVITATION CARD THAT DOESN'T REACH THE RELATIVES YOU DON'T LIKE?
THEY'RE RELATIVES, SO WHY ARE THEY SO HOSTILE TO EACH OTHER?!
IT'S SCARY...

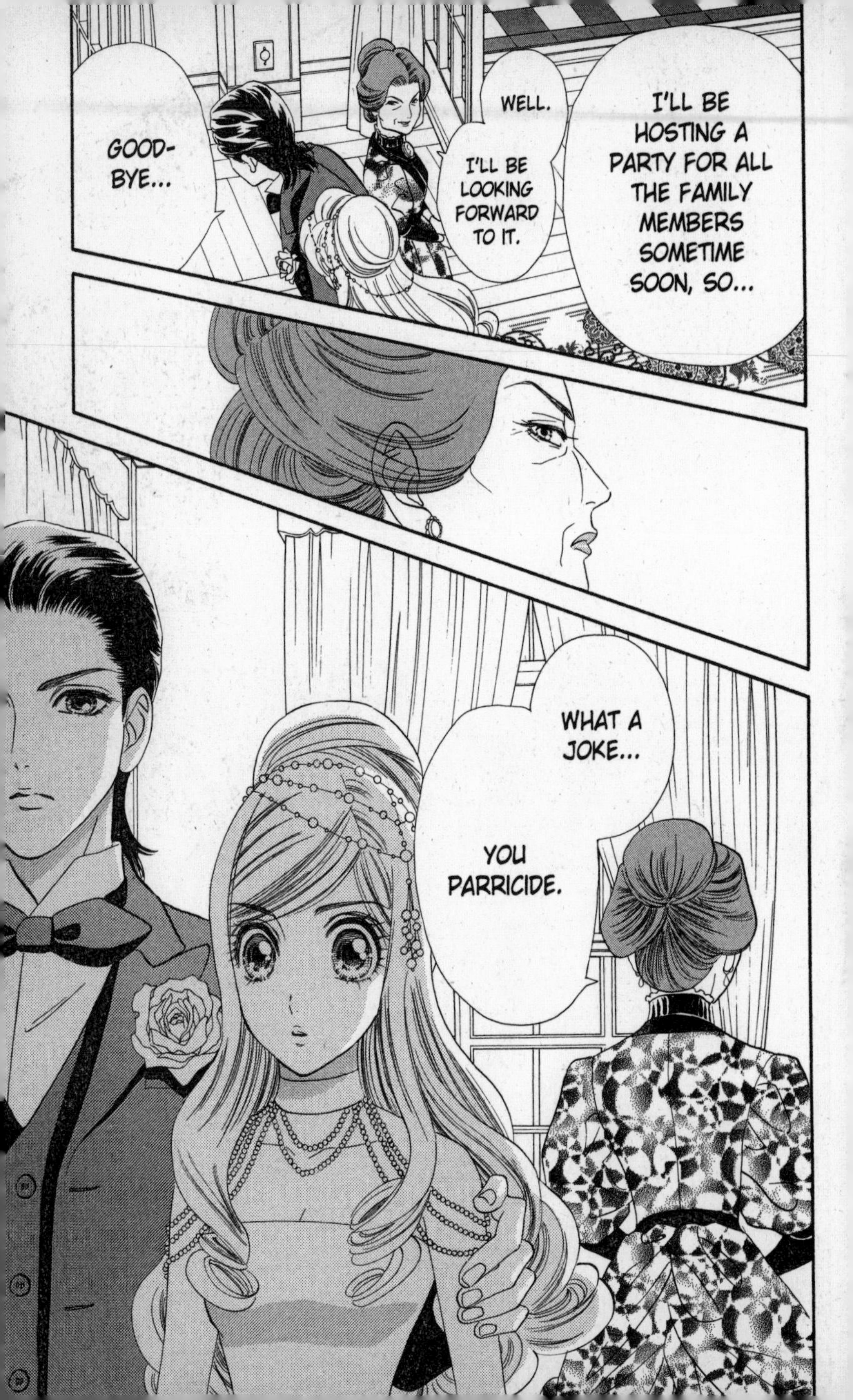
I'LL BE HOSTING A PARTY FOR ALL THE FAMILY MEMBERS SOMETIME SOON, SO...
WELL.
I'LL BE LOOKING FORWARD TO IT.
GOOD-BYE...
WHAT A JOKE...
YOU PARRICIDE.

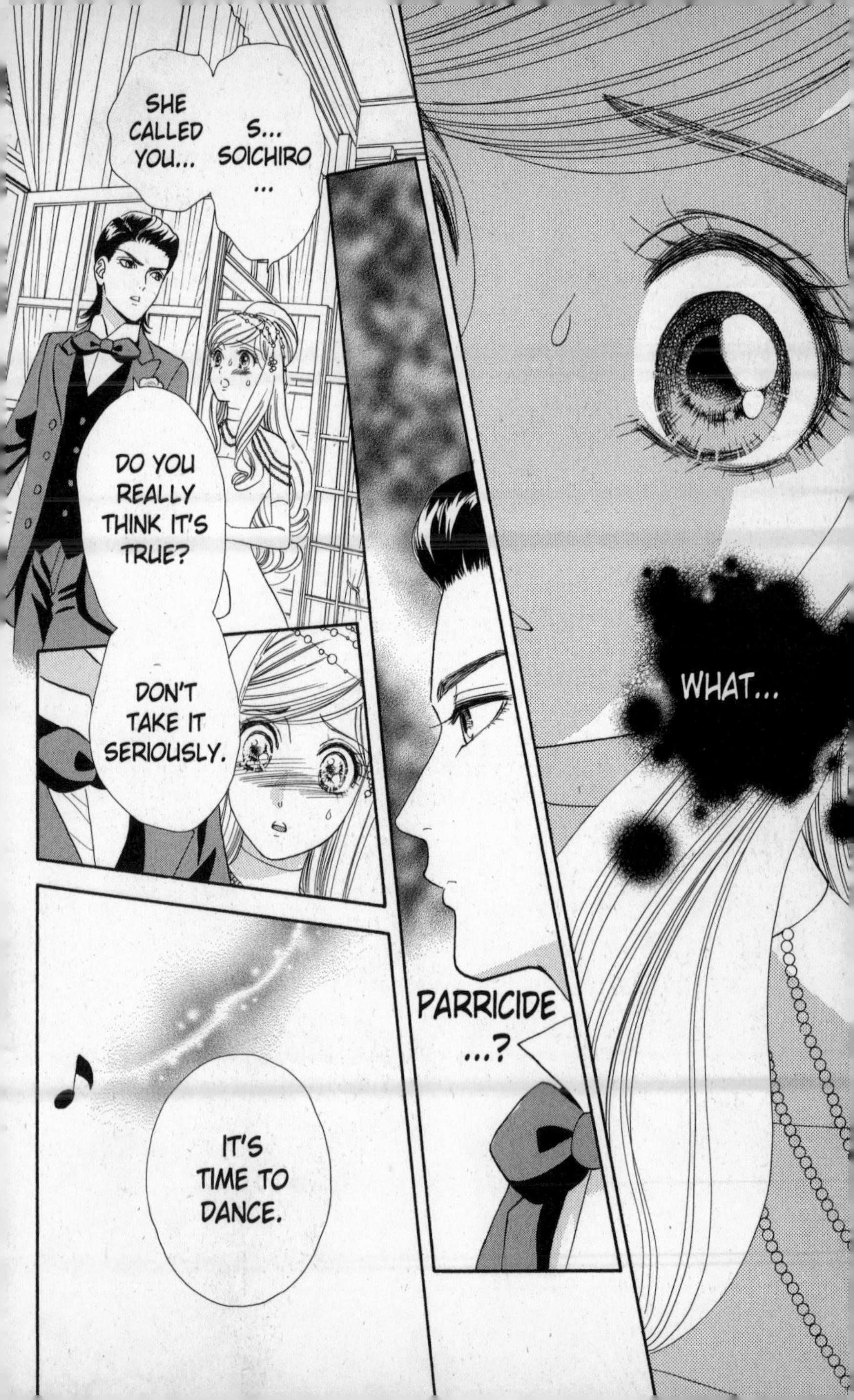
WHAT...
PARRICIDE ...?
SHE CALLED YOU... S... SOICHIRO ...
DO YOU REALLY THINK IT'S TRUE?
DON'T TAKE IT SERIOUSLY.
IT'S TIME TO DANCE.

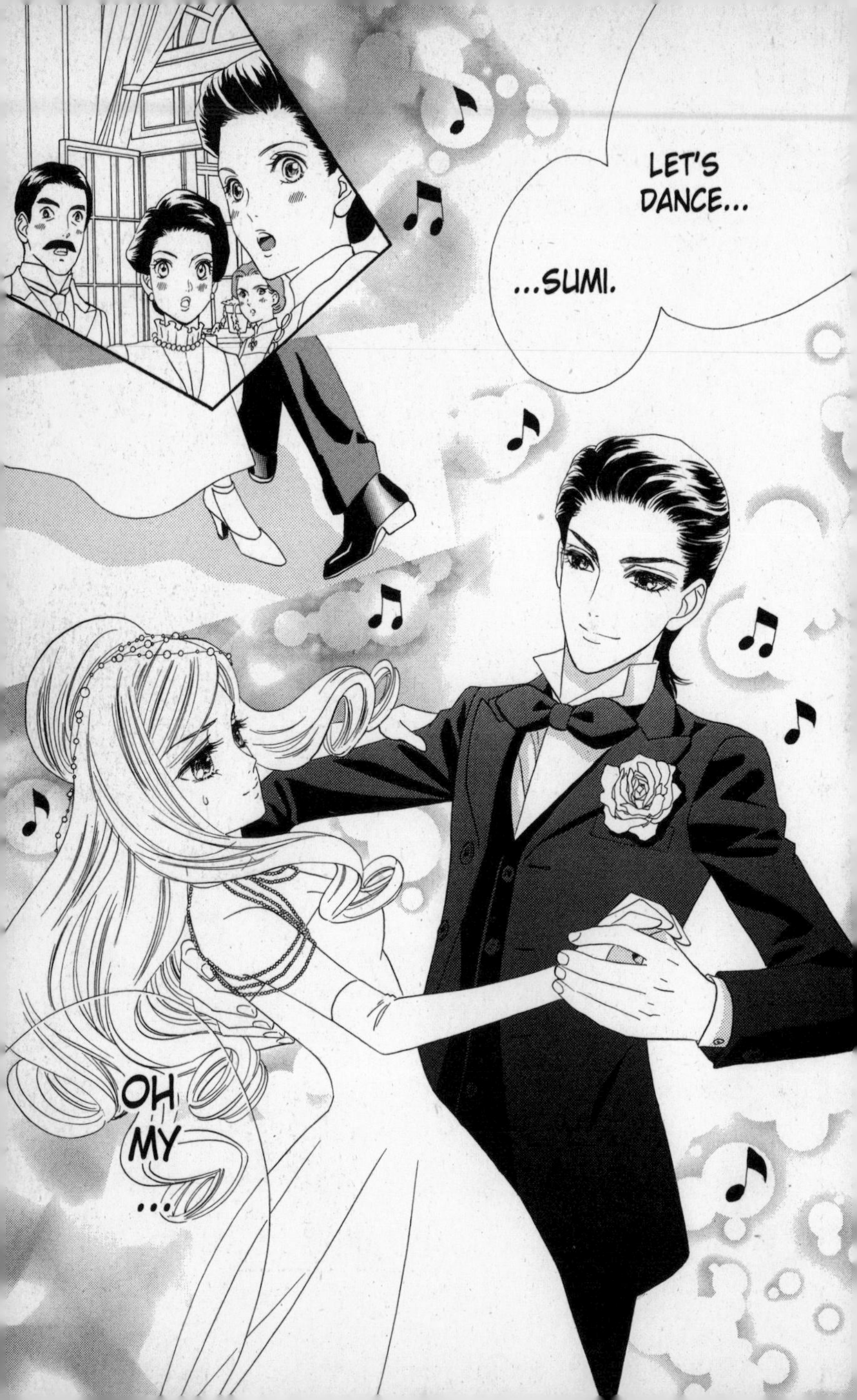
LET'S DANCE...
...SUMI.
OH MY ...

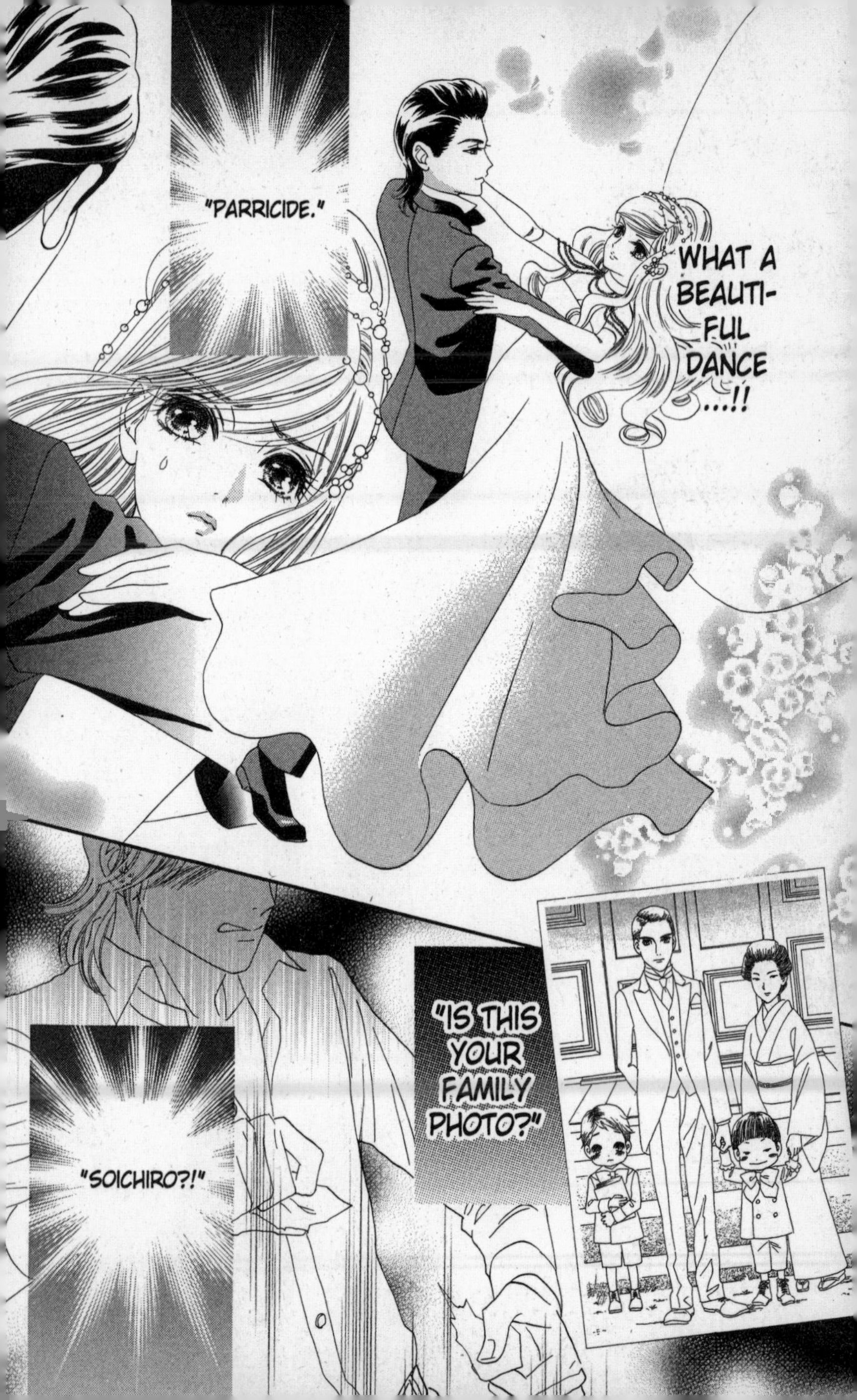
WHAT A BEAUTI-FUL DANCE ...!!
"PARRICIDE."
"IS THIS YOUR FAMILY PHOTO?"
"SOICHIRO?!"

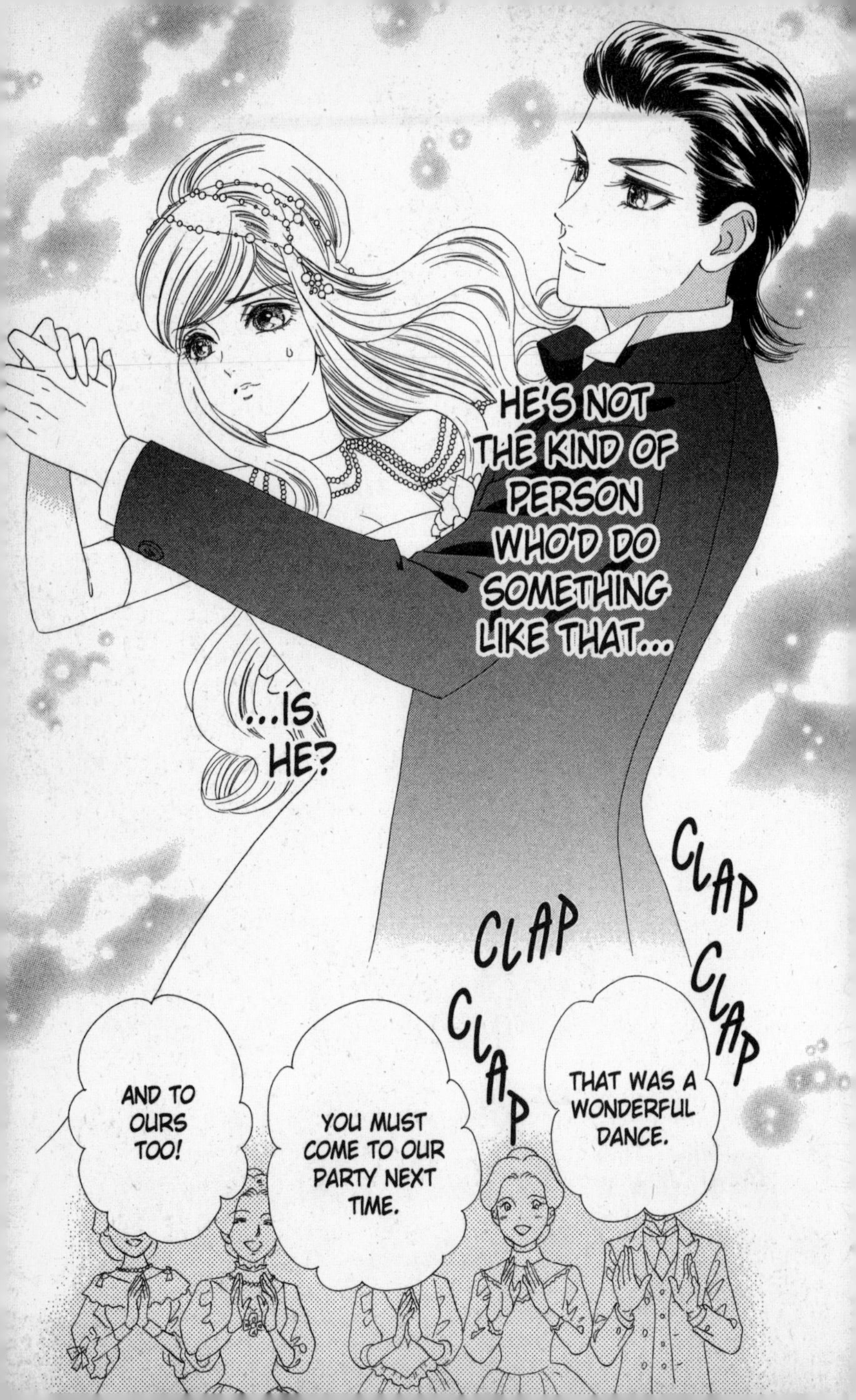
HE'S NOT THE KIND OF PERSON WHO'D DO SOMETHING LIKE THAT...
...IS HE?
CLAP
CLAP
CLAP
CLAP
THAT WAS A WONDERFUL DANCE.
YOU MUST COME TO OUR PARTY NEXT TIME.
AND TO OURS TOO!

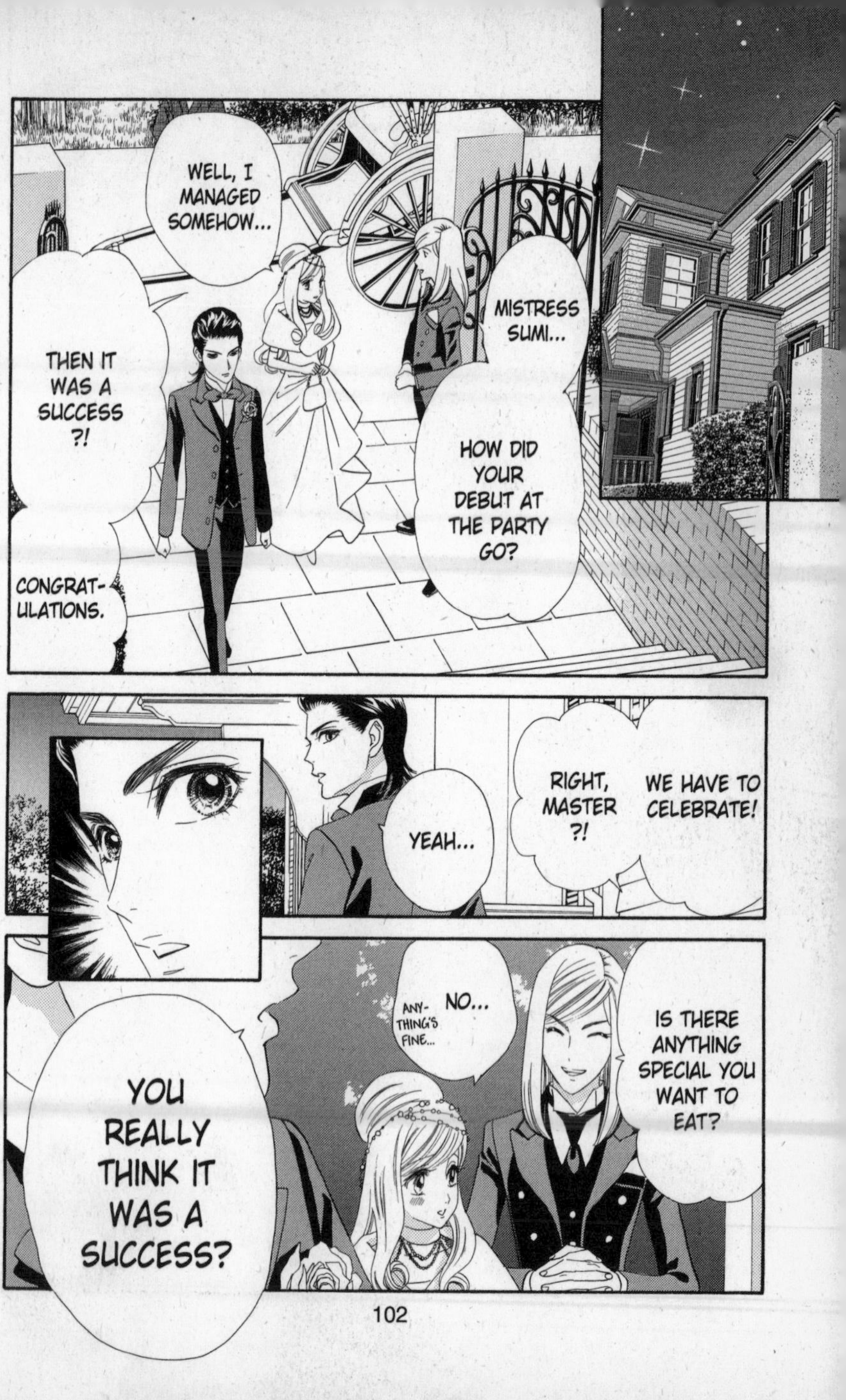
MISTRESS SUMI...
HOW DID YOUR DEBUT AT THE PARTY GO?
WELL, I MANAGED SOMEHOW...
THEN IT WAS A SUCCESS ?!
CONGRAT-ULATIONS.
WE HAVE TO CELEBRATE!
RIGHT, MASTER ?!
YEAH...
IS THERE ANYTHING SPECIAL YOU WANT TO EAT?
NO...
ANY-THING'S FINE...
YOU REALLY THINK IT WAS A SUCCESS?

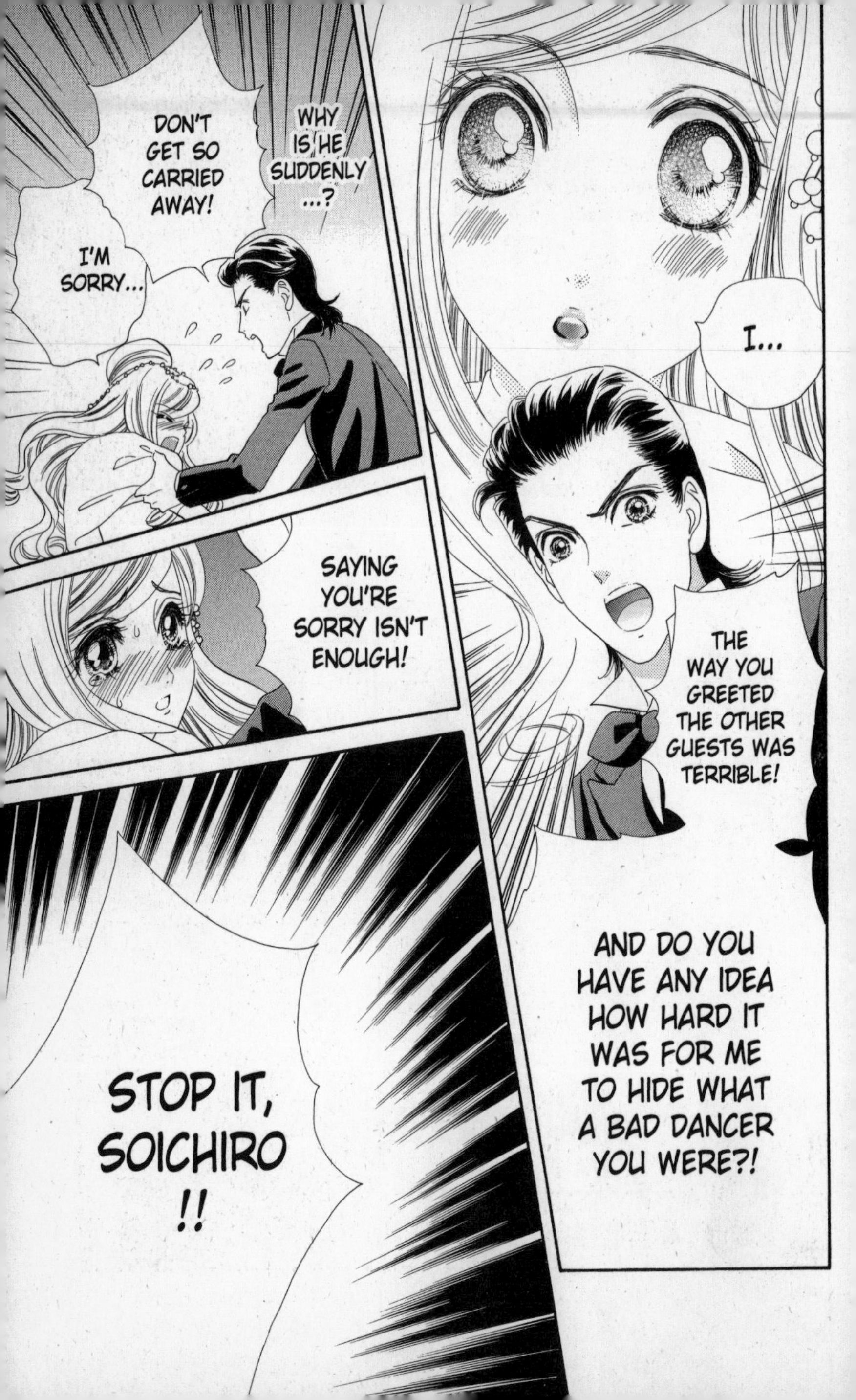
I...
THE WAY YOU GREETED THE OTHER GUESTS WAS TERRIBLE!
AND DO YOU HAVE ANY IDEA HOW HARD IT WAS FOR ME TO HIDE WHAT A BAD DANCER YOU WERE?!
WHY IS HE SUDDENLY ...?
DON'T GET SO CARRIED AWAY!
I'M SORRY...
SAYING YOU'RE SORRY ISN'T ENOUGH!
STOP IT, SOICHIRO !!

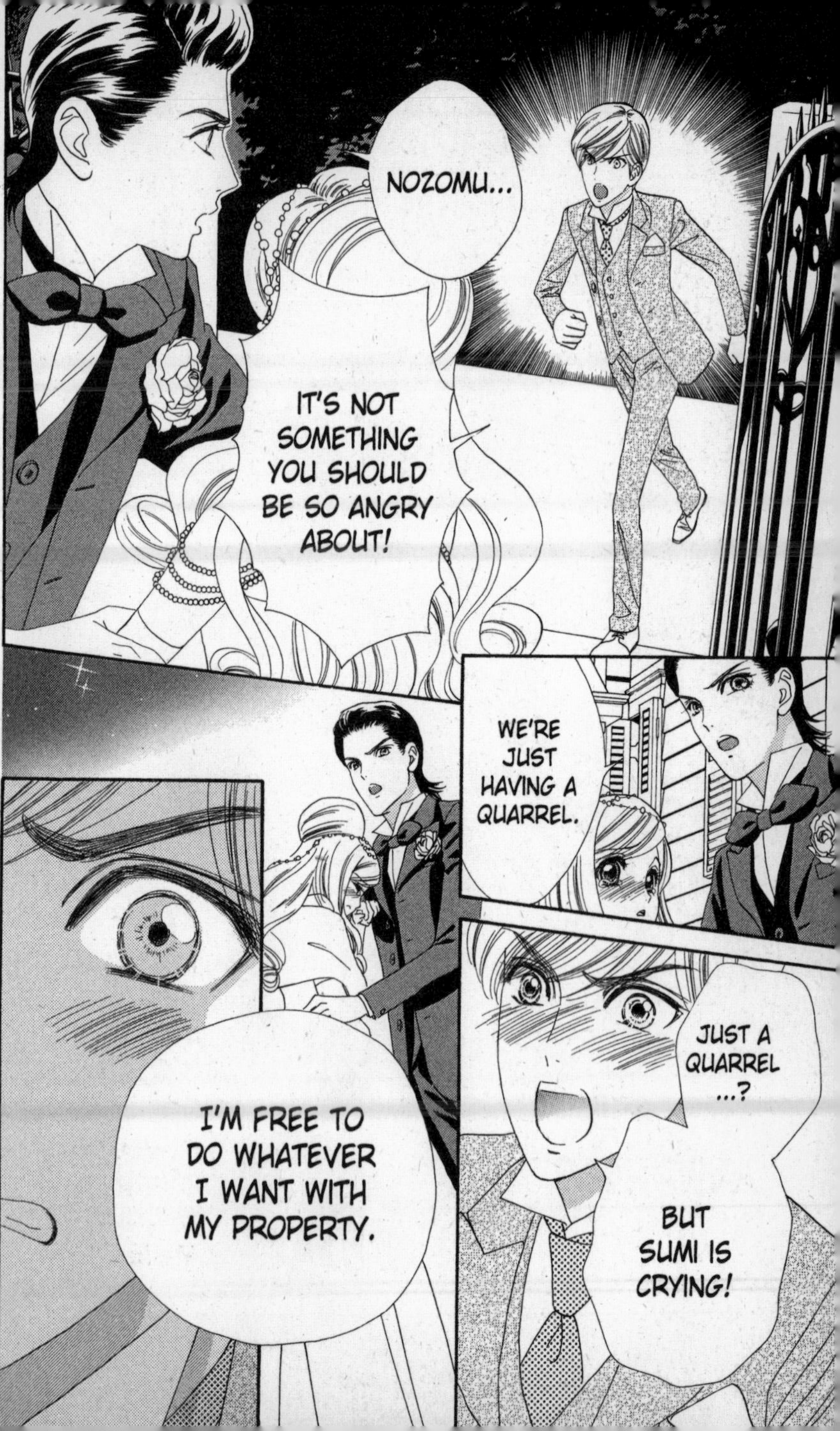
NOZOMU...
IT'S NOT SOMETHING YOU SHOULD BE SO ANGRY ABOUT!
WE'RE JUST HAVING A QUARREL.
JUST A QUARREL ...?
BUT SUMI IS CRYING!
I'M FREE TO DO WHATEVER I WANT WITH MY PROPERTY.

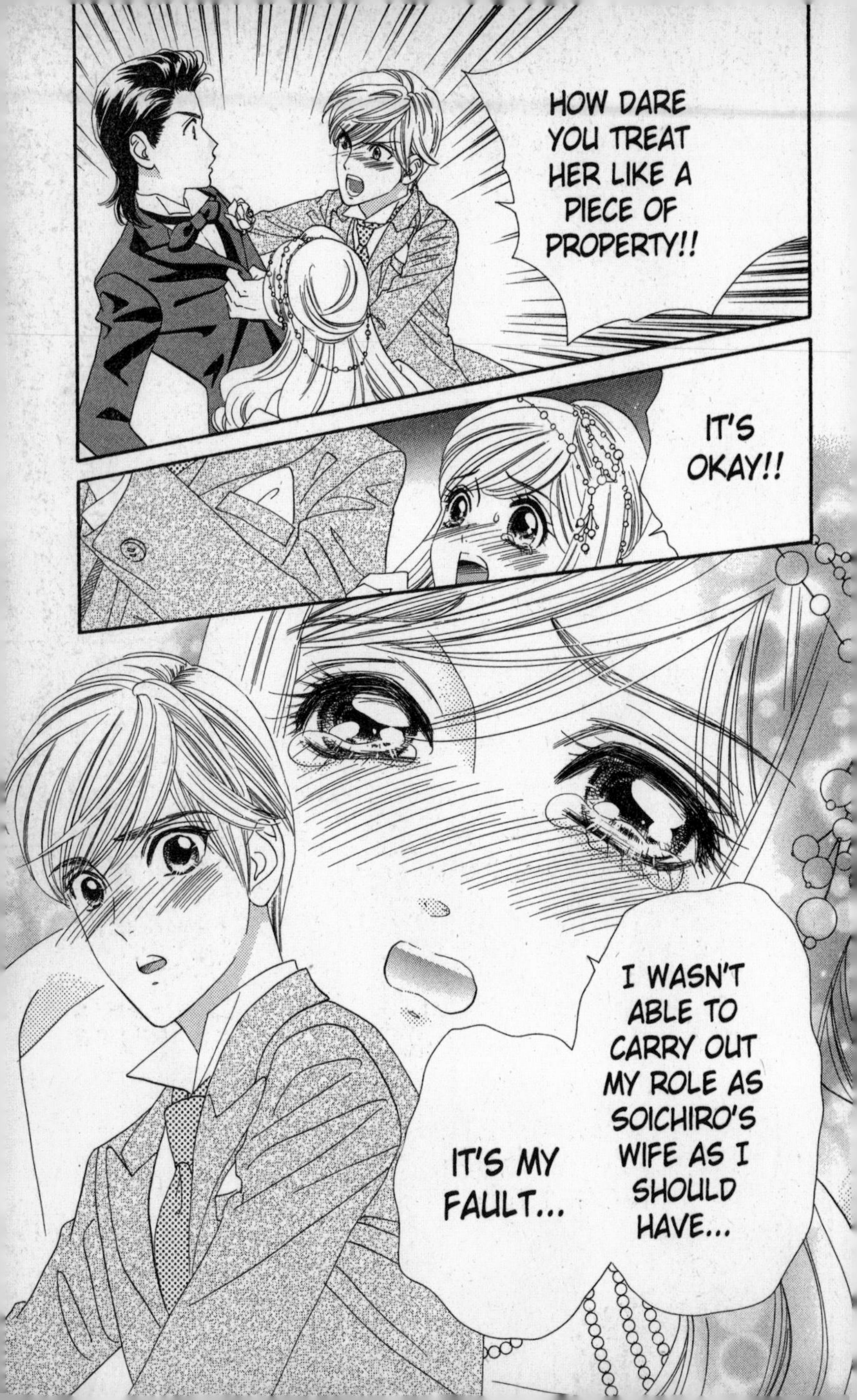
HOW DARE YOU TREAT HER LIKE A PIECE OF PROPERTY!!
IT'S OKAY!!
I WASN'T ABLE TO CARRY OUT MY ROLE AS SOICHIRO'S WIFE AS I SHOULD HAVE...
IT'S MY FAULT...

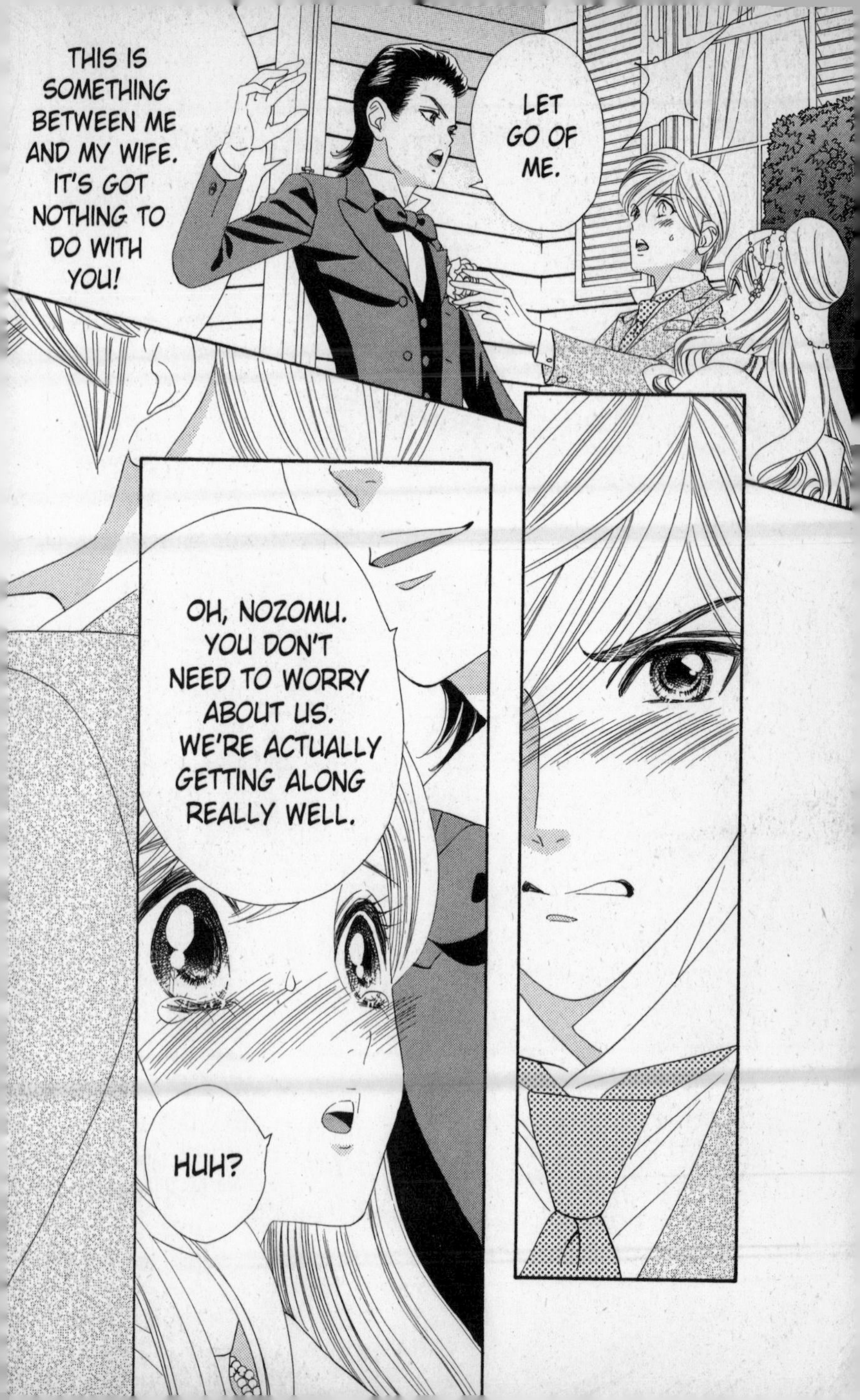
LET GO OF ME.
THIS IS SOMETHING BETWEEN ME AND MY WIFE. IT'S GOT NOTHING TO DO WITH YOU!
OH, NOZOMU. YOU DON'T NEED TO WORRY ABOUT US. WE'RE ACTUALLY GETTING ALONG REALLY WELL.
HUH?

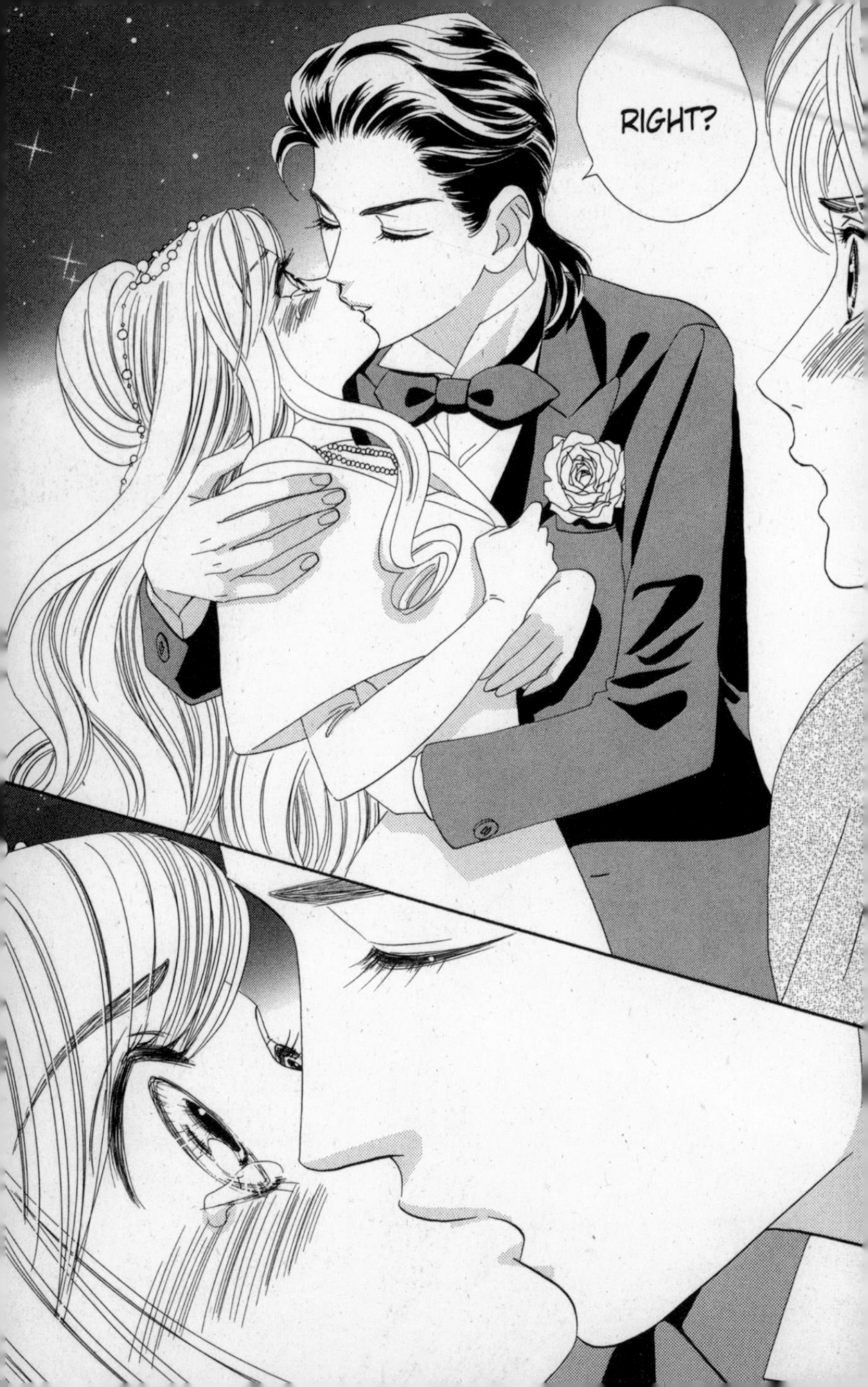
RIGHT?

STEP STAGE ☆ ④

HERE ARE ILLUSTRATIONS OF KOMAI THAT I DREW
DURING THE PREPARATION PART OF THIS SERIES.

No.

Date . .

BUTLER

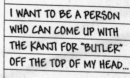

I WANT TO BE A PERSON
WHO CAN COME UP WITH
THE KANJI FOR "BUTLER"
OFF THE TOP OF MY HEAD...

RECENTLY, KOMAI'S
BEEN TURNING INTO A
COMEDIC CHARACTER...

I WANTED TO DRAW HIM AS
A COOL BUTLER THOUGH...

SORRY...

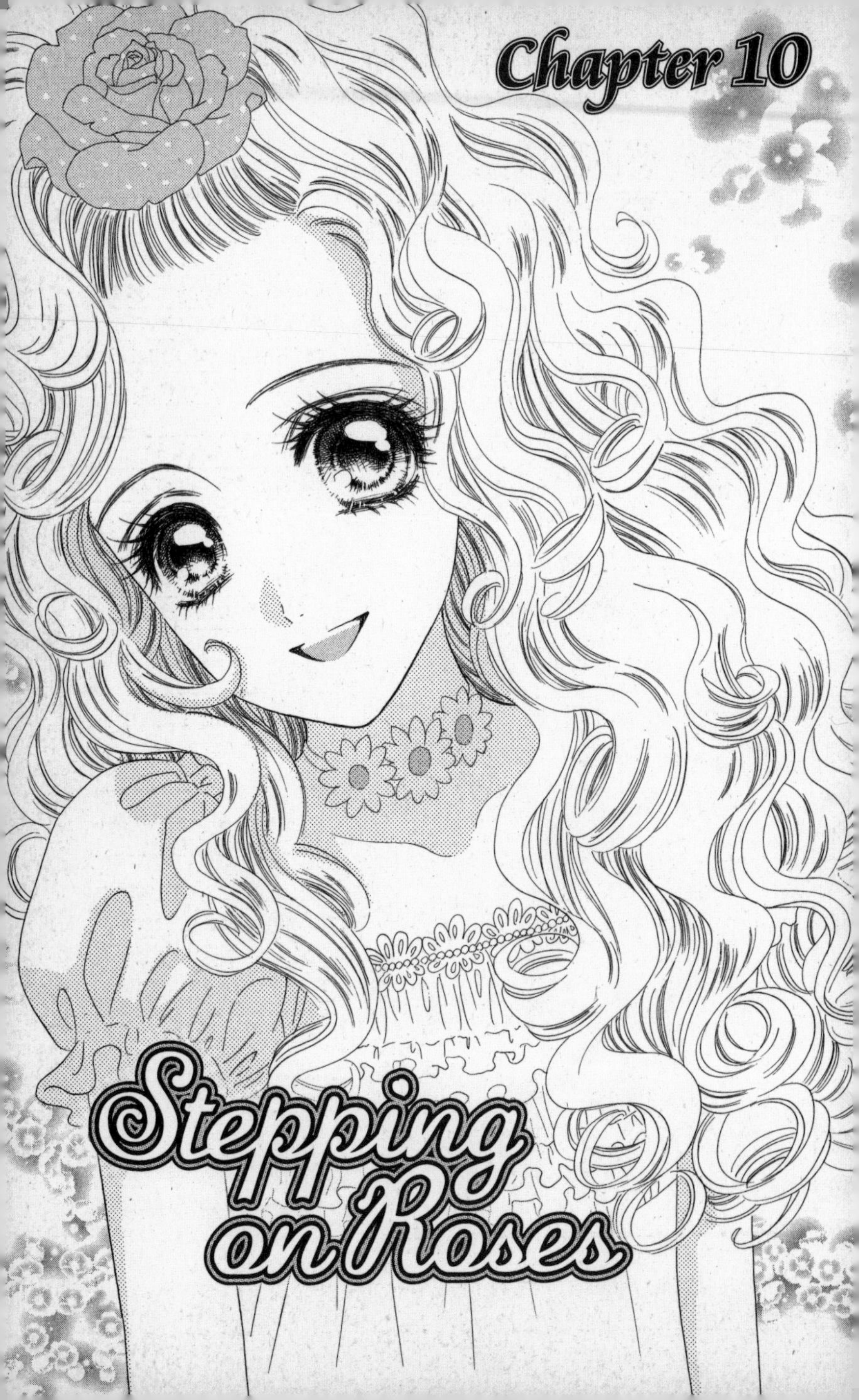
Chapter 10
Stepping on Roses

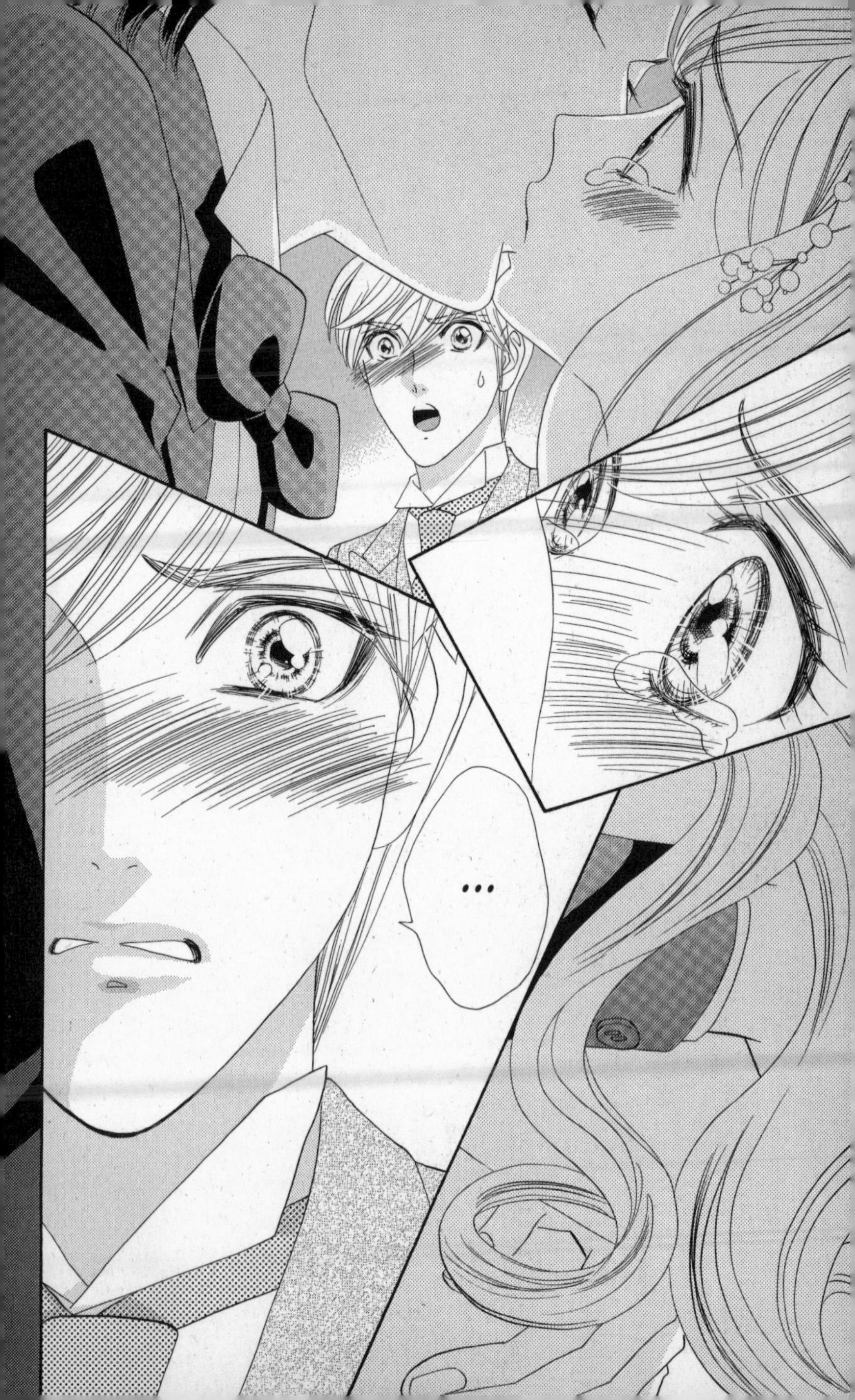
...

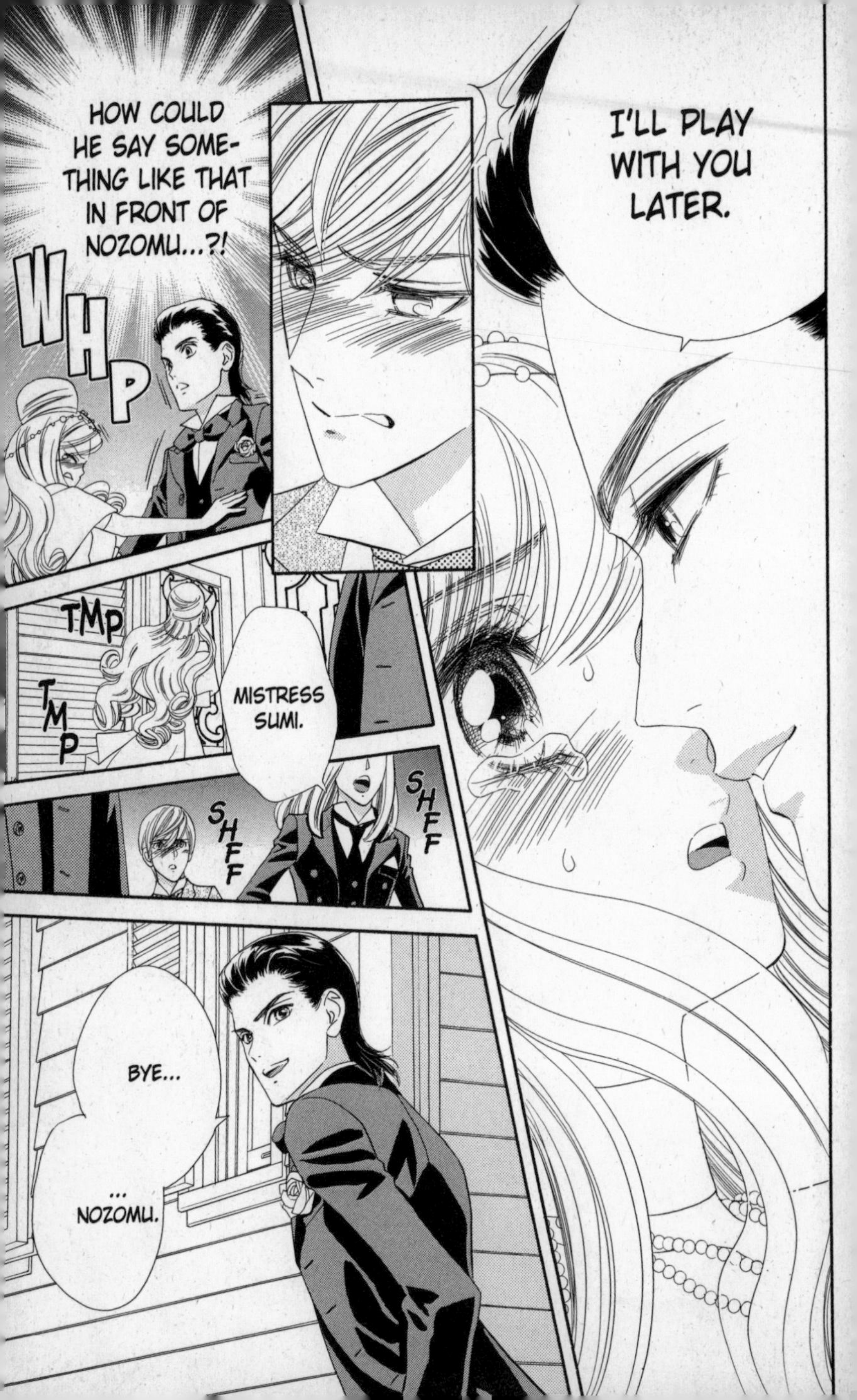
I'LL PLAY WITH YOU LATER.
HOW COULD HE SAY SOME-THING LIKE THAT IN FRONT OF NOZOMU...?!
WHP
TMP
TMP
MISTRESS SUMI.
SHFF
SHFF
BYE...
...NOZOMU.

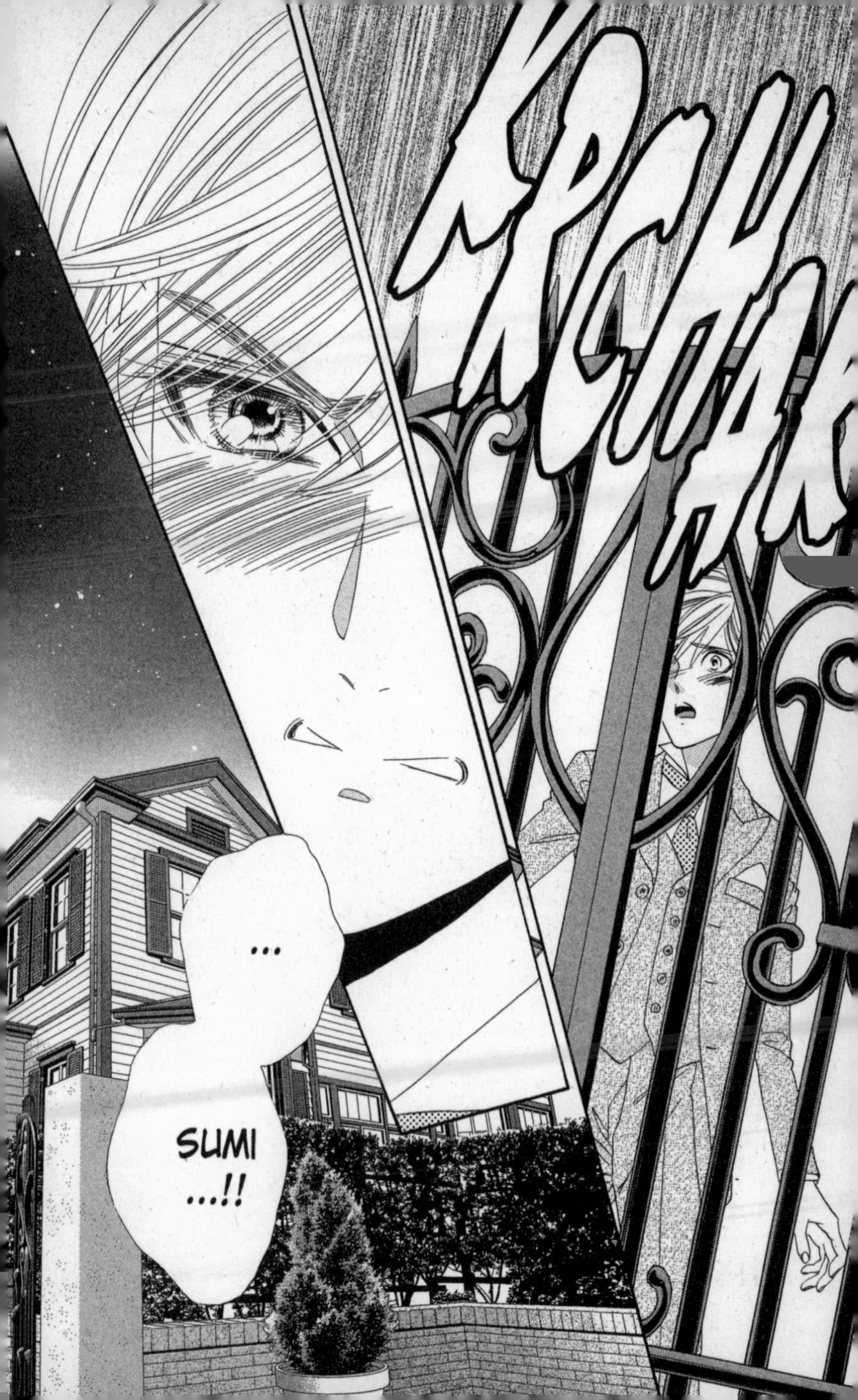
...
SUMI ...!!

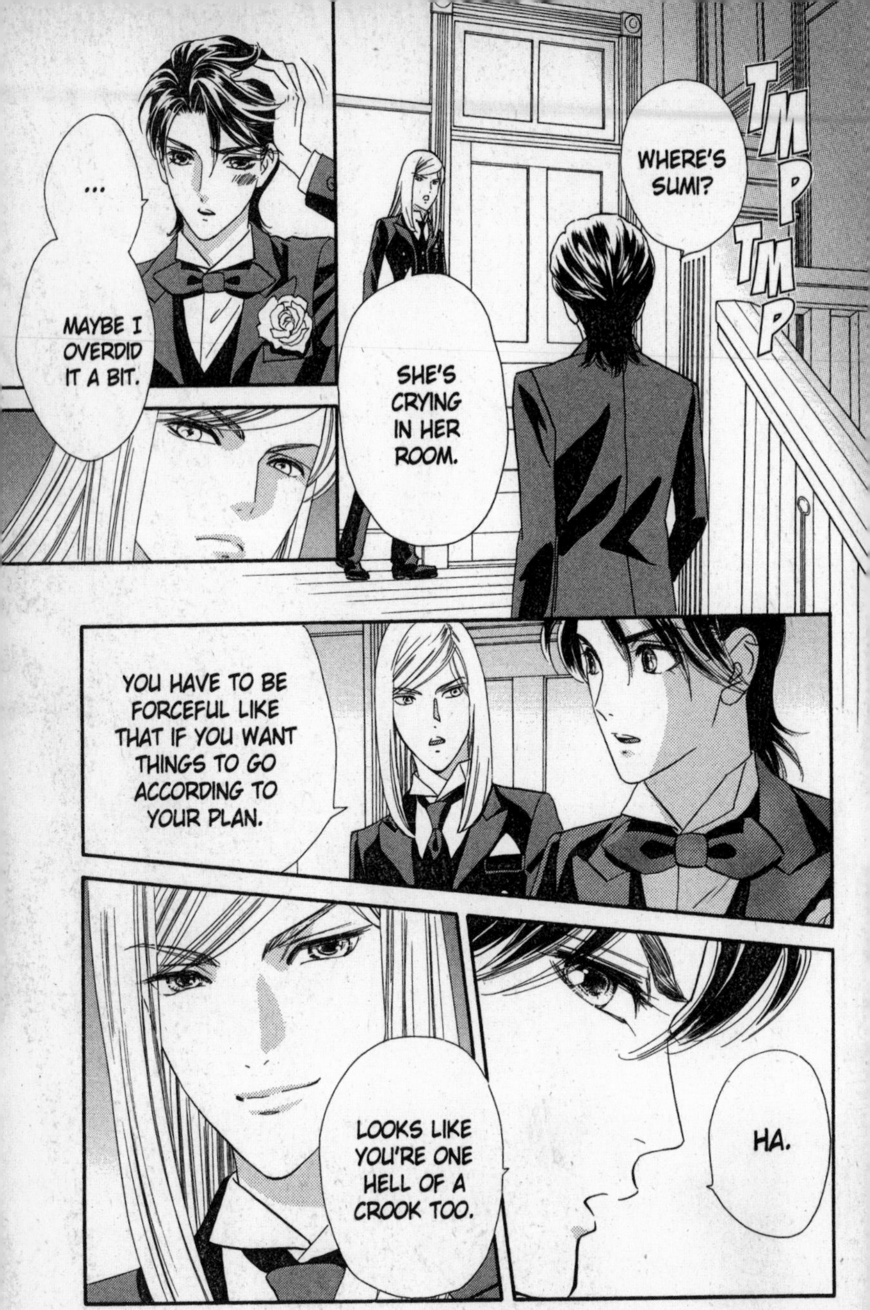
TMP TMP
WHERE'S SUMI?
TMP TMP
SHE'S CRYING IN HER ROOM.
...
MAYBE I OVERDID IT A BIT.
YOU HAVE TO BE FORCEFUL LIKE THAT IF YOU WANT THINGS TO GO ACCORDING TO YOUR PLAN.
HA.
LOOKS LIKE YOU'RE ONE HELL OF A CROOK TOO.

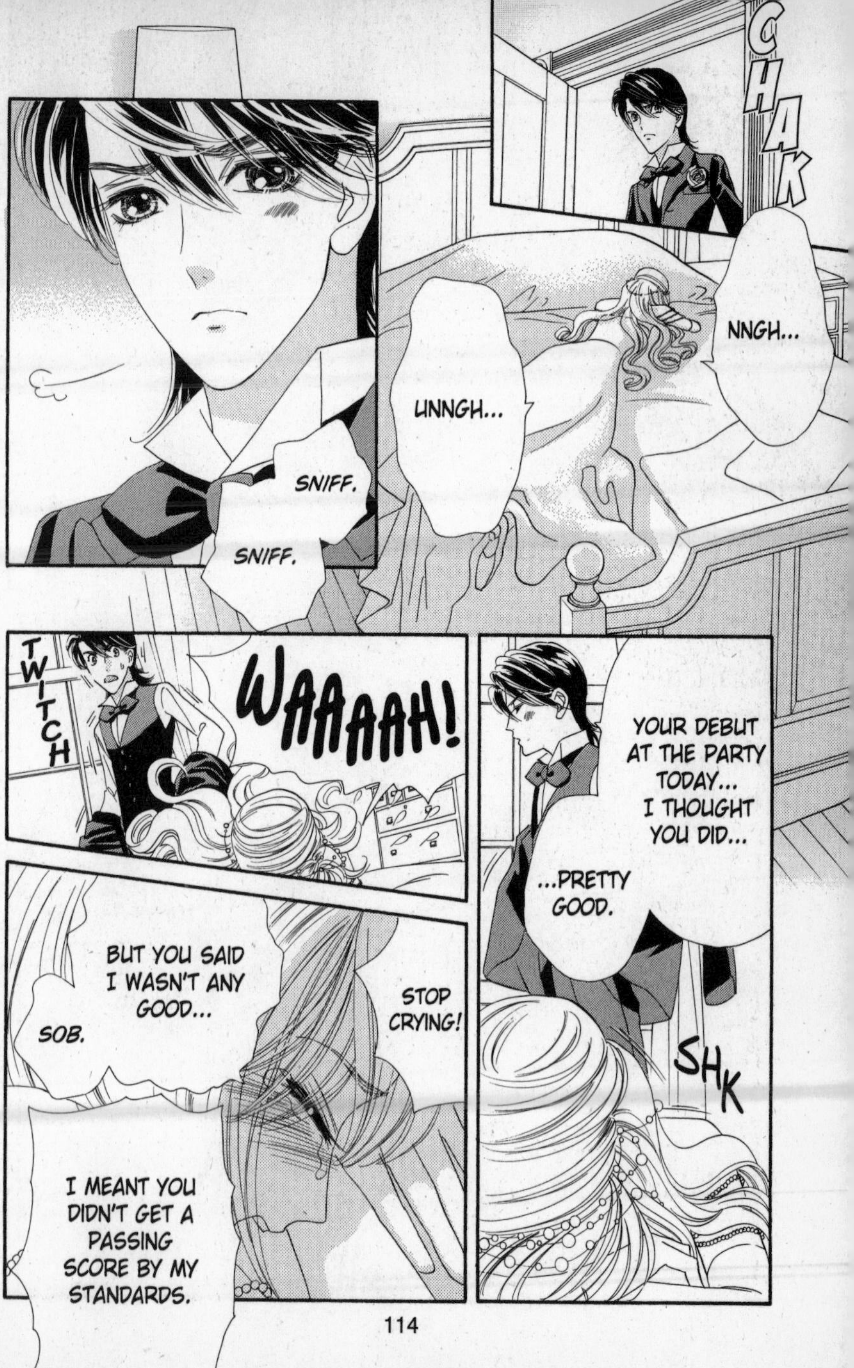
CHAK
NNGH...
UNNGH...
SNIFF.
SNIFF.
YOUR DEBUT AT THE PARTY TODAY... I THOUGHT YOU DID...
...PRETTY GOOD.
SHK
WAAAAH!
TWITCH
STOP CRYING!
BUT YOU SAID I WASN'T ANY GOOD...
SOB.
I MEANT YOU DIDN'T GET A PASSING SCORE BY MY STANDARDS.

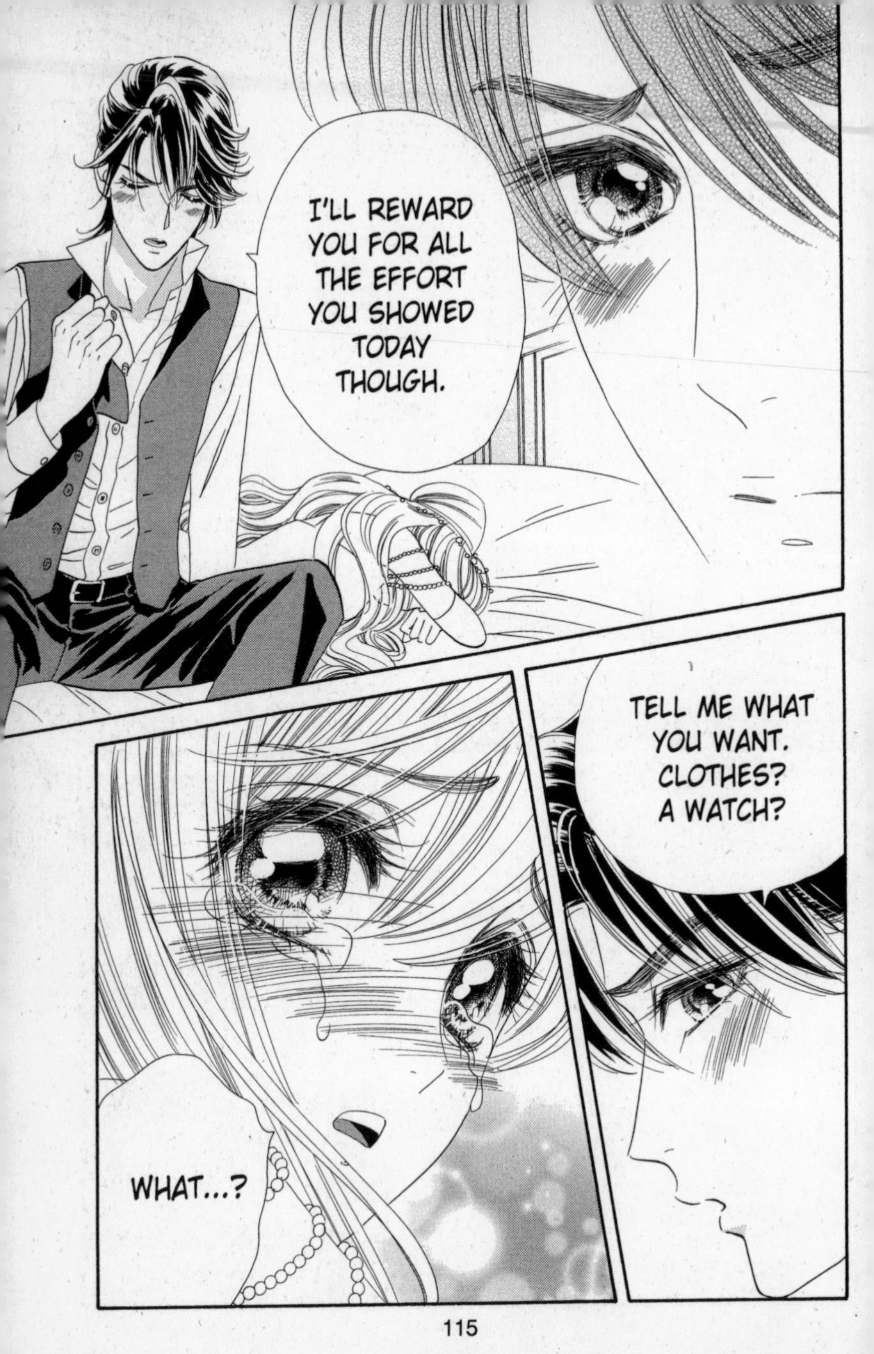
I'LL REWARD YOU FOR ALL THE EFFORT YOU SHOWED TODAY THOUGH.
TELL ME WHAT YOU WANT. CLOTHES? A WATCH?
WHAT...?

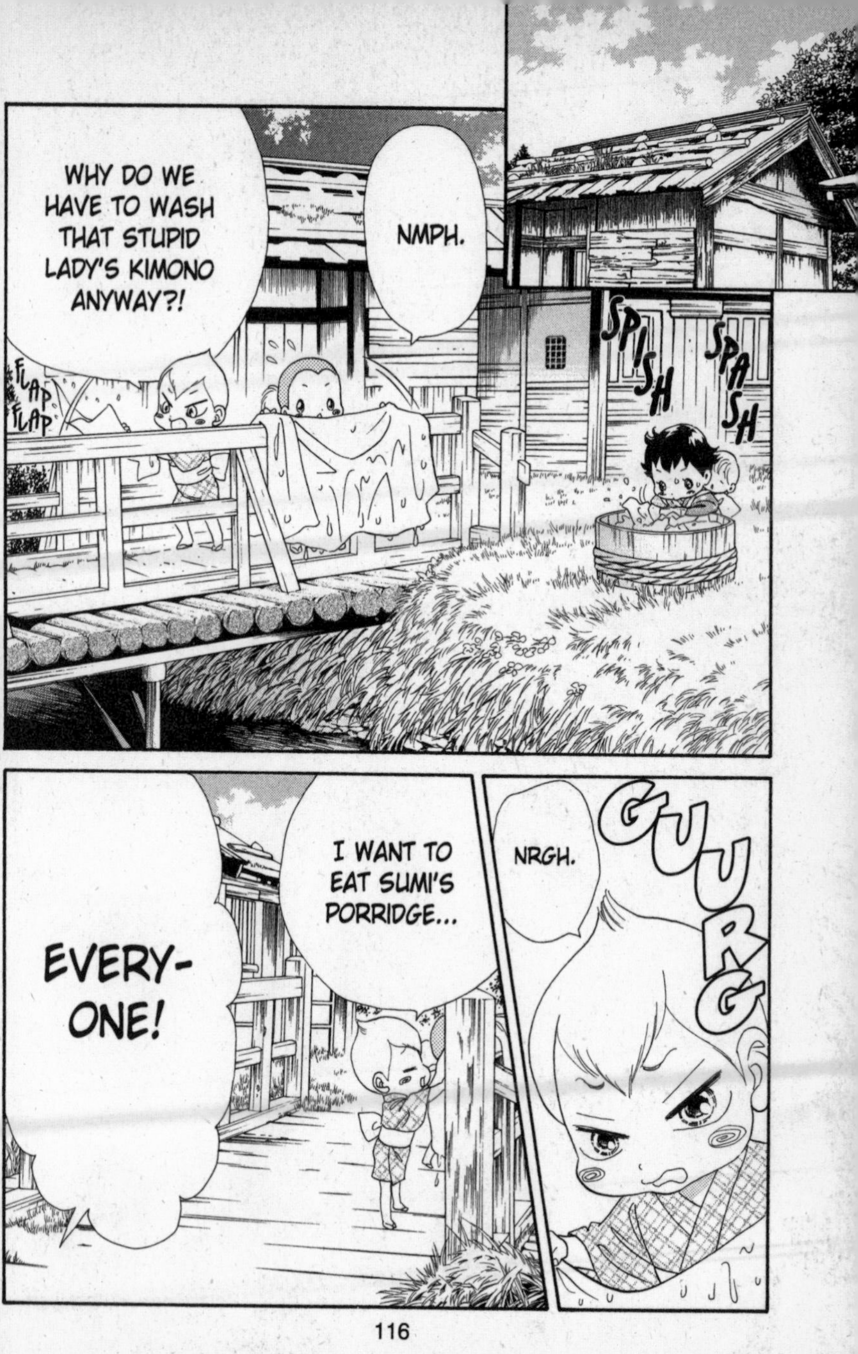
SPISH SPASH
NMPH.
WHY DO WE HAVE TO WASH THAT STUPID LADY'S KIMONO ANYWAY?!
FLAP FLAP
GUURG
NRGH.
I WANT TO EAT SUMI'S PORRIDGE...
EVERY-ONE!

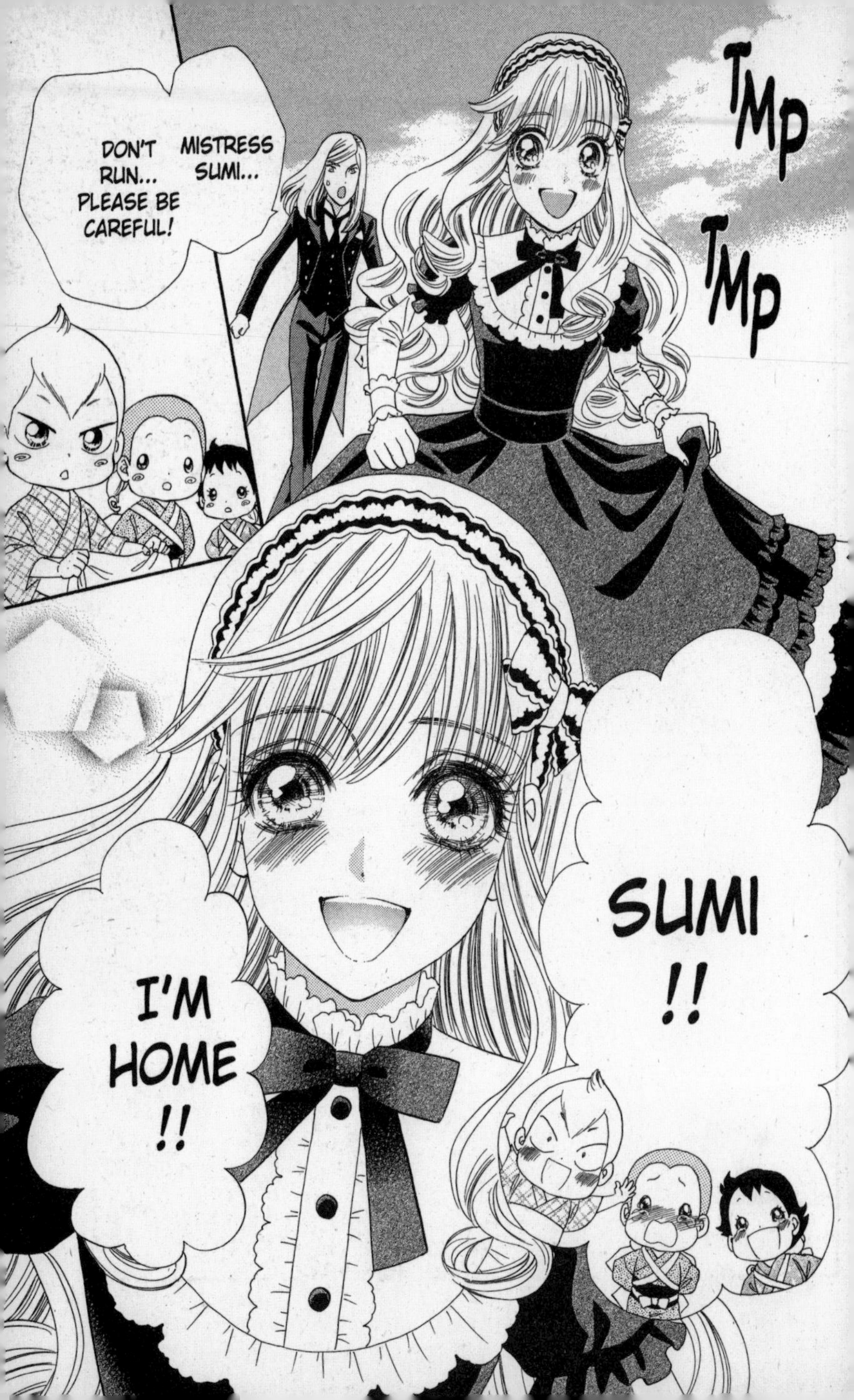
TMP TMP
MISTRESS SUMI...
DON'T RUN... PLEASE BE CAREFUL!
SUMI!!
I'M HOME!!

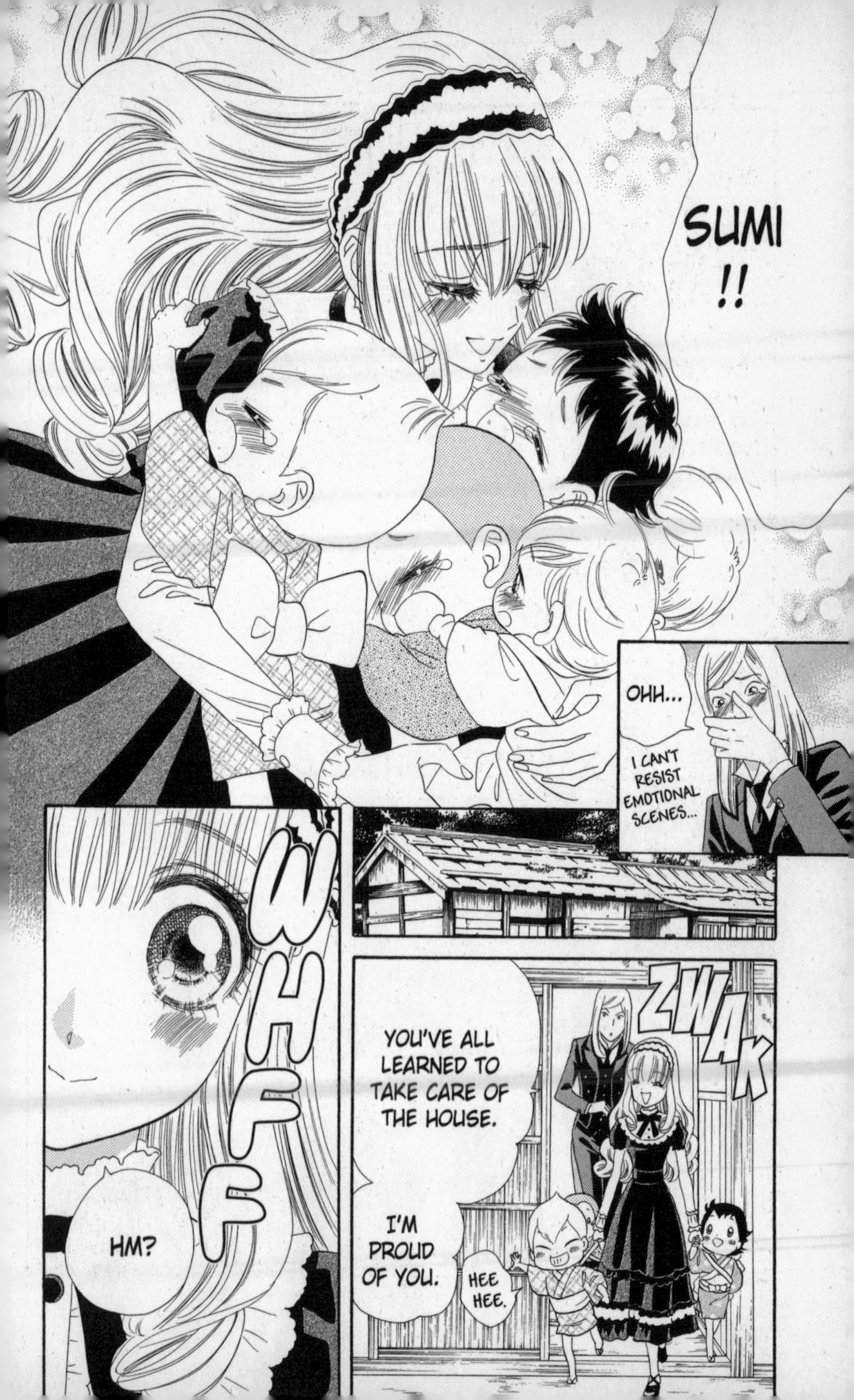
SUMI !!
OHH...
I CAN'T RESIST EMOTIONAL SCENES...
ZWAK
YOU'VE ALL LEARNED TO TAKE CARE OF THE HOUSE.
I'M PROUD OF YOU.
HEE HEE.
WHFF
HM?

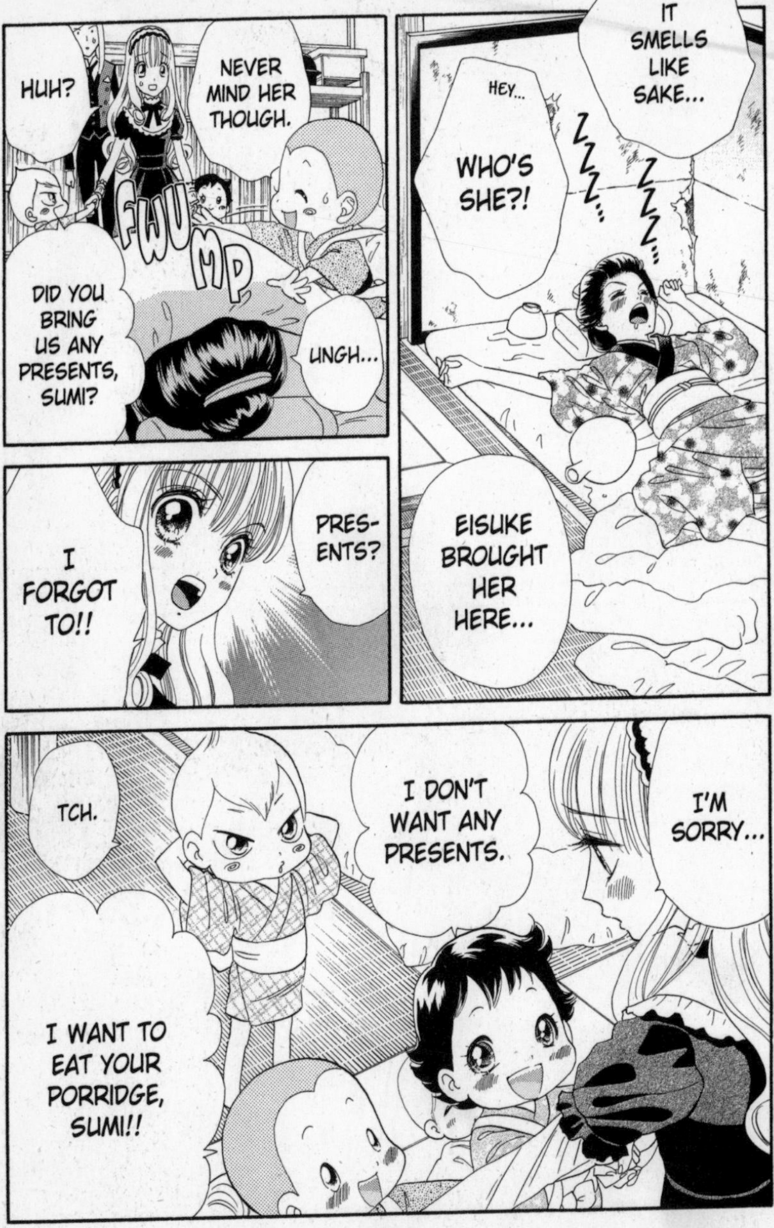
IT SMELLS LIKE SAKE...
HEY... WHO'S SHE?!
ZZZ...
ZZZ...
EISUKE BROUGHT HER HERE...
NEVER MIND HER THOUGH.
HUH?
FWUMP
UNGH...
DID YOU BRING US ANY PRESENTS, SUMI?
PRES-ENTS?
I FORGOT TO!!
I'M SORRY...
I DON'T WANT ANY PRESENTS.
TCH.
I WANT TO EAT YOUR PORRIDGE, SUMI!!

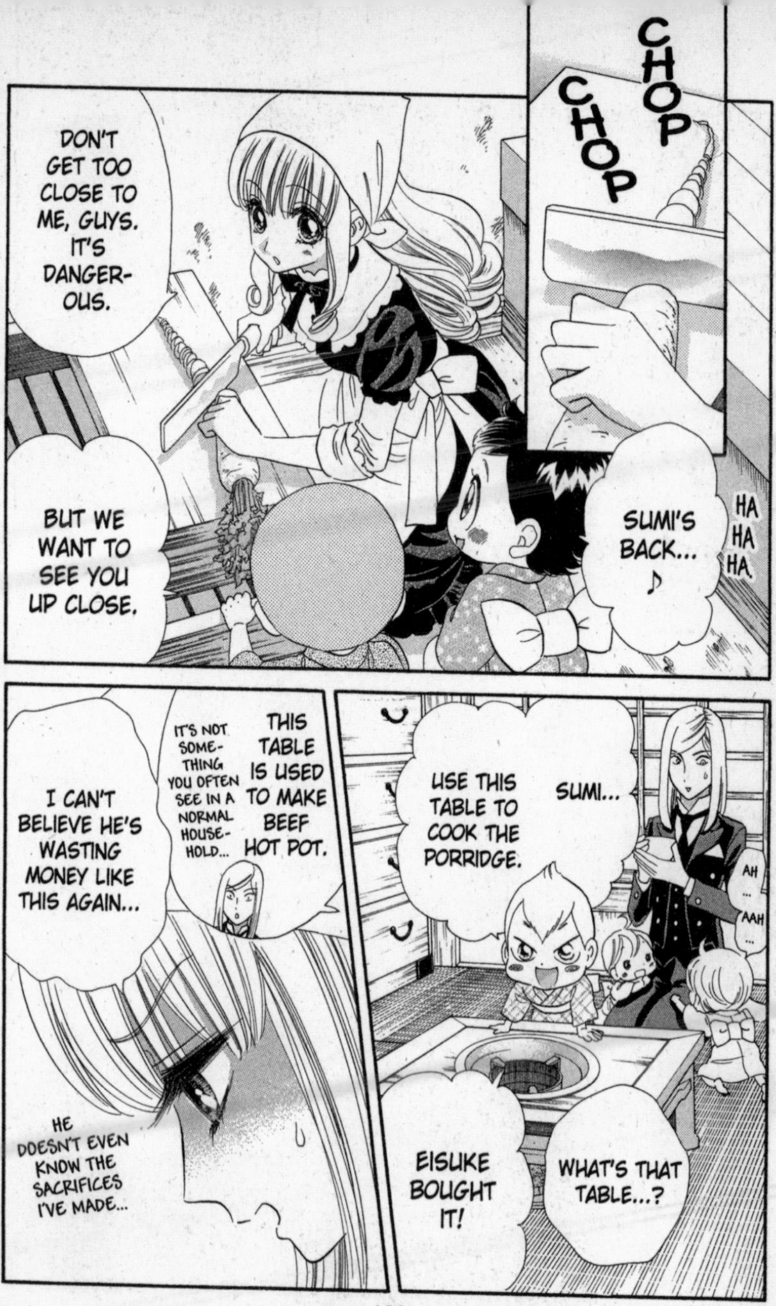
CHOP CHOP
DON'T GET TOO CLOSE TO ME, GUYS. IT'S DANGER-OUS.
SUMI'S BACK... ♪
HA HA HA.
BUT WE WANT TO SEE YOU UP CLOSE.
SUMI...
USE THIS TABLE TO COOK THE PORRIDGE.
AH... AAH...
WHAT'S THAT TABLE...?
EISUKE BOUGHT IT!
THIS TABLE IS USED TO MAKE BEEF HOT POT.
IT'S NOT SOME-THING YOU OFTEN SEE IN A NORMAL HOUSE-HOLD...
I CAN'T BELIEVE HE'S WASTING MONEY LIKE THIS AGAIN...
HE DOESN'T EVEN KNOW THE SACRIFICES I'VE MADE...

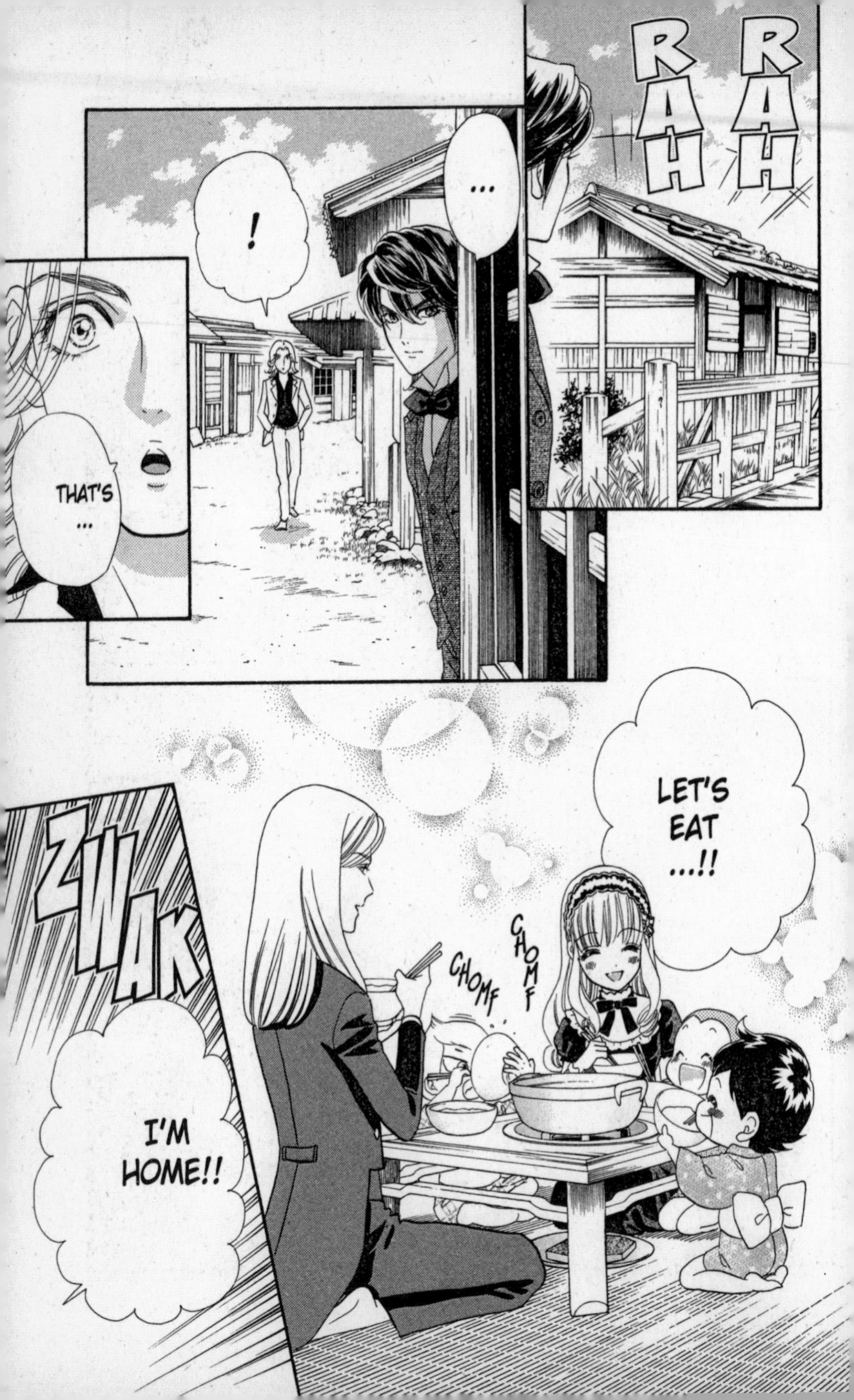
RAH RAH
...
!
THAT'S ...
LET'S EAT ...!!
CHOMF
CHOMF
ZWAK
I'M HOME!!

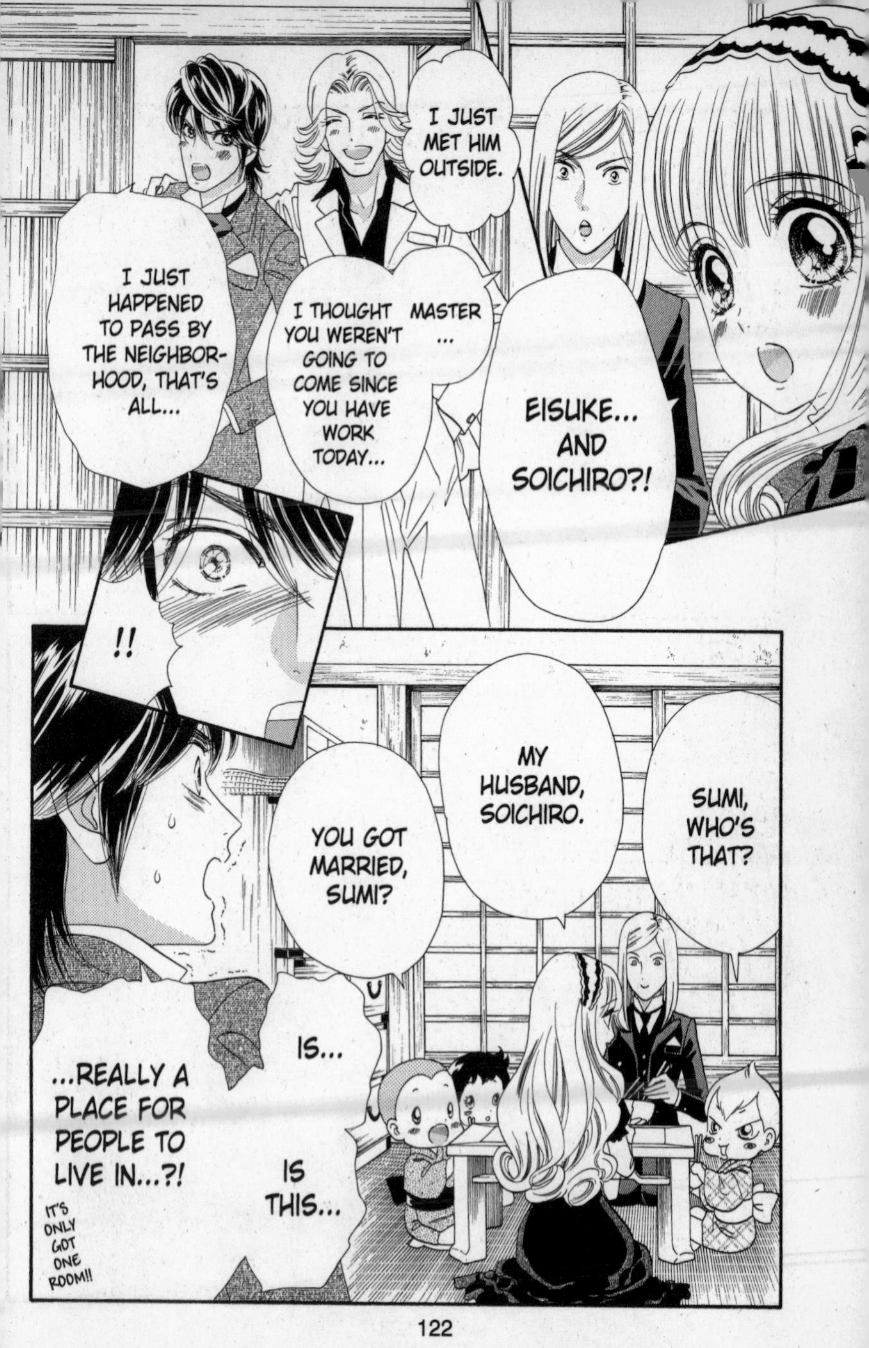
EISUKE... AND SOICHIRO?!
MASTER...
I JUST MET HIM OUTSIDE.
I THOUGHT YOU WEREN'T GOING TO COME SINCE YOU HAVE WORK TODAY...
I JUST HAPPENED TO PASS BY THE NEIGHBORHOOD, THAT'S ALL...
!!
SUMI, WHO'S THAT?
MY HUSBAND, SOICHIRO.
YOU GOT MARRIED, SUMI?
IS THIS...
IS...
...REALLY A PLACE FOR PEOPLE TO LIVE IN...?!
IT'S ONLY GOT ONE ROOM!!

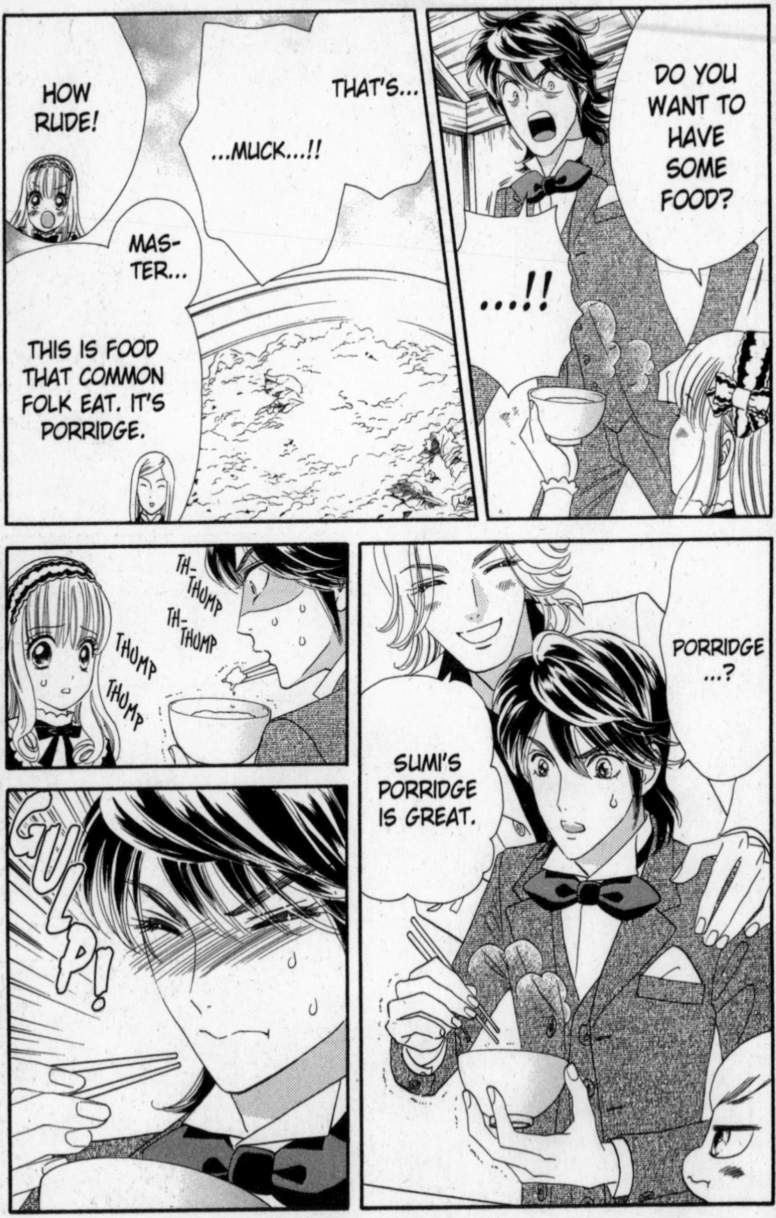
DO YOU WANT TO HAVE SOME FOOD?
...!!
THAT'S...
...MUCK...!!
HOW RUDE!
MAS-TER...
THIS IS FOOD THAT COMMON FOLK EAT. IT'S PORRIDGE.
PORRIDGE ...?
SUMI'S PORRIDGE IS GREAT.
TH-THUMP
TH-THUMP
THUMP
THUMP
GULP!

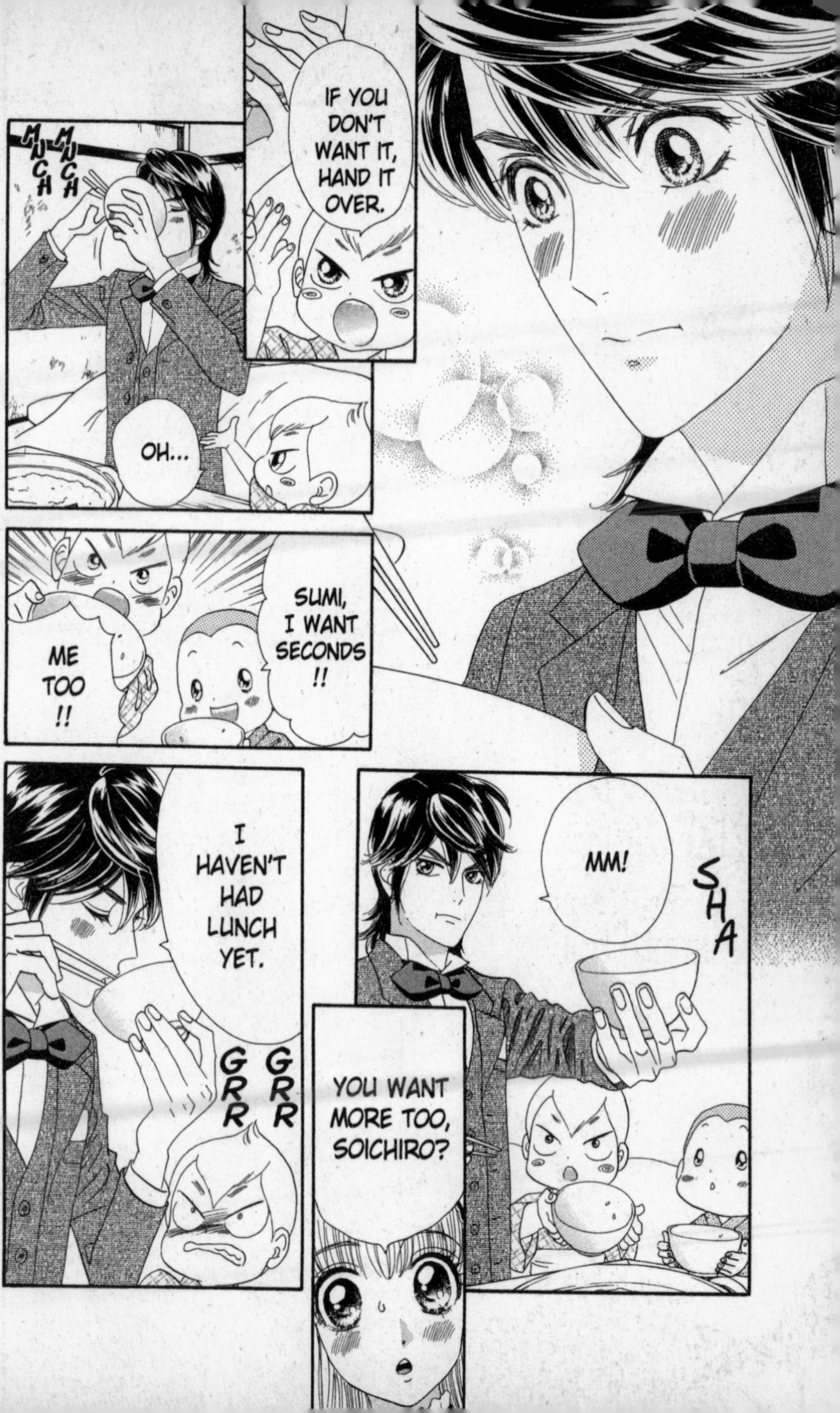
IF YOU DON'T WANT IT, HAND IT OVER.
MUNCH MUNCH
OH...
SUMI, I WANT SECONDS!!
ME TOO!!
MM!
SHA
YOU WANT MORE TOO, SOICHIRO?
I HAVEN'T HAD LUNCH YET.
GRR GRR

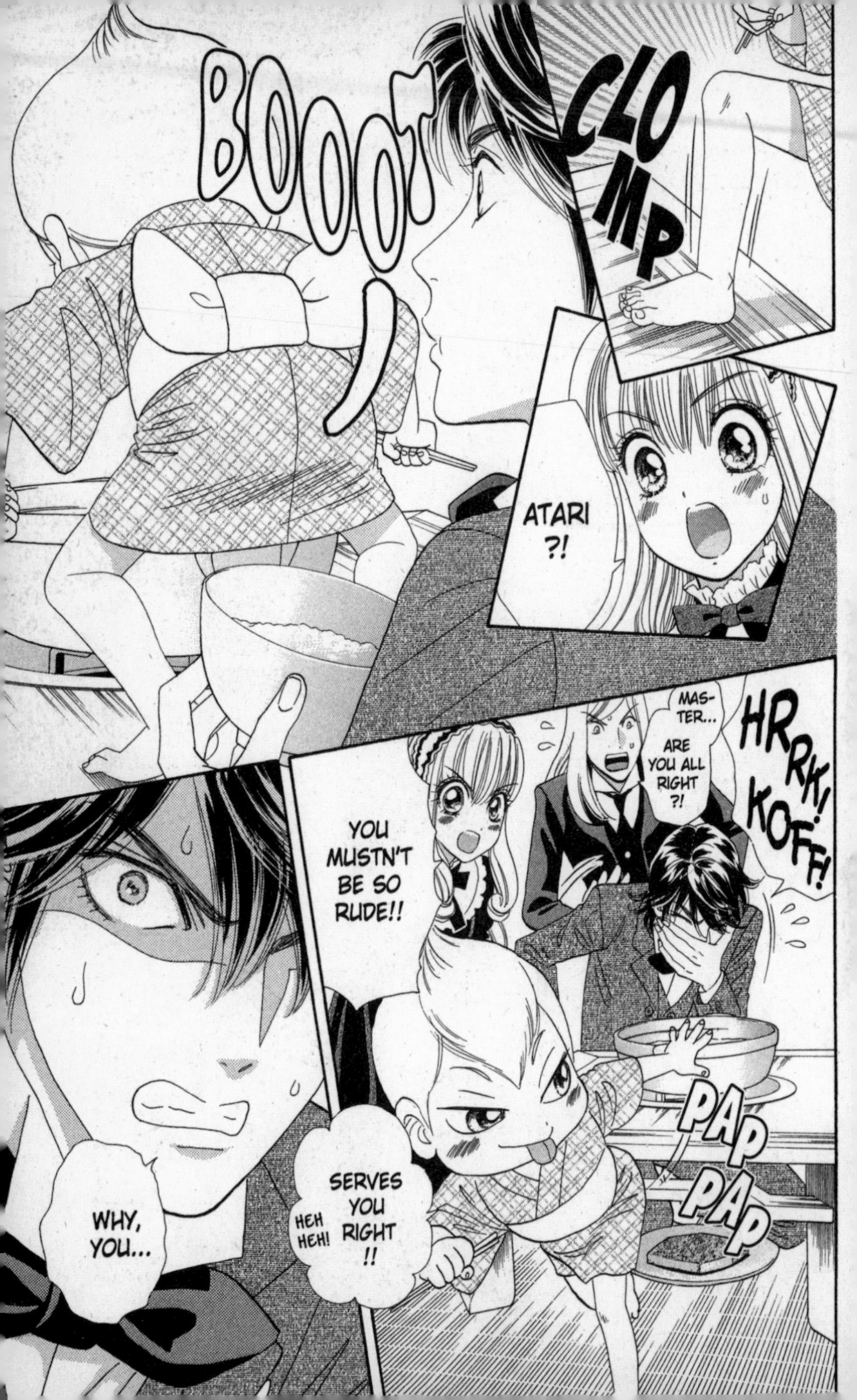
CLOMP
ATARI ?!
BOOOT
HRRK! KOFF!
MASTER... ARE YOU ALL RIGHT ?!
YOU MUSTN'T BE SO RUDE!!
PAP PAP
SERVES YOU RIGHT !!
HEH HEH!
WHY, YOU...

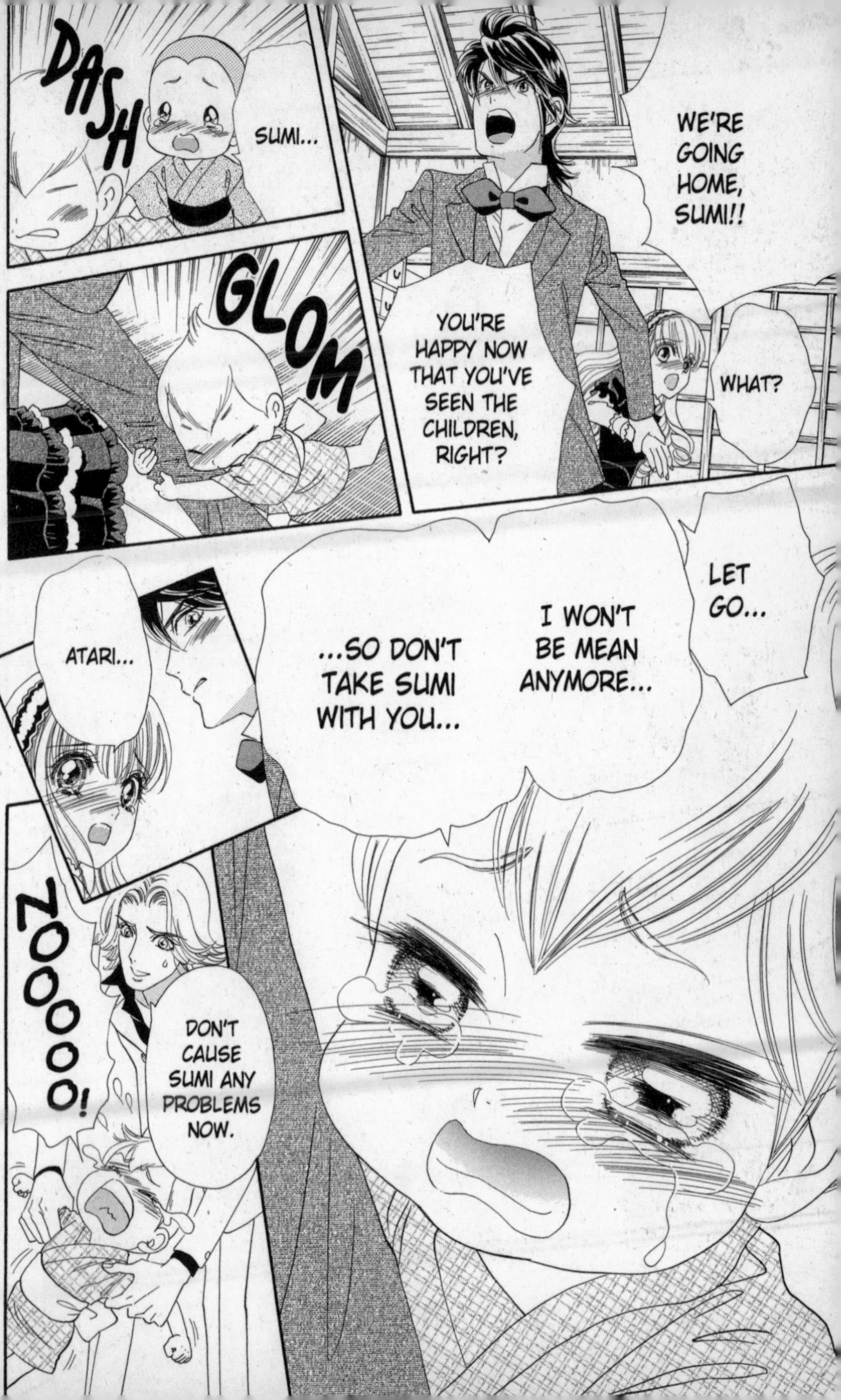

WE'RE GOING HOME, SUMI!!
YOU'RE HAPPY NOW THAT YOU'VE SEEN THE CHILDREN, RIGHT?
WHAT?
DASH
SUMI...
GLOM
LET GO...
I WON'T BE MEAN ANYMORE...
...SO DON'T TAKE SUMI WITH YOU...
ATARI...
ZOOOOO!
DON'T CAUSE SUMI ANY PROBLEMS NOW.

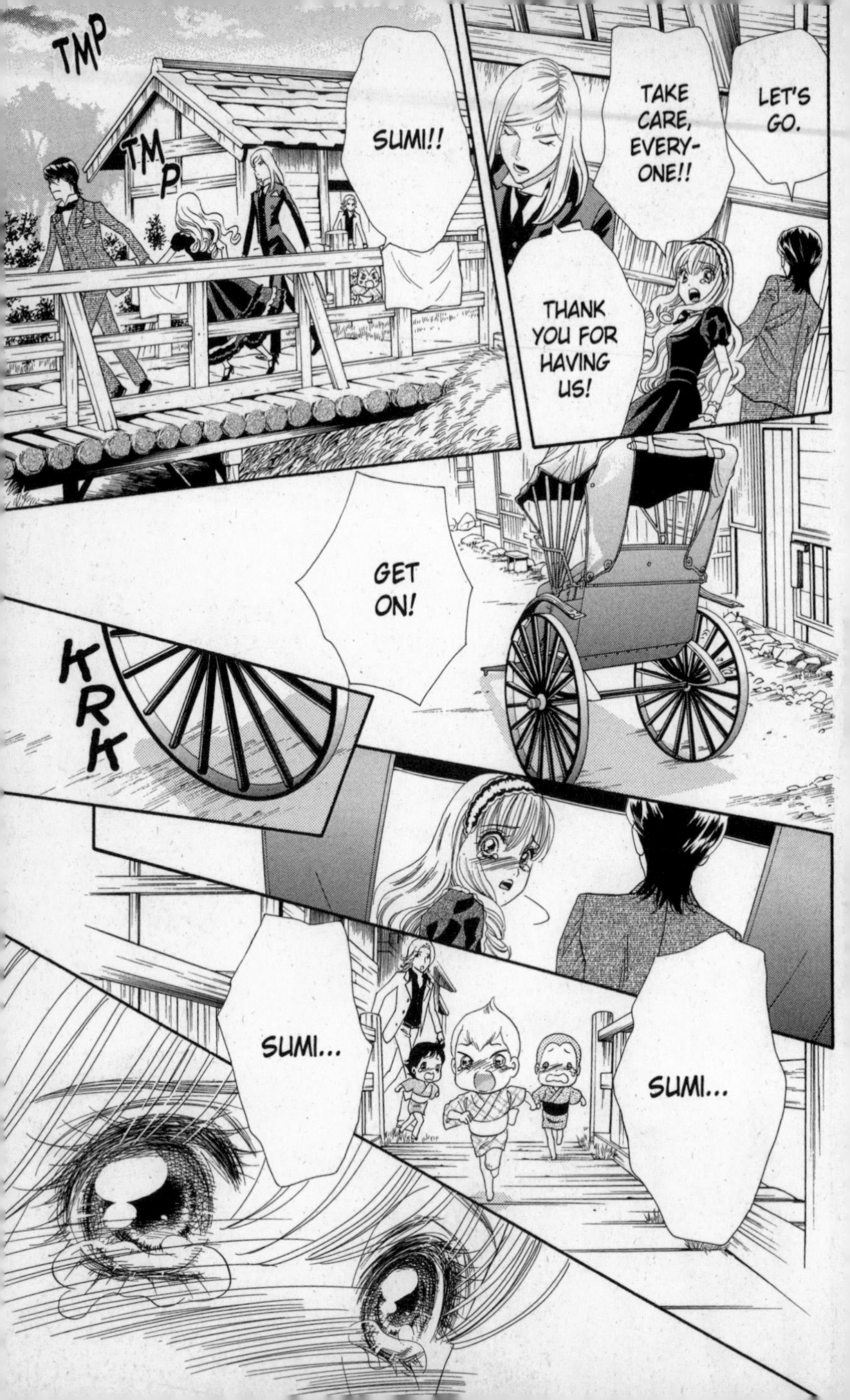
LET'S GO.
TAKE CARE, EVERY-ONE!!
THANK YOU FOR HAVING US!
SUMI!!
TMP
TMP
GET ON!
KRK
SUMI...
SUMI...

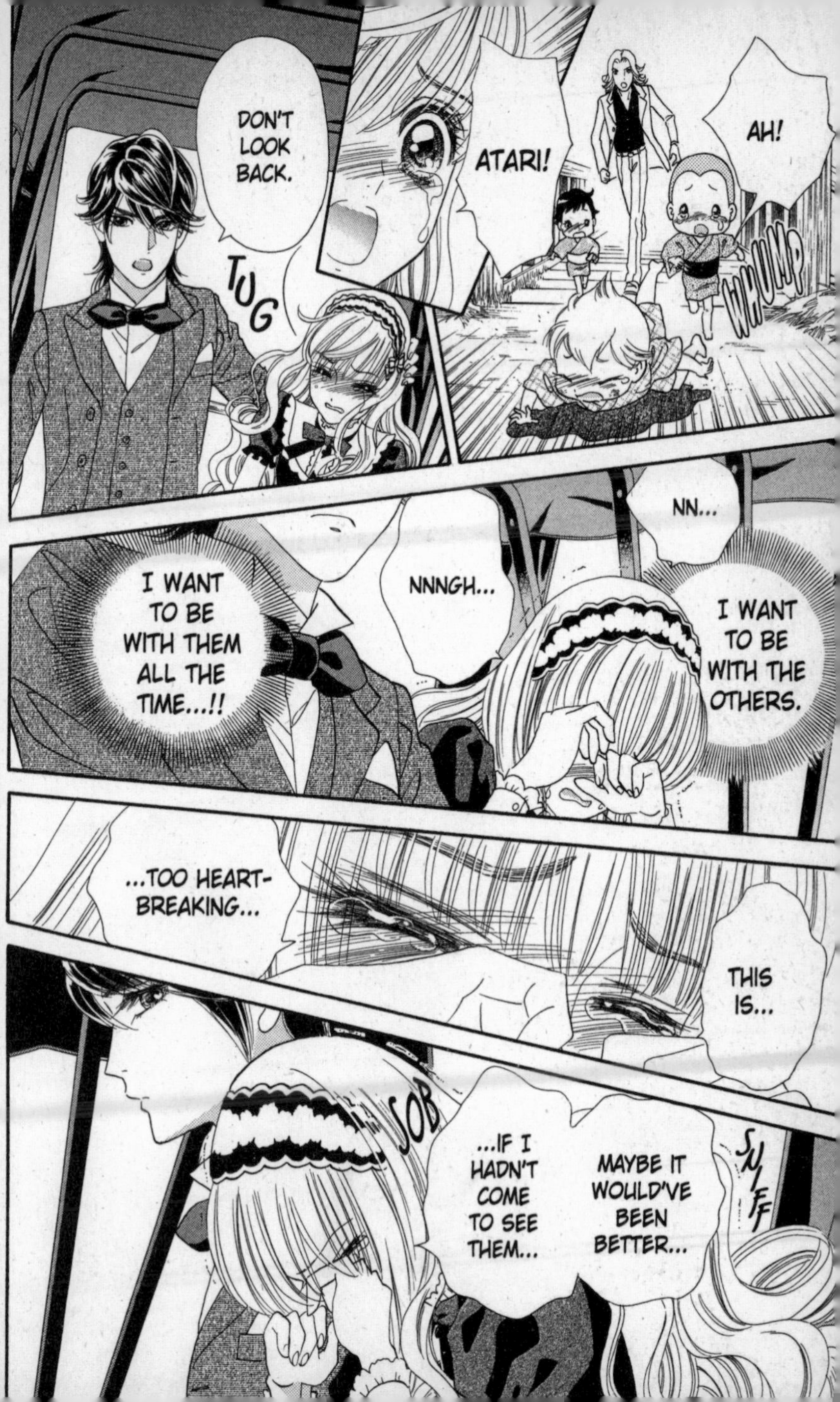
AH!
WHUMP
ATARI!
DON'T LOOK BACK.
TUG
NN...
I WANT TO BE WITH THE OTHERS.
NNNGH...
I WANT TO BE WITH THEM ALL THE TIME...!!
THIS IS...
...TOO HEART-BREAKING...
SNIFF
MAYBE IT WOULD'VE BEEN BETTER...
...IF I HADN'T COME TO SEE THEM...
SOB

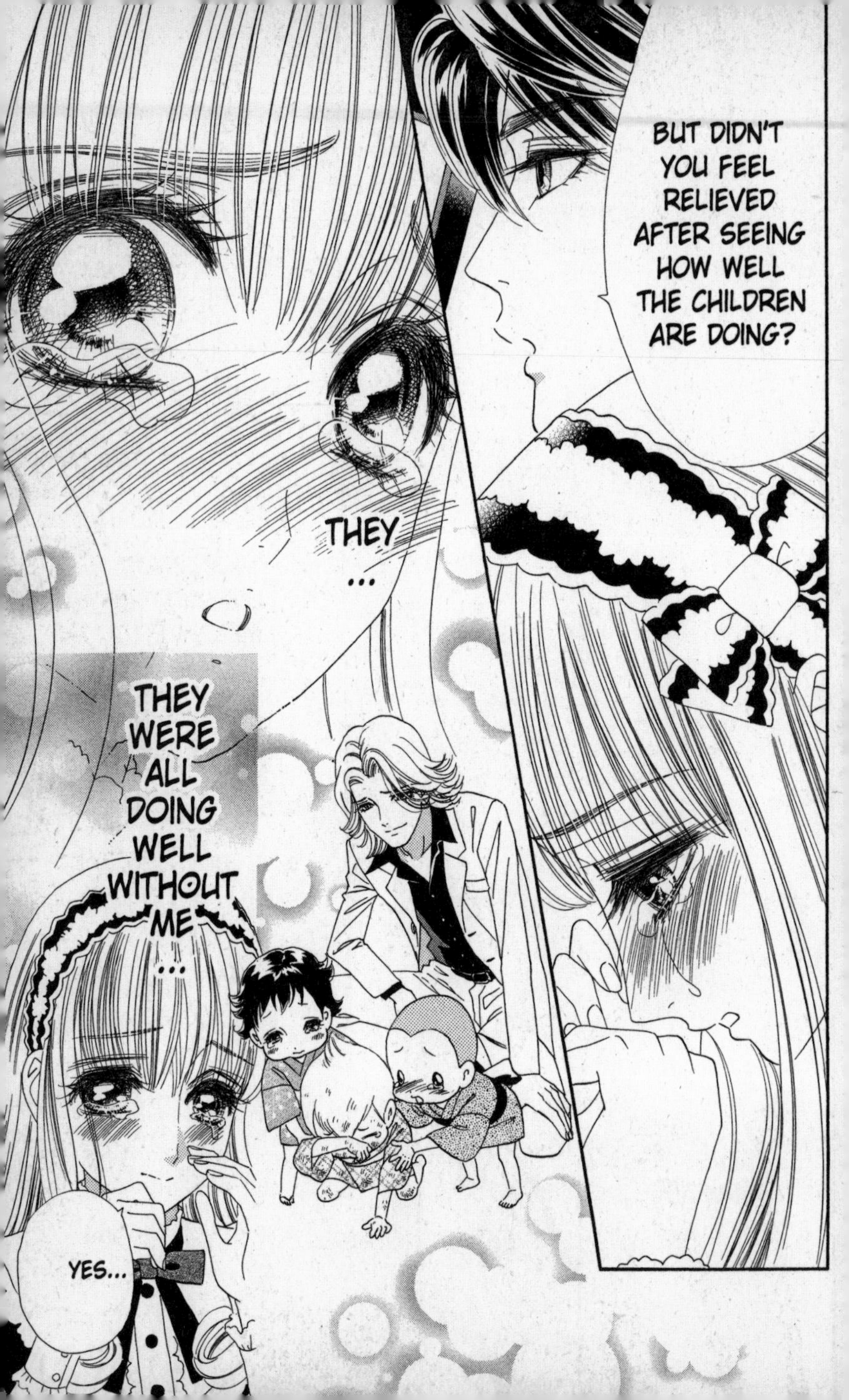

BUT DIDN'T YOU FEEL RELIEVED AFTER SEEING HOW WELL THE CHILDREN ARE DOING?
THEY ...
THEY WERE ALL DOING WELL WITHOUT ME ...
YES...

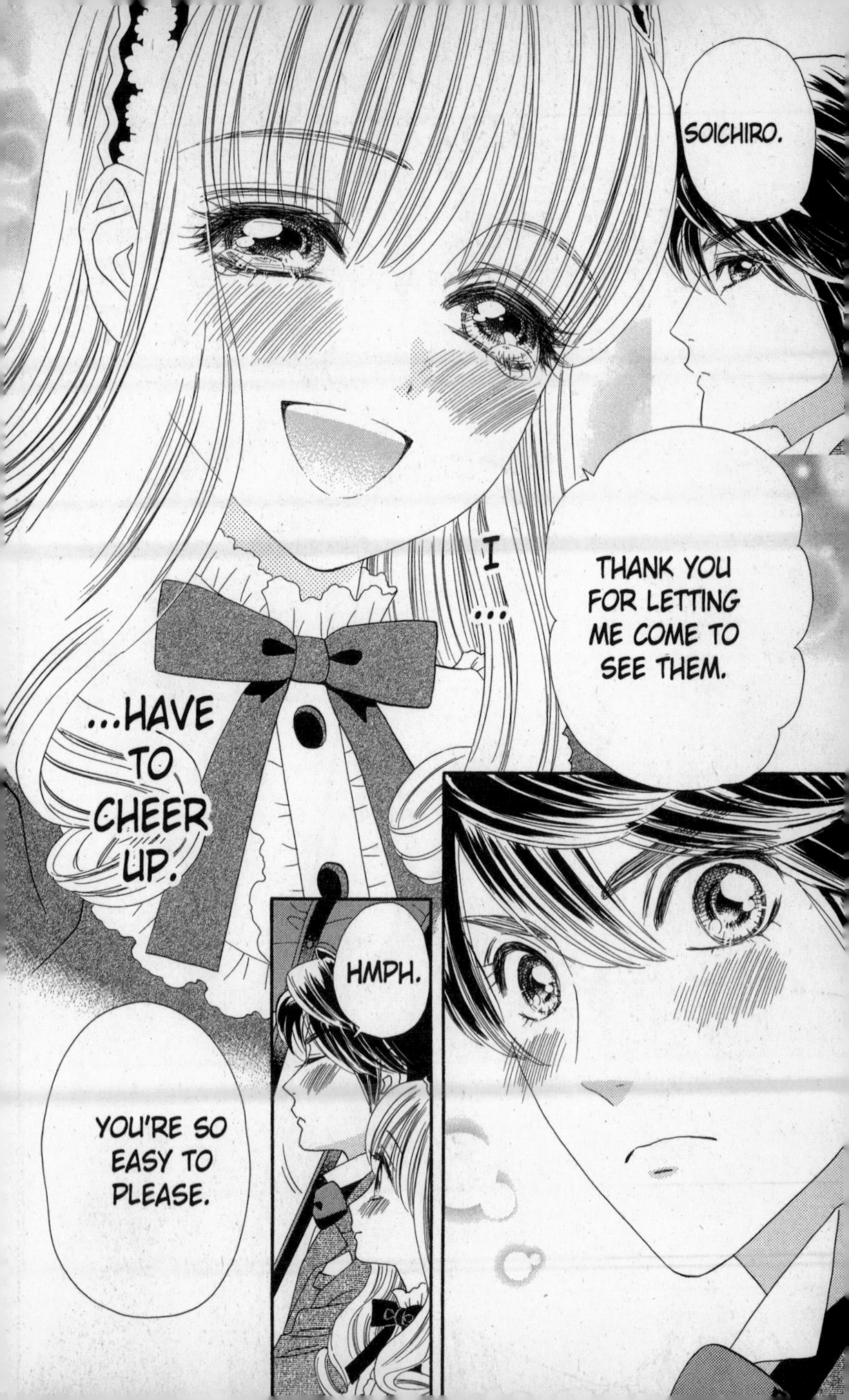
SOICHIRO.
THANK YOU FOR LETTING ME COME TO SEE THEM.
I...
...HAVE TO CHEER UP.
HMPH.
YOU'RE SO EASY TO PLEASE.

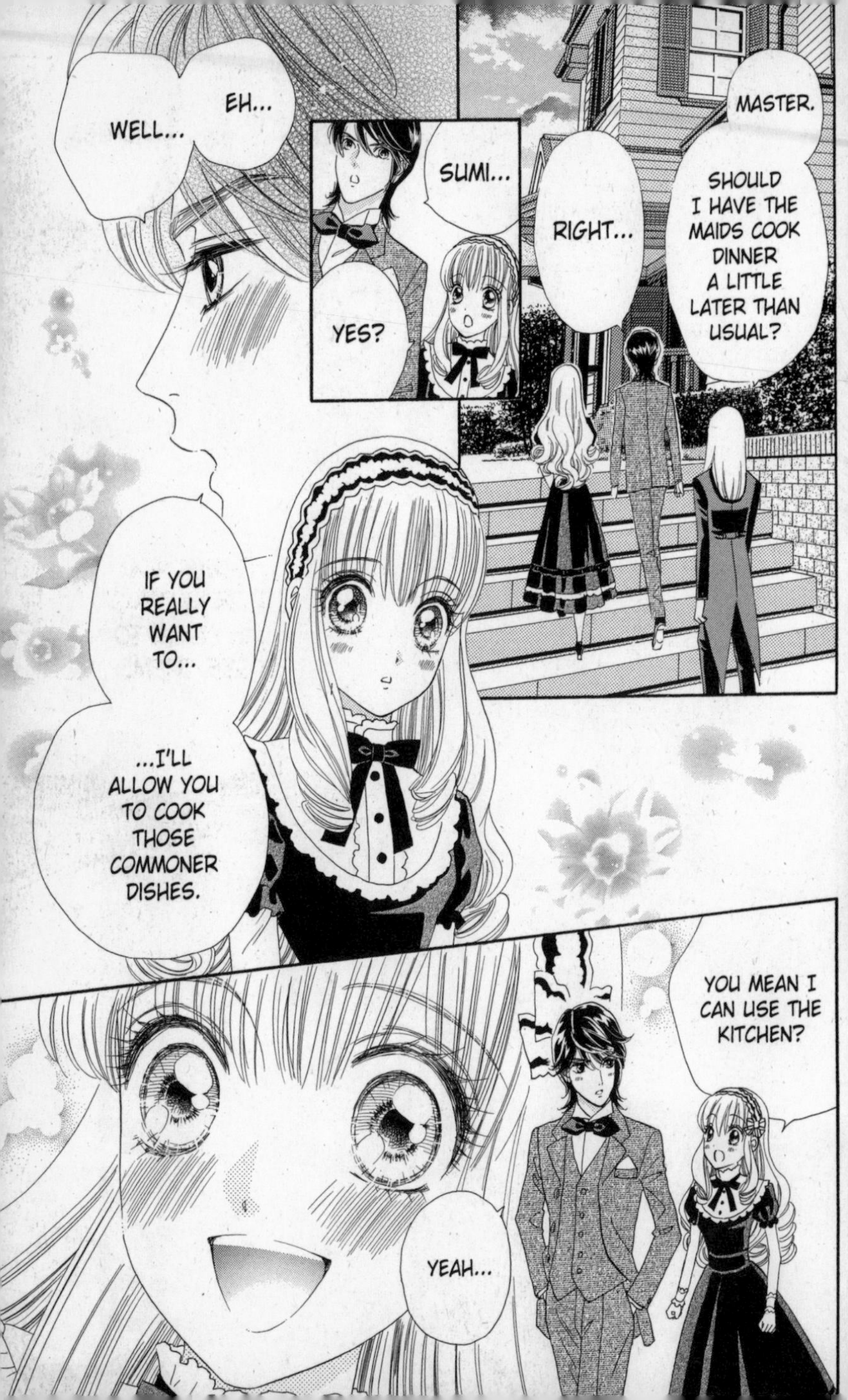
MASTER.
SHOULD I HAVE THE MAIDS COOK DINNER A LITTLE LATER THAN USUAL?
RIGHT...
SUMI...
YES?
EH... WELL...
IF YOU REALLY WANT TO...
...I'LL ALLOW YOU TO COOK THOSE COMMONER DISHES.
YOU MEAN I CAN USE THE KITCHEN?
YEAH...

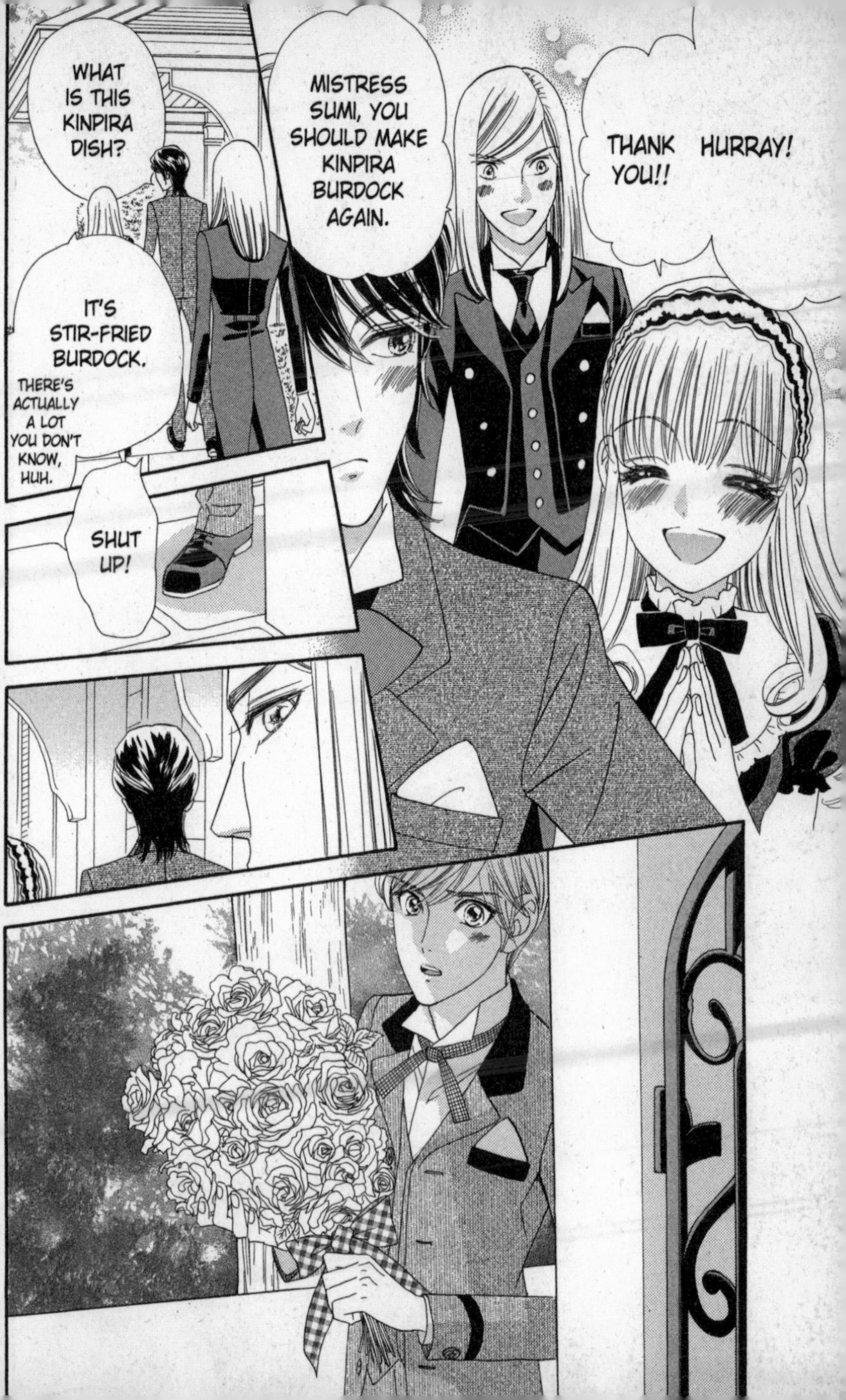
HURRAY!
THANK YOU!!
MISTRESS SUMI, YOU SHOULD MAKE KINPIRA BURDOCK AGAIN.
WHAT IS THIS KINPIRA DISH?
IT'S STIR-FRIED BURDOCK.
THERE'S ACTUALLY A LOT YOU DON'T KNOW, HUH.
SHUT UP!

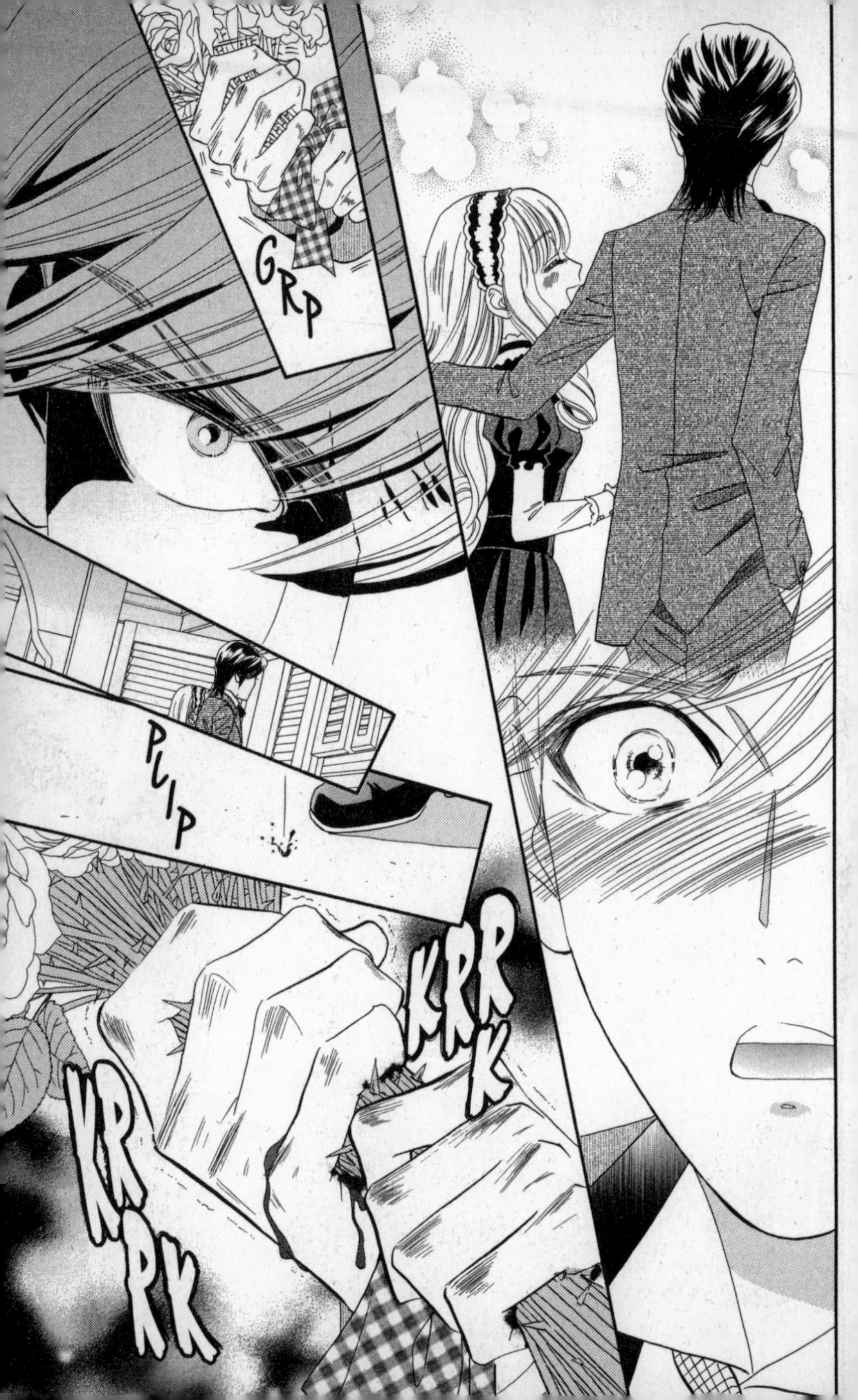
GRP
PULIP
KRRK
KRRK

STEP STAGE☆⑤

No.

A ROUGH SKETCH OF THE COLOR ILLUSTRATION USED FOR THE SERIES ANNOUNCEMENT IN THE MAGAZINE.

Date

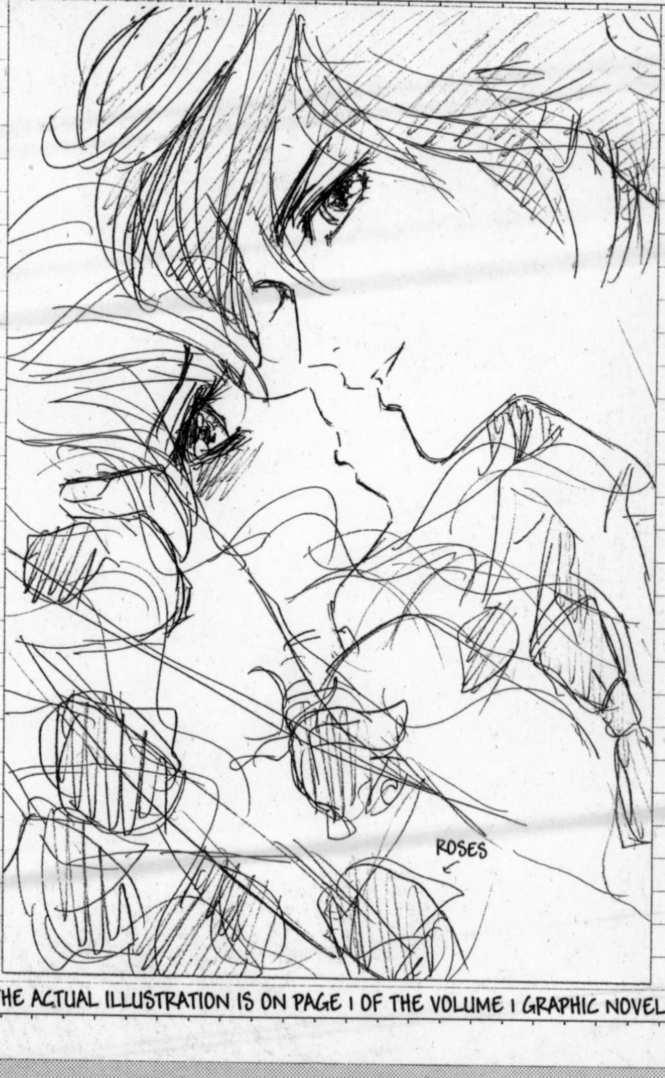
ROSES

THE ACTUAL ILLUSTRATION IS ON PAGE 1 OF THE VOLUME 1 GRAPHIC NOVEL.

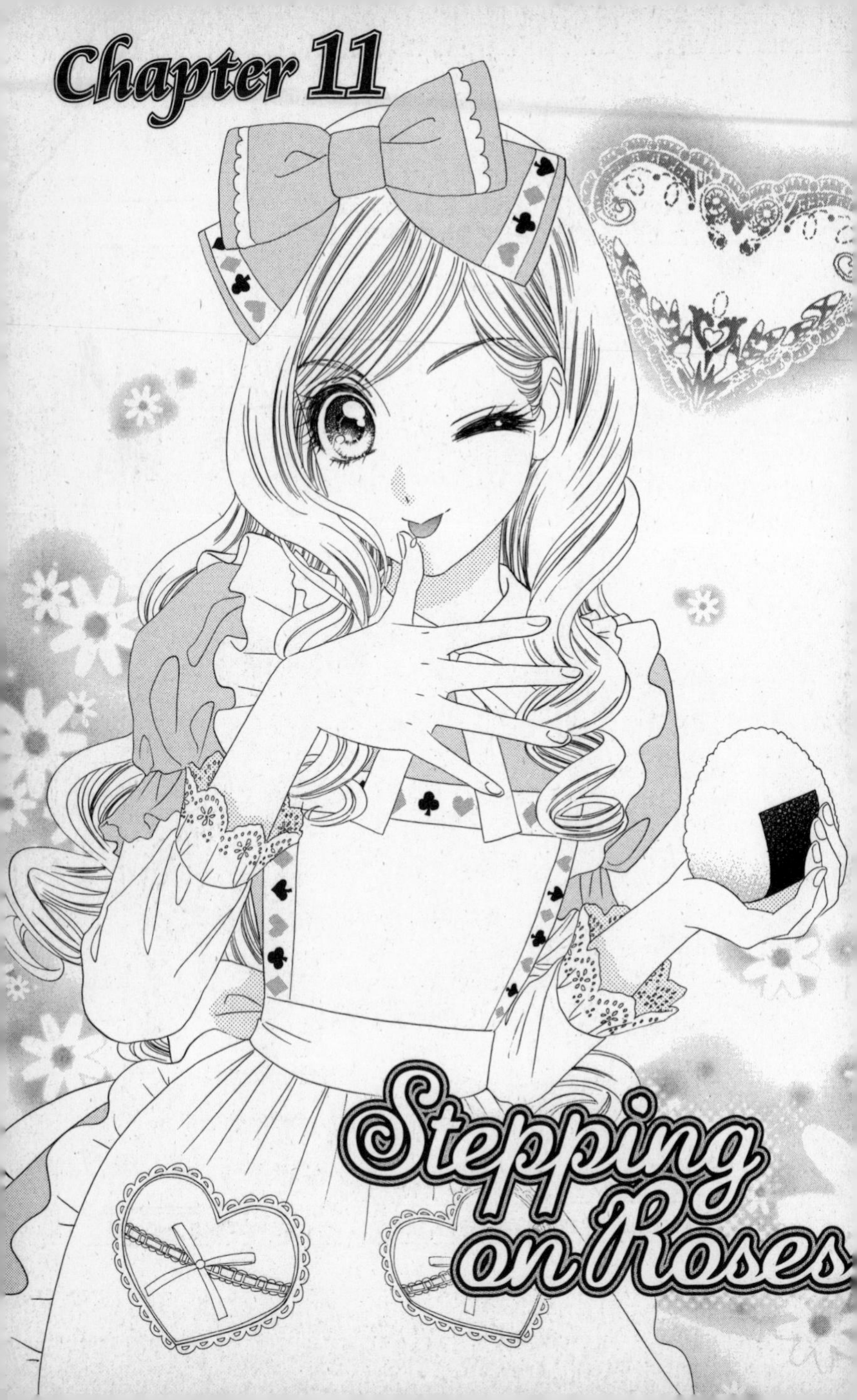
Chapter 11
Stepping on Roses

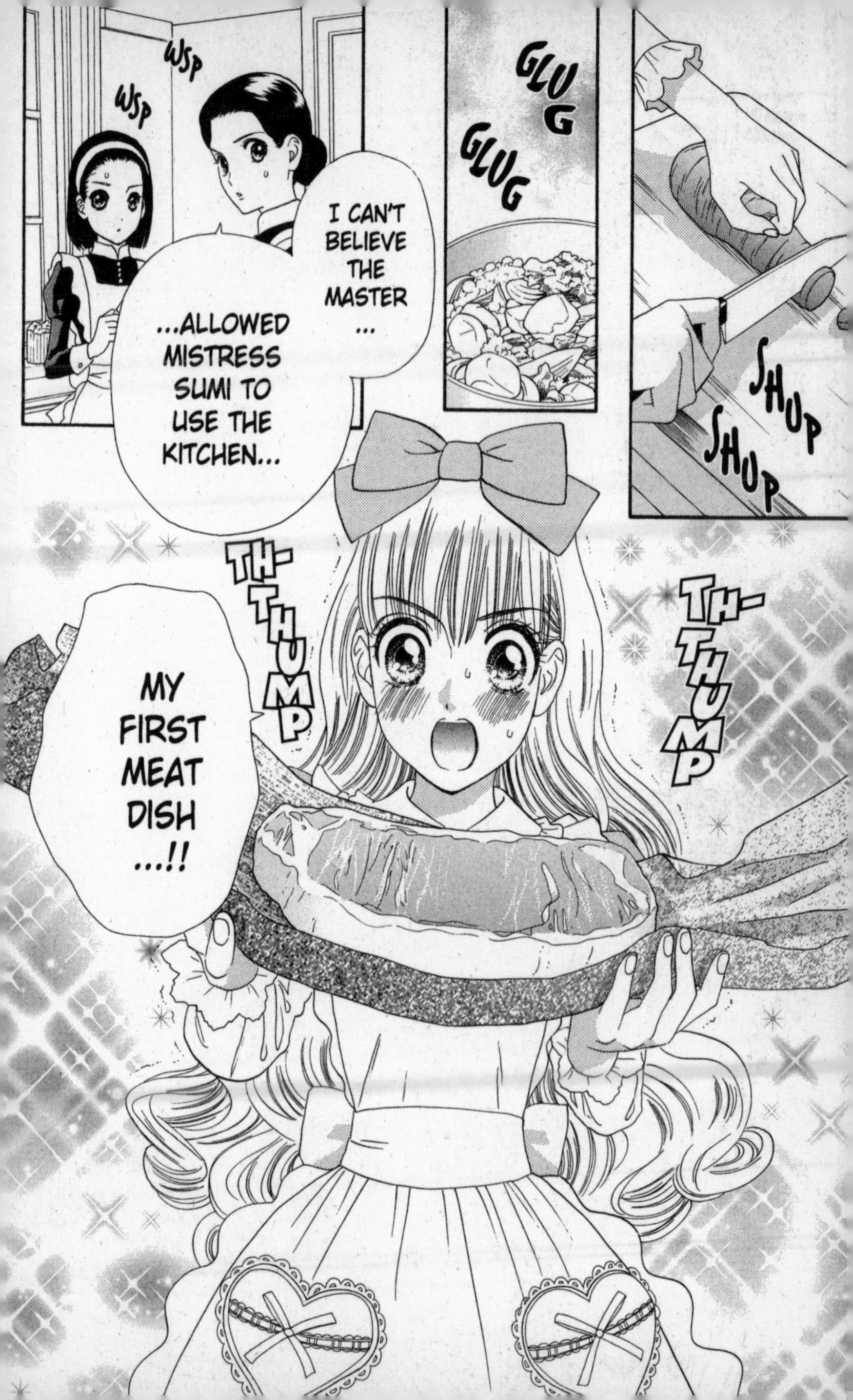
SHUP
SHUP
GLUG
GLUG
WSP
WSP
I CAN'T BELIEVE THE MASTER...
...ALLOWED MISTRESS SUMI TO USE THE KITCHEN...
TH-THUMP
TH-THUMP
MY FIRST MEAT DISH...!!

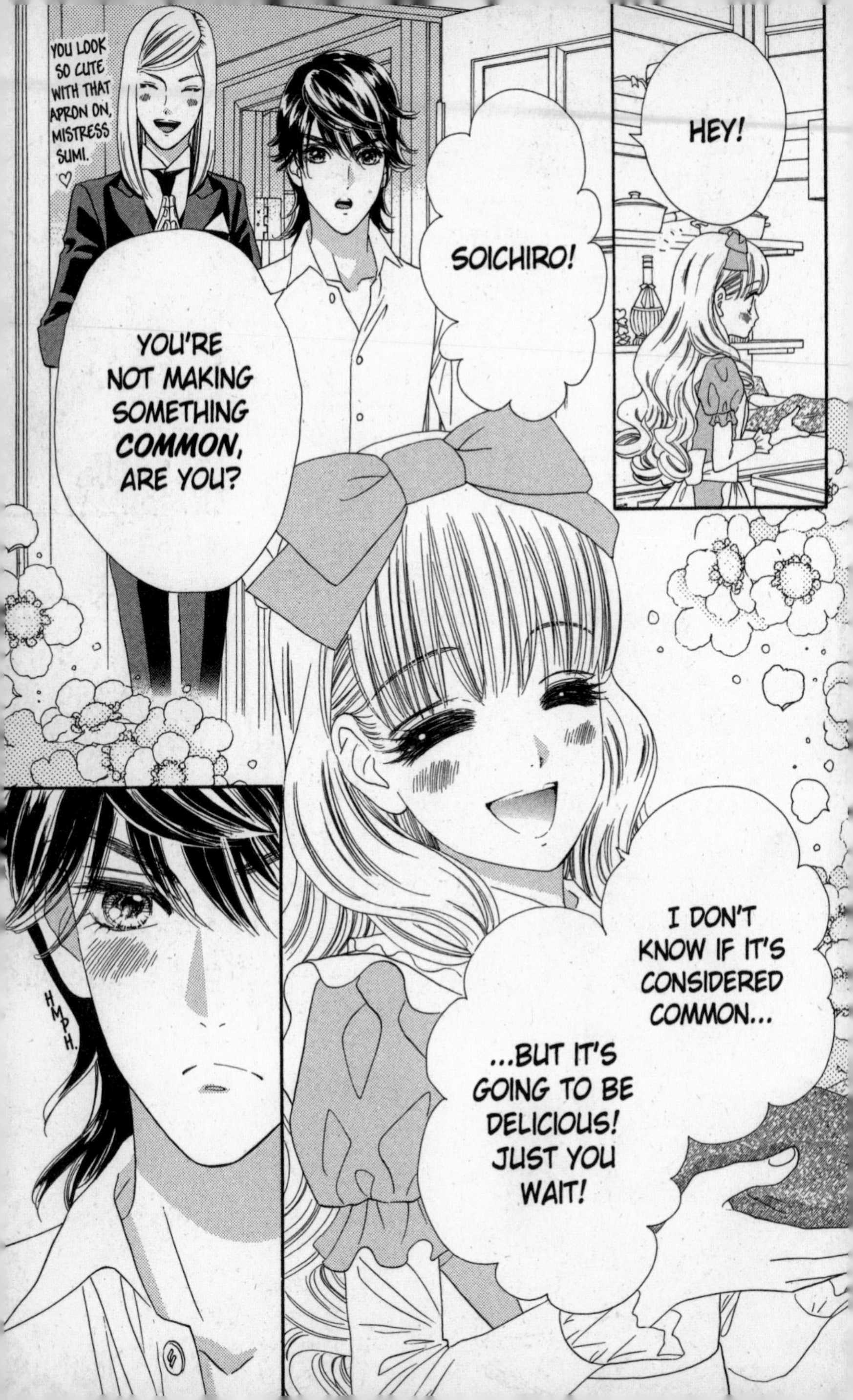
HEY!
SOICHIRO!
YOU LOOK SO CUTE WITH THAT APRON ON, MISTRESS SUMI. ♡
YOU'RE NOT MAKING SOMETHING COMMON, ARE YOU?
I DON'T KNOW IF IT'S CONSIDERED COMMON...
...BUT IT'S GOING TO BE DELICIOUS! JUST YOU WAIT!
HMPH.

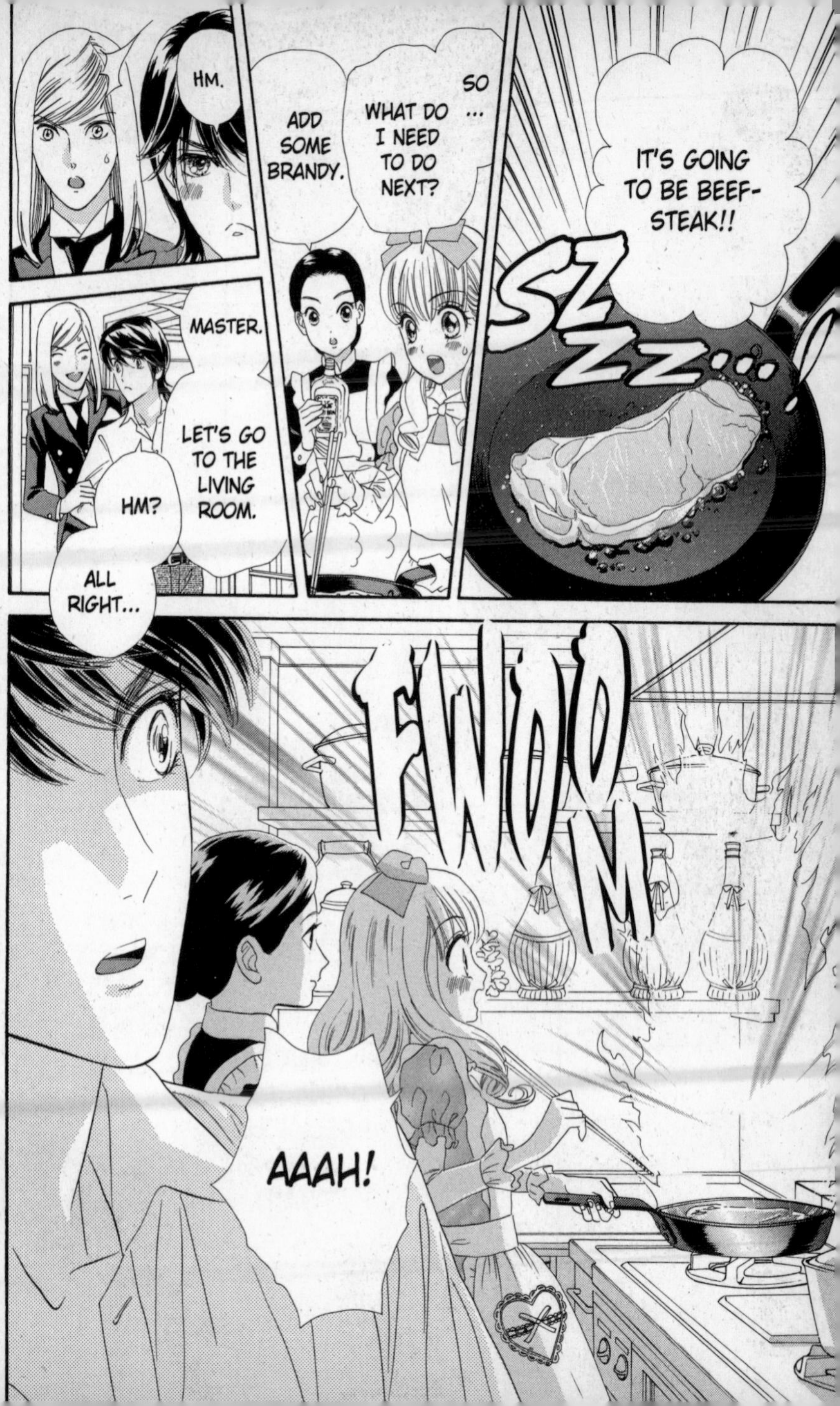
IT'S GOING TO BE BEEF-STEAK!!
SZZZ...!
SO ...
WHAT DO I NEED TO DO NEXT?
ADD SOME BRANDY.
HM.
MASTER.
LET'S GO TO THE LIVING ROOM.
HM?
ALL RIGHT...
FWOOOM
AAAH!

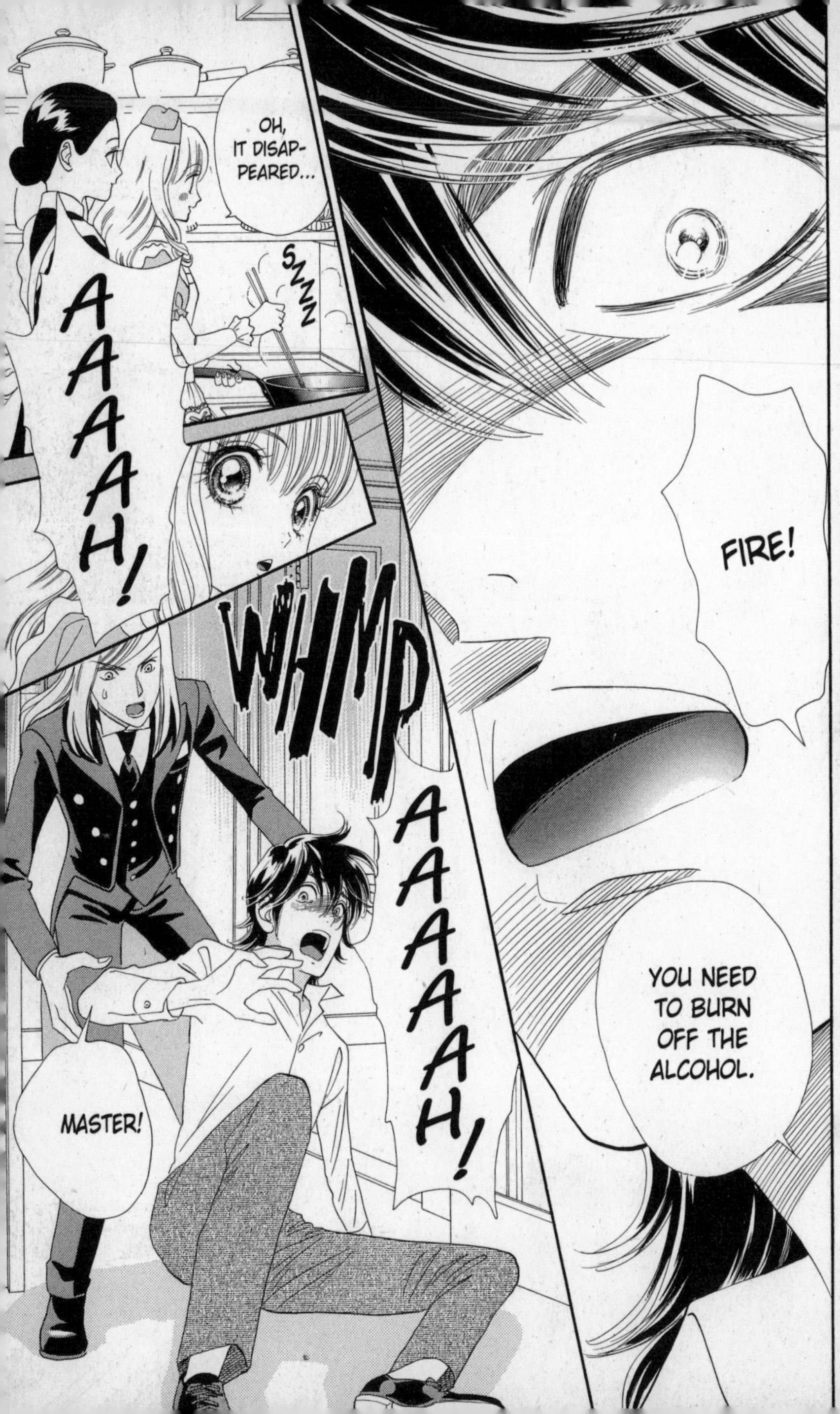
FIRE!
YOU NEED TO BURN OFF THE ALCOHOL.
OH, IT DISAP-PEARED...
SZZZ
AAAAH!
WHMP
AAAAAH!
MASTER!

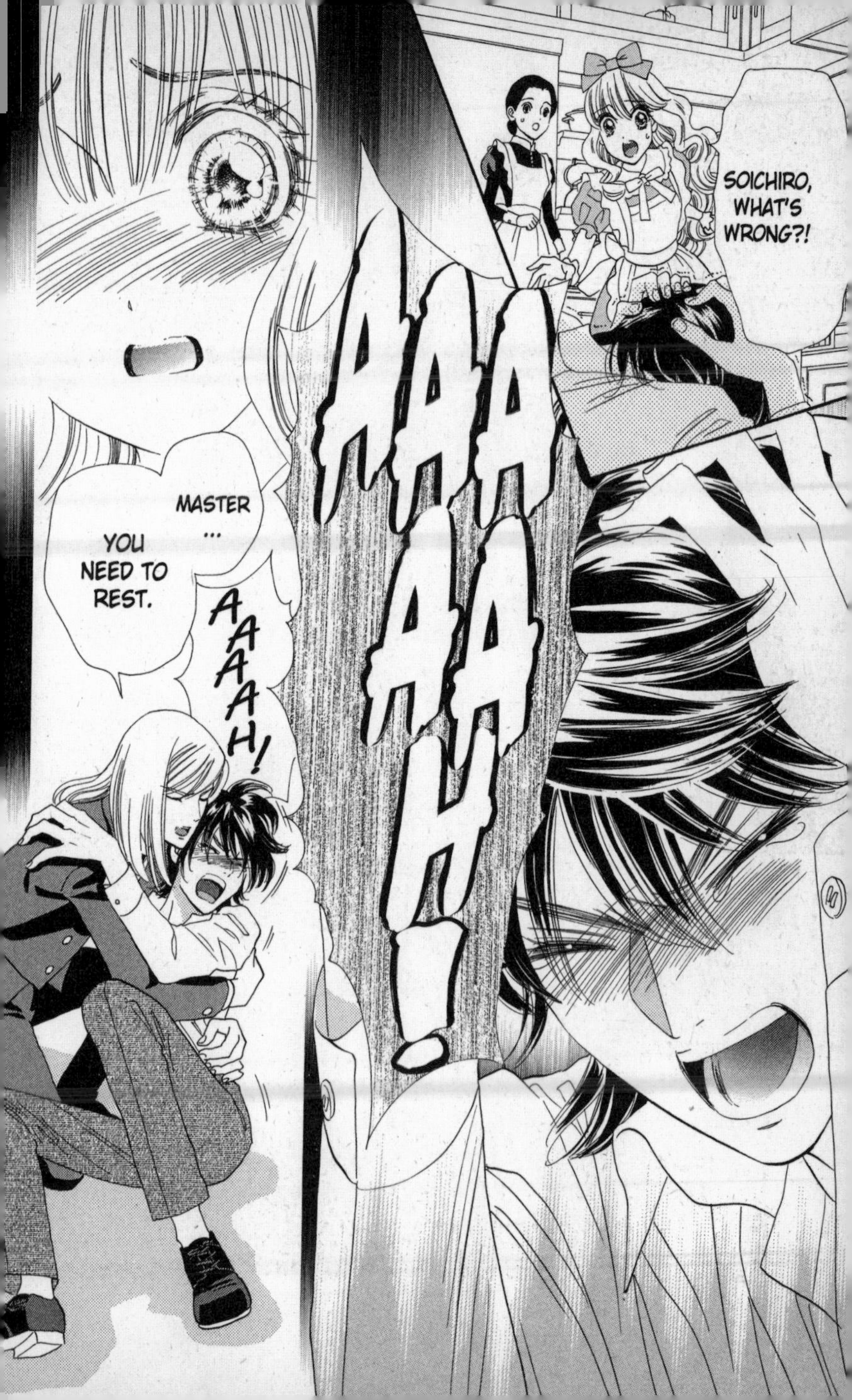
SOICHIRO, WHAT'S WRONG?!
AAAAAH!
MASTER...
YOU NEED TO REST.
AAAAH!

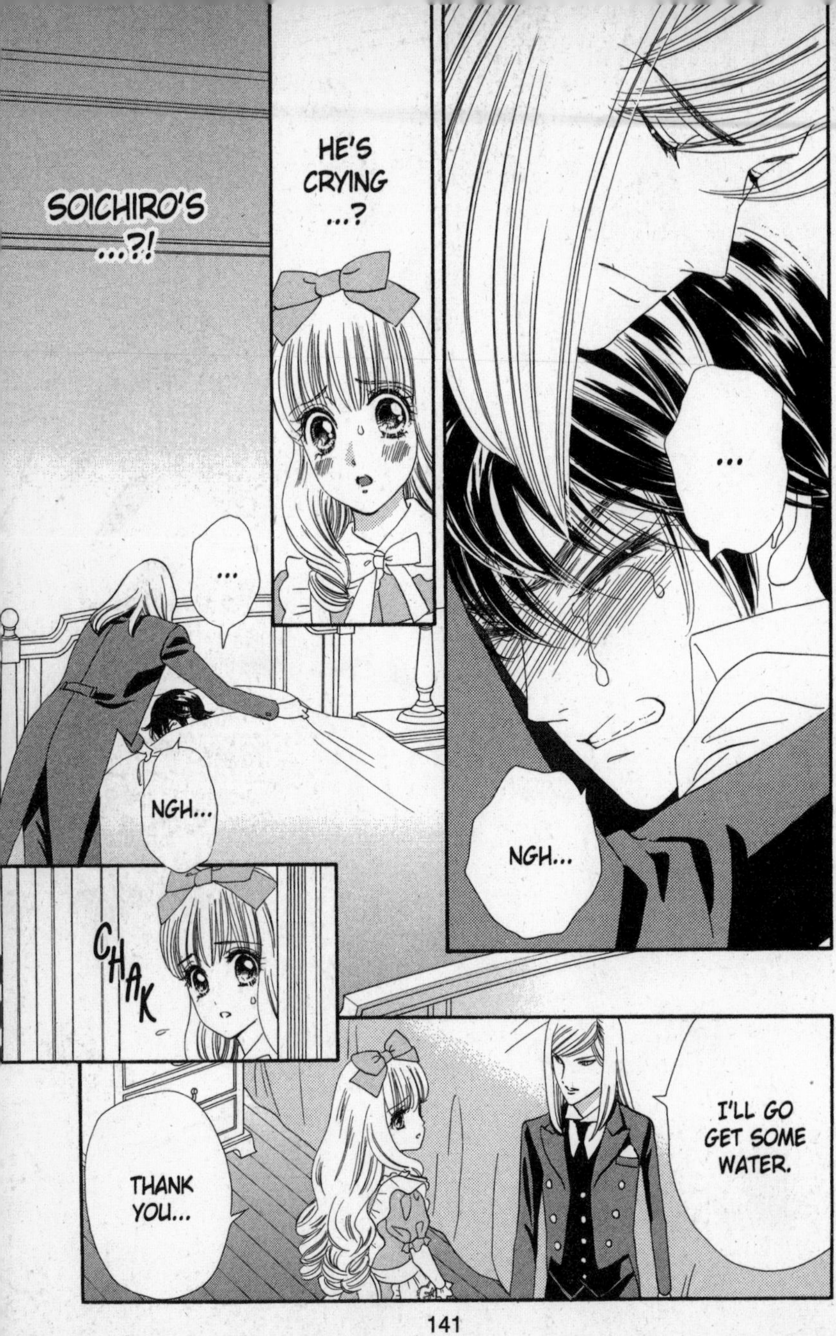
...
NGH...
HE'S CRYING ...?
SOICHIRO'S ...?!
...
NGH...
CHAK
I'LL GO GET SOME WATER.
THANK YOU...

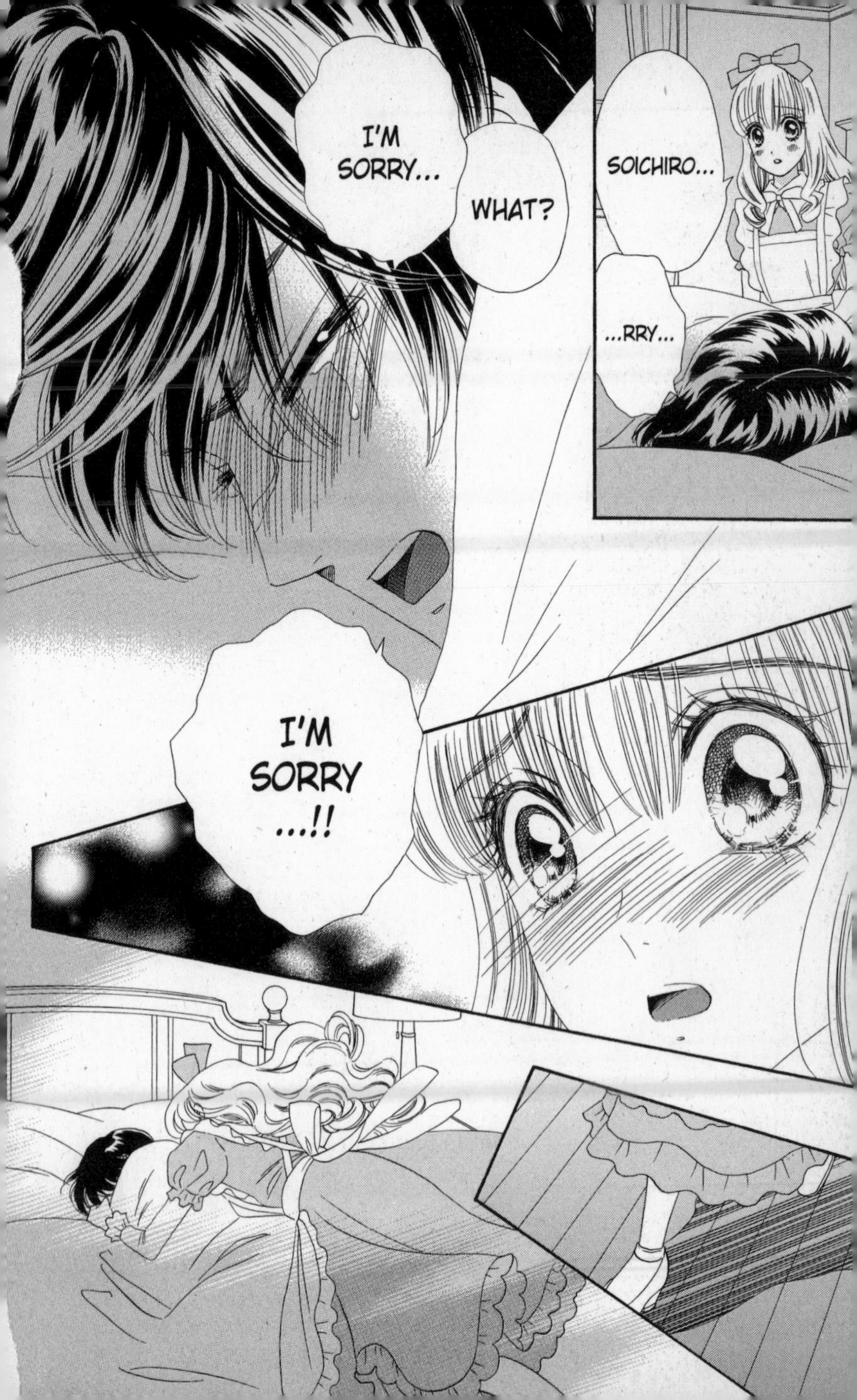
SOICHIRO...
...RRY...
WHAT?
I'M SORRY...
I'M SORRY ...!!

ZZZ...

ZZZ...

CHAK

HE'S
SWEATING
ALL OVER
...

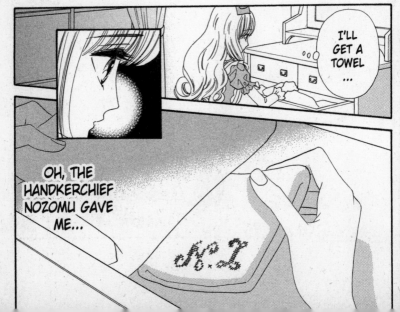

I'LL
GET A
TOWEL
...

OH, THE
HANDKERCHIEF
NOZOMU GAVE
ME...

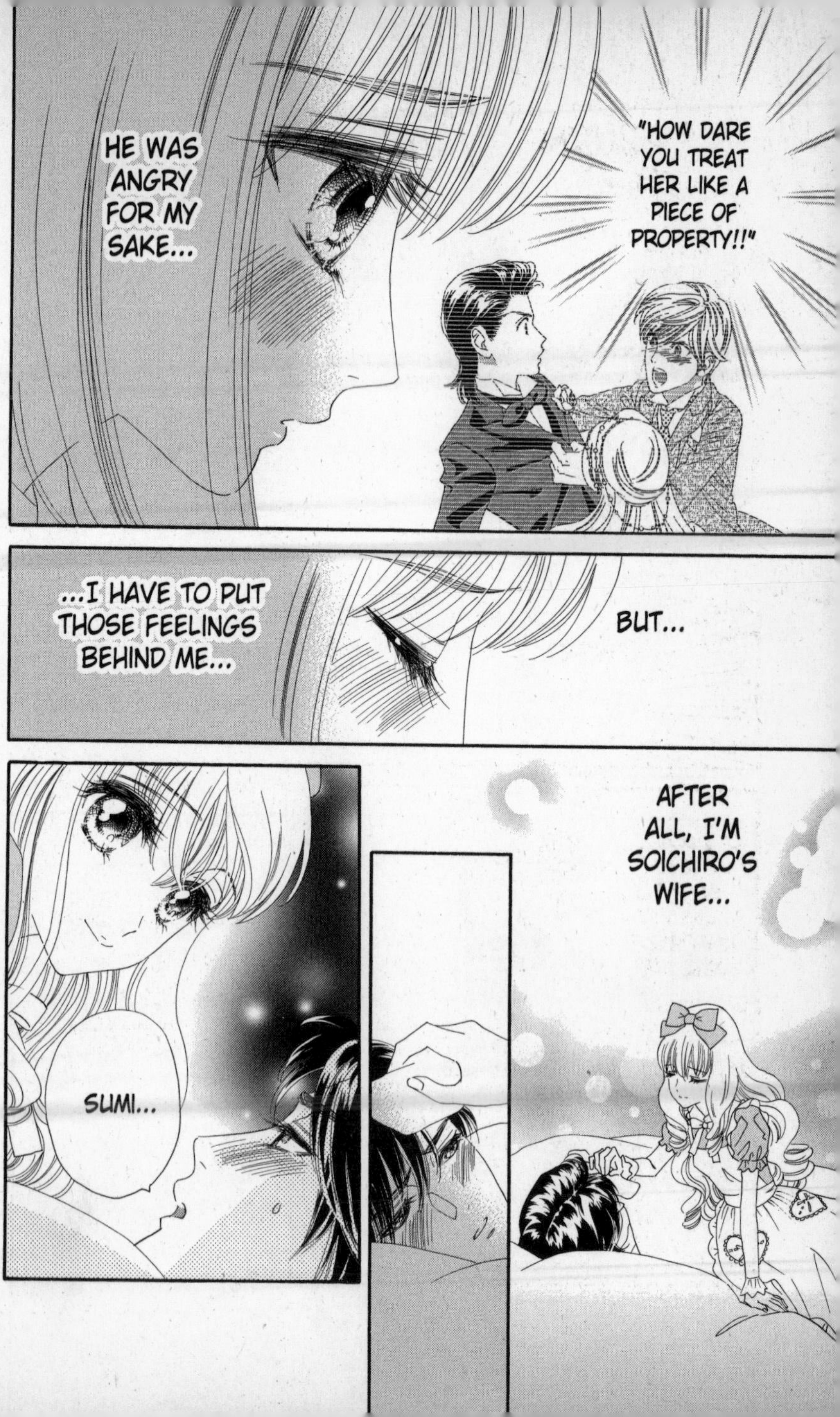
"HOW DARE YOU TREAT HER LIKE A PIECE OF PROPERTY!!"
HE WAS ANGRY FOR MY SAKE...
BUT...
...I HAVE TO PUT THOSE FEELINGS BEHIND ME...
AFTER ALL, I'M SOICHIRO'S WIFE...
SUMI...

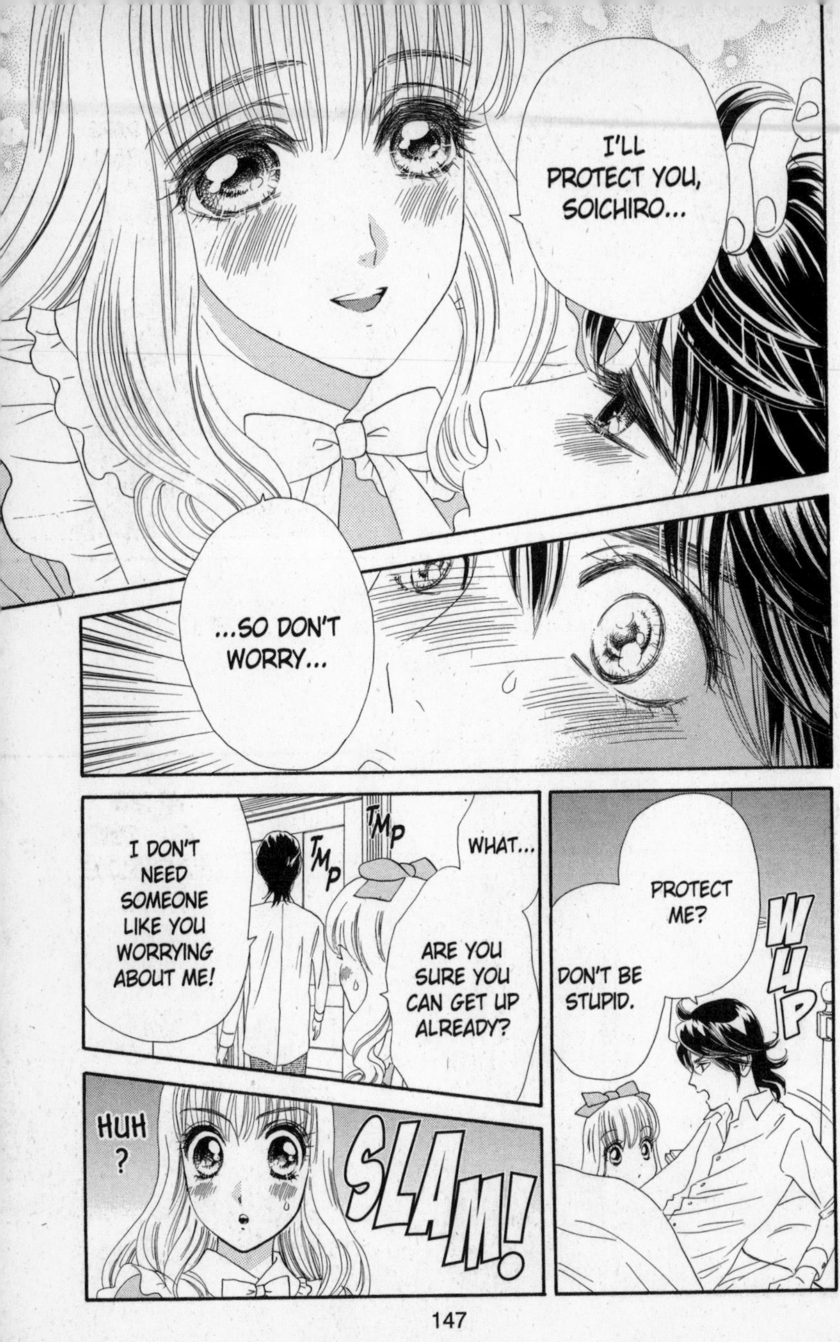
I'LL PROTECT YOU, SOICHIRO...
...SO DON'T WORRY...
PROTECT ME?
WUP
DON'T BE STUPID.
WHAT...
ARE YOU SURE YOU CAN GET UP ALREADY?
TMP
TMP
I DON'T NEED SOMEONE LIKE YOU WORRYING ABOUT ME!
SLAM!
HUH?

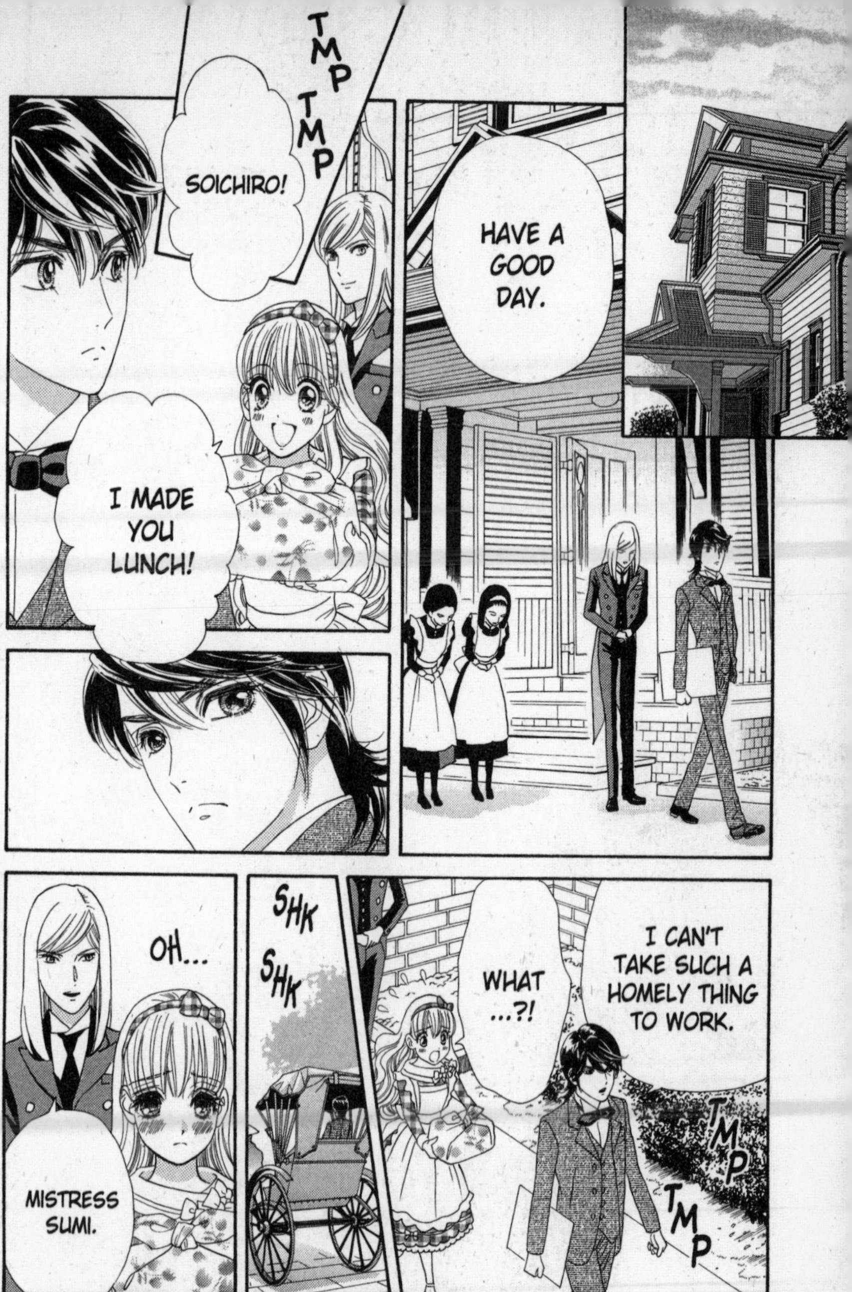
HAVE A GOOD DAY.
TMP TMP
SOICHIRO!
I MADE YOU LUNCH!
I CAN'T TAKE SUCH A HOMELY THING TO WORK.
WHAT ...?!
TMP TMP
SHK SHK
OH...
MISTRESS SUMI.

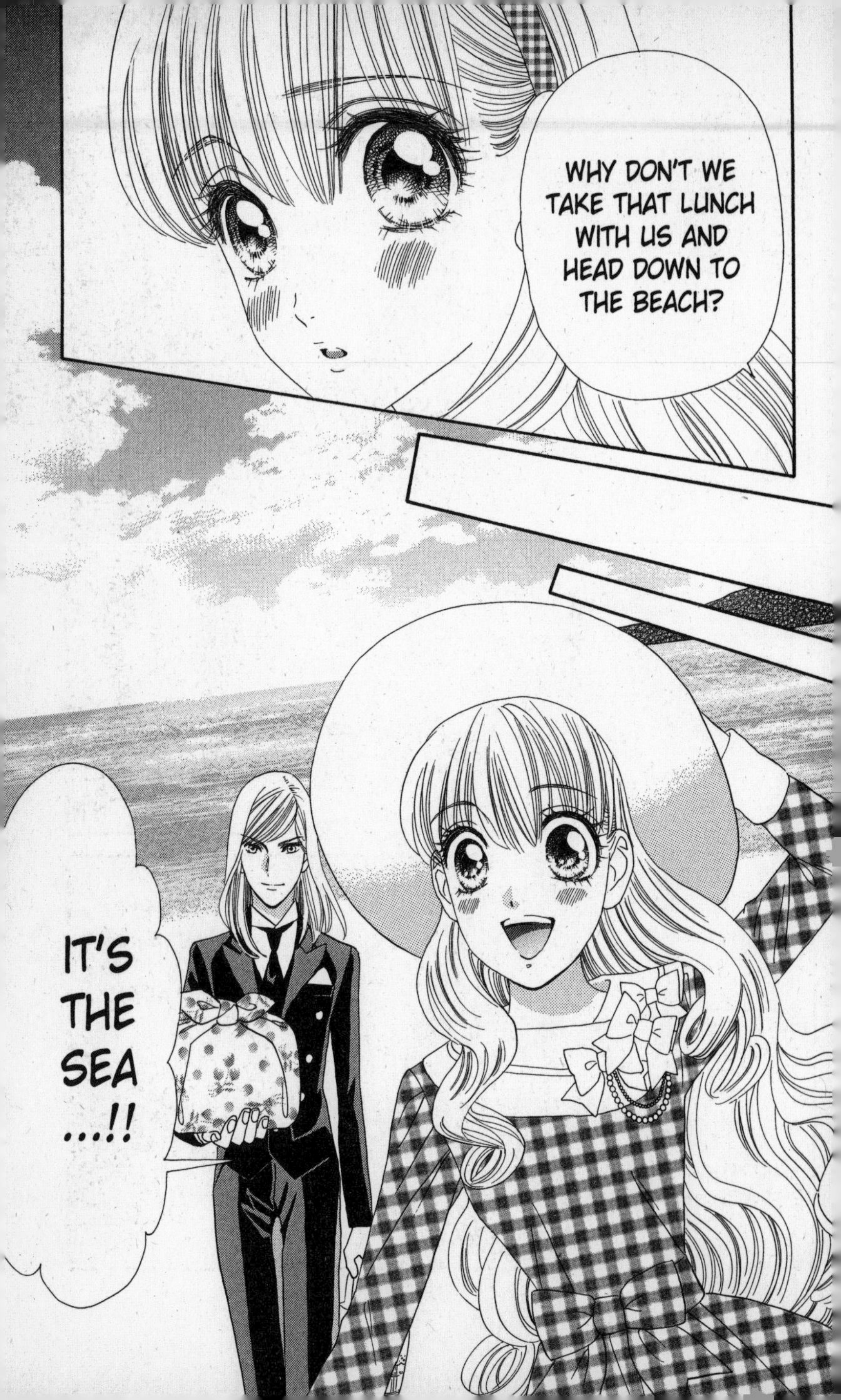
WHY DON'T WE TAKE THAT LUNCH WITH US AND HEAD DOWN TO THE BEACH?
IT'S THE SEA ...!!

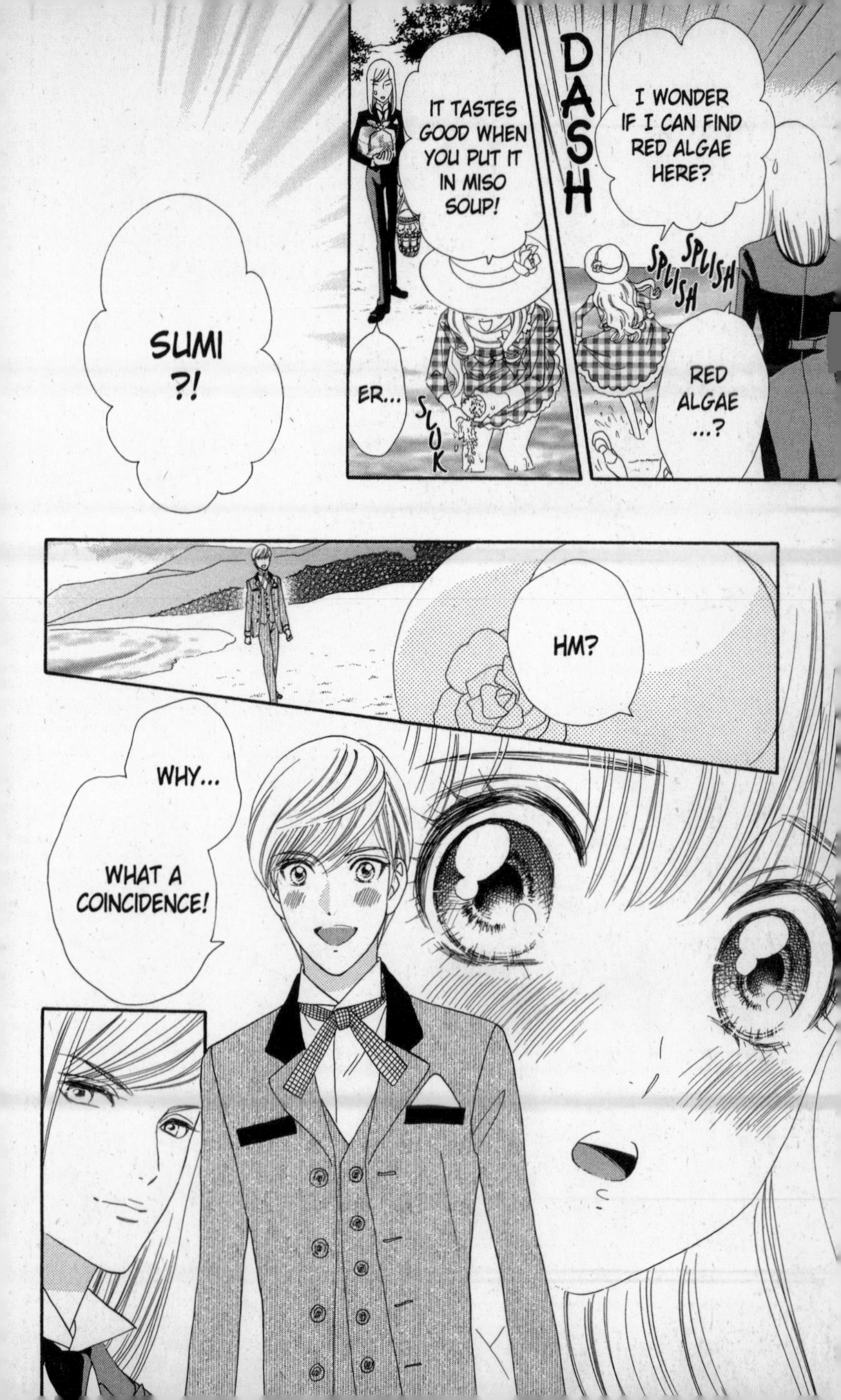
I WONDER IF I CAN FIND RED ALGAE HERE?
DASH
SPLISH SPLISH
RED ALGAE ...?
IT TASTES GOOD WHEN YOU PUT IT IN MISO SOUP!
SLUK
ER...
SUMI ?!
HM?
WHY...
WHAT A COINCIDENCE!

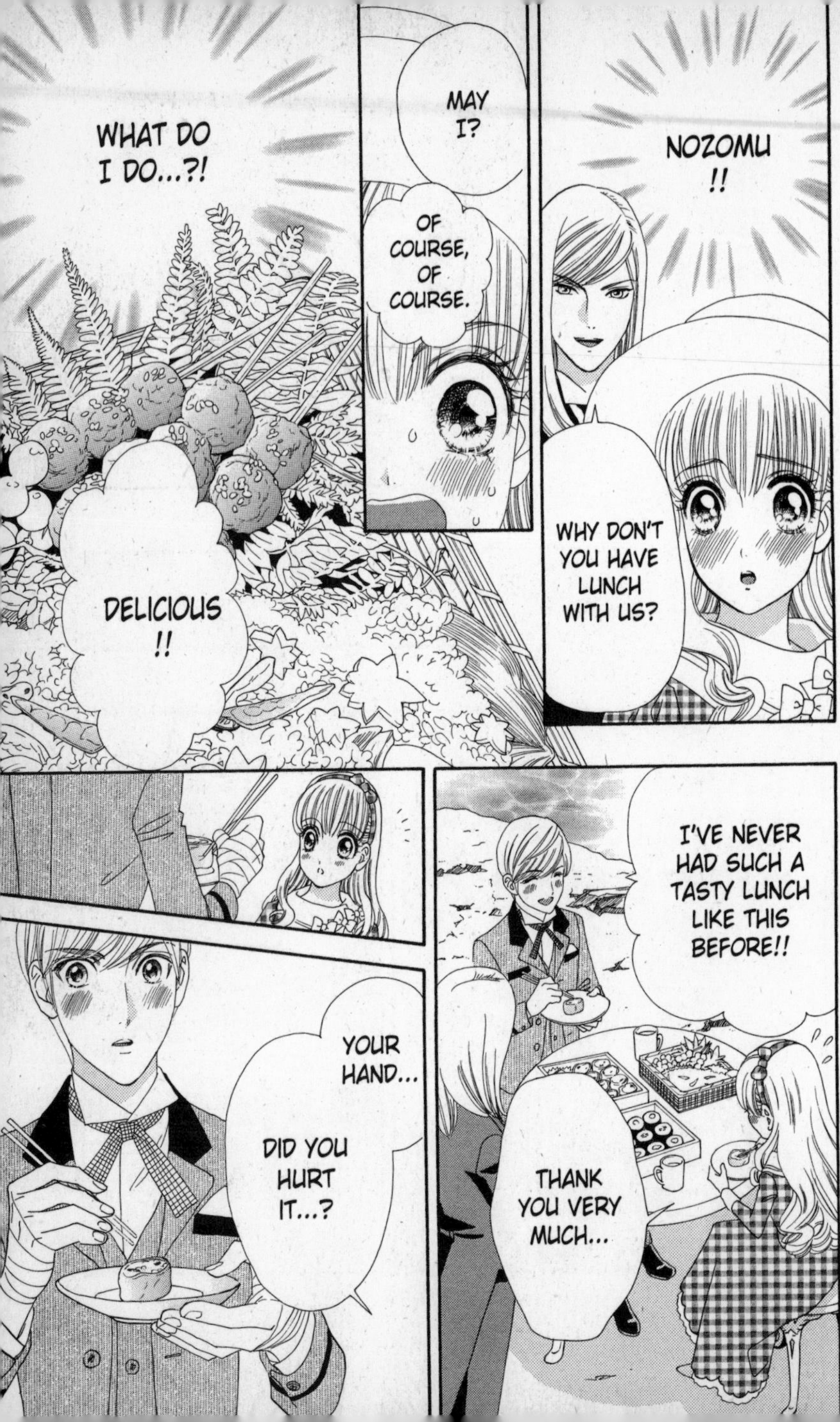
NOZOMU!!
WHY DON'T YOU HAVE LUNCH WITH US?
MAY I?
OF COURSE, OF COURSE.
WHAT DO I DO...?!
DELICIOUS!!
I'VE NEVER HAD SUCH A TASTY LUNCH LIKE THIS BEFORE!!
THANK YOU VERY MUCH...
YOUR HAND...
DID YOU HURT IT...?

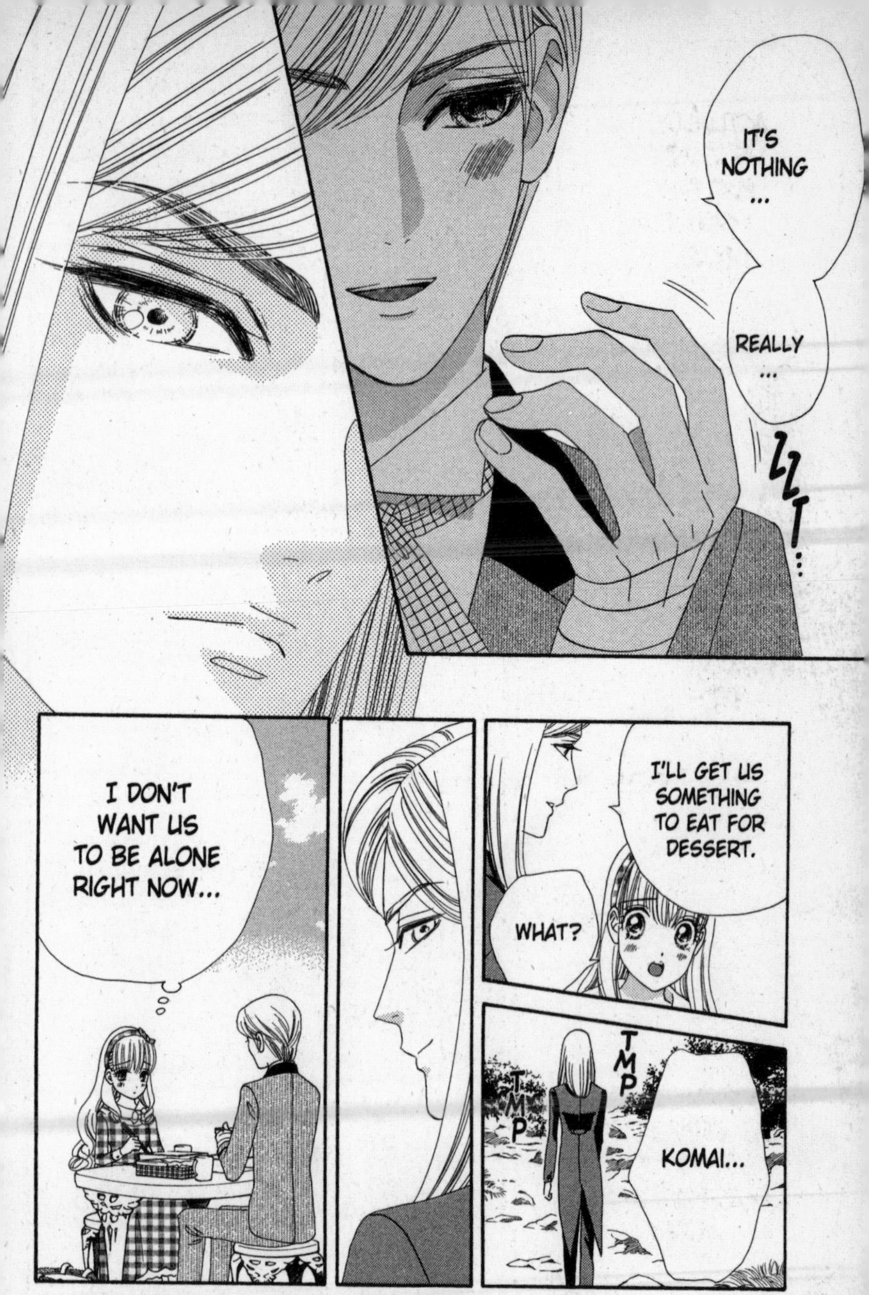
IT'S NOTHING ...
REALLY ...
ZZT...
I'LL GET US SOMETHING TO EAT FOR DESSERT.
WHAT?
TMP
TMP
KOMAI...
I DON'T WANT US TO BE ALONE RIGHT NOW...

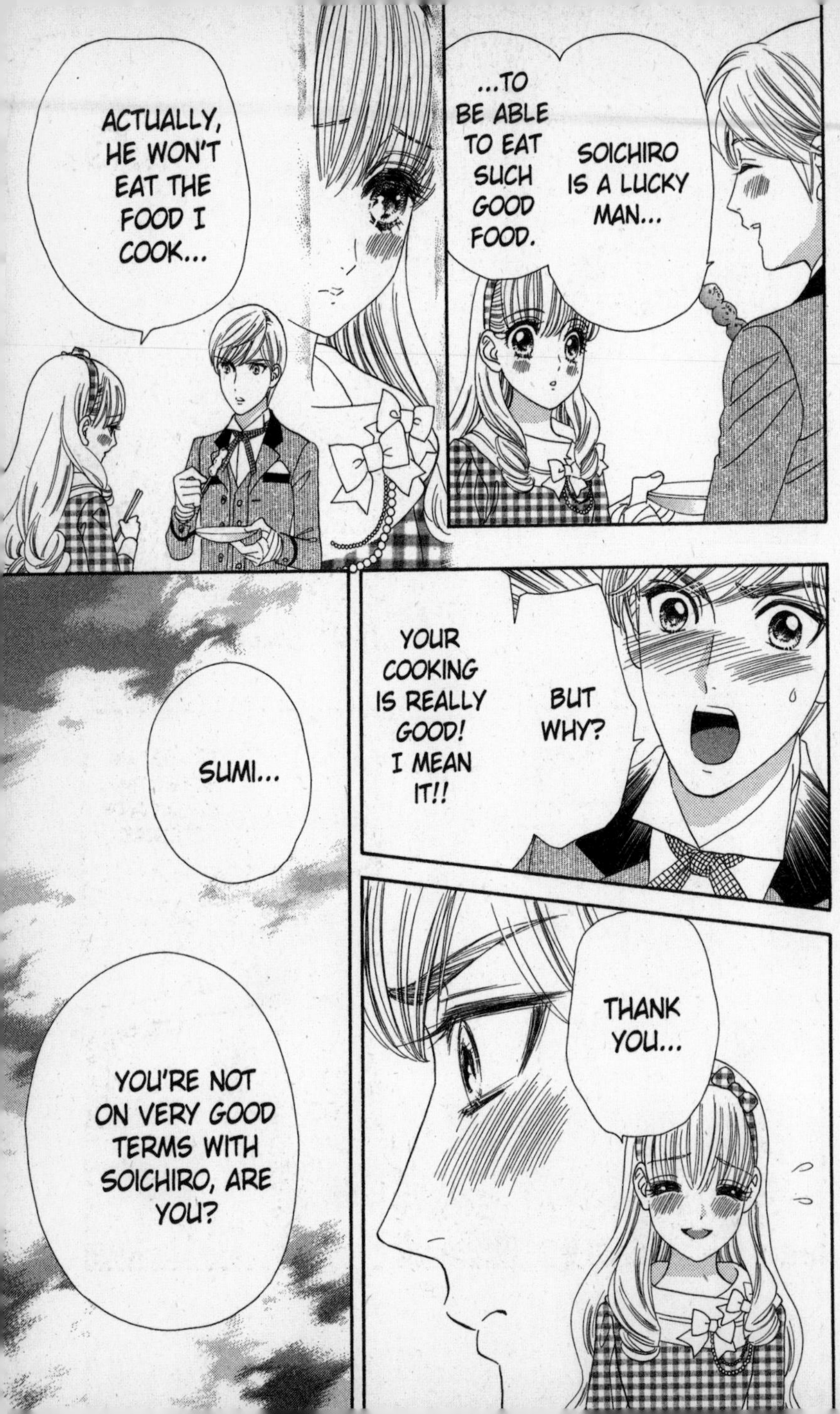
SOICHIRO IS A LUCKY MAN...
...TO BE ABLE TO EAT SUCH GOOD FOOD.
ACTUALLY, HE WON'T EAT THE FOOD I COOK...
BUT WHY?
YOUR COOKING IS REALLY GOOD! I MEAN IT!!
THANK YOU...
SUMI...
YOU'RE NOT ON VERY GOOD TERMS WITH SOICHIRO, ARE YOU?

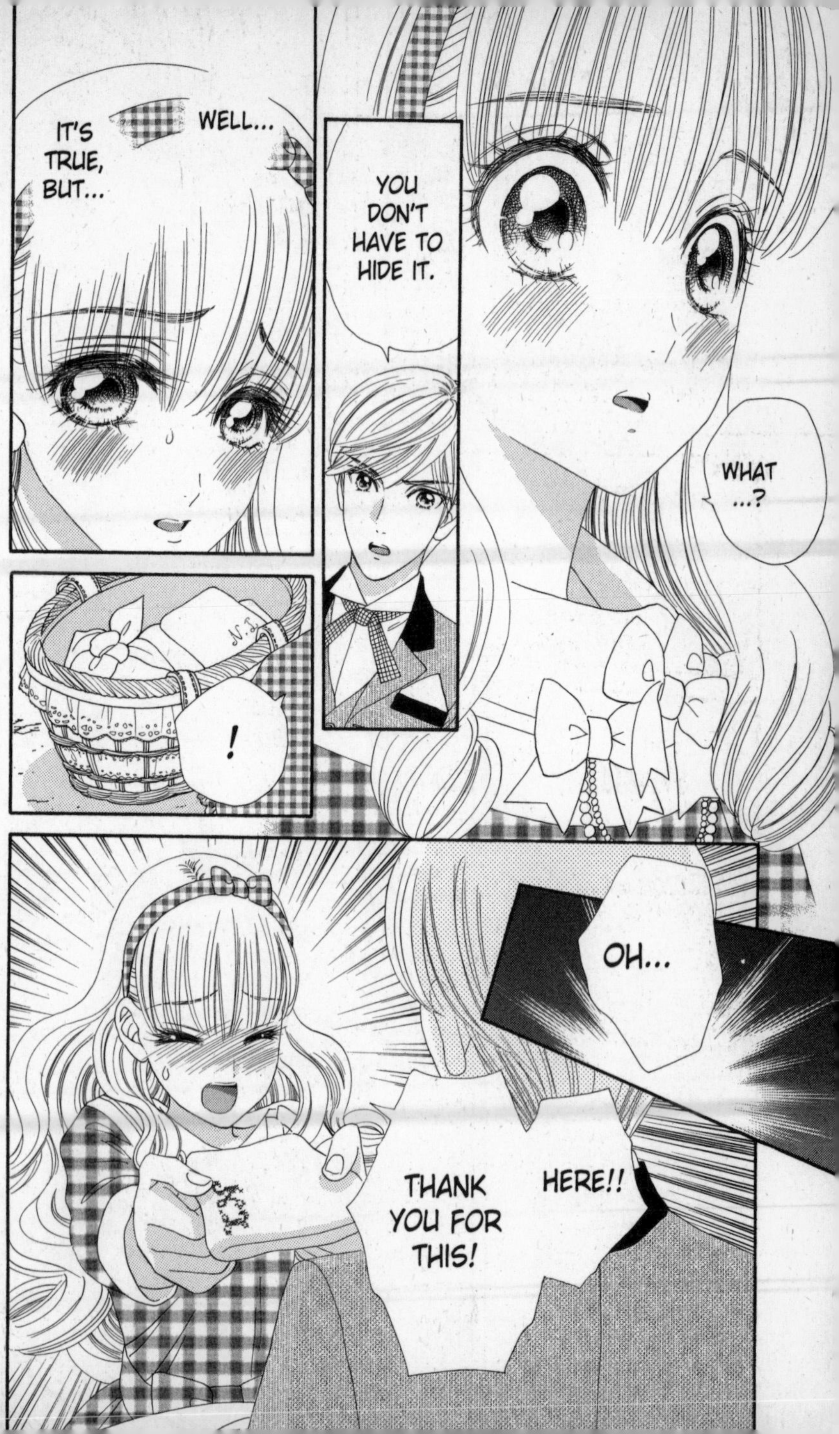
WHAT ...?
YOU DON'T HAVE TO HIDE IT.
WELL...
IT'S TRUE, BUT...
!
OH...
HERE!!
THANK YOU FOR THIS!

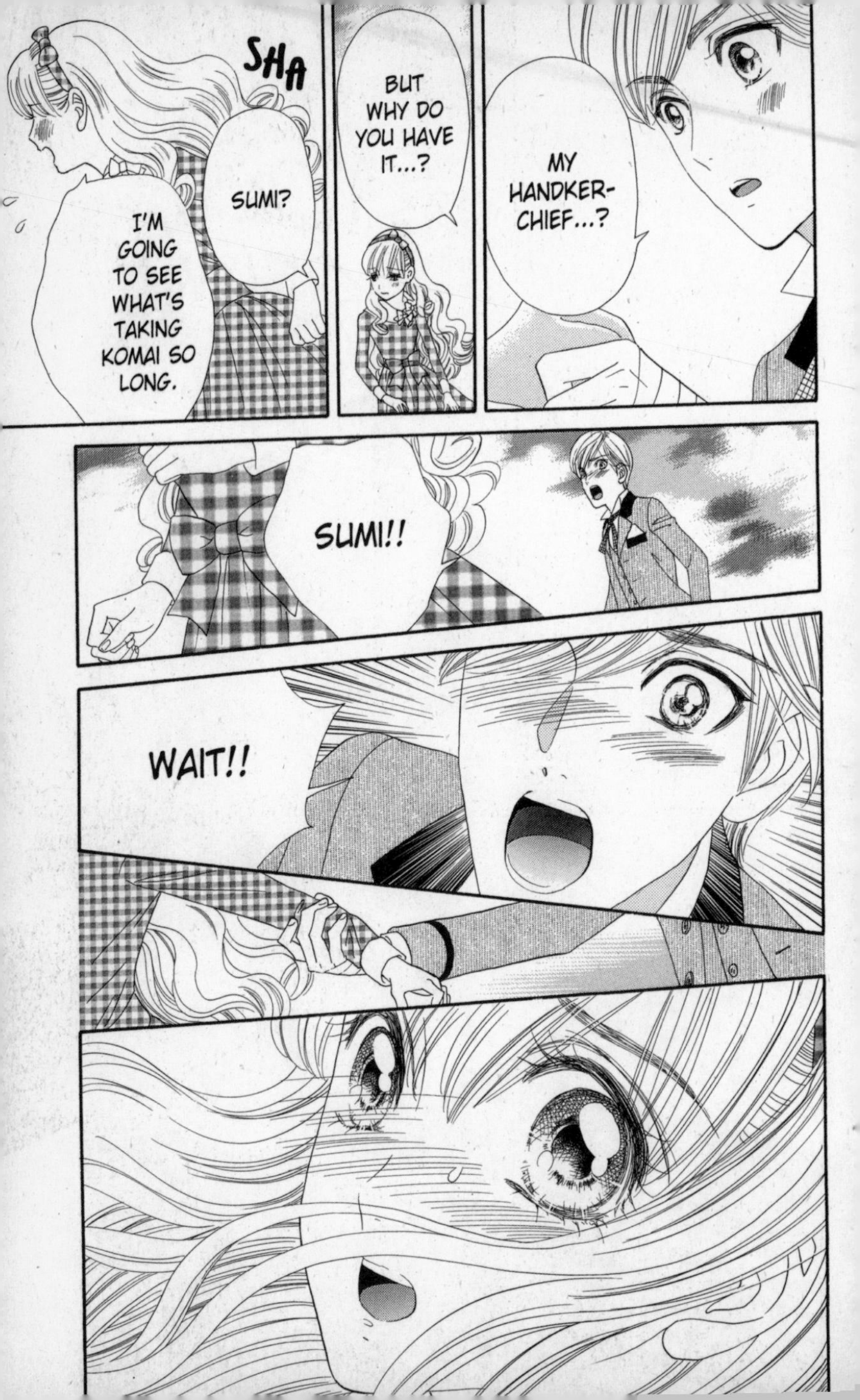
MY HANDKER-CHIEF...?
BUT WHY DO YOU HAVE IT...?
SHA
SUMI?
I'M GOING TO SEE WHAT'S TAKING KOMAI SO LONG.
SUMI!!
WAIT!!

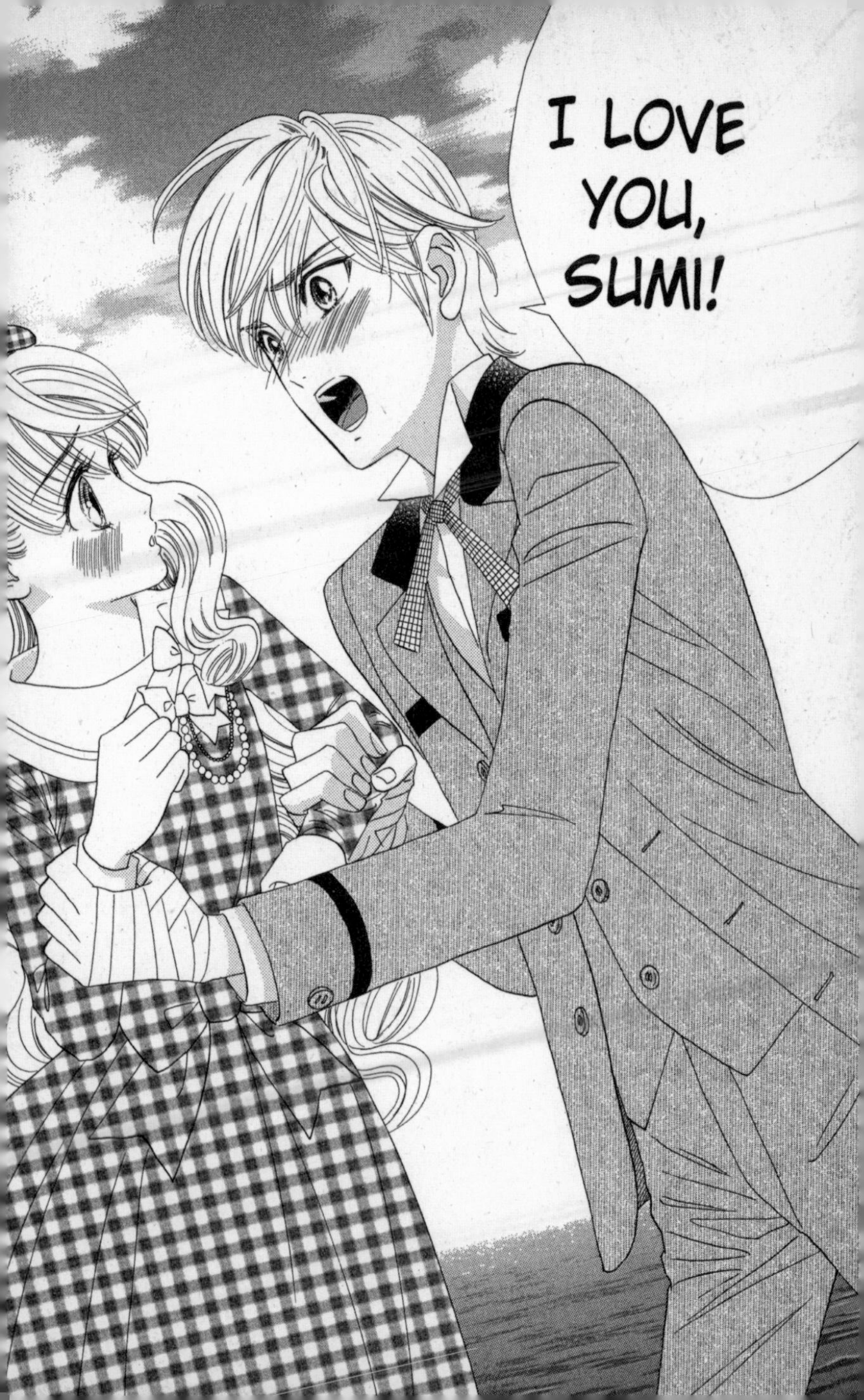
I LOVE YOU, SUMI!

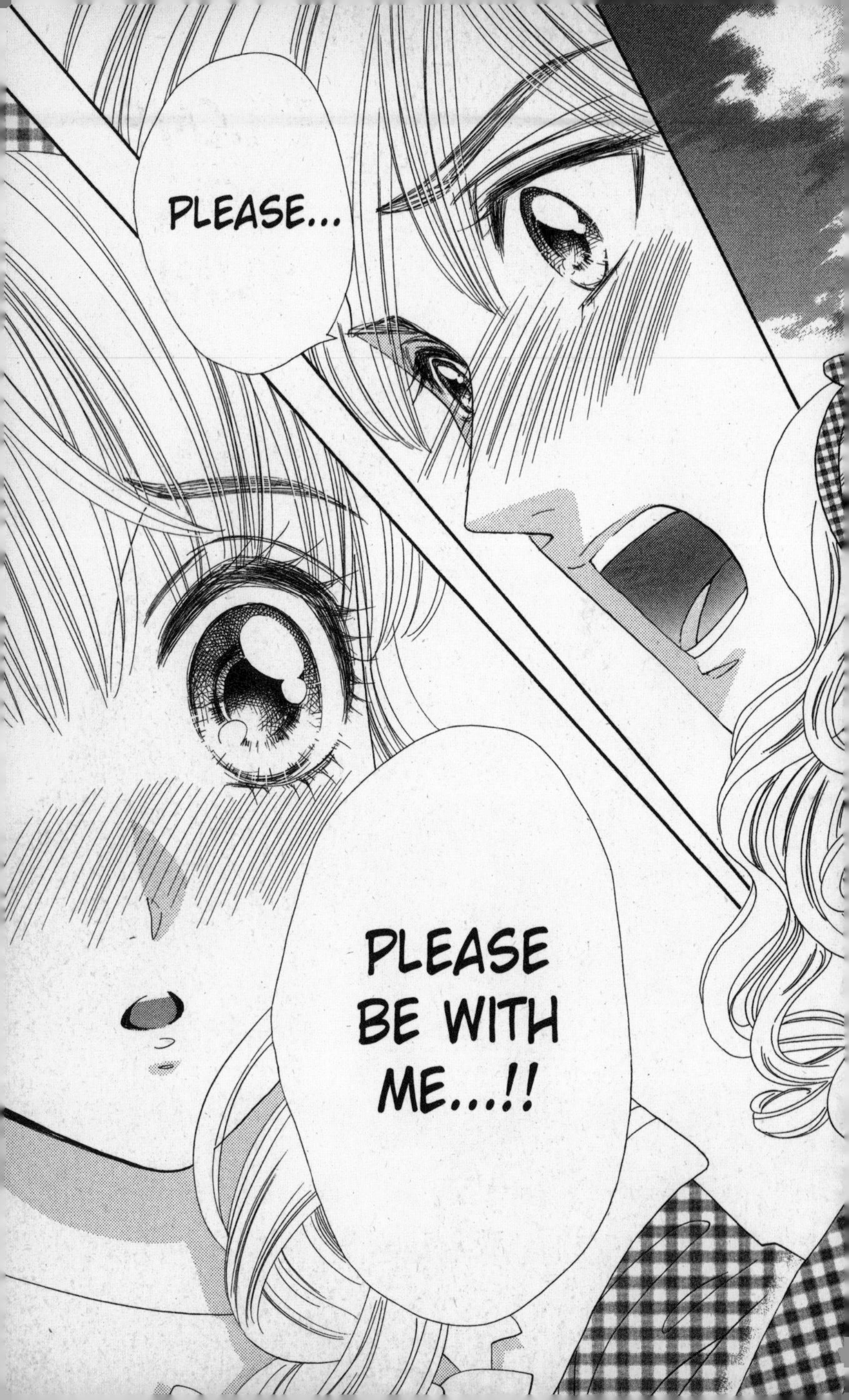
PLEASE...
PLEASE BE WITH ME...!!

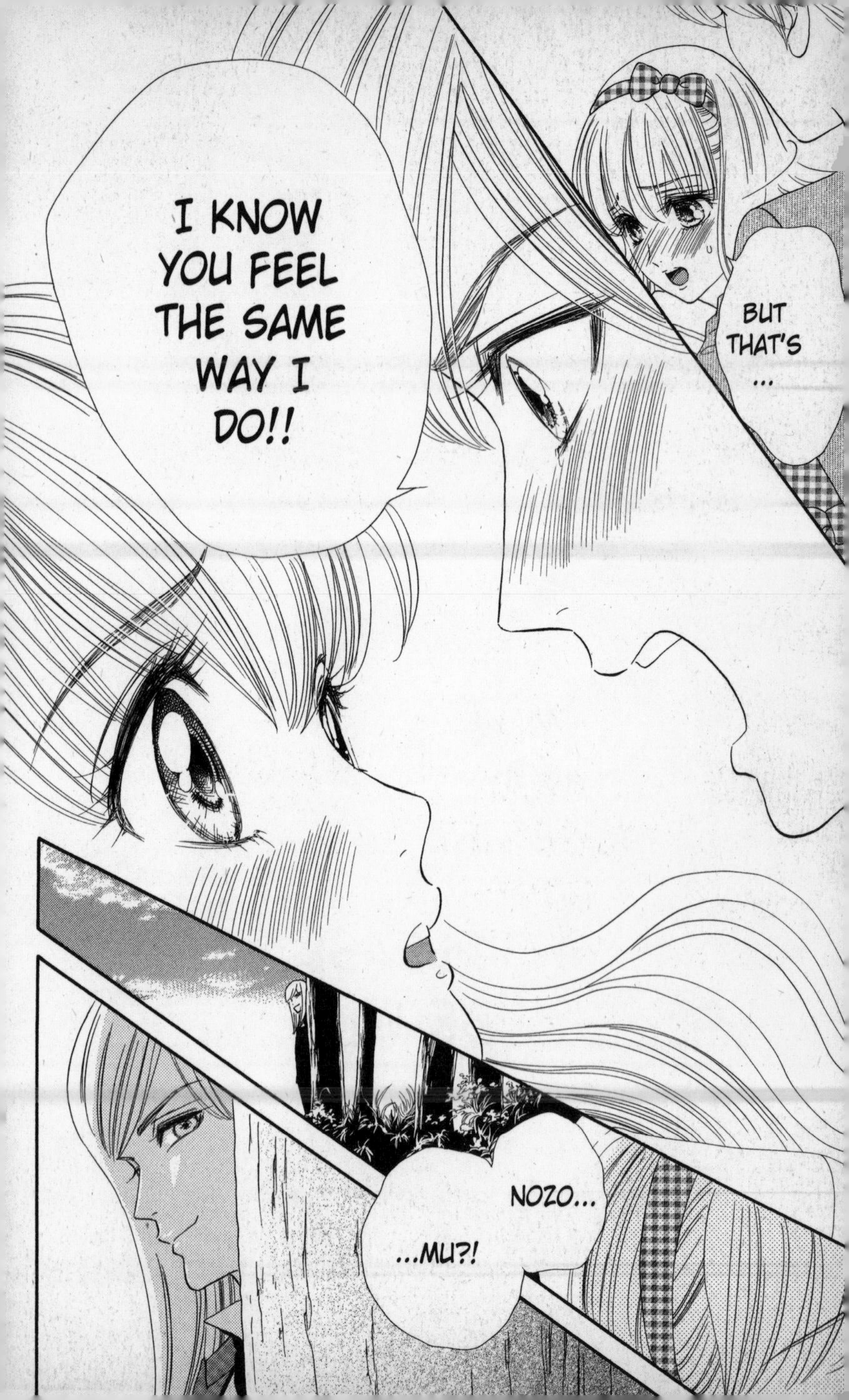
BUT THAT'S ...
I KNOW YOU FEEL THE SAME WAY I DO!!
NOZO...
...MU?!

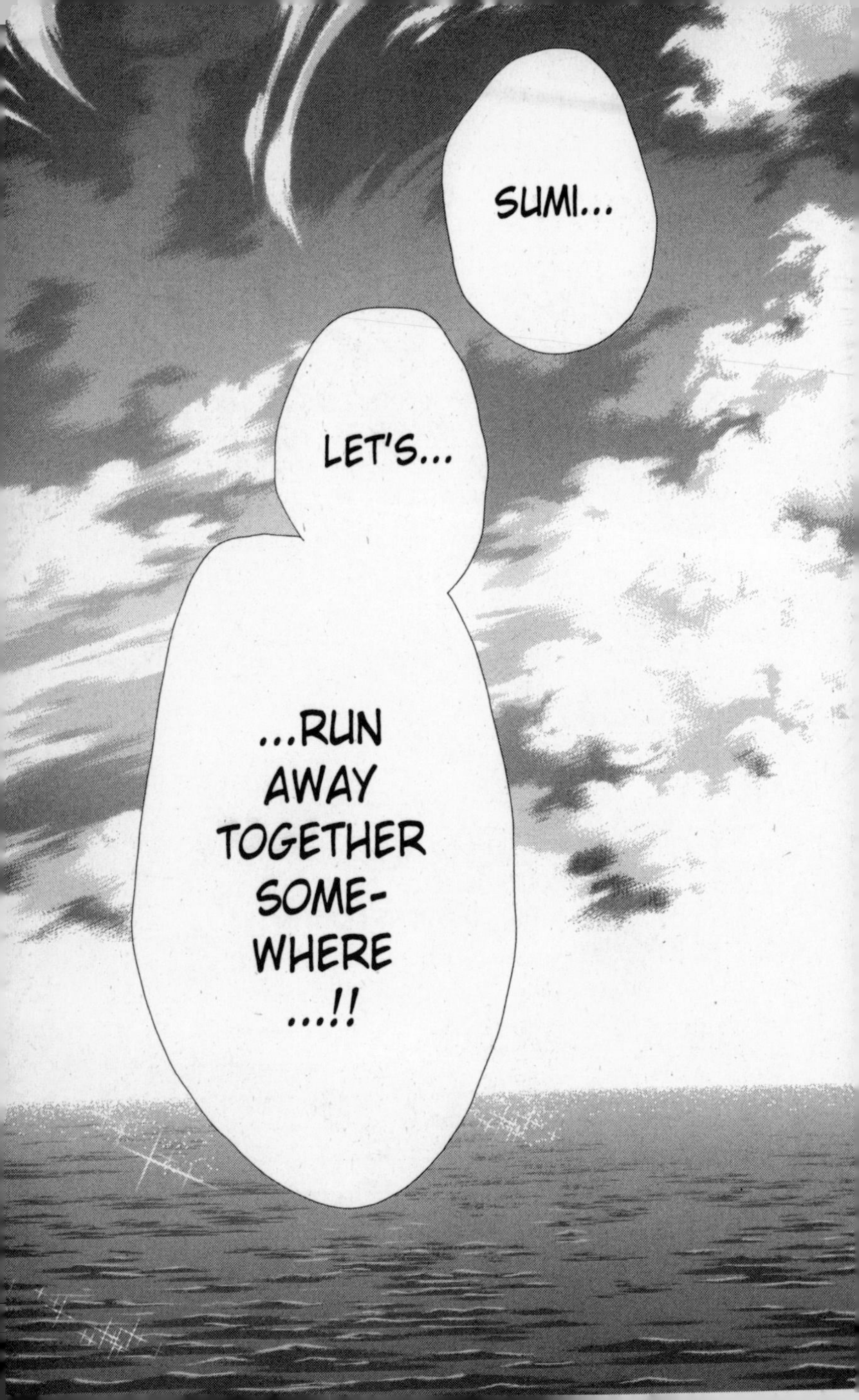
SUMI...
LET'S...
...RUN AWAY TOGETHER SOME-WHERE ...!!

ONLY A LITTLE MORE TO GO UNTIL THE END OF VOLUME 2.

THE STORY IN THIS VOLUME HAS TAKEN SUCH AN
ABRUPT TURN THAT IT'S KIND OF SHOCKING.
EVEN I'M LOOKING FORWARD TO HOW VOLUME 3 WILL
TURN OUT. IF YOU HAVE ANY REMARKS OR REQUESTS,
PLEASE SEND THEM TO THE FOLLOWING:

RINKO UEDA
C/O STEPPING ON ROSES EDITOR
VIZ MEDIA
P.O. BOX 77010
SAN FRANCISCO, CA 94107

READING THE REMARKS OF MY READERS IS A BIG
SOURCE OF ENCOURAGEMENT FOR ME. I'LL TRY
TO ANSWER ALL THE QUESTIONS I CAN IN THE
GRAPHIC NOVEL.

SEE YOU ALL IN VOLUME 3!

Rinko ☺ Ueda

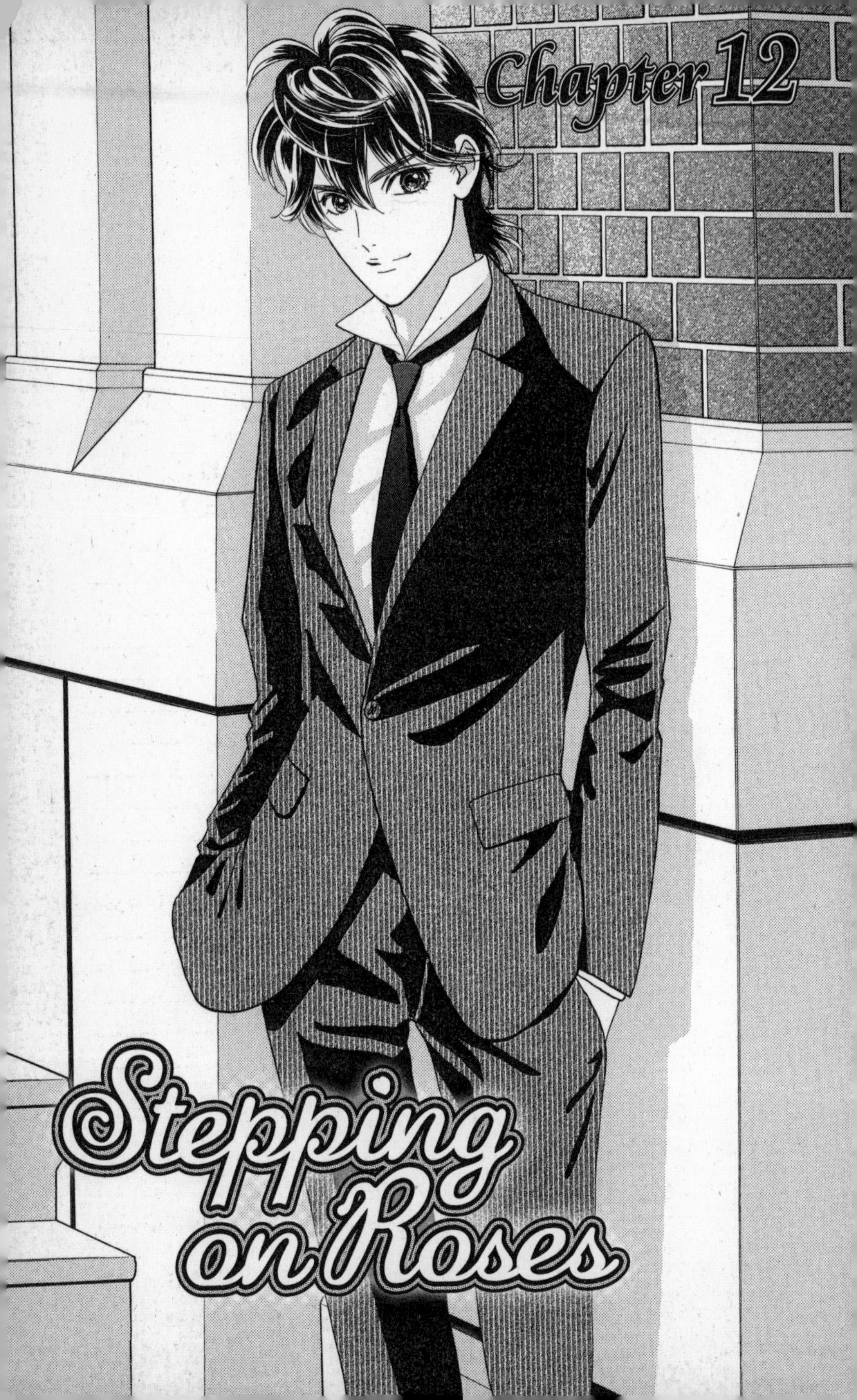
Chapter 12
Stepping on Roses

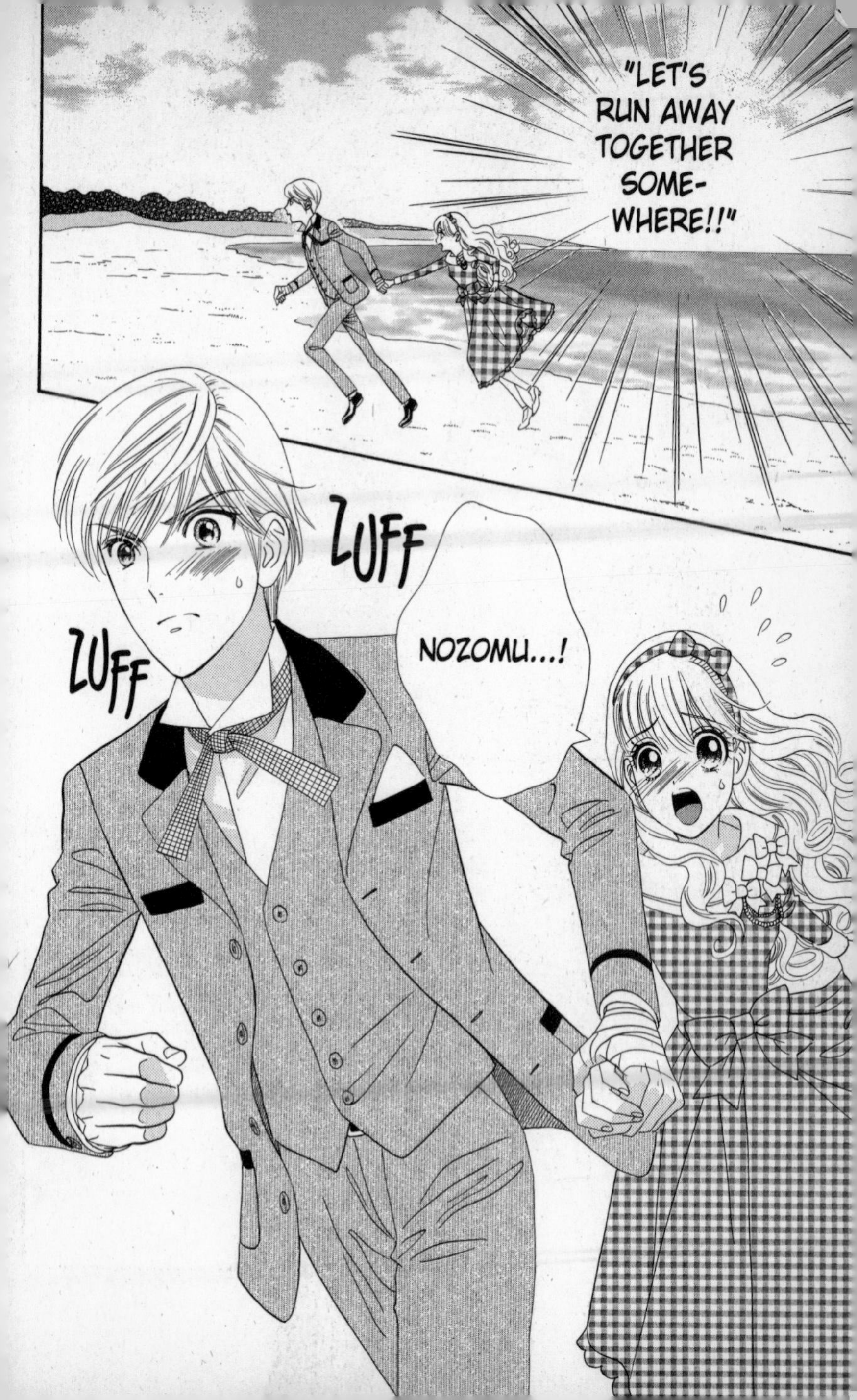
"LET'S RUN AWAY TOGETHER SOME-WHERE!!"
NOZOMU...!
ZUFF
ZUFF

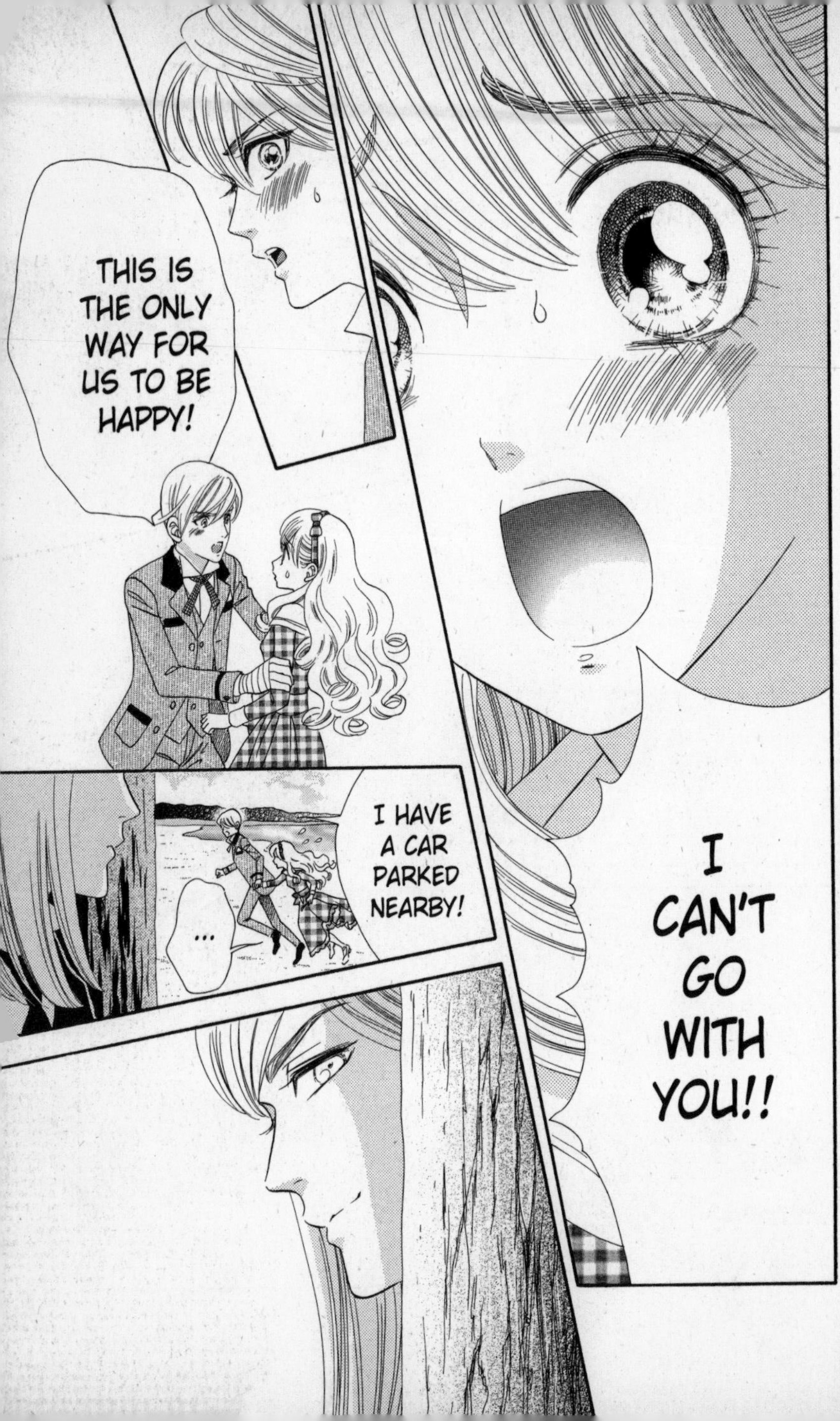
I CAN'T GO WITH YOU!!
THIS IS THE ONLY WAY FOR US TO BE HAPPY!
I HAVE A CAR PARKED NEARBY!
...

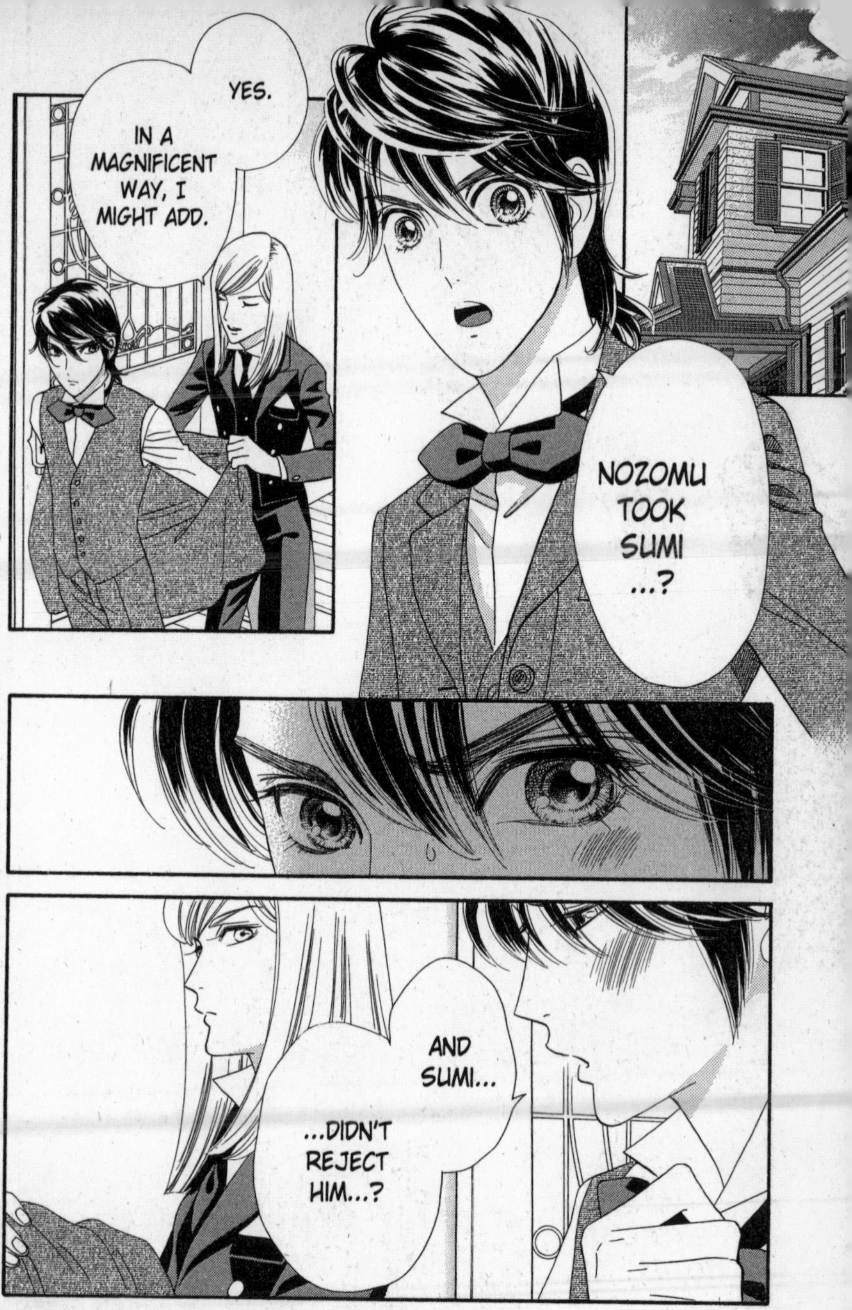
NOZOMU TOOK SUMI ...?
YES.
IN A MAGNIFICENT WAY, I MIGHT ADD.
AND SUMI...
...DIDN'T REJECT HIM...?

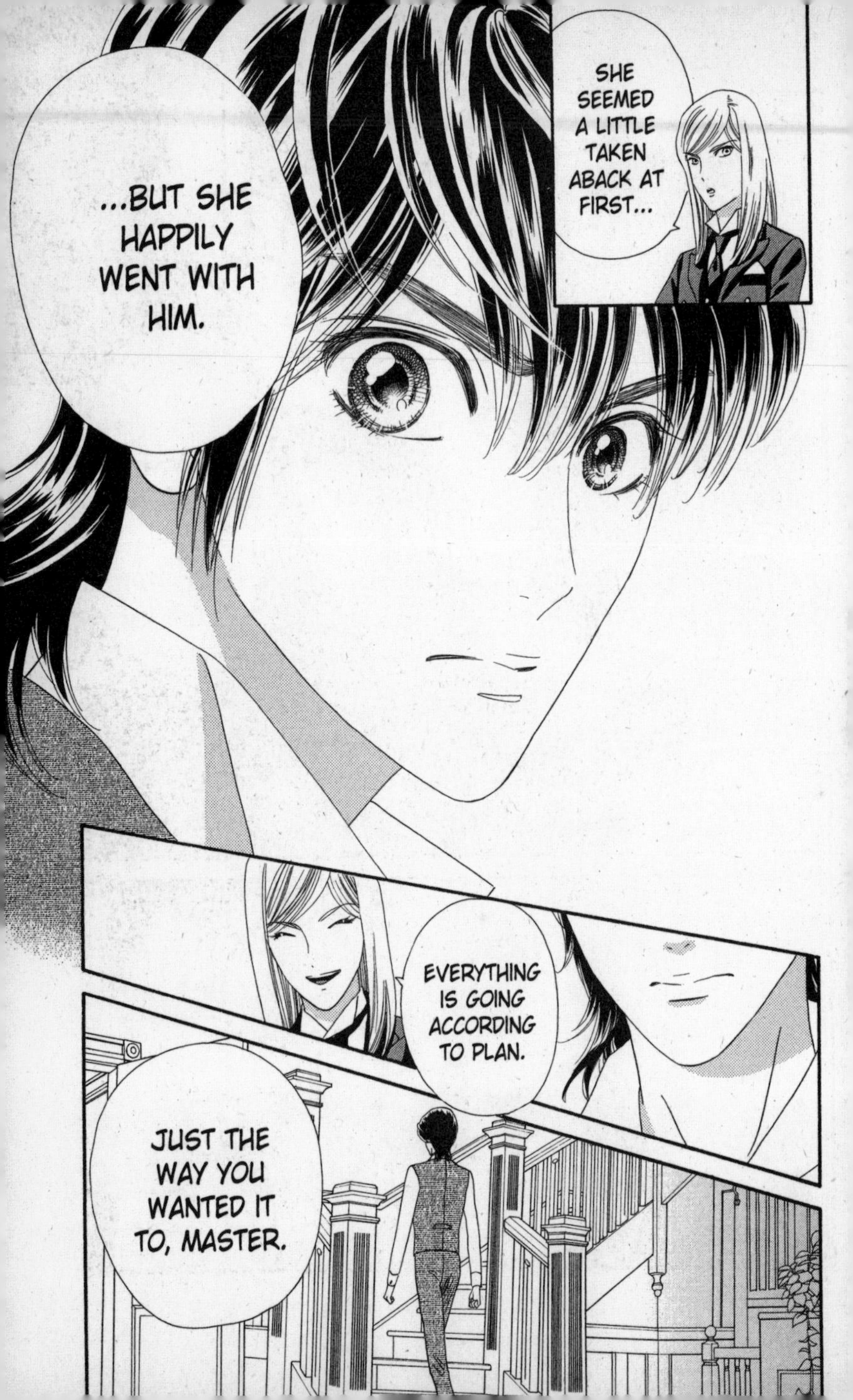
SHE SEEMED A LITTLE TAKEN ABACK AT FIRST...
...BUT SHE HAPPILY WENT WITH HIM.
EVERYTHING IS GOING ACCORDING TO PLAN.
JUST THE WAY YOU WANTED IT TO, MASTER.

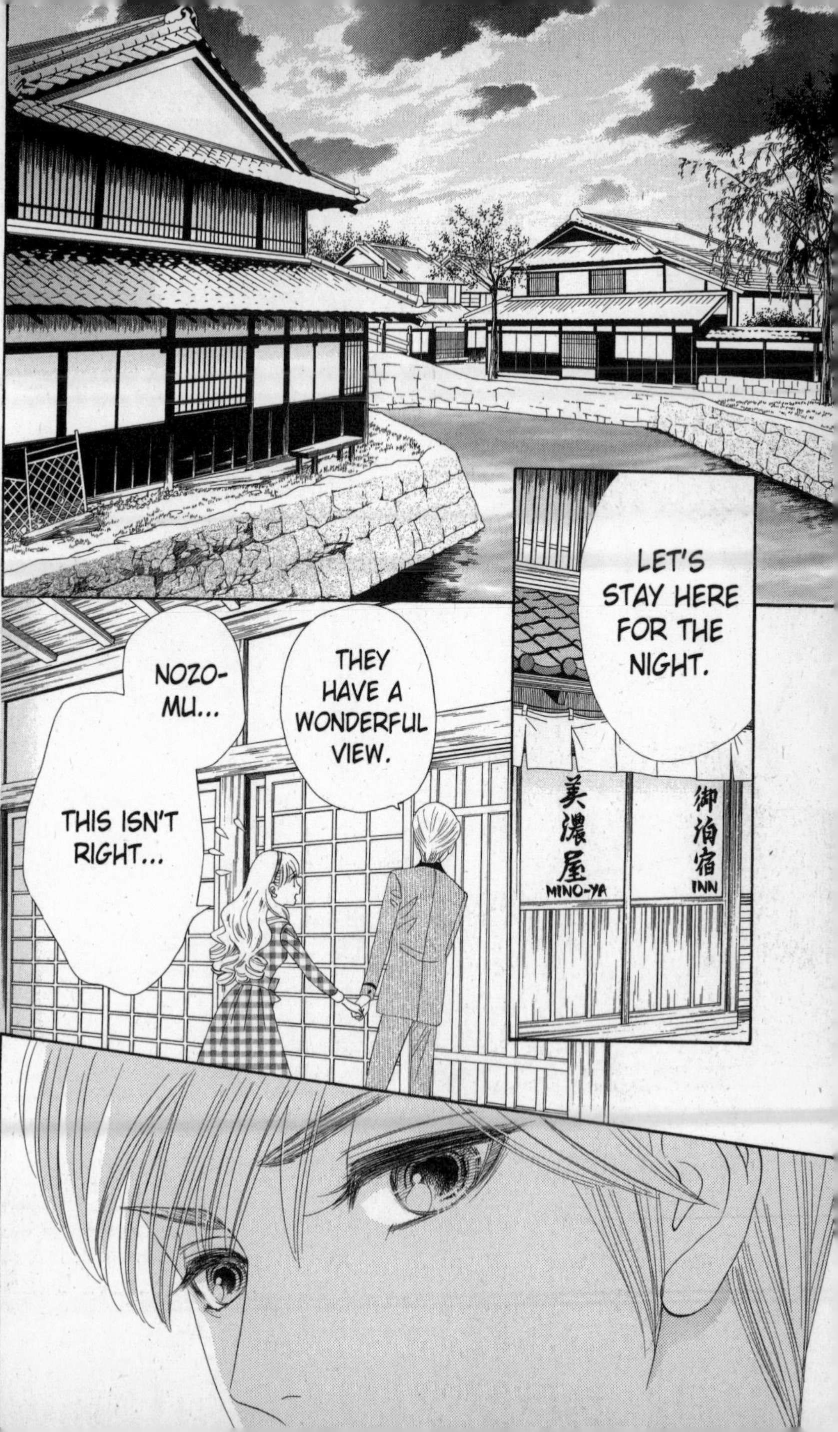
LET'S STAY HERE FOR THE NIGHT.
御泊宿
INN
美濃屋
MINO-YA
THEY HAVE A WONDERFUL VIEW.
NOZO-MU...
THIS ISN'T RIGHT...

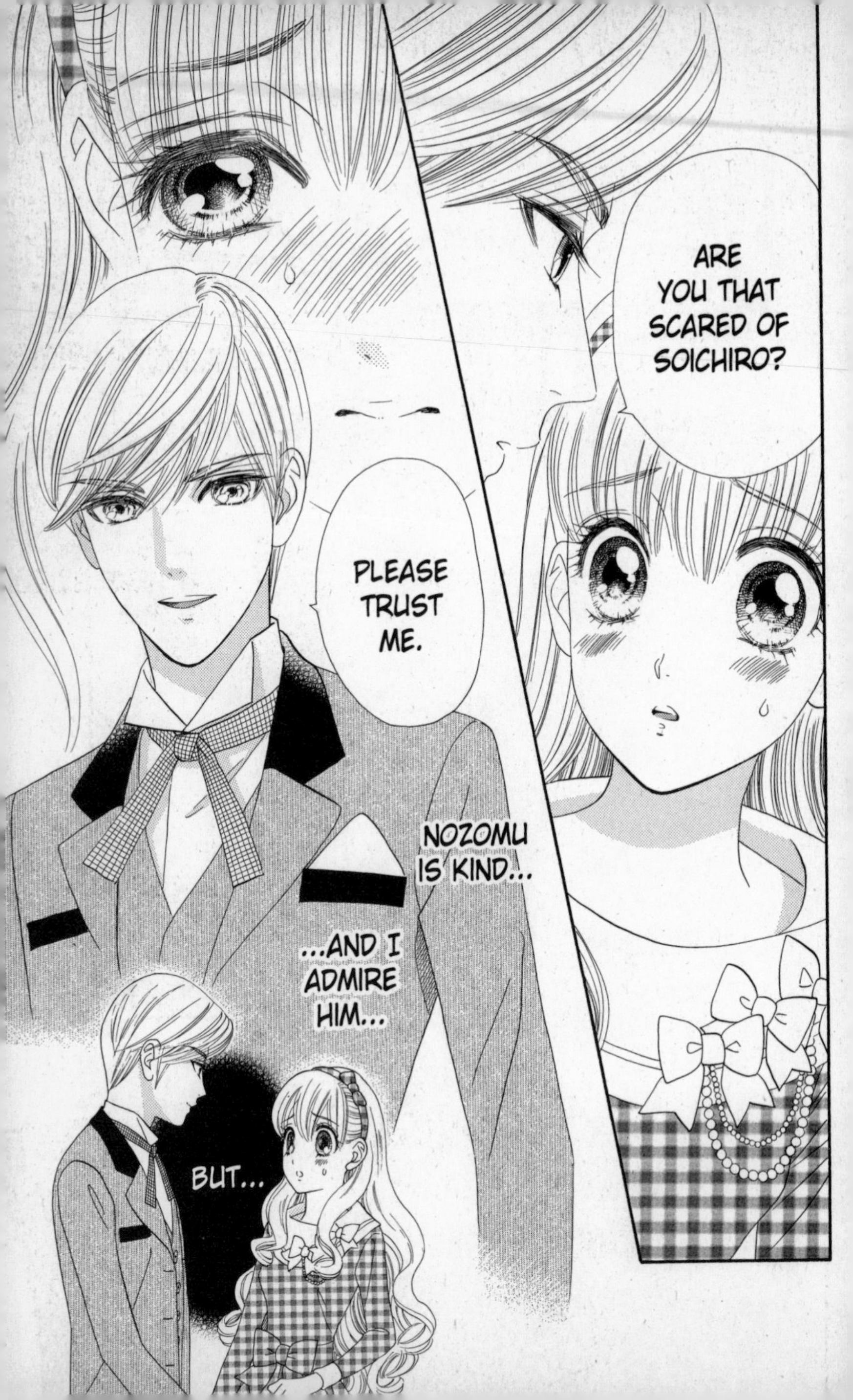
ARE YOU THAT SCARED OF SOICHIRO?
PLEASE TRUST ME.
NOZOMU IS KIND...
...AND I ADMIRE HIM...
BUT...

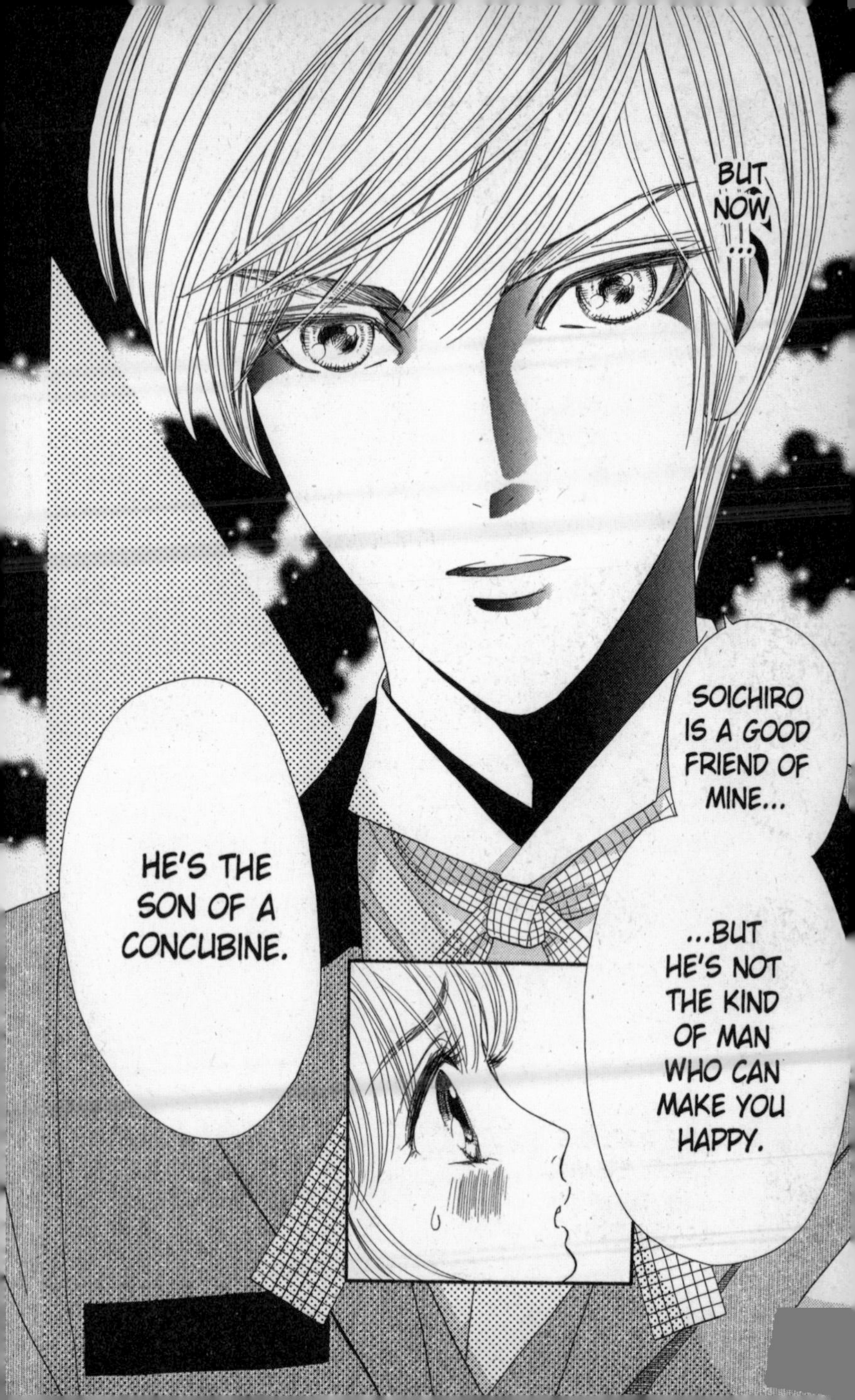
BUT NOW...
SOICHIRO IS A GOOD FRIEND OF MINE...
...BUT HE'S NOT THE KIND OF MAN WHO CAN MAKE YOU HAPPY.
HE'S THE SON OF A CONCUBINE.

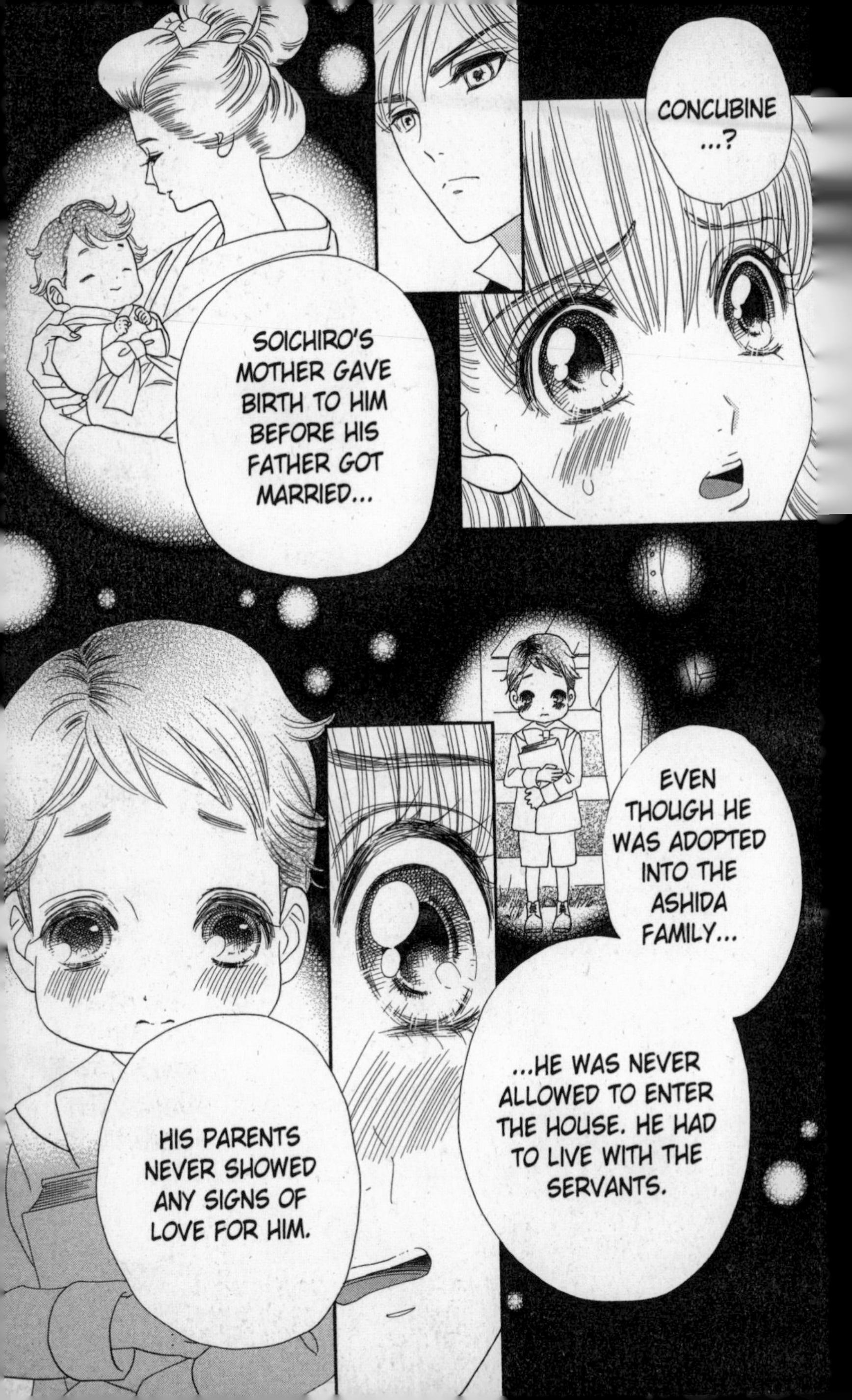
CONCUBINE ...?
SOICHIRO'S MOTHER GAVE BIRTH TO HIM BEFORE HIS FATHER GOT MARRIED...
EVEN THOUGH HE WAS ADOPTED INTO THE ASHIDA FAMILY...
...HE WAS NEVER ALLOWED TO ENTER THE HOUSE. HE HAD TO LIVE WITH THE SERVANTS.
HIS PARENTS NEVER SHOWED ANY SIGNS OF LOVE FOR HIM.

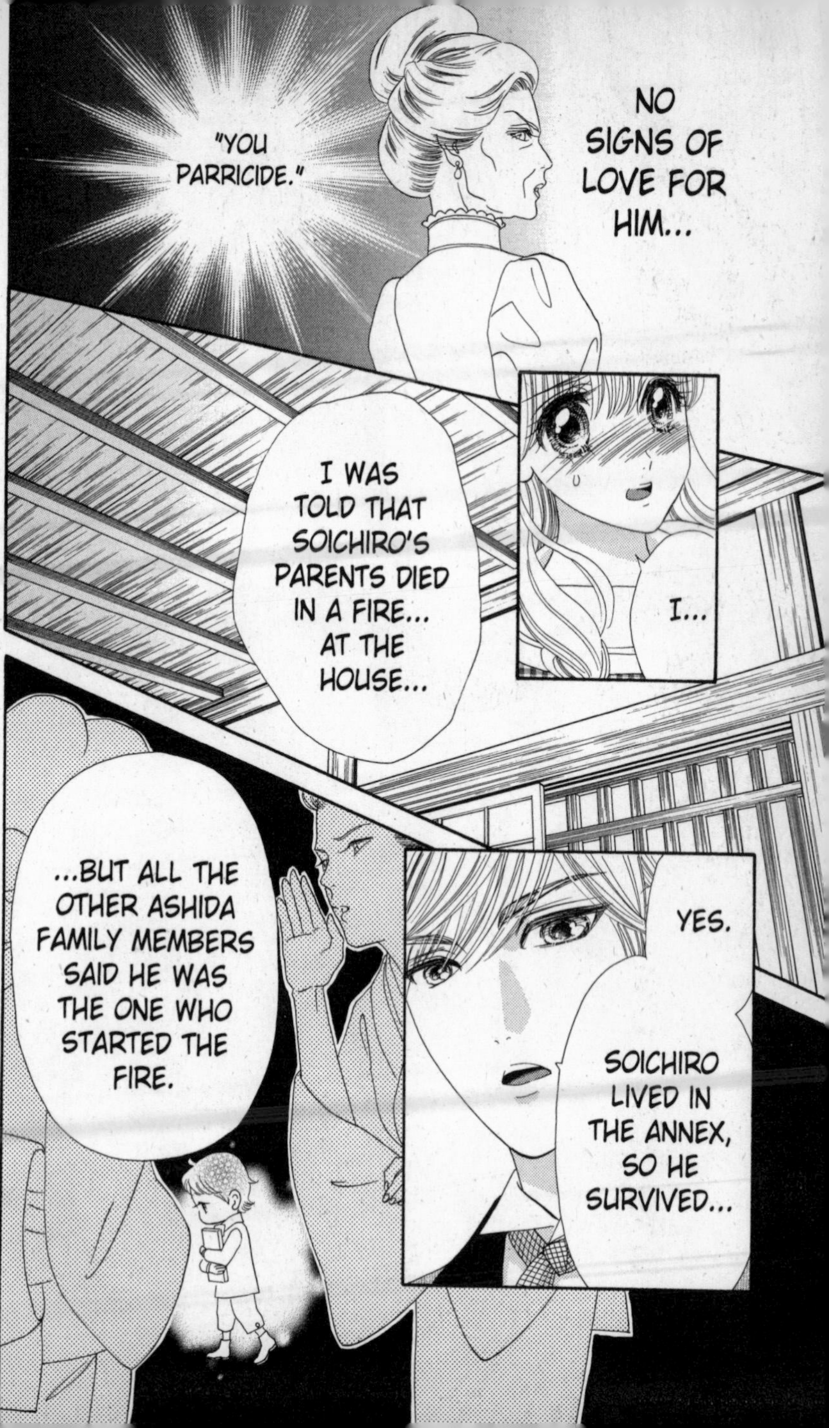
NO SIGNS OF LOVE FOR HIM...
"YOU PARRICIDE."
I...
I WAS TOLD THAT SOICHIRO'S PARENTS DIED IN A FIRE... AT THE HOUSE...
YES.
SOICHIRO LIVED IN THE ANNEX, SO HE SURVIVED...
...BUT ALL THE OTHER ASHIDA FAMILY MEMBERS SAID HE WAS THE ONE WHO STARTED THE FIRE.

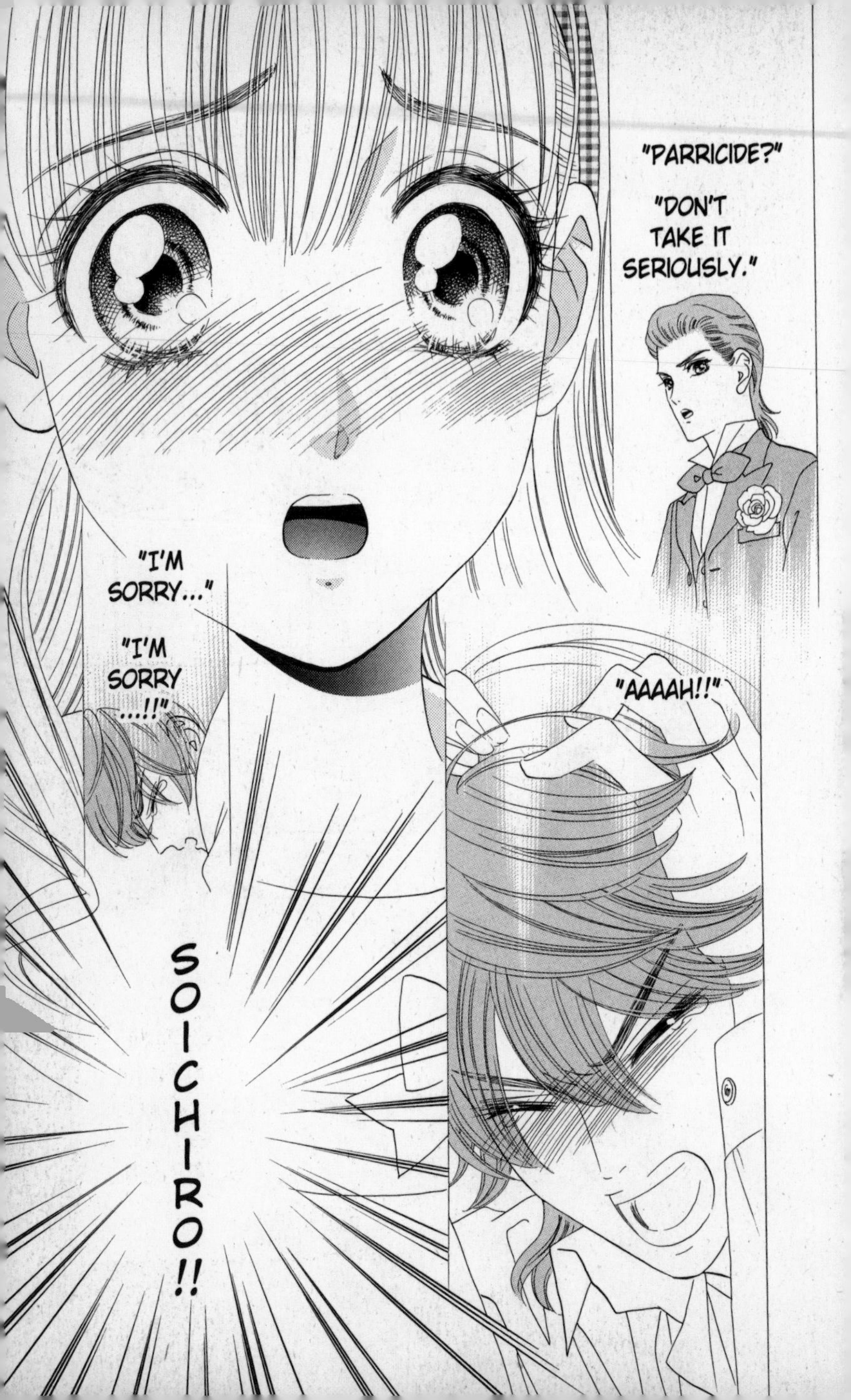
"PARRICIDE?"
"DON'T TAKE IT SERIOUSLY."
"AAAAH!!"
"I'M SORRY..."
"I'M SORRY ....!!"
SOICHIRO!!

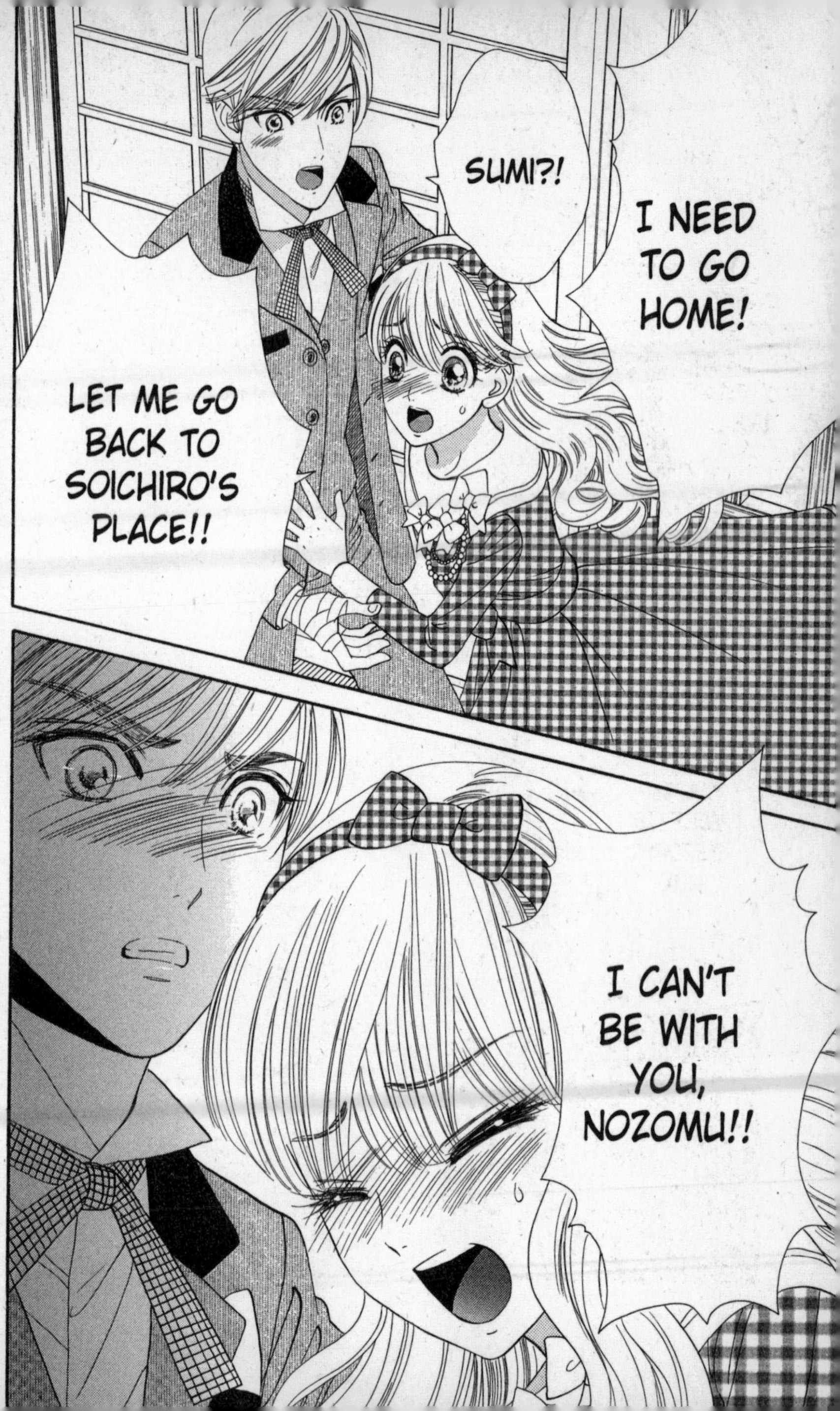
SUMI?!
I NEED TO GO HOME!
LET ME GO BACK TO SOICHIRO'S PLACE!!
I CAN'T BE WITH YOU, NOZOMU!!

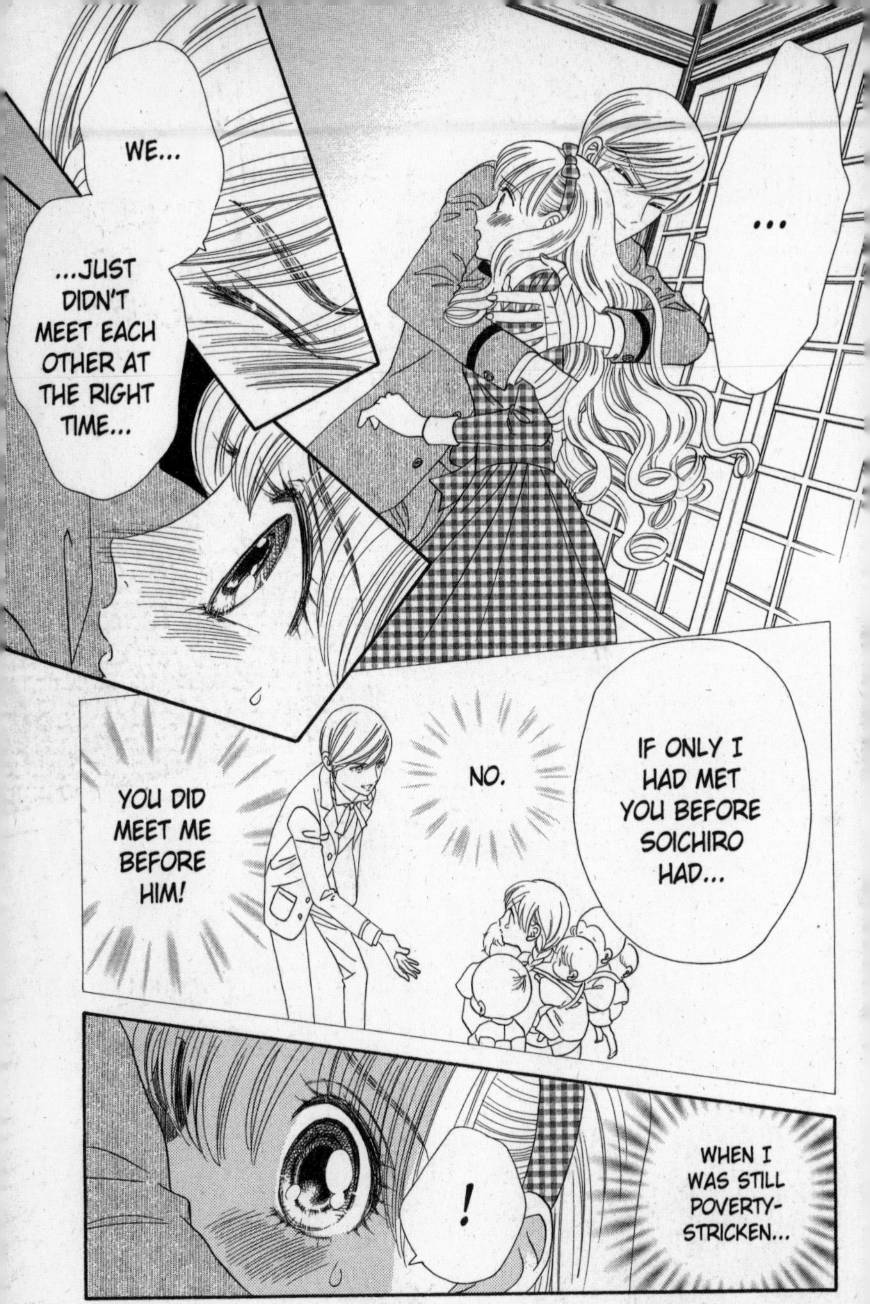
...
WE...
...JUST DIDN'T MEET EACH OTHER AT THE RIGHT TIME...
IF ONLY I HAD MET YOU BEFORE SOICHIRO HAD...
NO.
YOU DID MEET ME BEFORE HIM!
WHEN I WAS STILL POVERTY-STRICKEN...
!

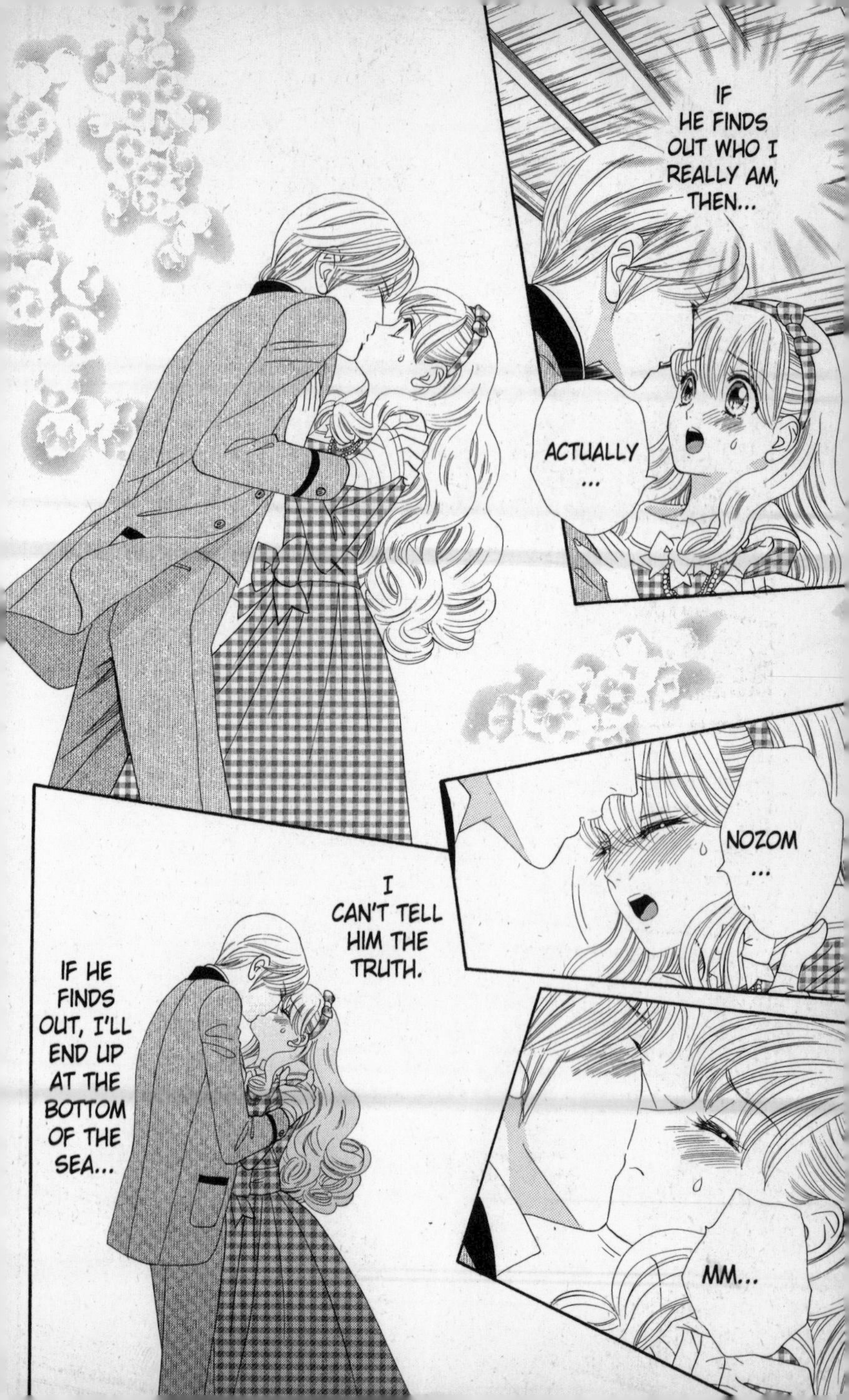
IF HE FINDS OUT WHO I REALLY AM, THEN...
ACTUALLY...
NOZOM...
MM...
I CAN'T TELL HIM THE TRUTH.
IF HE FINDS OUT, I'LL END UP AT THE BOTTOM OF THE SEA...

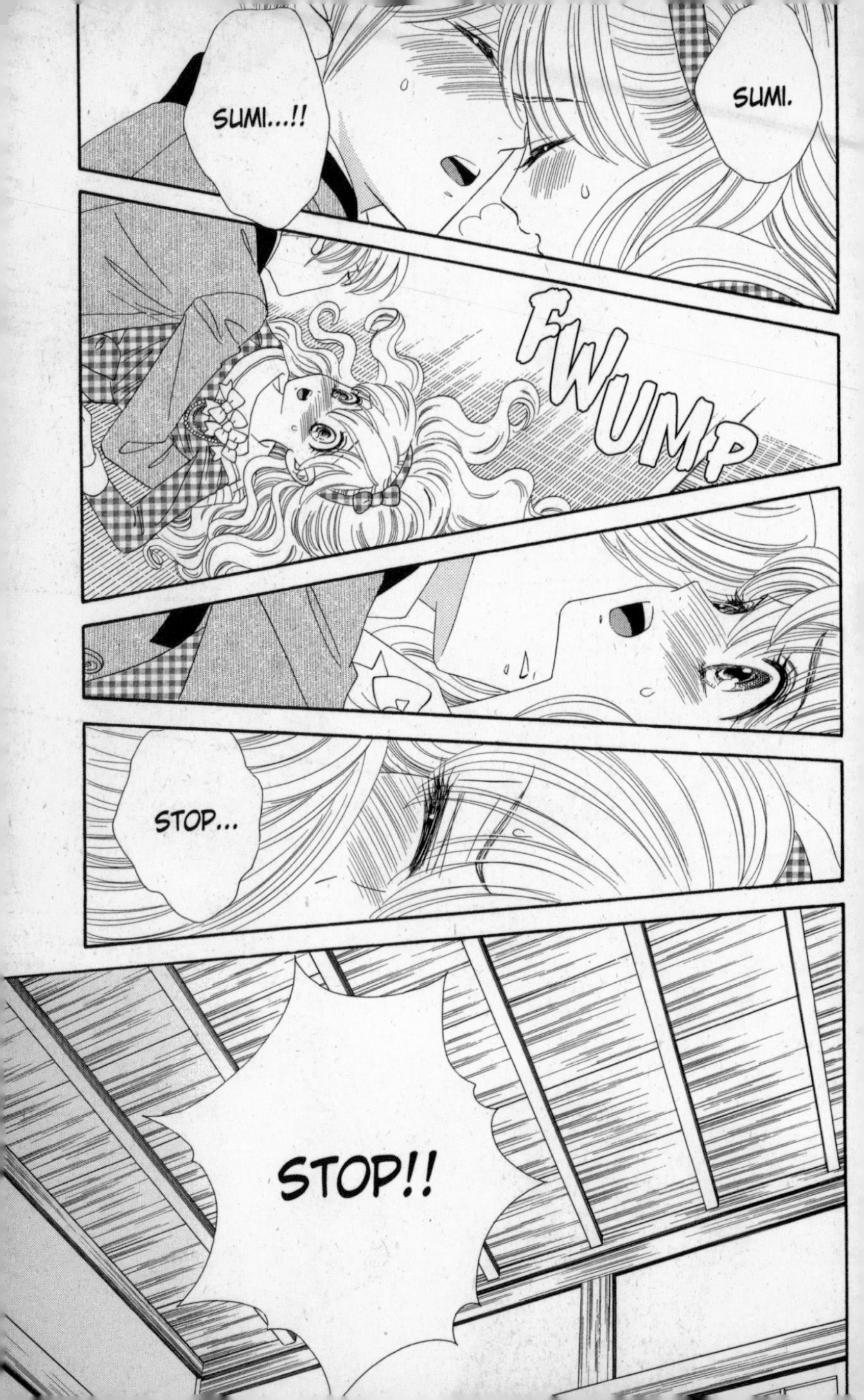
SUMI.
SUMI...!!
FWUMP
STOP...
STOP!!

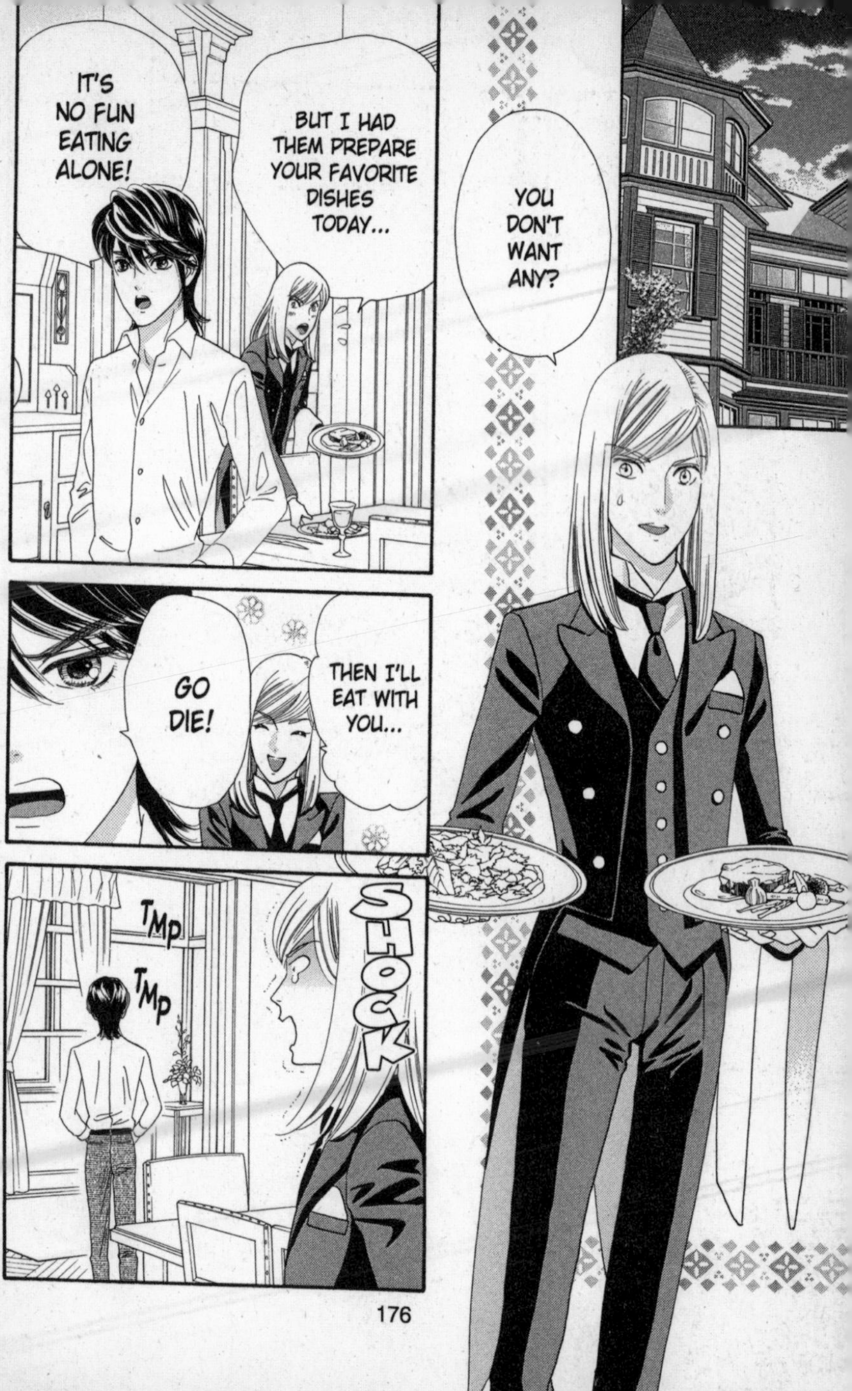
YOU DON'T WANT ANY?
BUT I HAD THEM PREPARE YOUR FAVORITE DISHES TODAY...
IT'S NO FUN EATING ALONE!
THEN I'LL EAT WITH YOU...
GO DIE!
SHOCK
TMP
TMP

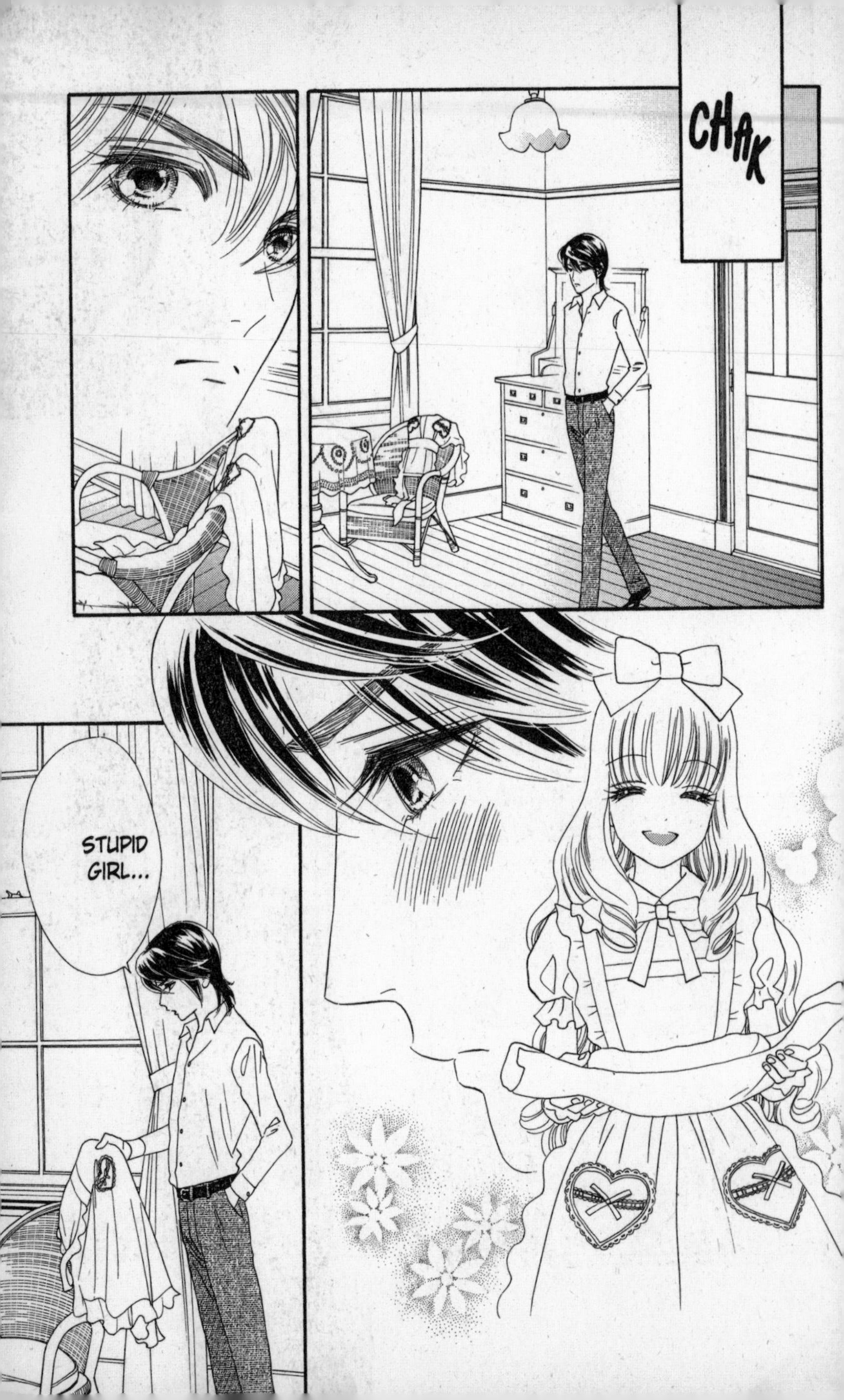
CHAK
STUPID GIRL...

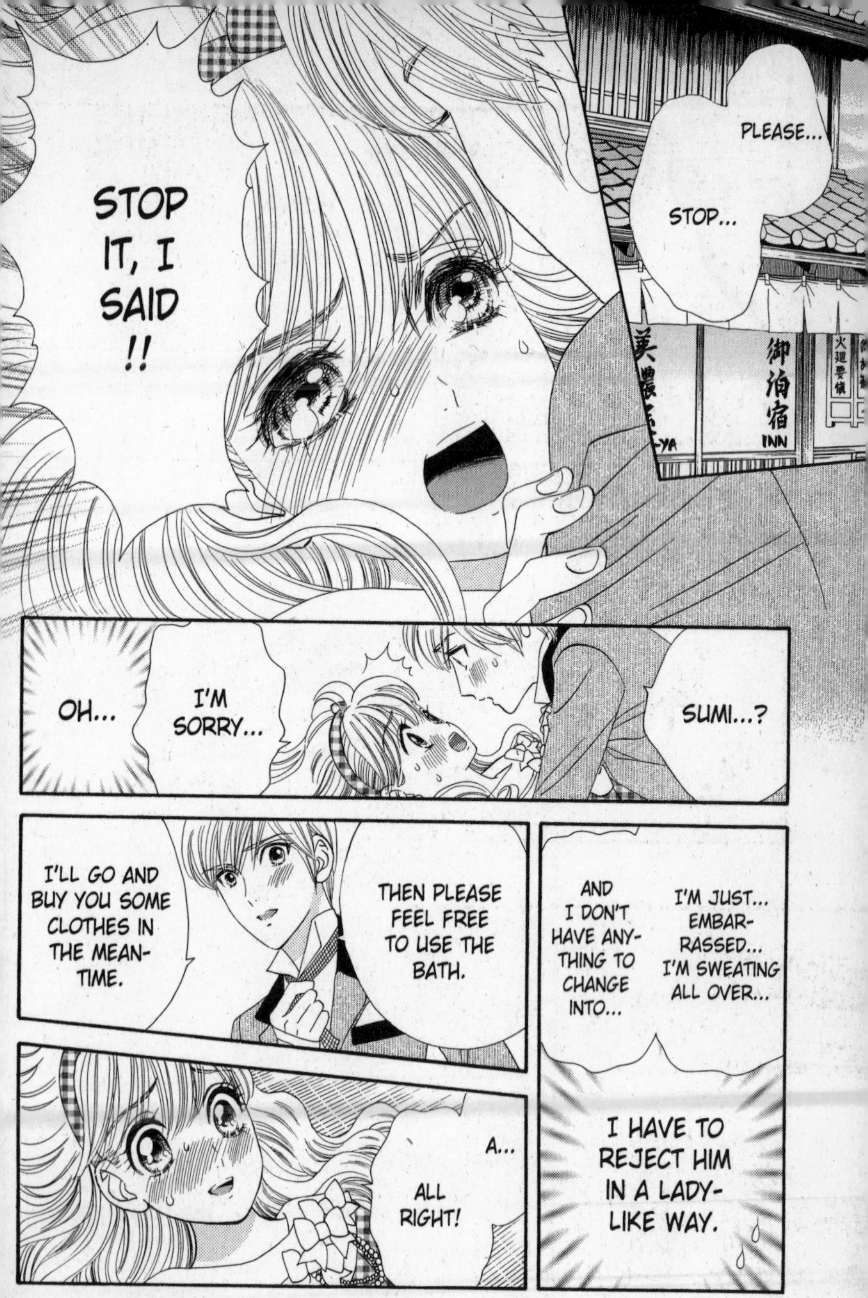
PLEASE...
STOP...
御泊宿
INN
火廻要慎
-YA
STOP IT, I SAID!!
SUMI...?
I'M SORRY...
OH...
I'M JUST... EMBARRASSED... I'M SWEATING ALL OVER...
AND I DON'T HAVE ANYTHING TO CHANGE INTO...
I HAVE TO REJECT HIM IN A LADY-LIKE WAY.
THEN PLEASE FEEL FREE TO USE THE BATH.
I'LL GO AND BUY YOU SOME CLOTHES IN THE MEAN-TIME.
A...
ALL RIGHT!

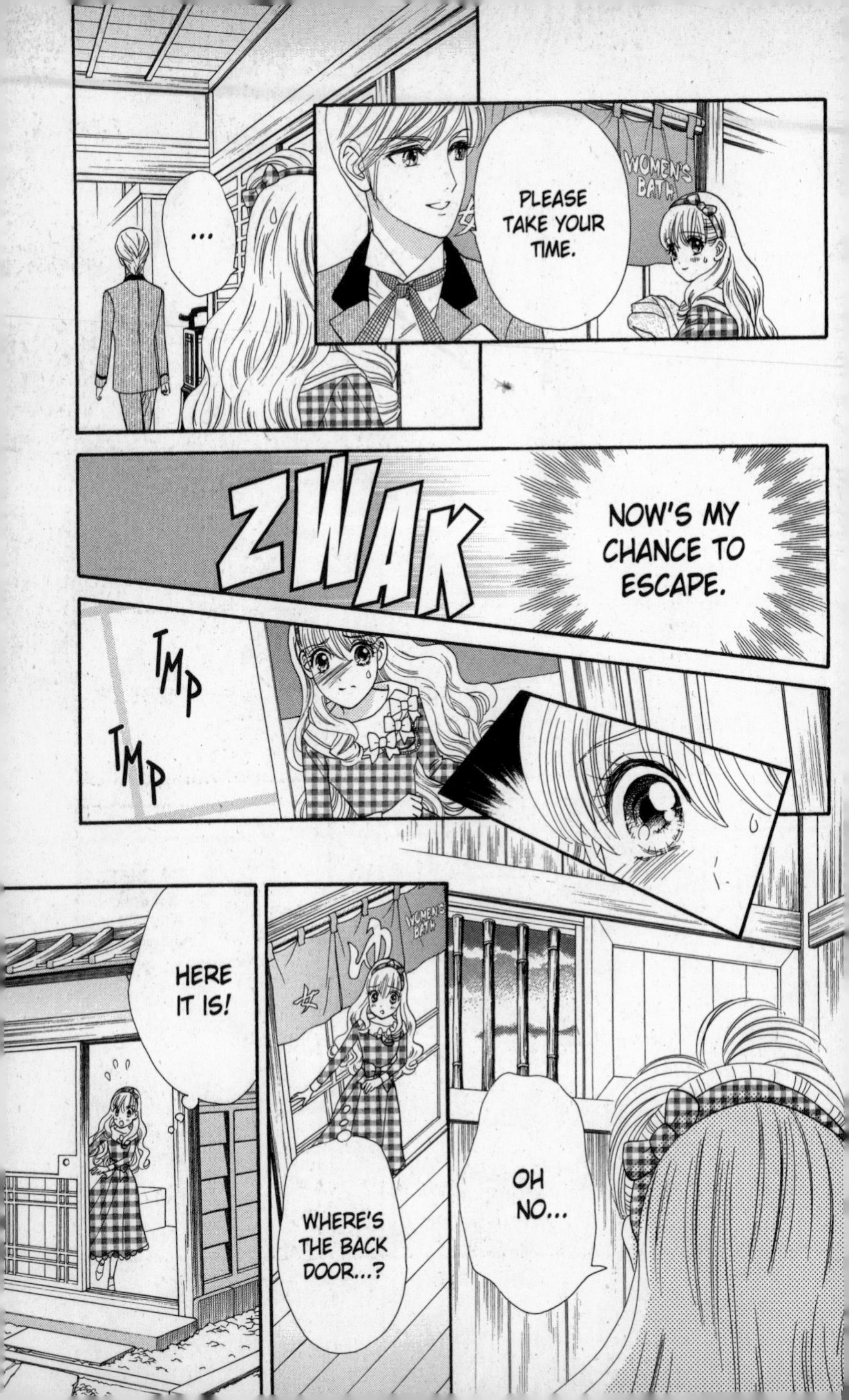
WOMEN'S BATH
PLEASE TAKE YOUR TIME.
...
ZWAK
NOW'S MY CHANCE TO ESCAPE.
TMP
TMP
OH NO...
WOMEN'S BATH
WHERE'S THE BACK DOOR...?
HERE IT IS!

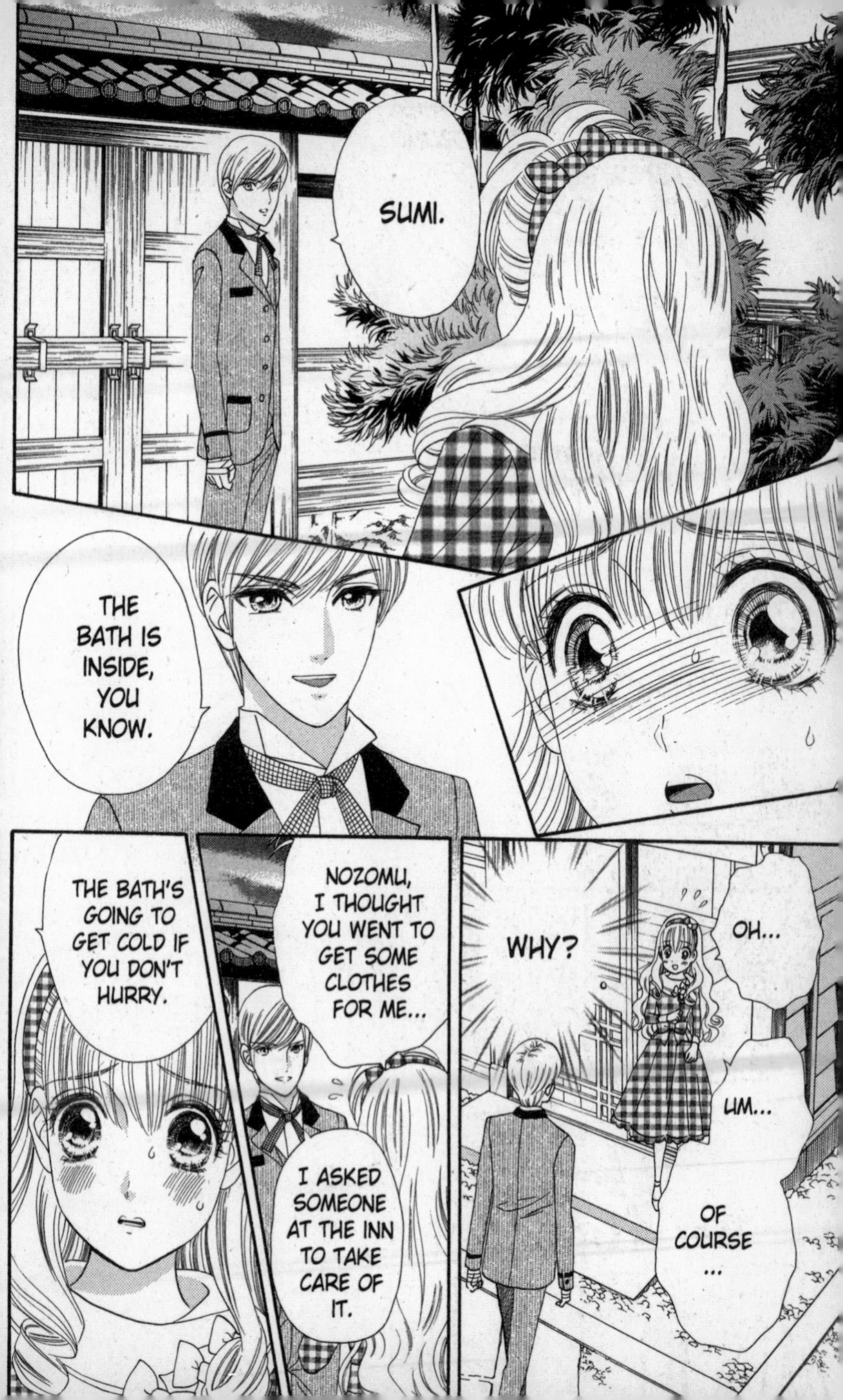
SUMI.
THE BATH IS INSIDE, YOU KNOW.
OH...
WHY?
UM...
OF COURSE ...
NOZOMU, I THOUGHT YOU WENT TO GET SOME CLOTHES FOR ME...
I ASKED SOMEONE AT THE INN TO TAKE CARE OF IT.
THE BATH'S GOING TO GET COLD IF YOU DON'T HURRY.

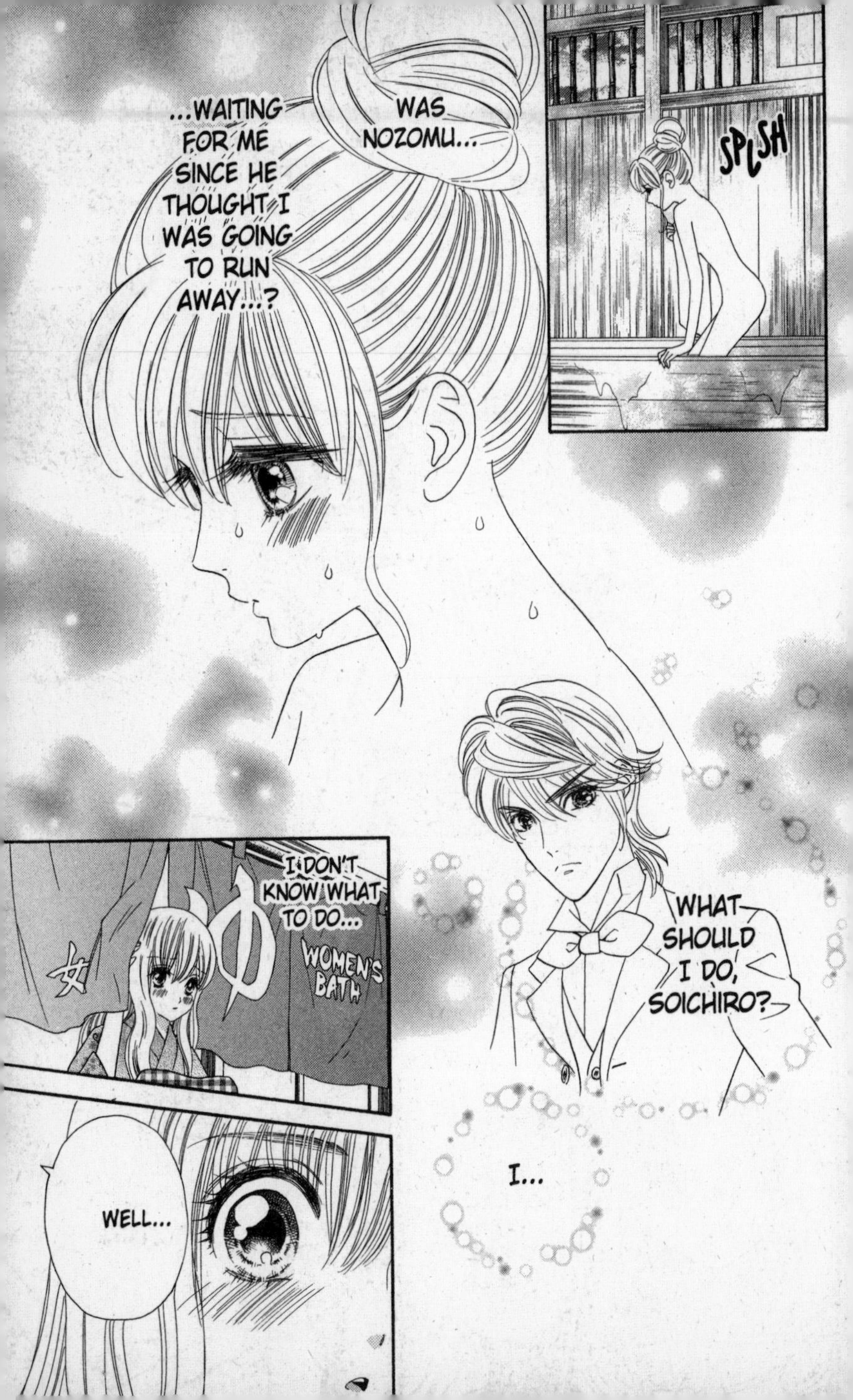
SPLSH
WAS NOZOMU...
...WAITING FOR ME SINCE HE THOUGHT I WAS GOING TO RUN AWAY...?
WHAT SHOULD I DO, SOICHIRO?
I...
I DON'T KNOW WHAT TO DO...
WOMEN'S BATH
女
WELL...

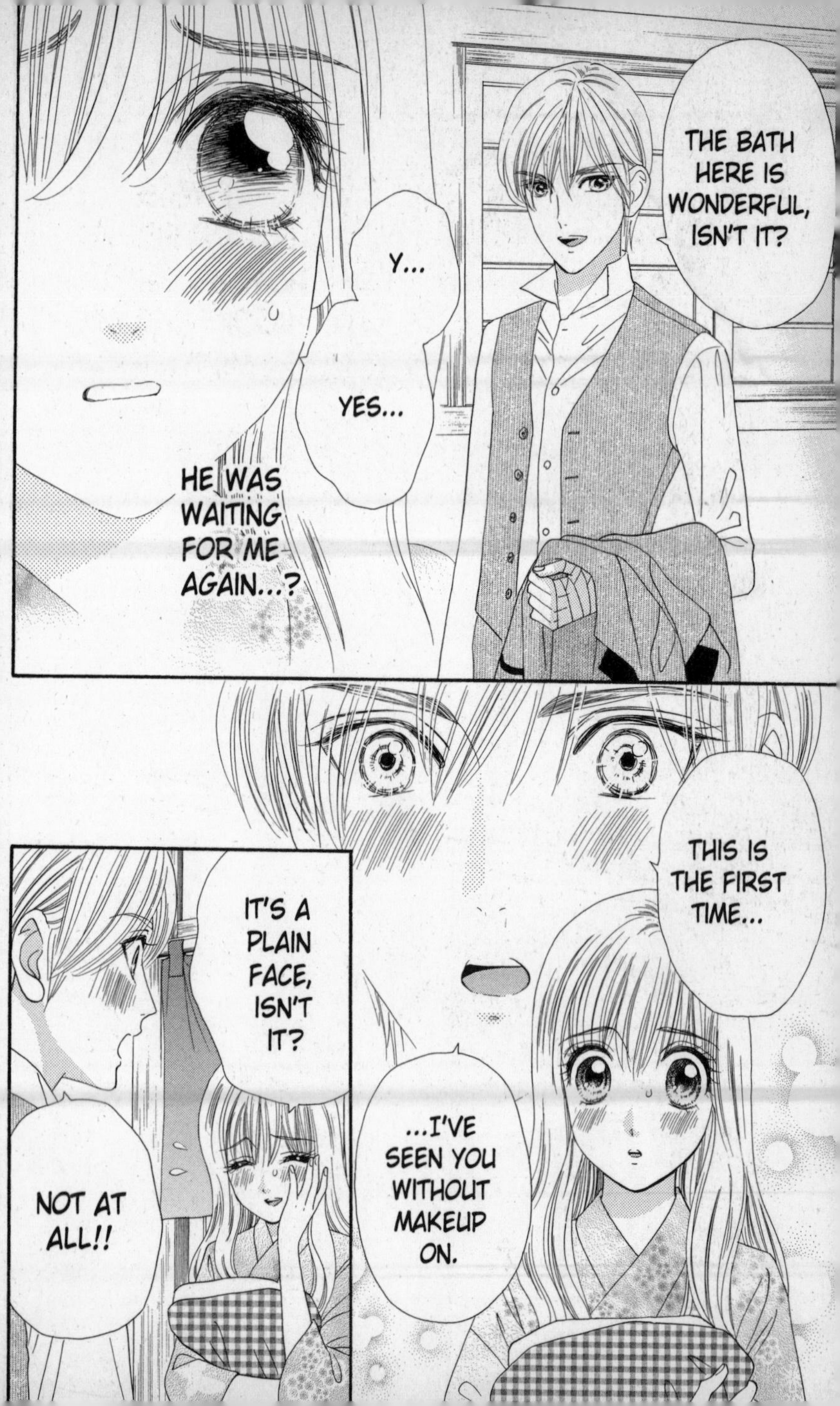
THE BATH HERE IS WONDERFUL, ISN'T IT?
Y...
YES...
HE WAS WAITING FOR ME AGAIN...?
THIS IS THE FIRST TIME...
...I'VE SEEN YOU WITHOUT MAKEUP ON.
IT'S A PLAIN FACE, ISN'T IT?
NOT AT ALL!!

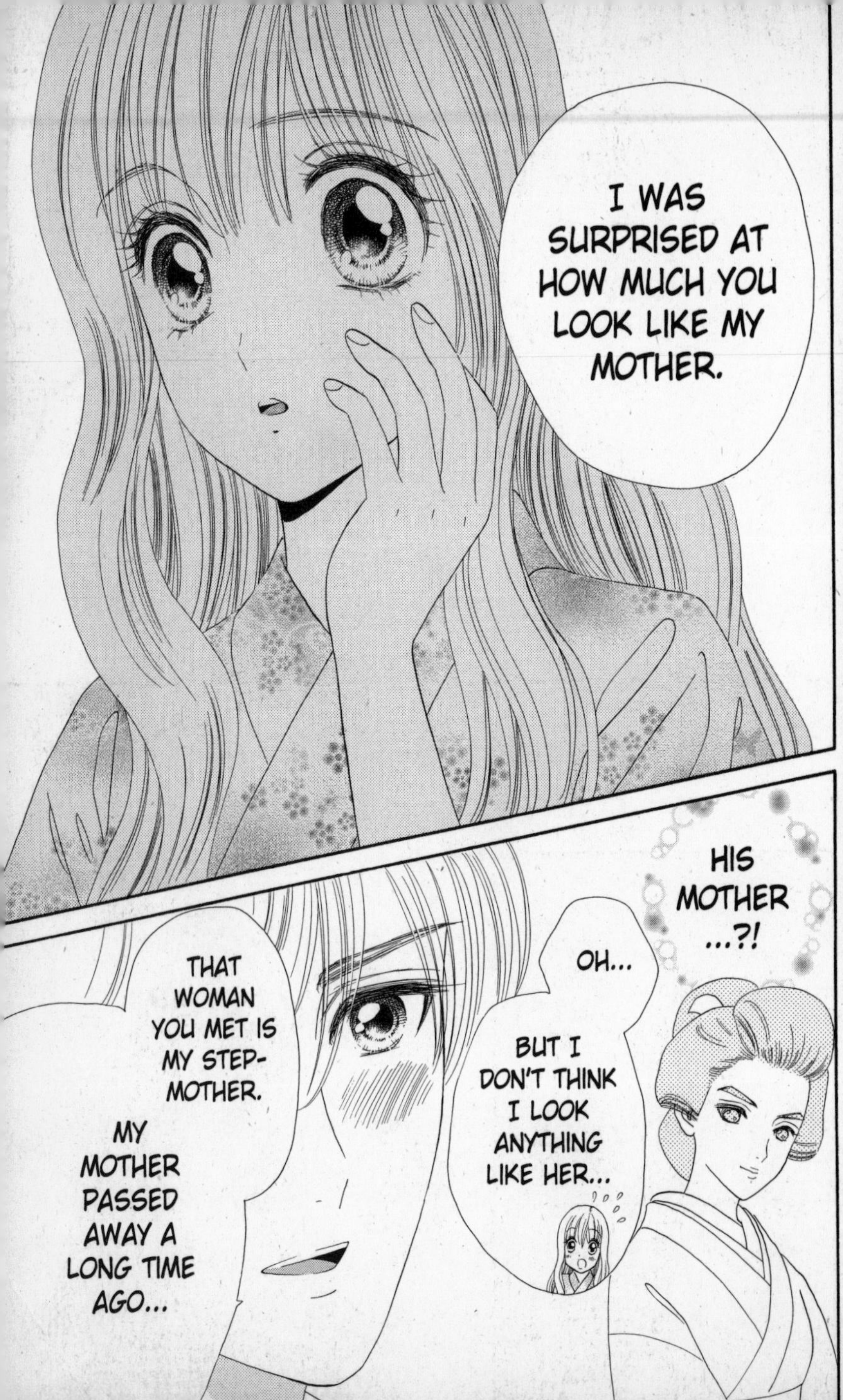
I WAS SURPRISED AT HOW MUCH YOU LOOK LIKE MY MOTHER.
HIS MOTHER ...?!
OH...
BUT I DON'T THINK I LOOK ANYTHING LIKE HER...
THAT WOMAN YOU MET IS MY STEP-MOTHER.
MY MOTHER PASSED AWAY A LONG TIME AGO...

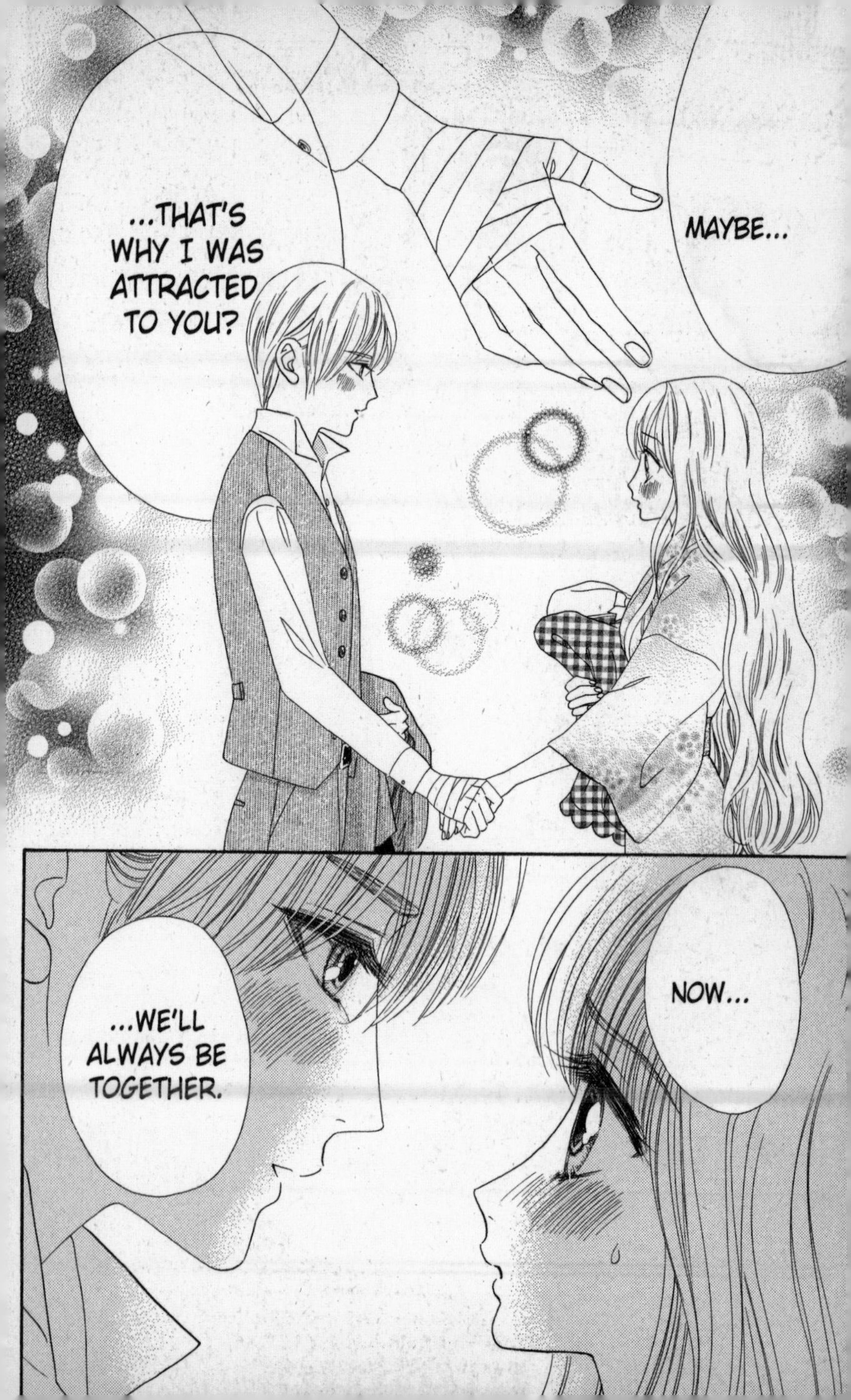
MAYBE...
...THAT'S WHY I WAS ATTRACTED TO YOU?
NOW...
...WE'LL ALWAYS BE TOGETHER.

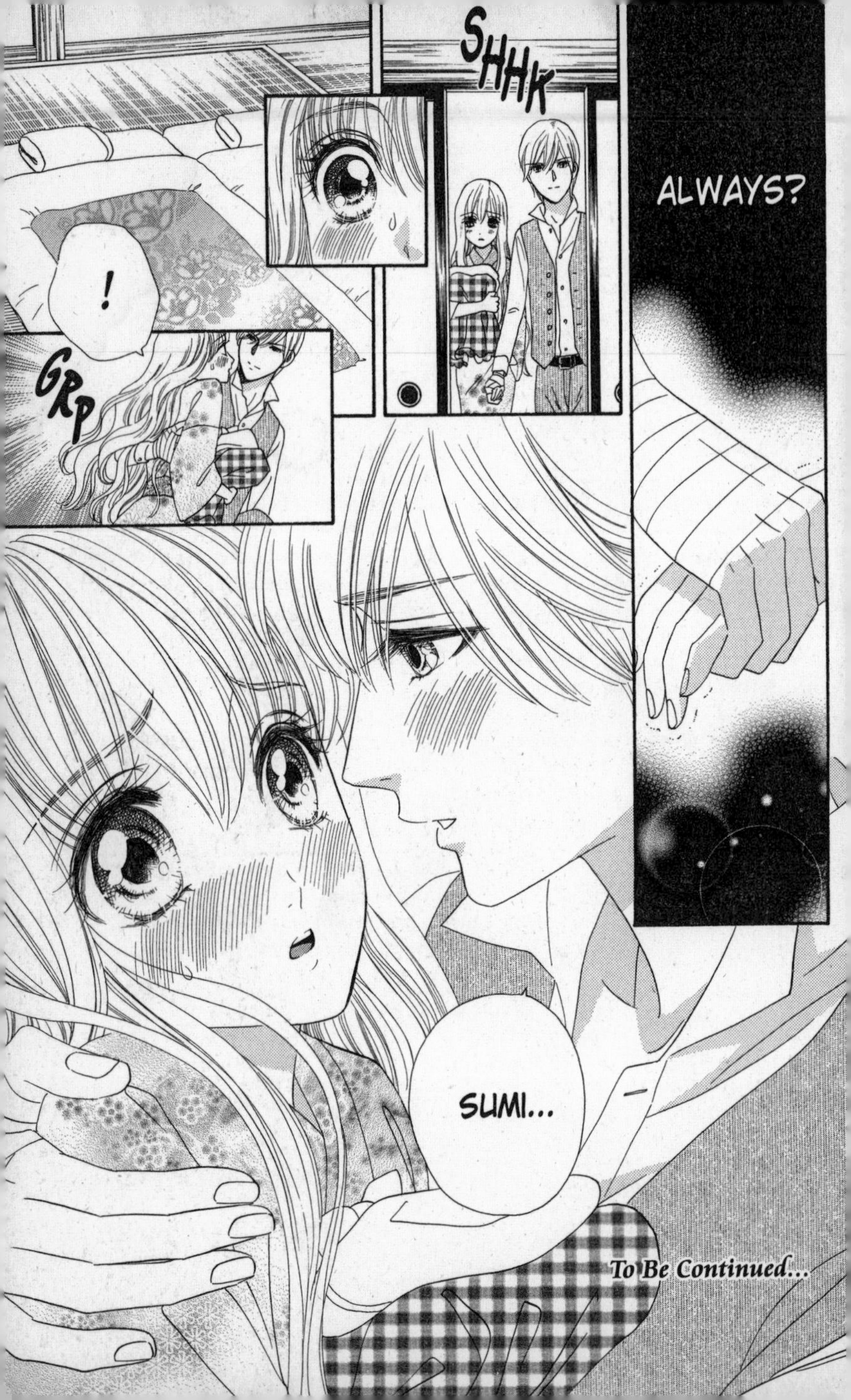
ALWAYS?
SHHK
!
GRP
SUMI...
To Be Continued...

Glossary

The setting of *Stepping on Roses* plays an important part in the story, as it showcases a unique time of change and transformation in Japan. Check out the notes below to help enrich your reading experience.

Page 82: Lucky names
Eisuke named the children using words that have lucky connotations. *Fuku* means "luck," *Tomi* means "wealth" and *Atari* means "jackpot." Also, *Manpuku* means "full stomach."

Page 120, panel 4: Beef hot pot
The beef hot pot Komai is referring to is called *ushi-nabe* or *gyu-nabe*, a stewed dish that originated in Yokohama.

Page 132, panel 1: *Kinpira*
A traditional Japanese cooking style that involves sautéing and simmering root vegetables such as burdock, carrots and lotus roots with a slightly sweet flavoring.

Page 11, panel 1: *Kuruwa*
The kanji character (廓) on the lantern means "an enclosed area," and it signifies the red-light district.

Page 56: Meiji Era
The Meiji Era (1868–1912) was a time of reform in Japan during which Western models and technology were studied, borrowed and adapted for the sake of modernization. One of the slogans of this period was *bunmei kaika*, or "civilization and enlightenment."

Page 56: Sumi
The kanji character for Sumi's name is 純, and it means "pure" or "chaste."

Page 56: Taro and Ichiro
Taro means "eldest son," and *Ichiro* means "firstborn." These name parts tend to be used in traditional Japanese names for the eldest son.

Everything up until the part where Nozomu clenches the roses in his hand should be considered the prologue of this story. Watch how the story unfolds from here on out. I'm thinking of creating a stereotypical story, but I like this kind of stereotype. Please feel free to send me your comments and suggestions.

-Rinko Ueda

Rinko Ueda is from Nara Prefecture. She enjoys listening to the radio, drama CDs and Rakugo comedy performances. Her works include *Ryo*, a series based on the legend of Gojo Bridge; *Home*, a story about love crossing national boundaries; and *Tail of the Moon* (*Tsuki no Shippo*), a romantic ninja comedy.

STEPPING ON ROSES
Vol. 2
Shojo Beat Edition

STORY AND ART BY
RINKO UEDA

Translation & Adaptation/Tetsuichiro Miyaki
Touch-up Art & Lettering/Mark McMurray
Design/Yukiko Whitley
Editor/Amy Yu

VP, Production/Alvin Lu
VP, Sales & Product Marketing/Gonzalo Ferreyra
VP, Creative/Linda Espinosa
Publisher/Hyoe Narita

Printed in the U.S.A.

Published by VIZ Media, LLC
P.O. Box 77010
San Francisco, CA 94107

10 9 8 7 6 5 4 3 2 1
First printing, July 2010

www.viz.com
www.shojobeat.com

RATED T+ FOR OLDER TEEN

PARENTAL ADVISORY
STEPPING ON ROSES is rated T+ for Older Teen and is recommended for ages 16 and up. This volume contains brief nudity and sexual themes.
ratings.viz.com

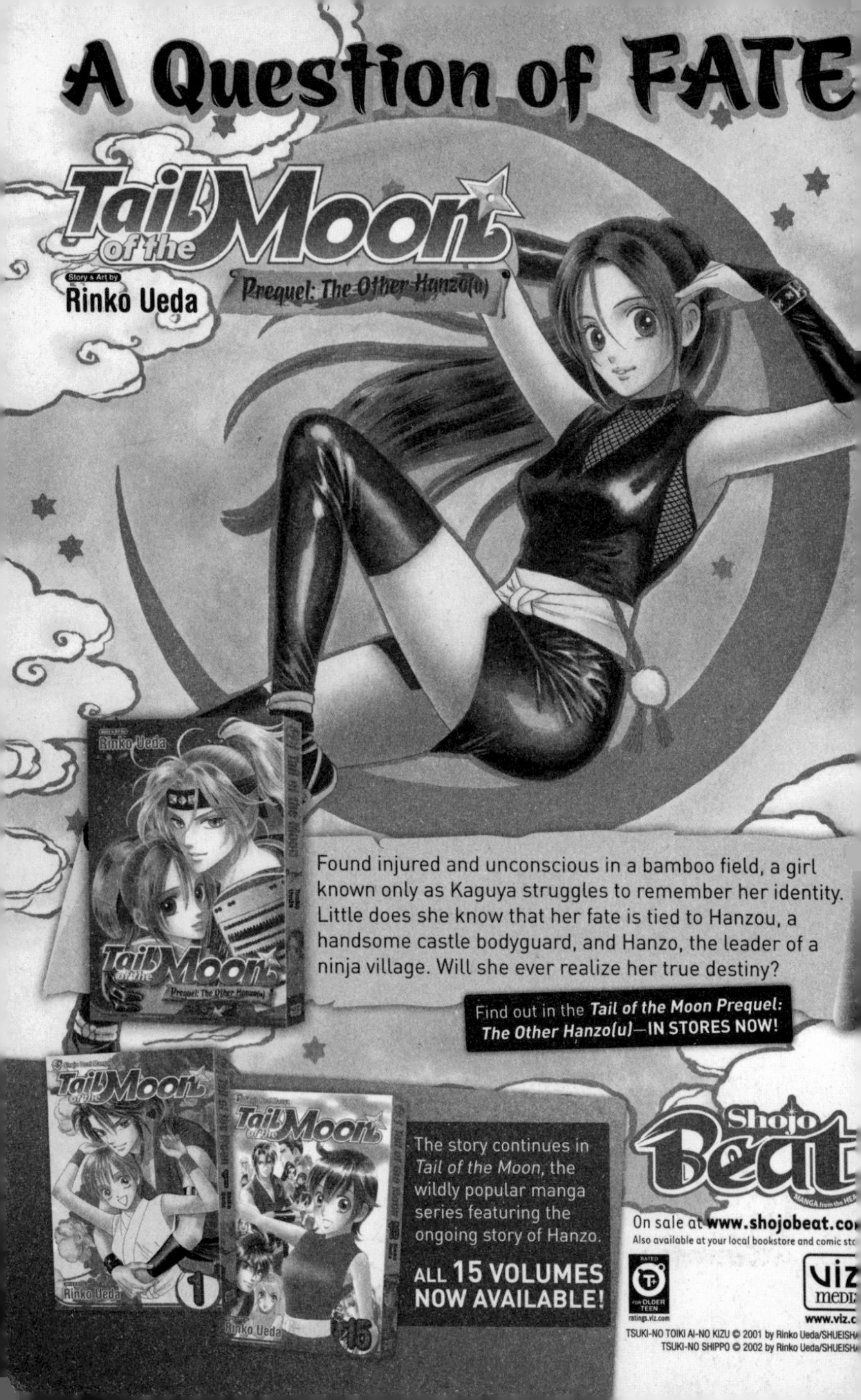
A Question of FATE
Tail of the Moon
Story & Art by
Rinko Ueda
Prequel: The Other Hanzo(u)
Found injured and unconscious in a bamboo field, a girl known only as Kaguya struggles to remember her identity. Little does she know that her fate is tied to Hanzou, a handsome castle bodyguard, and Hanzo, the leader of a ninja village. Will she ever realize her true destiny?
Find out in the Tail of the Moon Prequel: The Other Hanzo(u)—IN STORES NOW!
The story continues in Tail of the Moon, the wildly popular manga series featuring the ongoing story of Hanzo.
ALL 15 VOLUMES NOW AVAILABLE!
Shojo Beat
On sale at www.shojobeat.co
Also available at your local bookstore and comic sto
RATED T+ FOR OLDER TEEN
ratings.viz.com
www.viz.c
TSUKI-NO TOIKI AI-NO KIZU © 2001 by Rinko Ueda/SHUEISH
TSUKI-NO SHIPPO © 2002 by Rinko Ueda/SHUEISH